Between Downs and Thames
Railways of Gravesend, the Hoo Peninsular & isle of Grain

By Rob Poole IEng MIET

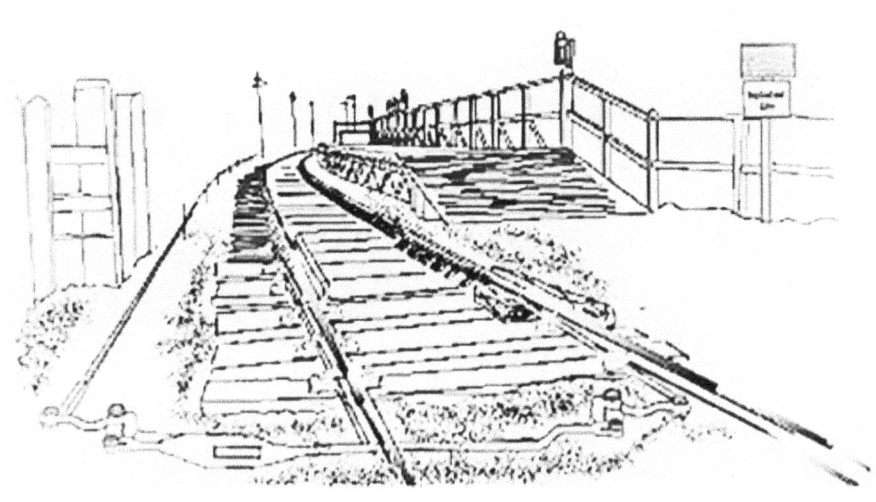

Uralite Halt's timber sleeper built platform circa 1928.

To my son Alan, who wanted to dig the tracks.

Copyright

Published 2016

Published by Rob Poole in conjunction with CompletelyNovel.com

Copyright@Rob Poole 2016

ISBN 9781849149440

All rights reserved. No part of this publication is to be reproduced, stored in a retrieval system or transmitted in any form or by any means, electronic, mechanical, photocopied recorded or otherwise without the prior permission of the author.

Images

Photographs and images have been obtained from various sources. Those obtained directly from the original photographer or an image library have been duly acknowledged. Some, however, have been acquired on the open market and a quantity remain anonymous. If that is the case, these have been credited to the collection of the supplier. Should any photographs or images have been used without due credit or acknowledgement, then apologies are offered.

Front Cover

South Eastern & Chatham Railway 4-4-0 express passenger locomotive Class E1.

1899 map of the South Eastern & Chatham Railway network.

Back Cover

Class 395 'Javelin' on the inaugural High-Speed service of 29th June 2009. George Marcar

Frontage of Gravesend station in 1849.

2nd Edition 21st October 2016

3rd Edition 17th January 2017

Minor corrections and updates

Foreword

Rob Poole was born in Gravesend and educated at Southfields Secondary School followed by the North West Kent and Mid Kent Technical Colleges. Pursuing a career as an electrical technician then draughtsman and manager for a switchgear company he ultimately became an electrical engineer and manager for London Underground whilst he was busy attaining membership of the Institute of Engineering and Technology as an Incorporated Engineer.

His interest in railways developed during his formative years as it did with many of us of similar age when the less imaginative interests now available at our fingertips were not available to young boys who preferred to study our "prey" where it wandered free, so to speak. Pockets of steam still existed around Gravesend whilst over the "water" in Tilbury the last embers of the London, Tilbury & Southend commuter services and freight still relied heavily on coal fired locomotion.

A natural curiosity sometimes got the better of him, which would these days lead to serious trouble, as the occasional bout of trespassing was risked to gain entry to motive power depots (plain 'shed-bashing' at the time) whilst inadvertently accumulating a vast knowledge of locomotive engineering, the geography of the United Kingdom and a huge understanding of how the railways functioned and changed to suit the ever-changing requirements of both passengers and freight and often, sadly, to the whims of politicians.

Later in life Bob, as he is known to fellow members, joined GRES (the Gravesend Railway Enthusiasts Society) and since 1992 has been enrolled onto the committee, progressed to Secretary, Webmaster and is now our Chairman. My involvement has been relatively recent but his obvious enthusiasm was apparent from my initial induction and becoming aware of his desire to write this book I was very keen to offer my support for what is no mean undertaking. It was evident from the first draft that an enormous amount of research has been painstakingly carried out and that his experience giving talks on railways, general transport, defence and local history has given him the encouragement to keep going.

Both membership of the South Eastern & Chatham Railway Society and volunteering on the North Downs and Kent & East Sussex Railways have also proved beneficial in understanding the complex history of the area's railways as well as gaining a hands-on appreciation of the more down to earth matters of running trains.

Sources of research have been vast including the National Railway Museum archives, the National Records Office, Kent Archives, local libraries, Gale News Vault, Gravesend and Northfleet Historical Societies, personal interviews, the SE&CR Society and of course the membership of GRES. The hours of proof reading and editing have been more than pleasurable and certainly never a chore as references to Bob's personal heroes frequently appear in the text, for example Harry Wainwright and O.V.S. Bulleid.

Undaunted by the problems encountered along the road to publication I am pleased to report that his authorial ambitions have not diminished and further volumes are planned so watch this space!

Howard Cook Gravesend Railway Enthusiasts Society

Notes

This work recording the story of of the once extensive North Kent railway networks of the Hoo Peninsular, the Isle of Grain and neighbouring Gravesend, it also includes the villages and towns of Gravesend's hinterland, known since 1974 as Gravesham. To avoid repetition, I have simply referred to the combined areas of the Hoo Peninsular, the Isle of Grain and Gravesham as local, unless a specific site is being described.

To put these into a wider perspective, a brief historical background of the railways of Kent and South-east England is also woven into the story. Primarily focused on the public railway networks, where they are of a particular interest I have included some of the more fascinating industrial and military lines that once abounded in the area.

It has been almost impossible to keep strictly within the bounds of Gravesham and the Hoo peninsular and occasionally their boundaries have been stretched to include something of particular interest, and I trust you will indulge me in that. To try to put things into context, aspects of local history are also included and I hope this will assist those who are interested in railways, rather than being fascinated by them. With dates I have been parochial and those shown refer to when a particular railway arrived in the locality, not necessarily the date of say a railway company's inception.

The era of the railways predominance as a transport provider coincided with Imperial measurements and Sterling currency, I have used these where the record mentions them. Somewhat lazily, rather than attempting to convert these individually, a conversion chart is included in the appendix. Railways are great users of acronyms, and a glossary of terms can also be found in the appendix.

Many of the illustrations and maps are my own work, intended to convey my impression of a particular subject. Rosherville locomotive shed excepted, they are not to scale.

Acknowledgements

It would not have been possible to compile this book without the unselfish help and support of individuals, societies, institutions and libraries. I would like to especially thank all the staff and volunteers of the Gravesend library for their assistance in my researches, and my fellow members of both the Gravesend Railway Enthusiasts Society and the South Eastern & Chatham Railway Society.

Those individuals I would particularly like to single out are Dave Fisher and Barry Diplock for allowing me to use their collection of local railway photographs and tickets, without whose generosity this work could not have been produced.

Thanks also to Howard Cook for his valuable contribution by editing and proof reading the manuscript. Others I would like to include are James Elford, for providing me with his WWI information and Jim Greaves and Tony Riley of the SECR Society who have been unstinting in their help with access to records, drawings and photographs.

A special thanks also to David Willis for has willingness to provide me with information on the Chattenden & Upnor Railway and both Tony Larkin and Gordon Hales who have also been generous in allowing reproduction of some of their postcard and photographic collections.

For help with local historical information I would like to thank Chris Bull, Ken Mc Govern and Sandra Soder. My thanks also to those who have shared their memories and reminiscences.

My apologies if I have omitted to include you, this is purely an oversight on my part and please rest assured that I value the help of all my contributors.

October 2016.   R.H.P

Between Downs and Thames - Railways of Gravesend, the Hoo Peninsular and Isle of Grain

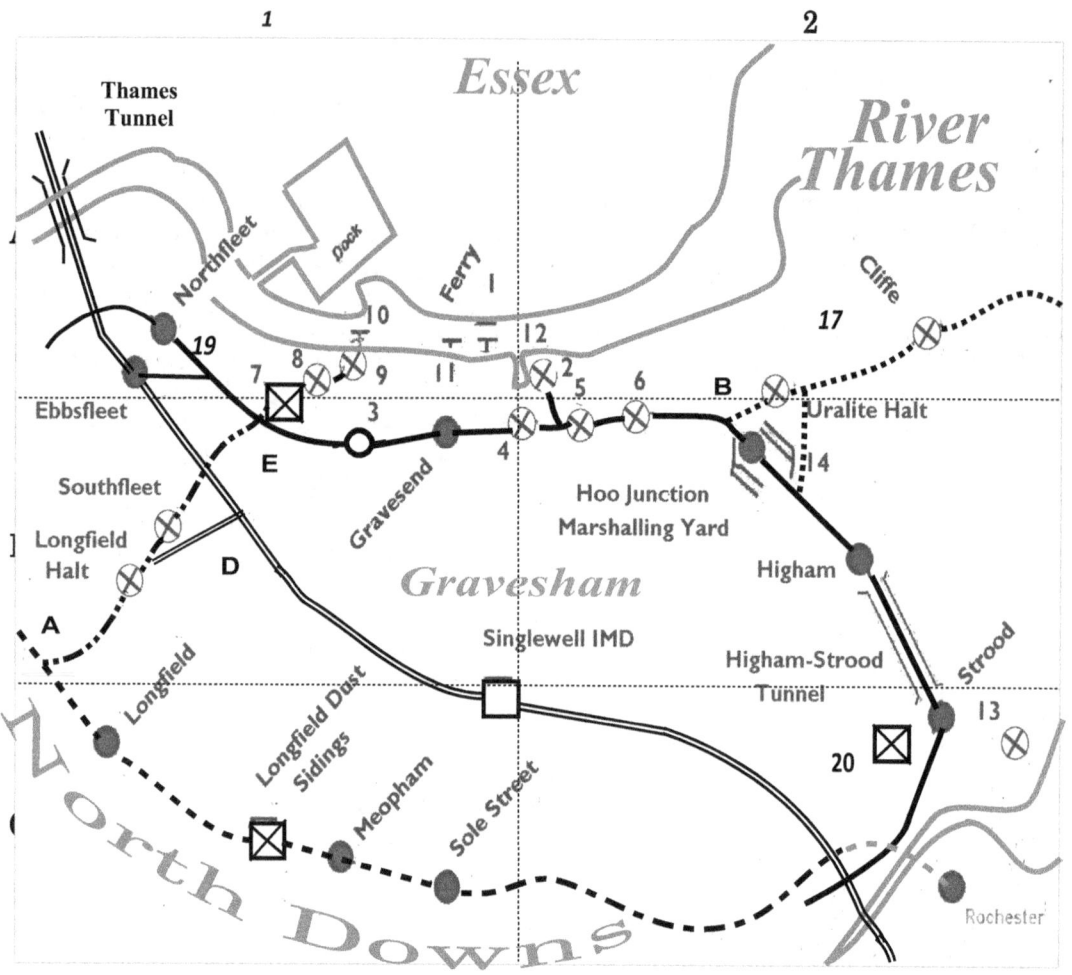

Locations Map - West

Between Downs and Thames - Railways of Gravesend, the Hoo Peninsular and Isle of Grain

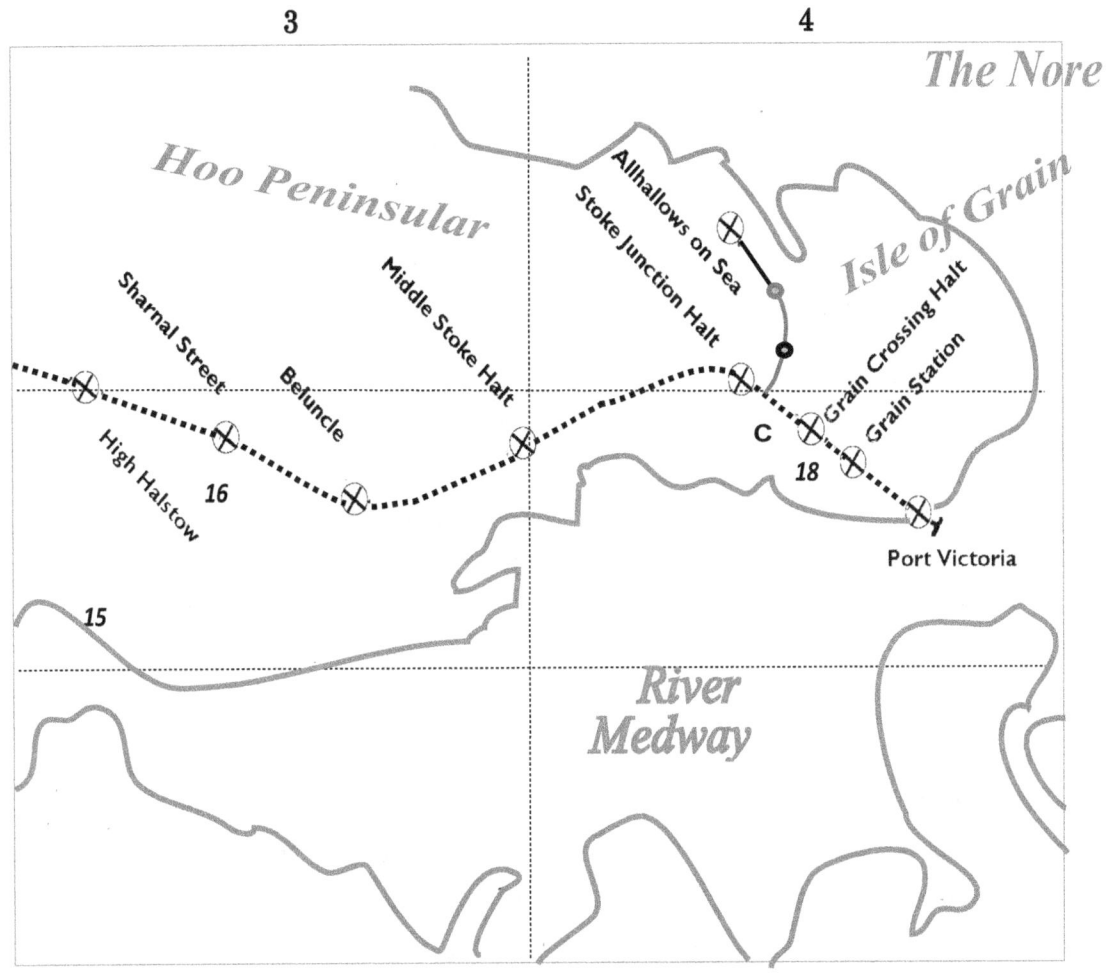

Locations Map - East

1 - Tilbury Landing Stage
2 - Gravesend G&RR Station
3 - Proposed SER Rosherville Station
4 - Milton Road Halt
5 - Denton Halt
6 - Milton Range Halt
7 - Perry Street Loco shed
8 - Rosherville Station
9 - Gravesend West Street Station
10 - West Street LC&DR pier
11 - West Street Pier
12 - Gravesend Town Pier
13 - Rochester G&RR Station
14 - Hoo Junction Staff Halt
15 - Upnor & Lodge Hill Railway
16 - Chattenden Naval Tramway & Kingsnorth Light Railway
17 - Brett Aggregates
18 - Hansons & Thamesport
19 - Lafarge spoil line
20 - Strood Locomotive Shed

A - Fawkham Junction   B - Hoo Junction   C - Stoke Junction   D - Southfleet Junction   E - Springhead Junction

Between Downs and Thames - Railways of Gravesend, the Hoo Peninsular and Isle of Grain

Contents

Page		Page	
1	Introduction	90	Stations & Halts
5	**Gravesham's Railways**	186	**Depots, Works and Marshalling Yards**
7	Gravesend and Rochester Railway 1845	186	Horlocks Locomotive Works
12	South Eastern Railway 1846	187	Perry Street Locomotive Shed
18	London, Chatham & Dover Railway 1861	189	Longfield Dust Sidings
21	Gravesend Railway 1886	192	Hoo Junction Marshalling Yard
33	South Eastern & Chatham Railway 1899	197	Singlewell Infrastructure Maintenance Depot
40	Southern Railway 1923	199	**Locomotives, Carriages and Multiple Units**
47	British Railways Southern Region 1948	225	**Gravesend-Tilbury Railway Ferries and Piers**
53	Privatisation 1996	227	Gravesend Town Pier
58	Channel Tunnel Rail Link (HS1) 2003	229	Tilbury Landing Stage
64	High-speed Suburban Service 2009	230	West Street Landing Stage
66	**Railways of the Hoo Peninsular & Isle of Grain**	231	West Street LC&DR Railway Pier
66	The Hundred of Hoo Railway.	235	Batavier Line steamer service to Rotterdam
69	The South Eastern Railway 1881	237	**Accidents & Incidents**
70	The South Eastern & Chatham Railway 1899	241	**Dreams & Schemes**
74	Southern Railway 1923	247	Notes on Nationalisation
77	British Railways 1948	248	Notes on Privatisation
78	Withdrawal of passenger services 1961	250	Bibliography
78	Latter Days	251	Appendices
79	Electrification Proposal 1980	253	Glossary
81	Transmanche Link	254	Index
81	Thamesport		
82	Chattenden Naval Tramway & Kingsnorth Light Railway		
84	The Chattenden & Upnor Railway (later Upnor & Lodge Hill Railway)		
87	The Hoo Ness Railway		

Between Downs and Thames - Railways of Gravesend, the Hoo Peninsular and Isle of Grain

Introduction

Gravesend Station's Rathmore Road frontage in 1849. The work of the architect Samuel Beazley, the exterior of the building is very little changed today. To the far left hand side can be seen the original masonry bridge that carried Darnley Road over the railway before this bridge was replaced in the 20th century. Gravesend Library

Overlooked by the scarp slope of the North Downs and bounded by the broad estuaries of the Thames and Medway rivers, Gravesham and the Hoo Peninsular, places of marsh and chalk lands, were once intersected by a maze of public, industrial and military railways and it is these highways of steel and iron that form the subject of this book.

Early railways, a revelation in a world where for millennia the speed of travel had been dictated by the pace of the horse, their impact on society must have been similar to that of the Internet today, opening up undreamed of travel and commercial opportunities. As the pinnacle of technological progress, they also attracted both the brightest and best to their service.

Railways came to the area at the dawn of the nineteenth century when, Thomas Pitcher, the owner of Northfleet Dockyard, quick to see their advantages, had the first local rail system built. Purchasing a second-hand stationary steam engine in 1802, he put it to work at Northfleet, where it hauled his loaded chalk wagons along a guided cable way to the Thames. Swanscombe was the site of the first local railway to use motive rather than stationary engine power. Opened in 1825 by James Frost, a pioneer of the modern cement industry, this was built at what was later to become White's cement works.

Initially using draught horses for traction, it later acquired steam locomotives of Lewin manufacture. An unusual 3 foot-8½ inch gauge system, the wheels of it's locomotives and rolling stock had outside flanges rather than the more conventional inside type. Serving the works well, it was still in use into the 1920's.

In 1844 came the first of the counties major rail routes, the London to Dover line of the South Eastern Railway (SER). The first true railway trunk route in Kent to reach the Channel coast, it was routed via Tonbridge and Ashford. Favouring a more northerly route, this was not the preferred alignment of its backers.

February 1845 brought to Gravesham it's first public railway, the small Gravesend and Rochester Railway (G&RR). Quickly becoming profitable, this five mile long railway hugged the bank of the Thames & Medway canal throughout its course to Strood.

With the attraction of the fast developing resort town of Gravesend and the conurbations of Medway, it would be thought that North Kent was an obvious target for the county's first major railway. Indeed, by an extension of the London &

Greenwich Railway, this was one of the South Eastern's preferred routes. However, this route faced powerful opposition from the politically vigorous local aristocracy, land owners and the owners of Gravesend and Rochester's flourishing road and river services. Gravesend's ancient Long Ferry § was one such rival; a river passenger service established in medieval times, it still plied its way between Billingsgate and Gravesend via the River Thames.

The Admiralty was also strongly opposed, their Lordships having no wish for any railway to extend beyond Greenwich. Neither was the Speaker of the House of Commons amenable, stating in 1836:

"No second outlet (for a railway) would be allowed to the south, the only one being the London & Croydon line, as it was considered dangerous to the country to have the land divided by railways"

With this statement, new railways were effectively excluded from both south London and north Kent. However, by buying the youthful Gravesend & Rochester Railway (G&RR) in 1846, the SER gained a toehold in the area and after overcoming considerable obstacles, the SER was at last able to open a secondary route, the North Kent Railway (NKR) of 1849.

Diverging from the SER's main line at Deptford, the NKR then pushed past St. Johns, Lewisham, Blackheath, Woolwich, Dartford and Gravesend until it finally reached its Strood terminus after crossing the marshlands of the Thames by way of the G&RR.

At this period, although picturesque and scenic, north-west Kent was not particularly agriculturally productive. It's largely open farmlands being blighted by relatively low fertility soils, the arrival of the NKR was to have a major impact on this Arcadia. In 1841 the combined population of the Hoo Peninsular, Gravesend, Northfleet and their local villages being just 27,219 souls, by 1911 this had grown to 55,000, an increase mainly attributable to the new railways who brought trade and industry in their wake.

The fledgling NKR, however, wasn't without competition, the river steamers putting up a particularly stiff opposition when sensing the loss of their passenger trade. However, this was a losing battle as river transport then was prone to delay or even complete stoppage from the

Granby Road Northfleet circa 1835. In the middle distance is Pitcher's tall engine house containing the engine which powered the cable-way which can be seen to its left. The site is now occupied by Kimberley Clarke's paper mill.

§ *The Long Ferry was met at Gravesend for onward travel to Dover by the Tide coaches. So named as their departure times varied with the tides on which the Long Ferry relied for travel between Gravesend and Billingsgate, they are believed to be amongst the first scheduled stage coaches to run in the UK and by the 1830's the Old Dover Road was the busiest turnpike road in the nation.*

thick, sulphurous smog's of the day. Should such a smog come down it wasn't unknown for steamboat travellers to find themselves stranded. Lewis Gilbert, a local traveller who had experience of both railway and river travel in the 1840's, recalled in 1911 his 1848 experience of travel between London and Gravesend:

"Passengers could go to Blackwall by boat and thence to London by train and in this (the train) the 3rd Class presented a variety, as it was furnished with a roof but no windows or seats, thus giving their occupants the chance to study the cattle trade! The passage by the boat was not so certain as to be satisfactory, because sometimes a fog would stop the boat on her passage, in which case you had the pleasure of hoping to get home next day".

By the 1850's, Gravesend and its environs a thriving tourist resort, the town was particularly popular with Londoners who flocked here in their thousands. Offering delights such as Clifton Marine Parade with its bathing facilities and reading rooms, the Rosherville Gardens, the Windmill Hill leisure complex and several smaller pleasure gardens, Gravesnd was in some ways the Disneyland of its day.

The hinterland of Northfleet was then a holiday and tourist area and unlikely as it may seem now, its attractive countryside to the south and west drew in many visitors, particularly to the village of Perry Street and the Springhead Gardens.

Attracted by this lucrative trade, came the NKR's first rival, the London, Tilbury & Southend Railway (LT&SR). Opening to Tilbury in 1854, the new railway also brought with it a railway operated steam ferry crossing the River Thames to Gravesend.

Transport improvements also took place on the Hoo peninsular following the 1882 opening of the Hundred of Hoo Railway, trains partly supplanting both the barges and carrier's wagons that had previously enjoyed a transport monopoly.

With the coming of this railway, agricultural developments became possible, trains being able to bring in the heavy machinery needed for improvements to the peninsular's soils and the drainage of its marshy pasture lands, this in turn generated an increase in farm produce traffic.

The opening of Tilbury docks in 1886 drew in yet more people to the area and with most of those employed in the docks residing in Gravesend due to a lack of housing in Tilbury, the ferry prospered as a result. By 1886, Gravesend was well served by public railways: the SER at Rathmore Road, the LC&DR at Gravesend West station and via its steam ferry service, the LT&SR at Tilbury from the Gravesend Town Pier and West Street landing stage.

The discovery in the late 18th century of the suitability of the local chalk for the manufacture

The LC&DR 0-6-0 locomotive "Constantine" a rebuild of the 1866 "Adrian" Class. Members of the "Constantine" Class are known to have worked the West Street Branch. Graces guide

of Portland cement was soon to create a large cement industry and with paper manufactories and other heavy industries also setting up premises in the area, by the early 20th century a maze of private lines and tramways, using a variety of rail gauges, had appeared to serve them.

With the start of the Great War in August 1914, the nations railways were to come under government control for the duration of the war, the local war industries then rapid expanding, the local railways quickly grew to serve them.

After the peace of 1919 the government of the day, wishing to maintain the advantages of the unified wartime system, amalgamated the over one hundred companies then providing the nations rail network.

Accordingly, on the 1st of January 1923, with the nations railways being streamlined into four large companies, the local public railways were assimilated into the Southern Railway (SR). During their brief reign, the SR brought to the area a new marshalling yard, 660 volt DC 3rd rail electrification, new locomotives, rolling stock, and a new station.

On the 3rd of September 1939, the horror of war came once again to the nation and the railways came under massive strain during the six long years of conflict that ended in 1945.

More change was to come postwar in 1948 when the area's public railways became a part of the Southern Region of the new British Railways. In the austerity years of the early 1950's, there was a dearth of investment in the railways and a local casualty was the 1953 withdrawal of passenger services from the West Street branch.

Another loss to the area was the ending of the Hundred of Hoo branch passenger services in December 1961. The branch then becoming freight only, it remains so today. On a brighter note, the June 1959 opening of Phase 1 of the Kent Coast electrification project brought travel benefits to the local passenger services by reducing journey times.

The West Street freight only branch, by now almost bereft of goods traffic, closed in the March of 1968. However, this was not the end of the branch. Partly re-opening in 1969 as a coal line as far as Southfleet station, it was later to see a role as part of HS1.

By the early 1970's, with the starting of the decline of local industries, many local industrial lines had closed, but against this trend, a new "Merry-Go-Round" ¶ line was to open in 1970. Bringing coal and gypsum to the Northfleet cement works via a new junction from the North Kent line, it was to remain open until 1992.

1970 also the year of the formation of the Gravesend Railway Enthusiasts Society, it is still going strong in 2016. With the prime intention of reopening a part of the Gravesend Railway, the North Downs Steam Railway Society, a local preservation group, it was formed in the early 1980's, unhappily, their efforts were to be in vain. In the 1980's, with revenues still declining, the public railways were transformed yet again when they were split into new business sectors. Another creation of the time was Railfreight, charged with running the UK's railway freight business.

The British Coal and British Rail (Transfer Proposals) Act 1993 brought the greatest change to the rail system since the 1948 nationalisation, the privatisation of the nation's railways.

Since the opening of HS1 in 2007, Gravesham has seen something of a rail renaissance, a variety of European cities now being only a few hours travel away. Inauguration of the UK's first high-speed domestic rail services coming in November 2009, this was to bring another huge benefit. Speeding journey times of local services. it also brought almost unheard levels of comfort.

Freight also saw expansion, 2012 seeing the re-opening of the disused 1970 Northfleet "Merry-Go-Round" line as part of an integrated waste disposal scheme, it was used to transport Crossrail's tunnelling spoil to Northfleet for onward travel by sea to Essex.

During the 2012 London Olympics, a high-speed shuttle service ran between Gravesend, Ebbsfleet and Stratford. Known as the "Javelin", this service used Hitachi Class 395 trains suitably graced with Olympic inspired emblems.

Gravesend station was to have a makeover during the winter of 2013-14, when it acquired a new platform, footbridge and other upgrade works as a part of Gravesend's Transport Quarter project. Looking to the future, Crossrail and perhaps even Thameslink may come to Gravesham, the land for an extra track from Abbey Wood having now been safeguarded.

So, with the benefit of a little background information, let us begin the story of the local railways.

¶ *A "Merry-Go-Round" rail system is a means of delivering bulk cargoes with the train moving at low speed while the load is discharged.*

Gravesham's Railways

Although there is some uncertainty over its actual guidance method, the first transport system in Gravesham to run vehicles on a rail or tramway was a cable hauled guided wagonway. Coming into operation in the early 1800's, this was the brainchild of Thomas Pitcher, the proprietor of Northfleet's Dockyard.

Installing a small, secondhand steam engine, purchased from a canal builder at an engine house at the bottom of Granby Road, Northfleet, this was used as the power for the operation. According to the *Gravesend Magazine,* this enterprise began in 1802 and if correct, this would make it one of the first steam powered operations of its type.

It's wagons loaded with chalk quarried from the local beds, they clattered along on this truckway towards Mr. Pitchers river-side wharf. In operation before 1820, prior to the availably of mass produced wrought iron rails, its wagons probably ran on either fragile cast iron rails or plates. The steam engine is long gone, but the engine house itself survived into the 20th Century. Now demolished, it was subsequently used as a school and a bakery, the course of the disused truck way itself was still discernable on Ordnance Survey maps of the 1930's.

In December 1824 the first scheme emerged to build a local trunk railway. Proposed by the Kentish Railway Company and with the eminent Thomas Telford appointed as its engineer, this line to link London and Dover, it's prospectus stating the following:

"To pass through Greenwich, Dartford, Gravesend, Rochester, Chatham, Canterbury and Dover with Branch Railways to Ramsgate and Margate."

Preference share certificate for the abortive 1835 London & Gravesend Railway

In the flowery language of the time, its backers described it as a necessity because:

"Due to the great and increasing commercial intercourse between England and France, the dangers attending the navigation from London to the Port of Dover, call for a medium of communication, at once safe, expeditious, and economical"

The Company claiming that purchase of their shares would be a handsome investment, all that was needed, the prospectus stated, was to raise a capital of £1 million by the purchase of shares priced at £100 each. The capital not forthcoming, neither was the railway.

Appearing in 1832 came a proposal for another London to Dover railway. This time using an alternative, if ponderous route, it was to start from Fenchurch Street and, then run via Limehouse to the Thames at North Woolwich. Crossing the Thames by steam ferry at Woolwich, its passengers would then have used the Kentish portion of this railway to reach Dover, it's route then taking them on a heading via Gravesend.

Differing significantly from earlier proposals, it was intended to be a plate-way. For those of you not familiar with the concept, a plate-way consists of "L" shaped rails, the wheels of the rolling stock of a plate way system sit on the bottom of the "L" whilst the upright acts to guide the wheels. This scheme too was also to pass stillborn into history.

Yet another scheme was put forward in 1835, a proposal for a London & Gravesend Railway. Getting as far as a preliminary share issue, the share certificate shown on page 5 gives some details. As with its predecessors, it did not come to fruition.

In the winter of 1843 came a proposal for a Rosherville to Chatham Railway. Dubbed as a "monstrous absurdity" by the *Maidstone Journal*, it was to be mostly routed in tunnel. Passing under Cobham village en route, with journey times between to the two termini quoted as just 15 minutes, this would have made it the area's first high-speed line. The distance between the two points being nearly 10 miles, its trains would have needed to have achieved an average speed close to 45 mph to achieve a 15 minute journey time, and this in a period when contemporary railways were struggling to reach 20 mph averages.

Yet another venture was the Gravesend, Strood, Rochester & Chatham Railway's proposal of 1844. Starting from a terminus midway between Gravesend town centre and the Terrace Pier, upon departing Gravesend it would have headed off towards the River Medway where on arrival, after crossing the river above Rochester Bridge, it was to terminate close to the Gibraltar Inn, Chatham.

When in 1844, the eminent civil engineer, William Cubitt, arrived in north Kent, his remit was to survey a route for the Great Kentish Atmospheric Railway. An alternative to a steam locomotive powered railway, it would have propelled its trains by using the principle of differential air pressure. As an extension of the London and Croydon Railway, the initial plan was to route the railway by way of Beckenham and Chatham to Dover. Cobham would have had a station on its main line, with Dartford and Gravesend served by branch lines.

When the final prospectus was issued, the route had gravitated northwards with Dartford, Gravesend, Chatham and Ashford now situated on its main line. However, when the railway's Bill was presented to a Parliamentary committee in 1845, it was rejected on the basis of an adverse Board of Trade report.

This left the way clear for two rival projects, the South Eastern's North Kent Railway and a rival scheme, the London, Chatham & North Kent Railway (LC&NKR). However, before either scheme could come to pass, a much smaller competitor, the Gravesend & Rochester Railway opened its own local line.

The Gravesend & Rochester Railway 1845

The name of this railway was something of a deception, as by calling itself the Gravesend & Rochester Railway, its owners were stretching the truth just a little. In fact it terminated at Strood, there being no railway bridge across the Medway until 1858. However, including Rochester in its title was a good marketing ploy.

As a creation of the Thames & Medway Canal Company, the fates of both intertwined, a history of the canal may be appropriate. Building the canal partly as a response to the threats to shipping in the Thames estuary from French privateers during the Napoleonic wars, the Thames & Medway Canal Company had hoped to prosper from the provision of this safer and shorter route.

Its proposer Ralph Dodd, this was the same engineer involved with the failed Gravesend to Tilbury road tunnel of 1799. His input was, however, probably limited to the planning stages only. Not having actually finishing much of what he started, today his name is commemorated by the Dodds gin brand.

Completed under the guidance of its engineer, Ralph Walker, it was unusual for its time by being of sufficient width to take full-size sailing barges between the Thames and Medway rivers.

Building the canal included the construction of an impressive 2.2 mile long tunnel. Later to become the present railway tunnel, it was bored through the chalk massif between Higham and Strood. The work of William Tierney Clark, an engineer who was also amongst the earliest designers of suspension bridges, it's line was laid out by an astronomers telescope, the first time this method was used.

At its opening in 1824 it was the second longest canal tunnel in the UK; the 3.12 mile Standedge tunnel in Yorkshire still holding that title. Before the railway passed through, the tunnel was a popular spot for local anglers who used lanterns to attract fish in the waters of the canal.

The canal was to be bedevilled by leakages and the problem of timing navigation through its entrance locks. With high tides occurring at different times on the Rivers Thames and Medway, should a barge miss the tide, then having to wait in the canal basin for the next high tide, this wait could be longer than the time taken under favourable conditions to sail around the Hoo peninsular.

Opening nine years after the Napoleonic wars had finished, the canal had by then lost its main *raison d' être* as a wartime diversionary route and having cost £260,000 to build, the recouping of this huge sum unlikely to be achieved by using the canals route solely as a waterway, sharing its route with a railway was seen as its salvation.

Fortunately for the canal company, it was able to use a clause in its enabling Act of 1800 allowing it to construct an *"inclined plane or railway"*. However, this wasn't the first proposal for a railway following the canals route.

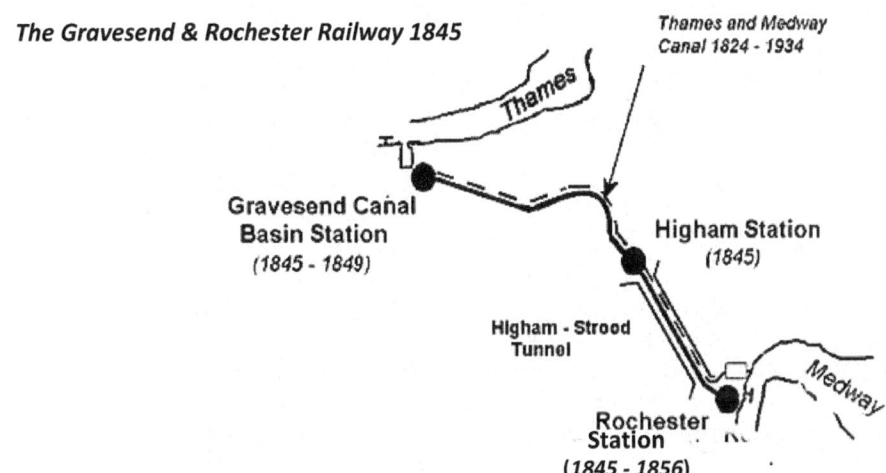

The first to surface (not from the canal!) was the Gravesend & Strood Railway. A worthy enterprise it was announced in 1836 when the *Maidstone Journal* published its prospectus. To be followed in 1840 by a proposal for a Gravesend & Rochester Railway, this was the first use of the name.

So it was in 1841 that the canal's directors approached John Rastrick for an estimate to build their railway. An eminent civil engineer, he is best known for his work on the Brighton line. Also a locomotive designer, Rastrick was one of the judges at the 1829 Rainhill locomotive trials.

Rastrick estimated the cost of the works at £120,000 and there the matter rested for a time. Agreement to the conversion of the canal was reached neither quickly nor quietly, only being achieved in the February of 1844 after a stormy meeting of the canal's shareholders finally agreed to build the railway. Soon afterwards, with the canal company changing its name to the Gravesend and Rochester Canal & Railway Company (GRC&RC), work began on the line. As anticipated, John Rastrick was appointed as engineer, the contractor being Fox Henderson & Co. The railway was to have three stations; termini at Gravesend (Denton) and Strood, with an intermediate station at Higham which was to have the lines only passing loop.

Construction proceeded quickly, and by the March of 1844, tracks were being laid to the south of the canal, opposite to its tow path. It's construction, however, was not of a high standard, wooden dowels being used to fix the rail chairs to sleepers and as we shall see later, the cause of problems and accidents, they were to become the Achilles heel of the line.

At completion, the Board of Trade surveyed the works and their inspector, General Paisley, concerned about the tunnels ability to cope with the passage of trains, had mortar balls fired into the tunnel's chalk walls and roof! These tests must have allayed the Generals fears, as he then allowed track laying to start. Unique in the UK as the only instance of the conversion of a canal

Newspaper advertisement announcing the 1845 opening of the Gravesend & Rochester Railway. Interestingly, it shows a mixed train with 1st and 2nd Class carriages, a goods wagon and a road carriage on a flat bed wagon. *Tony Riley collection*

GRAVESEND & ROCHESTER RAILWAY.

SECOND CLASS 6D.   FIRST CLASS 9D.

Including the Fare by the Steamer, which leaves the Sun Pier, Chatham, for the Rochester Station 15 minutes before the departure of each up Train and returns on the arrival of each down Train.

(Calling at the SHIP & BLUE BOAR PIERS.)

From Rochester Station.

7, 7½, 8, 9, 10, 11, 11½, 12, 12½, 1, 1½, 2, 2½, 3, 3½, 4, 4½, 5, 5½, 6, 6½, 7½, 8½

From Gravesend Station.

7½, 8½, 9½, 10½, 11, 11½, 12, 12½, 1, 1½, 2, 2½, 3, 3½, 4, 4½, 5, 5½, 6, 6½, 7, 8, 9.

ALL THE TRAINS STOP AT THE HIGHAM STATION.

The Brompton, Chatham and Rochester Omnibuses Leave the LORD NELSON, BROMPTON, at Thirty Minutes previous to the starting of the following up-trains, viz.; 7, 8, 9, 11, 1, 3½, 4½, 5½, 6½, and the Station at ROCHESTER upon the arrival of the down-trains, viz.—7½, 9½, 11, 11½, 12½, 1½, 3½, 4½, 5½, 6½.

FARE, 3d.

MAIDSTONE.—The WONDER Omnibuses will leave the Haunch of Venison and New Inn Coach Offices direct for the Rochester Station, at 6, 7½, 9½, 10½, 12, 1, 2, 3½, 5.

The Strood terminus of the G&RR in 1845. This engraving shows the Strood portal of the Higham to Strood canal tunnel and the timber framework supporting the tracks leading into the tunnel. What appears to be a carriage shed is to the left of the picture.

tunnel for railway use, the General's caution was understandable. Moreover, his anxieties over the strength of the tunnel's structure were not without foundation, chalk falls having been the cause of frequent closures of the tunnel. With tests successfully concluded, it had been intended to start running public services in August 1844, but this was delayed while further remedial works were carried out.

Finally completed in the December of 1844, according to Smetham's *History of Strood,* trial running started on Christmas Day 1844, and driven by one Faithful Kirkham, the railway's locomotive foreman, the first locomotive to pass through the tunnel was either *Trafalgar* or *St Vincent.* A journey not without mishap, the locomotive's chimney striking the chalk roof of the tunnel as it emerged at Strood, nine inches had to be hastily cut off the locomotive's chimney before its return. The locomotive coming from the direction of Gravesend, this would infer that this locomotive, at least, had been delivered to Gravesend by sea.

After a final Board of Trade inspection in the early January of 1845, clearance was given for the railways public opening for the 23rd of January 1845. However, yet another delay was to prevent opening only this time it was a dispute over non-payment of monies by the G&RR to the line's contractor that delayed matters. The *Maidstone Journal's* report on the event tells us that when payment was not forthcoming, the contractor seized Gravesend station, and a party of his navvies, armed with pickaxes, spades, crowbars, etc. went down the line intent on destroying Rochester station. Furthermore, to stop the G&RR running trains, locomotive pars removed by the contractor's foreman, the contractor then refused to give up possession of either station or stolen parts until he was paid.

With the situation now tense, it was the local magistrates who resolved the dispute by ordering the parties to negotiate a solution. After agreement was reached, Gravesend station given up and the stolen locomotive parts returned, on the 29th of January 1845, the railway re-opened for further trials.

With the locomotive *Camperdown,* suitably bedecked, being given the honour, after further trial runs followed by two days of free public rides, the G&RR eventually ran its first paying public service on Monday the 10th of February 1845. Opening in atrocious weather conditions, a contemporary newspaper account described the event thus:

"The Rochester and Gravesend Railway was opened on Monday with the usual formalities, and notwithstanding the intense severity of the weather, a considerable number of passengers passed up and down during the day whilst

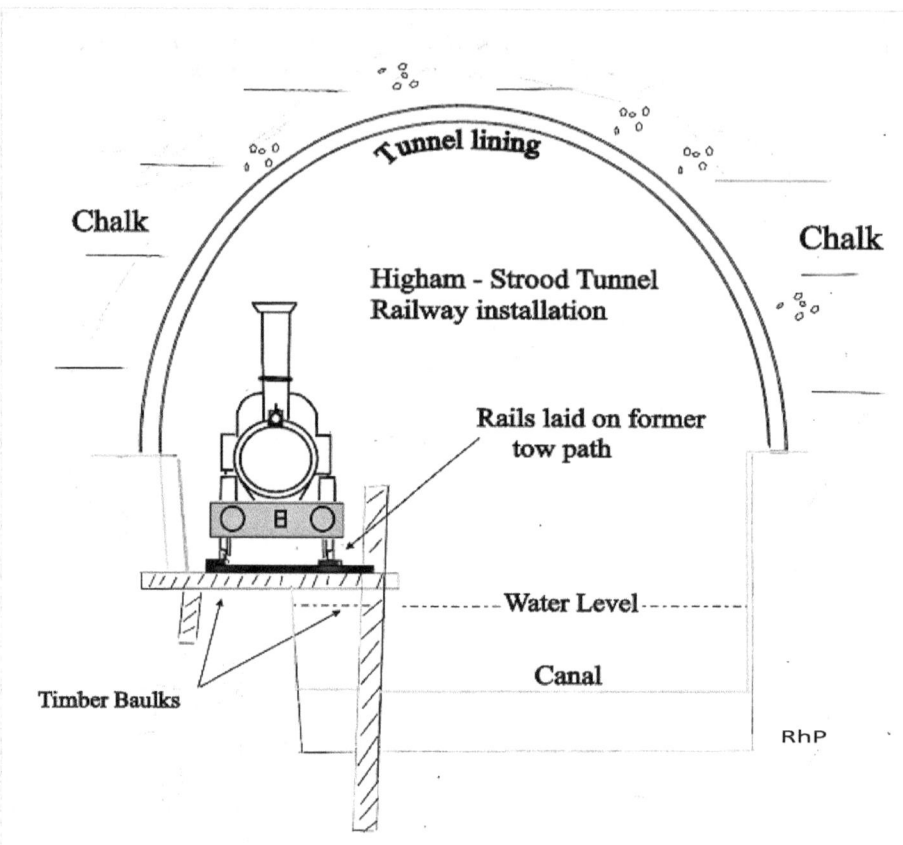

the lookers-on mustered in strong force at the various points on the line where the train was visible".

Providing connections with London, the conurbations of Gravesend, Rochester, Sheerness and other major towns of the county, the G&RR was part of an early form of an integrated transport system that used rail, road and waterborne transport links.

As the fastest of the links, the railways termini were conveniently located within walking distance of the river piers at Gravesend and Strood, where after alighting, passengers could continue their journey by a variety of transport methods. To connect with the awaiting stage-coaches at Rochester, a short walk over Rochester's Medieval bridge was all that was required, while those destined for the Isle of Sheppey could use a steamboat service by way of Chatham to Sheerness.

Vandalism was not unknown on the G&RR, passengers frequently opening the carriage's doors while in the Higham to Strood tunnel with calamitous results. After considerable damage to carriage doors, and near misses with passenger's heads, carriages had bars fitted to their windows and their doors locked before departure to deter this behaviour. A convicted vandal was James Bowney. A 24 year old labourer, tried for throwing a stone at the railway at Gravesend, the *London Standard* of the 11th of March 1846 reported his penalty as a sentence of six months hard labour.

To avoid structural damage to the Higham to Strood tunnel, its locomotives were fitted with special smoke deflectors to divert their exhaust away from its chalk walls and the train's carriages.

The G&RR timetable for 1845 shows an intensive service of 18 trains a day with a forecast journey time of 20 minutes between the two termini. There is no mention of signalling on the G&RR, its trains starting away with the ringing of a bell. Presumably there must have been some hand signalmen, especially at the Higham to Strood tunnel portals. The tradition of ringing a bell before a train departed was to last well into the 20th century and as late as 1952, a bell was still being rung five minutes before train departures at Westcliffe station, Essex.

Deviating away from our story slightly, the most prominent accident of recent times to occur in the Higham to Strood tunnel came in 1999 when a major chalk fall caused the calamitous derailing of a four carriage passenger train. Thought to have been caused by a water course diversion during external building works, its 56 shaken passengers had to be rescued from the tunnel.

Pending investigations, a temporary 20 mph speed limit was imposed and when surveys identified instability, a decision was taken to line the tunnel walls throughout with concrete segments. Closing in January 2004 for both re-lining and permanent way renewal works, it re-opened in January 2005.

A journey through the tunnel in its early railway days was found to be unpleasant by some and an account of travel through the tunnel in 1847 was given by William Orr:

"The ride through the dreary tunnel with the dark waters of the canal beneath us, and an insecure chalk roof above our heads, enlivened as it is by occasional shrieks from the engine's vaporous lungs, and the unceasing rattle of the train, is apt to make one feel somewhat nervous. The first glimpse of bright daylight that breaks upon us, relieves us from a natural anxiety as to the chances we run of being crushed by the fall of some twenty tons of chalk from above, or being precipitated into twenty feet of water beneath"

William certainly had cause for trepidation. On the 28th of July 1855 a train composed of nine carriages derailed in the tunnel, the locomotive then burying itself into the chalk walls. Fortunately, no one was seriously injured and the cause of this incident was traced to the failure of the fragile wooden dowel pegs used to fasten rail chairs to sleepers.

Although the G&RR's life as an independent concern was short it was, however, successful. Profits quickly increasing, these were sufficient by 1846 to purchase a further locomotive, the *Van Tromp,* and to consider the purchase of more 3rd class trucks and a further locomotive. With success came thoughts of expansion, an extension to Gravesend town centre being considered, when the pioneering railway engineer, Robert Stephenson, was consulted on this, one of his recommendations was to fill in the canal tunnel for use by a double track railway only.

The SER, wishing to use the G&RR as a part of their North Kent Railway, made an offer of purchase, and on the 17th of May 1846, the sale of both railway and canal was ratified at the handsome price of £310,000. With the passing of Act 9 &10 Vic. Cap. 339 on the 3rd August 1846, the sale of the G&RR then authorised, it was vested into the SER on the 27th September 1846.

Herepath's Journal for 1849 shows the SER had made a wise purchase; G&RR passenger numbers having risen by 30,337 over the numbers for 1848, receipts had increased by £895-10/s.

The Gravesend terminus of the Gravesend & Rochester Railway seen from the Thames entrance lock to the canal

The South Eastern Railway 1846

The 1840's were an era of cheap money, the bank rate then being a very reasonable 3¼ percent, and by the passing of the 1844 Bank Charter Act, ¶ the Peel government created stability and increased confidence in the pound sterling. Directly affecting the speculative world of railway construction finance, it increased the availability of loans.

Great profits were being forecast in the prospectuses of the quickly proliferating railway schemes of the day this caused a great deal of frantic speculation. Small investors becoming desperate to possess railway stocks and shares, this period is known as the era of "Railway Mania". A period of financial volatility, this was when the SER proposed a new line into Kent.

An already established railway, the SER was originally incorporated in June of 1836 as the South Eastern and Dover Railway, the company changed it's name shortly afterwards to the South Eastern Railway (SER).

Embodied to promote and build a London to Dover Railway, it duly did so, but only after being pressured by Parliament into sharing the route with the London & Brighton Railway as far as Redhill. Their wholly owned part of the line now reduced to a Redhill-Tonbridge-Ashford-Dover section, construction starting in 1838, the line reached Dover in February 1844.

In January 1845, the SER took over the lease of the existing London and Greenwich Railway, this giving them control of their main line into London Bridge and what now was a branch line to Greenwich.

Having had tried earlier to use this branch to extend eastwards, the SER attempted to do

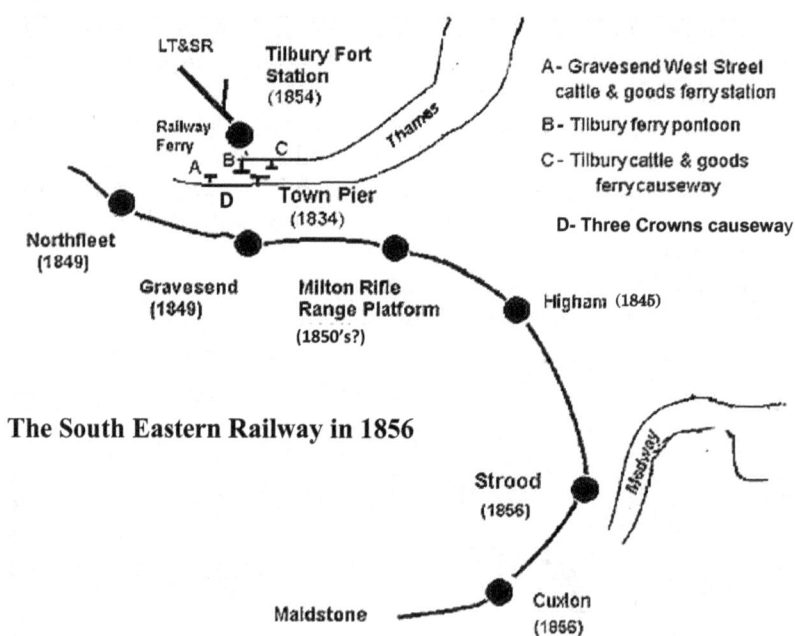

The South Eastern Railway in 1856

¶ *This Act restricted the right to issue bank notes to the Bank of England only. Prior to this, joint stock banks had the right to issue their own bank notes. With these banks increasing rapidly in numbers from the early nineteenth century, the amount of paper money in circulation exceeding the amount of gold bullion held by the Bank of England, this resulted in a recession.*

so again in 1845, but strong opposition from both Greenwich Hospital and the Admiralty frustrated this once more and it was to be 1878 before an extension to this line opened to Charlton.

To enable the SER to project a railway further into North Kent, a secondary main line was started in 1848. Known as the North Kent Railway (NKR), it avoided contentious locations by being built away from Greenwich and its associated problems.

The first major railway to pass through Gravesham, it is still with us today as the North Kent line. Starting at Deptford at the aptly named North Kent Junction, it diverges from the former SER main line in an easterly direction on its way to Strood. Passing through Lewisham by way of St Johns, the line then describes a near half circle to add the towns of Blackheath, Charlton and Woolwich along its line of way.

Heavily engineered in the vicinity of Greenwich and Woolwich, this was mandated in order to avoid Greenwich Observatory, the astronomers there being concerned that the passing of trains would upset their delicate instruments.

The military also caused difficulties for the SER by insisting that the area they used for manoeuvres at Woolwich was to remain both intact and unaltered.

Once again heavily engineered to meet the Army's requirements, the line runs in either cuttings or tunnels for most of its route between New Cross and Woolwich. Liberally provided with infrastructure works, the line courses through ten major tunnels on its 30 mile route, all but two being in suburban areas.

After leaving behind the urban sprawl of London's suburbs and their Kentish borderlands, after passing Gravesend the more open and expansive terrain of the Thames marshlands are reached. Then passing Higham, the line runs through the 2.2 mile Higham- Strood tunnel to its Strood terminus.

Previously a canal tunnel, it was converted wholly to railway use in 1846. An expensive conversion, Herepath's *Railway Journal* of 1846 records the cost of its widening and the upgrading of the former G&RR at £100,000. In operation before the link up of the G&RR with NKR in 1849, the SER had restarted the Gravesend to Strood services on the 23rd of August 1847 to recoup part of their outlay.

Identifying the engineer of the NKR is something that cannot be done with much certainty. One Hutton Vignolles the most likely candidate, a clue to this lies in his name appearing in Herepath's Railway Journal No. 304 Vol 7 of 1845 where the term "North Kent (Vignolles) Line" is used.

Something of a workaholic in the mould of Brunel, Vignolles was known to drive himself to the point of exhaustion. After falling asleep, sometimes he could not be woken, and when then rolled into bed, he had to have his Wellington boots cut off him!

Returning now to its rival, the LC&NKR, this also was a creation of Vignolles. Projecting this line to cross the Medway by way of a combined road and rail bridge, its route was then to follow the east bank of the Medway as far as Sheerness.

Map of a rural SER Gravesend Station in 1852; note the carriage shed by the Stone Street over bridge.

Favoured by both the Admiralty and Parliament, there was more than a good chance that it was the preferred proposal, and resort to bribery suspected to have given the preference to the NKR, Vignolles was a possible beneficiary. Appearing in front of a select committee in June 1845 §, he certainly spoke favourably of the SER's scheme, and upon receiving Parliament's blessing, the SER quickly pressed ahead with building the NKR.

Having had some five years experience of both running and building railways, it would be thought that the SER would be reasonably capable of opening the short NKR with little trouble. However, when it came to choosing contractors, this was not to be, and allowing nepotism to override financial prudence, they chose John Brogden, a son of one of the members of the SER board, to construct part of

§ *Select Committee on Railway Bills 11th June 1845.*

the line, when despite his offer being higher than either of the other two bidders, he won a contract to build part of the works. Somewhat predictably, when Brogden Junior failed to meet his contractual obligations, the SER had recourse to law in July 1849 to gain possession of their line.

Disputes concerning the price of land were a commonplace during the building of the early railways and the NKR was to be no exception. A typical example illuminating this was a conflict that arose over local land prices ¶ in the August of 1847. Having offered £6,000 to purchase the property of a Mr. Fowler, after some further surveys, the SER reduced their offer to £4,480 and in an attempt to gain the higher price, Mr. Fowler described this land as being *"very eligible for building"*. As we shall see, this was a common ploy used to enhance a properties value.

An aggrieved Mr. Fowler then taking his objections to law, the case being heard at Gravesend's Town Hall, it was considered of sufficient important for a jury to be sworn in and the Attorney General to become involved.

Unfortunately, the juries decision is currently unknown, but the SER may have achieved the lower price by using a compulsory purchase order. Familiar now for other purposes such as motorway building, the Land Clauses Consolidation Act of 1845 was first introduced to remove the need for private Parliamentary Acts for the purchase of disputed land required for railway building.

The land in question was an important part of the route. Forming a corridor between existing housing and Milton church, the railway crossing the Strood Turnpike road here on the level, a former crossing keeper's cottage existed here until the early 1970's. The crossing closing in 1865, it was superseded by the present over bridge.

Turning now to the NKR's route through Gravesham. Entering Gravesham from the west on a narrow ridge of chalk, this was not the case when built, the former arable farmland having been excavated away since on either side for chalk by the cement industry. After crossing over the HS1 railway at Galley Hill, the line then passes on an embankment and bridge over the valley of the small River Ebbsfleet. Once a source of major flooding, the Ebbsfleet in this area has now been diverted into a culvert.

After coursing past Northfleet station, the line then traversing another excavated chalk ridge, this was made famous when Bradshaw's 1863 guide waxed lyrical about Northfleet by stating:

"The extensive excavations about here, forming a sort of miniature Switzerland, not only give the scenery a wild and romantic aspect, but furnish valuable materials for the potteries."

Then entering a cutting, the railway crosses above the A2260 Thames Way road by way of a modern bridge. Recently opened, this road follows the alignment of the former Gravesend Railway. Continuing then in cuttings, it is near to a pedestrian footbridge at Mayfield Road that the summit of the NKR in Gravesham is reached at 65 feet above sea level.

A further third of a mile bringing the line to Gravesend station, the rails can be seen to be gently curving in under Darnley Road from the southwest. This, however, was not the lines intended alignment, the change of course being a result of the railway's surveyors siting the line away from its original route, intended to run parallel to the present A226 Overcliffe Road.

A product of a Gravesend builders attempt to make a financial gain from the railway's arrival by declaring the land was to be used for a housing development, the SER diverted the line onto its present course after refusing the builder's asking price. As we saw earlier in the case of Mr. Fowler, the purchase price then being enhanced, t h i s ploy was often used by those selling land to the railway.

Existing properties on the line's course occasionally required demolishing, and with some dwellings succumbing to the east of Gravesend at Chalk, the villagers petitioned the SER. Claiming that some "30 cottages" had been demolished to make way for the line, the SER replying that only "three to four houses" had been removed.

Leaving Gravesend station towards the east, the line then enters brick lined cuttings, where after passing under nine road bridges, it emerges at Milton to follow the 1849 SER route for a mile

¶ *Kentish Gazette August 1847*

or so until it joins the 1845 alignment of the G&RR near to the site of the former Denton level crossing.

The 1845 railway having hugged the canal's route throughout, the SER's 1849 formation removes a large loop in the original G&RR route close to Hoo Junction. Rejoining the G&RR formation just before Higham station, the NKR then passes through the Higham to Strood tunnel to emerge at Strood station. However, this was not the original terminus of the G&RR, the current station site dates from 1856 when it opened with what is now the Medway Valley line.

With most disputes largely resolved, the line completed and approval given for opening by the Board of Trade's inspector, a tour of the NKR and its stations was undertaken by directors and officials of the SER. Travelling by a special train hauled by no less than three locomotives, this cavalcade was either an insurance against breakdown or more likely purely a grand spectacle.

Once satisfied with their new railway, the directors allowed its opening throughout in July 1849, and North Kent was finally rail connected to the capital. The celebration in Gravesend was described as "a sumptuous banquet" provided for the directors of the SER by a grateful Gravesend Corporation in the Clifton Hotel, Gravesend.

Travel on the new railway was at quite a leisurely pace by today's standards; the average speed of early SER passenger trains being a brisk 20 mph, this was a surprising six miles an hour faster than the grand Great Western Railways (GWR) average speed of 14 mph.

Few people at this time were likely to have travelled at speeds greater than 14 mph, the maximum speed of contemporary mail coaches and the highest speed most people are likely to have experienced would have been around 25 mph, the speed of a galloping horse.

In 1864 the SER extended its domain into London's West End by opening the Charing Cross Extension Railway. A continuation from London Bridge station, it crossed the Thames via Hungerford Bridge. Access to the City was achieved in September 1866 by way of a further extension using Cannon Street Bridge to access Cannon Street station. To the east, however, little had changed. Any direct rail journeys further into Kent from Strood had to be undertaken either via the SER's Medway Valley route, or by pedestrian interchange between the LC&DR and SER stations, as despite numerous requests from Rochester Corporation, to provide a link as no rail connection existed between the two stations.

Mr. N. E. Toomer, then the Mayor of Rochester, becoming somewhat frustrated with the intransigence of both the SER and the LC&DR over this issue, decided to take his grievances to the Railway Commissioners, who in January 1876 granted an order for the re-opening of the disused 1861 rail link between the LC&DR and the SER at Strood. Only used for passenger transfer, it became known thereafter as the "Toomer Loop" in recognition the Mayor's achievement.

This connection had not been an easy one to achieve, the LC&DR having no wish for the SER to gain access to the Medway Towns traffic, the Chairman of the LC&DR remained adamant right up until 1898 that SER trains were not to be given running powers over LC&DR metals.

While on the subject of railway management, a few words on their set-up may be appropriate. At the dawn of the railways there were few other large organisations beyond H.M armed forces, and this was the model that the SER used for its management structure as did other railways of the time.

This naturally led to a hierarchical employee grade system with senior managers being referred to as officers. An archaic style of management, as many veteran railwaymen will remember it survived until recent years. Like the army, many orders were issued in writing and direction for railwaymen came from the Rule Book, a manual that succinctly detailed their duties. For instance, the SER Rules and Regulations of November 1857 states that every employee was to read the Rule Book monthly and were to be tested on their knowledge of it on a three monthly basis. For those unable to read, it was to be read to them.

Between Downs and Thames - Railways of Gravesend, the Hoo Peninsular and Isle of Grain

Dating from 1895 is a transcription from J. Pearson Pattison's "The South Eastern Railway" showing timings for Gravesend to London Bridge trains via the North Kent and Sidcup Loop lines. Locomotive No. 38 refers to a Class 118 locomotive, then over 30 years old, No. 58 was a relatively new Q Class 0-4-4 tank engine. For more details on the Q Class refer to page 202.

Train			Run No. 143		Run No. 144	
From	Gravesend					
To	London Bridge					
Due to arrive			10.51		10.51	
Engine			Class 118 2-4-0		Q Class 0-4-4 Tank	
Load (coaches)			9		9	
Departure			10.18.4s		10.19.0s	
	Distance		Time from start		Time from start	
	Miles	Chains	Minutes	Seconds	Minutes	Seconds
Gravesend						
Northfleet	2	1	4	2	4	10
Greenhithe	4	11	6	51	7	3
Dartford	6	65	10	13	10	47
Crayford	8	51	12	37	16	37
Bexley	10	6	14	34	15	29
Sidcup	12	1	17	30	18	31
New Eltham	13	45	21	14	20	34
Eltham	14	41	21	14	21	44
Lee	16	21	23	33	23	47
St Johns	18	26	26	56	26	47
Spa Road	21	8	29	57	30	29
London Bridge	22	3	31	47	32	22
Arrival (actual)			10 49	51	10 51	12
Time taken			31	47	32	12
Time allowed			33	0	33	0
Signal delays			0	15	0	0
Gain			1	13	0	38

An example of an SER Class 118 locomotive mentioned in the performance chart above. Introduced in 1859, the drawing shows the class as it would have appeared in 1866 after rebuilding. Regular performers locally, at one time they formed the majority of the locomotive stock of the SER and they could be found hauling anything from the railway's most prestigious expresses such as "The Tidal" between London and Dover down to humble goods services. By 1895 the class had been much reduced, and all were gone by October 1905 when No. 247A was condemned after working as Redhill station pilot.

RhP

However, on the plus side, the railways did provide their staff with uniforms and this was a major reason for joining the railway in an era when personal clothing was an expensive item. Depending on their grade, new uniforms were issued annually in May, with new topcoats being provided every two years. A great status symbol for the day, for those who needed them for time-keeping, pocket watches were issued. Despite the issue of watches to its staff, the punctuality of the SER remained lamentable and it was accused of ignoring its commuters needs by giving preference to its continental traffic.

To investigate this claim, or more likely, to sensationalise it, on the 16th of August 1888, a young newspaper reporter undertook a journey by stopping train from Gravesend to London. Dubbing this train the "Flying Watkin", this was no doubt a tongue in cheek reference to the SER chairman, Sir Edward Watkin.

Describing the train as being composed of 15 vehicles, only two of which were of a similar height or matching livery, a mixture of passenger and goods rolling stock, its make-up included a cattle van coupled next to the last vehicle, a 3rd Class carriage.

Due to leave at 12:15 pm, its departure was delayed while milk churns were loaded and two gentlemen finished their beer! The train's journey to Dartford taking 35 minutes, speeds dropped to 12 mph on rising gradients. Finally arriving at Charing Cross after a near two hour journey, the maximum speed reached a giddy 30 mph, the trains motion at this velocity was such that oil spilled from the carriage's lamps.

The train's locomotive described as a six wheeled "boneshaker", its makers plate displayed a date of 1850. If correct this may identify it as a member of the SER's *Folkestone* Class. Originally constructed as 4-2-0 Crampton types, these locomotives were rebuilt between 1868 and 1869 as 2-4-0's.

Engaged in a bitter competition with its two rivals, the LC&DR and the LB&SCR, the SER expended much capital in feuding. Having made all three impecunious, a Bill came before Parliament in 1868 seeking co-operation between these three companies and the LS&WR. However, this was to fail when the SER refused to limit their fares to those of the LS&WR. Not the last attempt at creating more harmonious relations, other fruitless attempts were made in 1875 and 1887.

This rivalry did, however, act as a spur with each company offering either faster journey times or lower fares, and by the end of the 19th century, with nearly identical services provided to the towns they served, this was becoming ruinous for both companies.

Therefore, with bankruptcy looming, on the 1st of January 1899 a working union between the LC&DR and the SER was agreed. Each company keeping it's board of directors, the railway was to be run by a joint Management Committee, and on the 5th of August 1899, when the South Eastern & London, Chatham and Dover Railway Act was passed, the amalgamation between the two was confirmed under the name of the South Eastern and Chatham Railway.

The London Chatham & Dover Railway 1860

Thus far the SER had enjoyed a monopoly of rail traffic in the Gravesham area, its only railway competitor being the LT&SR via the Gravesend to Tilbury ferry. Whilst the ferry gave access to the cheaper fares of this Essex railway, it was not seen as a serious threat by the SER, as passengers using the LT&SR facing a crossing of the often foggy River Thames, a return journey was uncertain before the 1956 Clean Air Act alleviated these notorious smog's.

However, 1858 saw a much more serious railway competitor appear on the scene. This was the East Kent Railway Company, whose stated intention was to cross the Medway and then build a railway from Canterbury to Strood to link up with the SER.

Having recently started on building an extension railway from Strood to their main line at Paddock Wood via the 1844 Maidstone branch, the SER did not see the need for such a line, a belief they based upon their estimate that the potential revenues from East Kent were insufficient to justify building both a bridge over the Medway and a railway extending eastwards. Ironically, they did just this at great expense in 1891 when building what was the most wasteful of their competitive ventures, the doomed Chatham extension.

East Kent and the popular Thanet resorts were poorly served by railways in the 1850's. To travel from London to Ramsgate by railway throughout involved a tiring and expensive journey of 102 miles, whereas it was a little over 75 miles by road. Furthermore, the City of Rochester and the naval dockyard at Chatham having no rail link nearer than Strood, the medium sized towns of Faversham and Sittingbourne were completely without rail communication, as was Sheerness and its naval dockyard. This situation causing the local populace and the areas businesses to agitate for a railway of their own, the East Kent Railway (EKR) was incorporated in response to this.

A Bill for the construction of this new railway was introduced to Parliament by the EKR in 1853. Intending to connect to the Cinque Port town of Faversham by a branch, the plan was later altered to include Faversham on its main line.

For some unfathomable reason, the SER took a most relaxed view of this new railway venture, as they were probably supremely confident of its inevitable failure. The proposer's of the EKR seem to have also shared this view, offering a lease on the line to the SER for a trifling 5%. Convinced they could purchase the line for a pittance after its failure, the SER refused. How many times must the SER have rued missing the opportunity of killing off their main rival before its birth?

Even without any serious opposition, it looked as if the EKR's Bill would be thrown out by Parliament, but a petition from the inhabitants of East Kent was given a sympathetic ear and persuaded the House to allow a deposit of the plans.

The new line was also looked on with favour by the military as it was "*deemed of great national importance for the defences of the kingdom*" by aiding the rapid movement of troops and martial equipment between the Woolwich Royal Arsenal, Chatham Dockyard and the port of Dover. At a time of heightened tension with the French Empire, this must surely have weighed heavily with Parliament's decision.

Thomas Crampton appointed as engineer for the line, he in turn deputised Joseph Cubitt as the designer of the magnificent four span iron railway bridge to cross the Medway at Rochester. At the insistence of the Admiralty, this iron bridge also included a lifting portion for the passage of tall-masted ships. Opening on the 29th of March 1858, trains then started running to Strood from Faversham on the partially complete EKR.

The Act of Parliament that authorised the building of the EKR also granted access rights or running powers for EKR carriages and other rolling stock to travel over the NKR, be it only behind SER locomotives.

Supposedly, the carriages of the EKR having equality of access to the NKR with those of the SER, the Act also stipulated the provision of through ticketing and holding of SER trains for connections with EKR services or vice versa.

With the apparent success of the new EKR line, the SER seems to have become deliberately obstructive, insisting that EKR passengers de-train at Strood and purchase SER tickets for onward travel, thus missing their connections. This was to be a foretaste of the rivalry that was to exist between the two companies for the next 40 years.

Aggrieved by the SER's behaviour, the EKR then instigated a Board of Trade enquiry. Unfortunately for the EKR, the enquiry found against them and this affirmed to the EKR that it needed its own route from Strood to London.

Approaching Parliament in 1857 with a Bill to enable the building of this extension line, once again the SER offered little opposition, their acquiescence is believed to be due to an agreement with the EKR that they would offer no resistance to any SER plans for possible extensions into east Kent.

An Act to enable the EKR's new line was duly passed in July 1858, after which the line became known as the London Extension. As conceived by its designer, Thomas Crampton, it was to pass through North Kent to Shortlands, where it would connect to the West End of London & Crystal Palace Railway, thus giving the EKR access to Battersea and thence to Victoria station by way of a connection with the Victoria Station & Pimlico Railway. With these plans accepted, on the 1st of August 1859, the EKR changed its name to the grander sounding London, Chatham and Dover Railway (LC&DR).

The contract for the lines construction was placed with Messrs. Peto & Betts, their agent, Mr. C. Watson directing the building works. As with the construction of all lines of this era, the use of significant mechanical aids was largely unknown, the construction of the LC&DR relying largely upon the muscle power of man and horse.

Building of the line was not without mishap; an embankment at Strood collapsing overnight, by morning a black ooze was to be seen floating in its place. Stabilised only after extensive piling had been undertaken, a brick viaduct replaced the embankment. ¶

Another difficult section was the deep cutting on Sole Street Bank between Cobhambury and Sole Street. Had the level here been only a few feet lower, the railway would have been in tunnel. Earl Darnley of Cobham Hall implacably opposed to the LC&DR, he short sightedly refused permission for a Cobham station.

Completed in sections, the railway opened through North Kent on the 3rd of December 1860, although access to the new line did not come locally until the opening on the 1st of February 1861 of Sole Street station, with Meopham station following on the 6th of May 1861.

A local newspaper of the 3rd of December 1860 gave this description of the line on opening:

"The portion which will be opened today will entirely divert traffic from the North Kent to the London, Chatham and Dover line. Its length is nearly twenty-two miles, the cuttings and embankments being of a very substantial nature, there being scarcely a mile of level line between Strood and Bickley and the whole line has been very carefully laid out"

In the June 1927 edition of the Hartley Parochial magazine, an article by an elderly lady, recalled the building of the railway, saying that the people were very pleased at the making of

¶ *Gravesend Magazine – How the iron road came to Kent.*

the railway, and after church they walked to the site to view progress.

The new line was not an easy one to work compared to the rival SER line, and as noted in the newspaper report of 1860, it was both heavily engineered and steeply graded throughout Gravesham. The first part of its route following a steep incline of the North Downs, this was a slope that became known to generations of railwaymen as Sole Street Bank.

A major challenge to locomotives and their crews in the steam era, its ruling gradient, the steepest part of the incline at 1:100 over the five miles between the Medway Valley and Sole Street station, this was the steepest main line bank on the LC&DR. The locomotives and their crews were given a breather at Sole Street station, the lines summit in Gravesham. Briefly then running on the level, upon leaving Meopham Station, by way of embankments and cuttings, it finally departs Gravesham at Longfield Hill.

Never a very prosperous company, the original EKR's financial situation had been shaky from its beginnings with the line's contractors often going unpaid, things were to get worse for the LC&DR.

The parliamentary Acts that authorised a company to build a new railway containing certain clauses limiting the new company's loan raising capacity to not more than a third of the company's authorised share capital, agreement to these clauses was mandatory, and before any loans could be taken out, as a safeguard, evidence had to be provided to a Judge that at least 50% of the capital required had been paid into the company's bank.

Trying to circumvent these requirements was to be the cause of the severest of the LC&DR's financial woes, this transgression was exposed when building a new line between London Bridge and Victoria.

Messrs Peto and Betts, in a somewhat close collaboration with Crampton were selected as contractors for this line and to finance it, a cunning subterfuge was used. Shares and debentures were issued in the names of Peto, Betts and Crampton and the LC&DR accounts were written up to make it look as though the associated cash payments from the trio had been made to the railway. The non-existent money was then supposedly lent back to them to fund the construction of the line, whereas in fact, no money had actually changed hands.

Being somewhat casual about their financial affairs, although no evidence for this exists, it is possible Peto & Betts used a similar scheme to finance the London extension.

All went well until 1866, when the unexpected and disastrous collapse of the LC&DR's bank, Overend, Gurney and Co, caused the last major run on a UK Bank before Northern Rock's 2007 collapse. Then becoming public knowledge that the LC&DR was borrowing money illegally and funding construction works by devious means to get round Parliament's loan restrictions. Then refused further loans, the LC&DR became insolvent.

Consequently, the LC&DR board and its solicitors pursued Peto, Betts and Crampton for damages, making personal claims against the trio for the stupendous sum of £6,661,941. The guilty trio eventually admitting to owing the sum of £365,000 to the LC&DR, somewhat grudgingly, this was the figure accepted by the company. The affair ruining the reputation of both Peto and Betts, both died in obscurity. Although a bankrupt, Crampton's reputation surviving, he continued in business.

The LC&DR or the "Chatham" as it was alternatively known, was much criticised for its lamentable carriage stock and poor punctuality. However, having an excellent safety record, it was in part due to use of the superior Westinghouse air brake and implementation of the Sykes "Lock and Block" signalling system. A sophisticated scheme, this included electrical and mechanical safety interlocks between signals, track and trains. Bankruptcy never far away, in 1898 the LC&DR agreed to share operations with the SER and the two companies becoming known as the South Eastern and Chatham Railway on the 1st of January 1899, the first joint working was in October 1898, fierce gales in the Channel diverting an LC&DR boat train over SER metals into Folkestone.

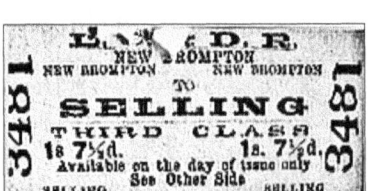

London Chatham & Dover ticket from New Brompton to Selling. New Brompton is better known today as Gillingham. Dave Fisher collection

The Gravesend Railway 1886

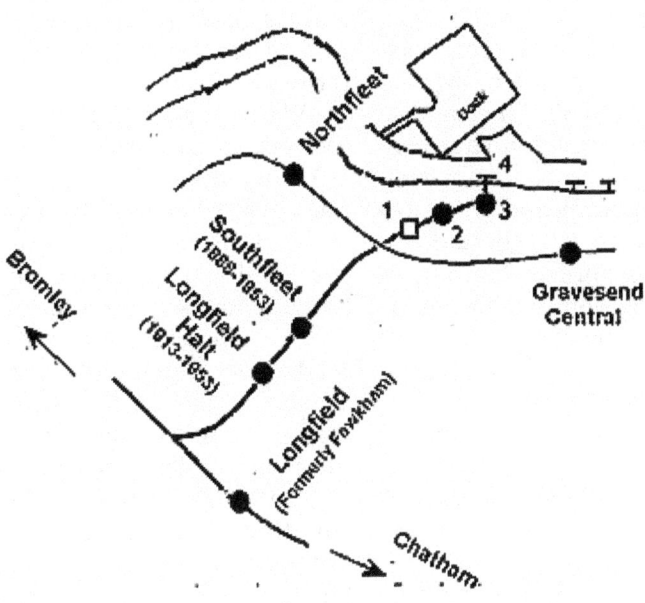

1 - Perry Street Loco Shed (1886-1926)
2 - Rosherville Station (1886-1933)
3 - West Street Station (1886-1967*)
4 - West Street Pier (1886-1966)

Goods only from 1953

No doubt the LC&DR viewed with some envy the SER's abundant rail-borne trade with the then rapidly growing conurbations of Gravesend and Northfleet, they themselves having no rail connection to either.

After the 1882 opening by the SER of its Hundred of Hoo Railway to Port Victoria, the LC&DR were resolved to construct their own competing line upriver at Gravesend. As we have seen, with its access to the Thames, the town was a popular tourist resort, possessing attractions such as the Rosherville Gardens and many other pleasure spots to tempt the day tripper. Taking into account the towns considerable commercial and industrial traffic, Gravesend was certainly a tempting destination and to access this traffic, a branch from the LC&DR was proposed in 1881.

Obtaining an Act of Parliament ¶ for this branch in July 1881, this authorised the Gravesend Railway Company to build a double track railway of almost five miles in length between Gravesend and Fawkham. Also assented to, but never built, was a short branch to a pier at Northfleet.

Starting from a connection with the LC&DR main line at Fawkham Junction, the line was originally to have terminated at a Princes Street, Gravesend station. However, as a cost saving measure the lines terminus station was later relocated to Bath Street on the site of the Fair Field. This also deleted, the line's terminus station was finally built at Stuart Road.

That by now familiar aristocrat, the Earl of Darnley, then made an appearance. As owner of the land needed by the railway, he tried using the timeworn ploy of announcing that the land needed by the new railway having already been earmarked for development, it was by this stratagem he hoped to elevate its value. His claim, however, like that of many others before him was unsuccessful.

Access to the River Thames was the other major force behind building the new Gravesend

¶ *Gravesend Railway Act 1881 44-45 Vic.C.144.*

Railway and in July 1882, the 1881 Act was amended to permit a 160 yard extension of the railway to a riverside pier.

The impetus to construct this pier was driven largely by the LC&DR's desire to bypass the Continental Agreement of 1863. A compact agreed with the SER, this stipulated that the receipts from the boat train traffic from the Channel ports between Hastings and Margate were to be shared between the two companies.

As Gravesend was outside of this boundary, it was exempted from the agreement, as would any revenues from steamer services attracted by the LC&DR to the town. Another incentive was the potential for revenue from conveying passengers of the Peninsular & Orient shipping line, whose magnificent ocean liners often lay at anchor in the deep water off Gravesend. As we shall see later, things weren't quite to work out with this new pier.

The contract to build the line was let on the 18th October of 1882 to a G. Barclay-Bruce, who as a contractor had a pedigree of building lines in South America, Europe and India as well as the East Somerset Railway. Obtaining another Act of Parliament shortly before starting the railway's construction phase, the LC&DR took ownership of the Gravesend Railway for the sum of £245,700, the Gravesend Railway was duly vested into the LC&DR on the 29th of June 1883.

On the following day, the 30th of June 1883, Lady Waterlow, the wife of the erstwhile Gravesend Railway's Company's chairman, Sir Sidney Waterlow Bart, ceremoniously cut the first sod at Gravesend West. Sir Sidney, also the local Member of Parliament, was later to reside at Trosley Towers and his coat of arms is still to be seen on the pedestrian bridge that crosses over Trottiscliffe Road.

Initially, the railway was to be provided with just two intermediate stations, Southfleet and Rosherville with a small locomotive shed provided at Perry Street for servicing the line's engines.

Construction work progressing in stages under the direction of the railways engineer, C.D. Fox, due to the nature of the terrain, the gently sloping scarp slope of the North Downs, this made the line another heavily engineered railway. The formation for most of its route running either in cuttings or on embankments, it fell at an almost constant incline between Fawkham Junction and Gravesend West station and natural ground level was only obtained at Fawkham Junction and it's Gravesend West terminus.

A lavishly equipped railway, befitting what was seen as an extension of the main line, it was officially opened on the 17th of April 1886, Lady Waterlow once again officiating by being assisted to drive the inaugural train. Following the obligatory opening ceremonies at Gravesend West station, the party then retired to the New Falcon Hotel for the usual celebratory lunch and congratulatory speeches. Coincidentally, also the opening day for Tilbury Docks, the party then bade farewell and crossed the river to Tilbury to join the celebrations there.

The 10th of May 1886 the day the public was admitted to the railway, this was only after the Earl of Darnley had tried to halt proceedings, his workmen erecting barriers in Stuart Road to foil public access to Gravesend West station. At the time, owning Stuart Road amongst others in the town, he disputed the railways right of use to this thoroughfare. After a tense half hour, the railway had these barriers removed and the railway opened for business, the dispute was later settled by arbitration.

Initially the new line offered a service of 14 daily weekday passenger trains direct to London, but by April 1892, these services had been cut back to ten daily departures. With a journey time to London Victoria from Gravesend West of 75 minutes, this compared unfavourably with its SER rival at Rathmore Road.

Looking at one such departure, the 9:30 am Gravesend to Victoria "cheap train", a discounted fare for a 3rd class journey on this service could be had for the princely sum of 1/-6d return. With a 1st class annual season ticket to Victoria priced at £4-10/-0d, it compared unfavourably with the equivalent SER's fare of £2 and 2 shillings, as did conveyance of small goods, the door to door delivery of a 14 pound parcel costing 4d.

Not everyone was happy with the arrival of the new railway, and in 1886 a letter was published in the *Gravesend Reporter* from "An Indignant Shareholder" who complained:

"Why was the Gravesend Railway and the magnificent pier at the end of it ever constructed? Everybody thought that when this railway was opened that at last we should have facilities given us for joining the main line down to Sevenoaks, Tunbridge Wells & from Swanley Junction, or down to Canterbury and Dover and the sea coast, from Farningham Road. An inspection however of the published timetable showed at once that any expectations of the sort were futile. For instance there is a down main line train that calls at Farningham Road at 10:46 am, and there is a train that leaves Gravesend at 10:40 am (the first for two hours to Farningham Road until 10 minutes after the down train has gone.)"

The correspondent then goes on to say that the London Tilbury & Southend Railway ran 38 trains each day, 12 of which were expresses. His parting comment, stating the obvious, was that the line had only been built to compete with the SER and LT&SR.

In 1886, a return excursion fare from Victoria station including admission to Gravesend's main tourist attraction, the Rosherville Gardens, cost 1/-9d. Competition for this market was keen, however, the London Tilbury & Southend Railway's fare from Fenchurch Street being a whole 3d cheaper at 1/-6d, this fare also included admission to the Gardens and a return ferry journey to Tilbury.

As the 19th century progressed, another source of revenue was to come to West Street. The Belle Steamer company, their paddlers called at the new pier to embark leisured passengers for voyages to either Yarmouth, Clacton or Felixstowe. Special services were put on by the LC&DR to connect with these steamer services. Advertised as "express", they were in fact semi-fasts. Using through ticketing, a 3rd class day tripper, once paying a 6/-0d fare at Victoria, could enjoy several hours at Clacton before returning to Victoria in the evening.

After the 1899 formation of the SE&CR, various new works were undertaken to improve the groups efficiency and effect connections between the two former rivals. Surveys being undertaken in 1903 in Gravesham to determine the feasibility of joining the former SER and LC&DR by a rail link, unfortunately it was not proceeded with, and had it been built, it would have given the town a direct connection from the SER station to London Victoria and perhaps part of the West Street branch, very probably electrified, would still be open today.

Goods revenue was important for the line, particularly later in its history when Thameside's industries had developed. The loads carried by the Gravesend Railway were varied and including coal, fish, general merchandise, farm produce, parcels, minerals and stone, another cargo was bagged cement.

A regular continental steamer trade having failed to materialise by the early years of the 20th century, the Gravesend Railway was by then seen as a branch rather than a main line, its loss of status reflected in being listed as the West Street branch in SE&CR timetables.

Fortunately, expansion of Gravesham's industries brought some additional revenue to the branch via manufactured goods traffic, and with the 1909 opening of Gravesend's Imperial paper mill, with rail connections made to the internal railway of the branch's most important customer, the traffic with the mill in 1913 contributed £24,000 to the SE&CR coffers.

Cement traffic from the nearby Tolhursts and Red Lion cement works was also important, as was the domestic coal and coke imported to coal merchants at Perry Street. General goods traffic also by then having increased, the SE&CR 1910 timetable lists an additional goods train arriving at Gravesend West for 3:20 pm.

However, passenger traffic had failed to develop as hoped, and by 1909 the passenger services having been reduced yet again to just six weekday London trains, this compared miserably with Gravesend Central station's 28 weekday London departures.

The final closure of the Rosherville Gardens in 1913 was a significant event for the branch. Bringing an end to its main source of passenger income, the direct passenger trains to London were then withdrawn and what passenger services remained were cut back to terminate at Swanley Junction station.

Very busy during the Great War, particularly with goods workings and troop trains, for a period during the conflict, the usual routes being closed during hostilities, letters, parcels and mail were brought to West Street Pier for onward shipment to the Netherlands.

Come 1922, an important new revenue stream came to Gravesend West, the Batavier

Line's overnight ferry to Rotterdam. A single through carriage provided from Victoria for its passengers, when this service became more popular, a dedicated boat train was provided.

In 1924, when Watling Street was widened to arterial road status as part of a government funded relief works programme, a major new railway bridge was built at Springhead to replace it's brick arch predecessor. Officially opened by the Prince of Wales, this riveted steel bridge, spanning the new road between Southfleet and Springhead, became a familiar local sight for many years.

By 1925, the branch's fortunes having revived somewhat, services increased to 12 trains daily, all these terminated at Swanley Junction with the exception of the one daily service to Victoria. Closure of the Rosherville Gardens having removed Rosherville station's main *raison d' être*, the resulting fall in passenger numbers did not justify its retention, and after a period of use as an un-staffed halt, on the 15th of July 1933, the 1915 wartime economy closure of Milton Road Halt excepted, Rosherville acquired the dubious honour of being the first local station to close.

Fruit being a staple traffic for the branch, this included cultivated blackberries whose orchards were for long a feature of the Southfleet and Swanscombe areas. In the late 1950's I surreptitiously visited these with my grandfather and very tasty these berries were. Now lost, they were grubbed-up during chalk extraction in the 1960's and 1970's.

Fruit and hop picking folk coming down from London by special trains during the season, camps for these casual workers existed at Longfield, Cobham, Higham and other local sites. A new traffic in the inter-war years was the import of coal to the Springhead sidings of the Central Electricity Generating Board. Long closed, these sidings were located close to where a high voltage switching complex stands today.

The branch visited by foreign locomotive types in Southern days, an ex-LB&SCR D1 Class 0-4-2 tank locomotive coming in 1928 with its two carriage set for crew training on the Westinghouse auto train (push-pull) system, another visitor was an ex-LS&WR M7 0-4-4 tank locomotive. Trialled on the branch in 1934, this large tank engine did not find favour with local railway management.

The Chatham main line electrified to Gillingham on the 27th of July 1939, the supply to the Fawkham traction section was taken from Springhead grid switching station. Fed by a large high voltage cable installed along the branch, it's presence was to be a major factor in the lines retention by BR long after train services had ceased.

When Dutch diamond merchants used the Batavier steamers and the boat trains to escape the Netherlands in May 1940 with their precious merchandise, the branch became known by railway staff as "The Diamond Line". The occupation of the continent bringing with it the suspension of the Batavier steamer service to Rotterdam and their boat trains, these were never to return.

Now without either boat trains or steamer services and the branch diminished in importance, wartime economy measures further reduced the already sparse service to just five weekday trains to Farningham Road only.

However, as in WWI, the branch saw an increase in goods and freight traffic and troop trains, some military traffic continuing into the early 1950's.

Incorporated on the 1st of January 1948 into British Railways, a partial revival in the branch's fortunes came two years after the end of hostilities. Although services were still running to a wartime timetable, the weekday passenger services destinations were extended once more to include Swanley.

The general Navigation Company's pleasure steamers returning once again to West Street Pier, the Saturday passenger services were increased to ten trains to connect with these.

However, despite these improvements, all was not well with the West Street branch, a

This Gibson style ticket is intriguing. As far as I am aware steam rail motors were not used on the branch, although converted rail car carriages were used on auto train workings, it is more likely to be the thrifty Southern using surplus ticket stock. Dave Fisher collection

passenger survey undertaken in 1952 revealing the branch's total annual passenger journeys to be just 21,069, with 57% of these journeys local to the branch, BR calculating that by ending passenger services, an annual saving of £11,000 could be realised, this spelt their doom. A proposal for closure then referred by BR to the Transport Users Consultative Committee, in the March of 1953, closure was approved, subject to the provision of additional local bus services.

There was, however, a fight back of sorts and objections to the closure were received from three Parish Councils, Dartford Rural District Council and the four persons who commuted regularly each weekday to Gravesend West from Orpington.

This challenge to the accuracy of the original survey giving the service a short reprieve while another survey was undertaken, regrettably, this only confirmed the first survey's data to be correct. Armed with this confirmation, BR ended the branch passenger services on the 3rd of August 1953. Their loss was an early casualty of BR's postwar cuts and was the first closure of a local branch lines passenger service.

Local authorities made attempts in the 1960's to re-open the branch passenger services, but these were all rejected by BR, who cited the cost of electrification as being the major obstacle.

The Southfleet Stationmaster's house in 1979. The others on the branch were of a similar style. All are now demolished. Dave Fisher

Goods services, however, surviving for a few more years; the ex-SE&CR C Class 0-6-0 locomotives remaining the predominant motive power, they were supplemented by occasional appearances of 2-6-0 locomotives.

By 1959 the branch's reduced status was confirmed when its award winning twin tracks were singled, and from 1960, the raucous notes of a steam locomotive's exhaust were to be heard no more, their duties taken over by Class 33 diesel locomotives. Together with infrequent visits by Class 73 electro-diesels, these were the last in a long line of locomotives to work on the entirety of this once lavishly provided branch.

The last major work on the branch came in 1965, when the 1924 built bridge over the A2 trunk road was lengthened to accommodate this roads widening to a dual carriageway.

The ending of BR's single wagon load services in early 1967 sounded the death knell for the branch, and from then until closure the only goods services were the occasional "as required" workings. Official closure coming on the 24th of March 1968, the severing of the track at Waterdales shortly afterwards thus isolating Gravesend from the Chatham main line.

This was not the end of the branch, however, a partial re-opening coming in 1969 when the line between Fawkham Junction and Southfleet

Fawkham Junction on the LC&DR main line in 1922. The tracks to the right of the picture form the connection with the Gravesend Railway. SE&CR Society

was put to use as a coal line for the Northfleet cement works and for the next seven years coal was regularly delivered here from the Midlands.

The coal depot and the branch closing in 1976, the by now derelict branch attracted the attention of a group of local railway enthusiasts, the embryonic North Downs Steam Railway Society (NDSR). Formed in 1980, the Society's aim was the partial re-opening of the branch as a preserved line to run steam tourist trains between Southfleet and Fawkham.

Opening negotiations with BR for a lease on the branch as outright purchase was not possible due to the presence of the HV cable to Fawkham traction sub-station, in the November of 1982, BR offered the NDSR a lease on the branch for the sum of £25,000. Unfortunately, the NDSR, were unable to raise this amount and after attempts at negotiating a lower figure failed, their hopes and dreams for a revitalised Gravesend Railway seemed to have ended.

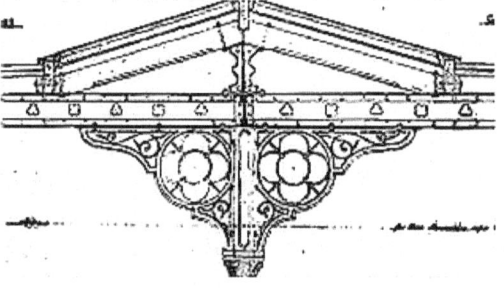

Gravesend West station cast iron platform canopy support detail.

However, unbeknown to the preservationists, a third party, Resco Railways, was also interested in the branch. A private company, they wanted to develop Southfleet station as a transport museum and after securing agreement with BR for purchase of the track and an infrastructure lease, Resco offered the NDSR a working partnership, which, however, was not taken up.

Resco then seeking permission to develop the site from Southfleet Parish Council, their application was refused as the small local roads were considered to be unable to cope with the expected large inflow of visitors.

Meanwhile, the NDSR became nomadic. Moving to a succession of sites, this included that at Cotton Lane, Stone, where I worked briefly as a volunteer during the 1990's. In 2016 the NDSR are in a flourishing partnership with the Tunbridge Wells and Eridge Railway Society, and constituted as the Spa Valley Railway Preservation Society in 1996, these two groups now jointly operate steam and diesel tourist trains between Tunbridge Wells and Eridge along part of the former Tunbridge Wells and Three Bridges Central line.

In September 1985, some years before the 1991 removal of the A2 over bridge, the West Kent Cyclists Touring Club launched a campaign to convert the branch's formation into a public cycle path between Gravesend and Longfield. However, the proposal came to naught.

During the late 1980's, much of the West Street branch's track was removed, some of it being taken by volunteers to the Kent & East Sussex Railway. Thereafter, the derelict line was left to slowly return to nature.

Nevertheless, once again the branch's fortunes were to change. As mentioned previously, in May 1994, Eurostar trains had started running to the continent from London Waterloo over the former SER main line. An unsatisfactory arrangement, it was seen as only a short term expedient until the Eurostar services transferred to the CTRL on its opening throughout.

When the CTRL project was split into two phases in 1998, this set back the CTRL's opening date and delayed the introduction of high speed Eurostar services on the CTRL for some time to come. To allow running a partial high speed service and stimulate passenger numbers, London Continental Railways looked for a temporary high speed link to connect with Phase 1 of the CTRL from Waterloo.

With the West Street branch's formation still intact south of the A2 road, this was seen as a suitable route and work began on reusing the branch for its new purpose in October 1998.

From Fawkham Junction, the high speed link follows the route of the Gravesend Railway, until just before Southfleet station, it curves away to connect with HS1 at Southfleet Junction. Fitted with dual power supplies, trains using the link derived their power from the domestic third rail 750 volt DC supply as far as the site of the former Longfield Halt, where a

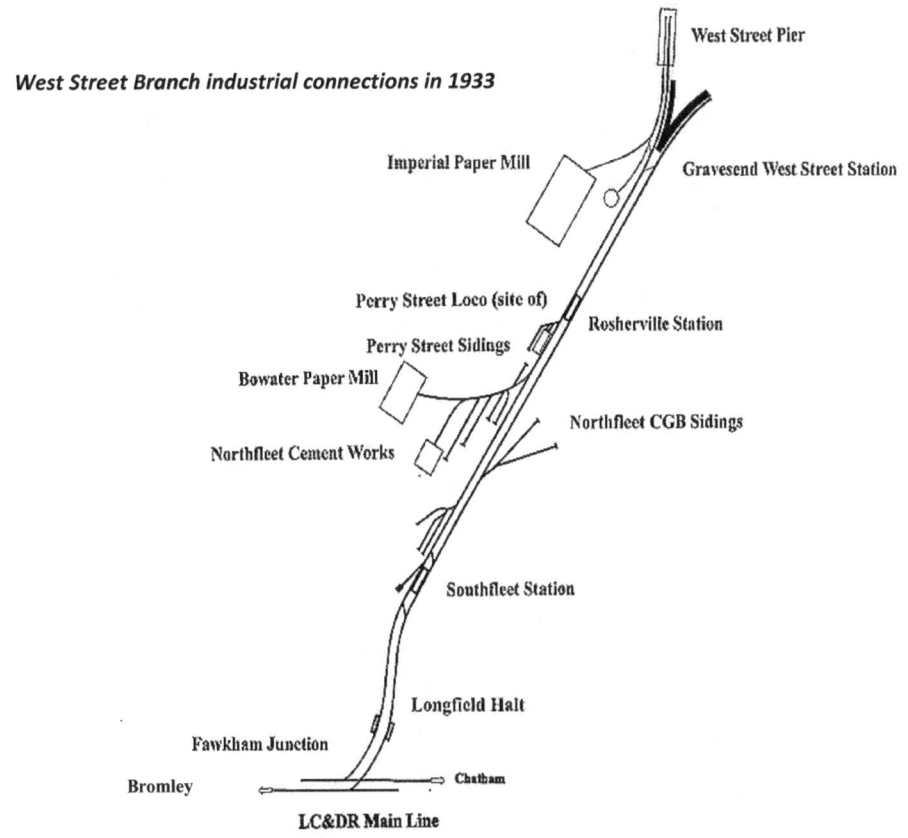

West Street Branch industrial connections in 1933

changeover was made to the CTRL's 25KV AC overhead traction supply.

Transition from Network Rail's colour light signalling to HS1's on-board signalling also took place here, with control transferring to an onboard system. Known as *Transmission Voie-Machine + Control de Vitesse par Balises* (control by beacons), it is an almost identical system to signalling used on the French *Ligne à Grande Vitesse* (LGV) high-speed lines.

With the link complete, on the misty Sunday morning of the 28th of September 2003, the first public 186 mph Eurostar service ran from Waterloo via Fawkham Junction and the Channel Tunnel to Paris. Continuing to see Eurostar services until HS1 opened throughout, the link closed in November 2007.

It's future is now uncertain; at one time used for engineer's trains and driver training, latterly it has been used for rolling stock storage.

The A2 over bridge as it appeared in September 1976. The view is looking towards Southfleet and shows the 1965 single track extension in the middle distance. Dave Fisher

The A2 bridge seen just before demolition. Taken down in two phases, the Southfleet end span was the first part to go in mid-January 1991. The removal of the Northfleet end span took place over the 2nd and 3rd of February 1991 and required the use of what was then one of the largest portable cranes in the UK, a monster of 500 tons lifting capacity, brought in from Newcastle. D. Gosden

The point where the Gravesend Railway once crossed over the SER North Kent line. This picture was taken near the bridge that currently carries Dover Road over Thames Way. Tony Riley collection.

The same location seen in August 2015, this shows the North Kent line crossing Thames Way via the bridge in the centre of the picture. The Gravesend Railway ran on the higher ground to the left of the picture. Author

The entrance to Southfleet station in September 1952. J. Aston

Gravesend West in the early 1950's. C Class No. 31102 shunts the cattle pen roads with the shunter in attendance. Barry Diplock.

Longfield Halt seen in 1922. The man on the Up platform looks well wrapped up against the elements. SE&CR Society.

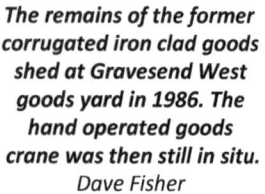

The remains of the former corrugated iron clad goods shed at Gravesend West goods yard in 1986. The hand operated goods crane was then still in situ. Dave Fisher

Abandoned chalk tipping wagons seen in 1973. GRES

A rather battered Barclay fireless locomotive No. 1, "Imperial", seen at the Imperial Paper Mill, Gravesend on the 21st of September 1963. The system was one of the last to close locally, operations not finishing until 1978. This locomotive was to find fame when it was purchased by a 14 year old Meopham schoolboy for £50 in July 1978, who donated it to the National Railway Museum at Shildon where it can be seen today. GRES.

Bowater's paper mill diesel locomotive No. 2 seen on their Thames jetty in the 1960's. Authors collection.

C Class 0-6-0 No. 31720 arrives at Gravesend West in 1951 on a Farningham Road freight working. The paper pulp storage yard of the Imperial Paper Mill can be seen in the background. *Barry Diplock*

A Koppel fireless locomotive at the Imperial Paper Mill Gravesend. The first of their type to be used in the UK, they were used extensively in locations such as paper mills, where the fire risk from a conventional locomotive was unacceptable. Their pressure vessels charged with steam from the mill's steam plant, they could operate for up to eight hours on a charge of steam. *Geoff Plumb*

On 28th September 2003, a Waterloo International bound Class 373 Eurostar is seen leaving the HS1 main line at Southfleet Junction. From here it will shortly enter the alignment of the former Gravesend Railway *Author*

The South Eastern & Chatham Railway 1899

Both of the constituents of the South Eastern & Chatham Railway having acquired a bad reputation somewhat unfairly for unreliability and poor services, it was hoped that by pooling their resources and the rationalising of services savings could be made, profitability generated and reputations enhanced.

Proceeds from traffic receipts shared out on the basis of 60% to the SER and 40% to LC&DR, loading gauge permitting, the movement of the two companies locomotives and rolling stock, once unheard of, occurred freely across the system. Some loss making duplicate lines closing, the most notable was the short SER extension from Strood (Rochester Bridge) to Chatham Central.

The coming together of these two companies should have given the new organisation an almost unassailable position in the local passenger transport business. However, changes were on the horizon.

A horse-powered tram service running the short distance between the two towns of Gravesend and Northfleet since 1883, in 1889 an attempt was made at Northfleet to provide an electrically powered tram service using a conduit pick-up in the road, but found to be unworkable, it was soon abandoned and the system reverted to horse traction in 1890.

A more serious competitor in the guise of the British Electric Traction Company arrived in Gravesham in 1901. Converting the existing tram system to standard gauge with an overhead DC power supply, by 1903 their new electric trams were plying tram routes to Denton, Swanscombe, the Old Prince of Orange and Pelham Road, with a further route along Dover Road to the tram depot.

The newcomer, seen by the SE&CR as a threat to their local passenger revenues, they responded in 1906 by opening a series of timber built halts to provide platforms for a novel new train. Known as a rail motor, although ultimately proving unsuccessful for reasons explained later, the halts built to serve them brought much needed access to the railway for the areas rural populations.

Unfortunately, the SE&CR was to continue to carry the baggage from its constituents for some time at least and remained a less than popular railway in the eyes of the public. An example of some of these misconceptions is seen in a letter to the *Gravesend Magazine* of 1911:

"Onward – That is the heroic motto adopted by the S. E Railway Co, and I, a season ticket holder have been waiting patiently enough for 30 years or more years to see them do it"

The correspondent was wrong on two counts; by 1911 the S.E. Railway Co. had become the SE&CR and their motto was no longer "Onward", but "Invicta".

The SE&CR, despite its bad press, was a reasonably enlightened employer. Railwaymen's pay was quite generous, the weekly wage for a passenger guard in April 1910 being £1-6/-0d, and for those with longer service, e.g. 10 years or more in the grade, £1-8/-0d was paid weekly. However, enhanced overtime rates were not paid unless more than 60 hours had been worked in a week, the additional time worked being paid at the rate of 1¼ for each extra hour.

A rather bizarre incident that SE&CR staff would have had to deal with occurred near Milton Road bridge in May 1908 when the first Up train of the day was accosted by a rampaging bullock. The animal having somewhat inconsiderately jumped over a fence by Norfolk Road, the resultant collision between train and beast was not one-sided, the animal managing to derail the fourth coach of the train. Occurring shortly before 5:00 am, the line had been cleared by the breakdown gang by 7:00 am. The fate of the bullock is not recorded.

A national coal strike starting in February 1912, its shortage resulted in service changes. Withdrawing most cheap fares for the duration of the strike and suspending the Gravesend to Dartford steam rail motor shuttle services, just one cheap fare was retained, the early morning workmen's tickets. Now known as the "Earlybird" ticket, then as now, passengers

A steam rail car similar to the type used for the services both to the 1906 halts on the North Kent line and the Hundred of Hoo branch. Later used to run a shuttle service between Gravesend and Dartford, during WWI they conveyed workers to the many munitions factories in the Dartford and Crayford area.

The competition. An electric tram in Pelham Road Gravesend in the early 20th century. GRES

An SE&CR Express with a D Class 4-4-0 locomotive in charge, it is resplendent in Wainwrights lined dark green passenger livery.

Between Downs and Thames - Railways of Gravesend, the Hoo Peninsular and Isle of Grain

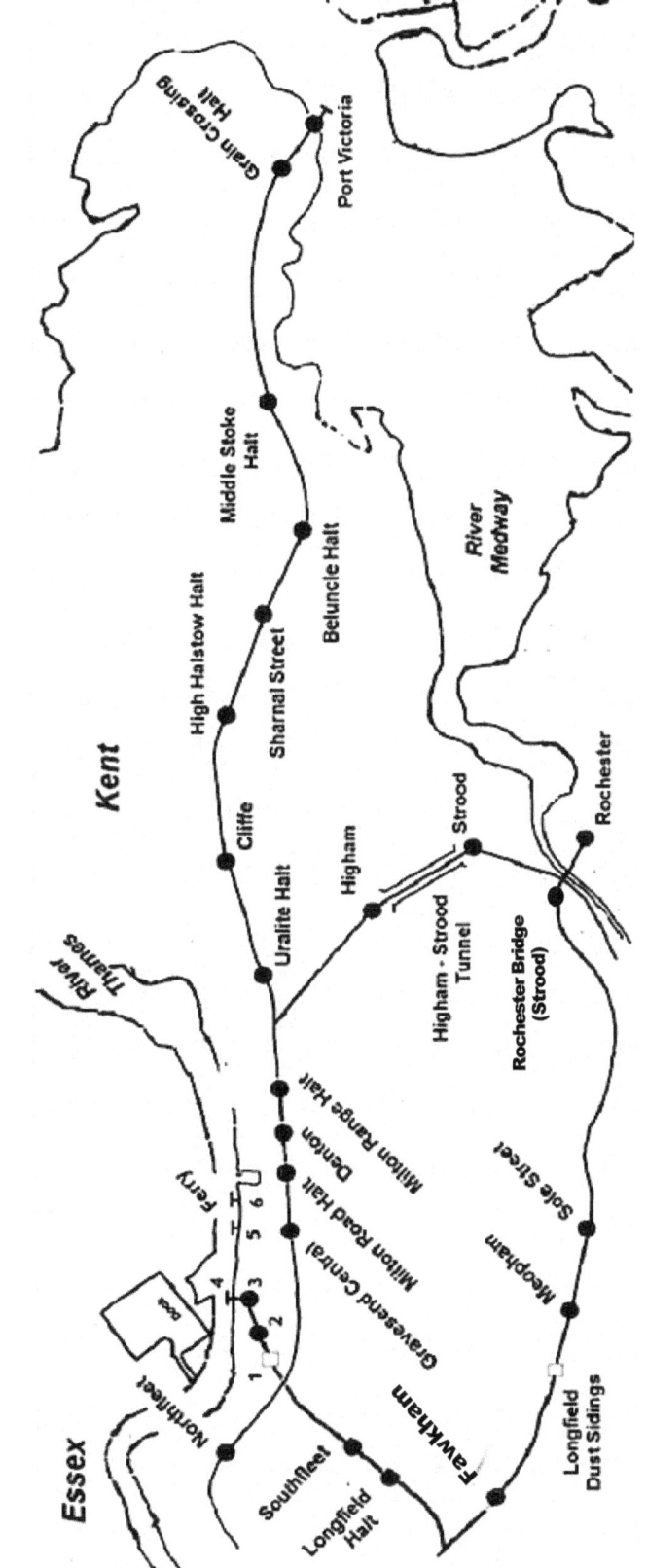

The South Eastern and Chatham Railway in 1913

1 Perry Street Loco shed   2 Rosherville Station   3 Gravesend West station   4 West Street LC&DR pier   5 LT&SR West Street Landing Stage   6 LT&SR Town Pier.

holding these workman's tickets were required to arrive at their London destination before 8:00 am. Goods traffic also affected, the timetables and fares did not return to normal until the strike ended in April 1912.

In August 1914 at the start of what was to be the UK's most ghastly of wars, posters advertising seaside excursions came down to be replaced by recruiting posters. At the beginning of the war, the railways were not too badly affected and train services ran very much as normal. Things were to change, however, and with railwaymen volunteering for military service, their roles were in some cases filled by women; in 1914 just 9,000 women working on the nations railways, by 1918 the number had risen to over 50,000. With wartime emergency regulations quickly introduced, one of the first changes made to passenger travel arrangements came when SE&CR staff were instructed that soldiers and sailors needing to entrain were to be found a place on the next train to their destination, even if that meant civilians could not travel.

Very much a railway war, government used the Regulation of Railways Act of 1871 as authority to take over control of the nation's railways and by appointing the Railway Executive Committee to oversee railway operations on the their behalf, they quickly

Special Notice for a train returning servicemen from leave to Chatham and Sheerness dating from May 23rd 1918.

South Eastern and Chatham Railway.

Private and not for Circulation. (No. 159 S.T.)

To the Officers and Servants of this and other Companies concerned.

INSTRUCTIONS TO STATION MASTERS, INSPECTORS, ENGINEMEN, GUARDS, SIGNALMEN, PLATE-LAYERS, GATEMEN, AND ALL OTHERS CONCERNED AS TO

A PRIVATE SPECIAL TRAIN FROM VICTORIA to SHEERNESS, SHEERNESS to GILLINGHAM, and CHATHAM to VICTORIA.

On Thursday, May 23rd, 1918.

TIME TABLES.

DOWN JOURNEY.				UP JOURNEY.			
Miles Distant from Victoria.	STATION or JUNCTION.	Special Train. a.m. arr.	dep.	Miles Distant from Sheerness Dkyd.	STATION or JUNCTION.	Special Train. p.m. arr.	dep.
M. C.				M. C.			
———	VICTORIA (No. 9 Departure Platform)	...	9 15	———	SHEERNESS DKYD. (No. 1 Platform)	...	1 15
3 14	Brixton	9 22		1 6	Queenboro' (Train Staff)	1 18	1 18
3 78	Herne Hill (Fast Line)	9 23½		6 66	Middle Junction (Train Staff)	1 27	1 27
8 54	Beckenham	9 33		7 09	Western Junction		1 28
12 44	Bickley Junction	9 38		9.31	Newington (Up Platform)	1 33	1 35
13 32	St. Mary Cray Junction	9 39		———	Newington (Up Lay-bye Siding)	1 37	2 12
17 52	Swanley	9 45		———	Gillingham (Up Line)	2 23	2 25
26 69	Sole Street	9 56		———	Gillingham (Down Line)	2 27	2 29
32 75	Rochester Bridge	10 3½		15 05	GILLINGHAM (Down Platform)	2 30	...
34 28	Chatham	10 6½		16 52	CHATHAM (Up Military Dock)	...	4 0
43 71	Western Junction	10 17		18 05	Rochester Bridge		4 4
44 14	Middle Junction (Train Staff)	10 18	10 18	24 11	Sole Street		4 12½
49 24	Queenboro' (Train Staff)	10 27	10 27	33 28	Swanley		4 23½
51 00	SHEERNESS DOCKYARD (No. 1 Platform)	10 38	...	37 48	St. Mary Cray Junction		4 29
				38 36	Bickley Junction (Fast Line)		4 30
				42 26	Beckenham Junction		4 35
				47 02	Herne Hill (Fast Line)		4 44½
				47 66	Brixton		4 46
				51 00	VICTORIA (No. 9 Departure Platform)	4 53	...

Speed must be reduced when approaching the Facing Points at Brixton Junction, Herne Hill North Junction and Western Junction; also over the Curves between Battersea Park and Brixton, between Kent House and Beckenham, and over Strood Curves.

Speed must be reduced when approaching the Facing Points at Middle Junction and Herne Hill (South and North Junctions), also over Strood Curves, between Beckenham Junction and Kent House, and over the Curves between Brixton and Battersea Park.

established their authority over the railway companies.

Set-up in 1912 as a precautionary measure and its members drawn from all walks of life, the executive used a government publication, the "Railway manual (war)" of 1911 ¶ for their guidance.

Wartime economy measures soon became apparent, with SE&CR carriages repainted into a dull brown colour, the once magnificent green lined locomotive livery turned a matt grey.

The line running close to the Medway estuary in places, trains travelling at night on the Hundred of Hoo branch were ordered to have their carriage blinds lowered from Hoo Junction onward to avoid aiding the enemy.

Although from 1915 all day and half day excursion tickets were withdrawn, many cheap tickets remained available. More austerity measures coming in on the 1st of January 1917, all fares were increased by 50% to cover increased operating costs. However, it wasn't until 1918 that a full emergency timetable came into effect.

The army having requisitioned some SE&CR locomotives and rolling stock for overseas use, to cover their loss locomotives from other companies were drafted in when shortages of motive power occurred, an example of this was the appearance of a Hull & Barnsley Railway 0-6-0 locomotive and accompanying brake van on the West Street branch.

All military trains received the code name "Imperial" and depending on priority, they were graded from A to D. On the SE&CR, an "Imperial A" coded train was a special private train, and given priority over all other traffic, nothing was allowed to impede its progress. Usually destined for one of the Channel ports, upon arrival, a Royal Navy destroyer awaited to take its passengers to France.

"Imperial B" coded trains a step down, "Imperial C" trains were allowed to take precedence over ordinary civilian traffic. "Imperial D" being the lowest category, they were given the best possible route, but were not permitted to take priority over civilian passenger trains.

Goods traffic saw a great increase during the conflict, the proximity of the vital armaments and munitions manufacturing works at Woolwich Arsenal, Crayford, Dartford and the Hoo Peninsular generating much new traffic.

Gravesend, Northfleet and Chattenden were all subjected to aerial attack by both German Zeppelin airships and Gotha aircraft. A railway embankment at Northfleet and the narrow gauge naval railway at Chattenden both being damaged during raids, a more serious attack occurred in the early hours of the 1st of November 1917. Their target an ammunition train at Gravesend station, fortunately for the station and the town the raiders missed their mark, the bombs damaging houses in Prospect Place instead.

Special leave trains were run for the armed forces, and on the opposite page is seen an SE&CR special instruction of the 23rd of May 1918 which advertises a private train returning servicemen from leave to their duties.

Ambulance trains would have also have been a familiar sight. Provided at first by the Red Cross and St. Johns Ambulance from public subscriptions, two further trains later supplied by the SE&CR, government later supplied the bulk of these vital vehicles. Converted from normal passenger rolling stock, ambulance trains usually consisted of up to ten vehicles, each train consisting of five ward coaches, two ordinary passenger carriages, a pharmacy car, kitchen car and coaches for the accommodation of the medical personnel.

Twenty-nine such trains operated within the UK. Their casualties being collected from either Dover or Southampton, they were then taken by rail to one of the 196 casualty receiving centres that were located throughout Britain.

The local reception centres at Greenhithe, Chatham and Well Hall, ambulance trains also ran to Longfield. Delivering casualties to the Voluntary Aid Detachment (VAD) hospital there, the harrowing sight of badly wounded men lying on the platforms was remembered by local people long afterwards.

Ingress Abbey at Greenhithe had sidings for both the VAD hospital in the Abbey buildings and the large temporary military hospitals at

¶ *This manual prescribed railway management in great detail, its preamble stating: "the efficient operation of a railway system can only be assured when the cordial co-operation of railwaymen is combined with the strictest obedience to regulations by the troops". For more information see www.babel.hathitrust.org*

A selection of SE&CR Edmundson style tickets.
Dave Fisher collection.

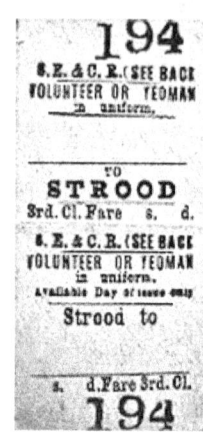

The Interior of a WWI ambulance train ward car.
Picture postcards from the First World War

Gravesend Central Station in 1922, the last year of ownership by the SE&CR. HJPR

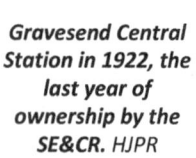

Stone and Joyce Green and the wounded from the Greenhithe trains were unloaded by railway staff. Doing this work voluntarily in their own time, casualties were gently lowered onto platforms especially built for the purpose.

Gravesend Hospital also treated thousands of sick and wounded soldiers and the small hospital at Milton Barracks, greatly extended, became a centre for the treatment of venereal diseases. Temporary VAD hospitals were also opened at Allhallows (the Parish Room) and at Cobham (the Meadow Rooms) where Australian wounded were treated. At Higham, the Hermitage was used as a temporary hospital, as was the Yacht Club and Hotel at Rosherville.

A total of 556 men of the SE&CR giving their lives during the First World War, some local men included William Eastwood, a porter on the Midland Railway, he was killed in action on 13th March 1918. Northfleet's war memorial remembering an SE&CR booking clerk, G. H. Fender, he died in 1920 from war related injuries.

With the coming of peace in November 1918, those railwaymen who had joined the colours and importantly survived, returned to their jobs, as did requisitioned locomotives and rolling stock. Those local men released from prisoner-of-war camps were given money, a ½ pound of tobacco or cigarettes plus a packet of chocolate by the Gravesend prisoners-of-war fund.

As the end of the conflict approached, acutely conscious of the need to find work for the returning heroes, the government started to take soundings from large organisations on their likely postwar labour requirements.

Perhaps this scheme was the initiative behind a proposal announced in an article in the *Gravesend Reporter* of the 5th of November 1921 which informed its readers that the SE&CR was considering the electrification of their lines out to a distance of a 30 mile radius from Charing Cross. Dependant on Government support, it was stated that the scheme, drafted in 1919, but delayed due to some post war issues, would provide work for several thousand men. Somewhat optimistically, it was also hoped that electrification would improve the speed and frequency of train services in the Gravesham area by between 40 and 60%.

Intended to be a four rail DC system, similar to the system used by the London Underground today, unlike the Underground, it was to have operated at a potential of 3,000 volts. However, when large scale electrification did occur after the formation of the Southern Railway in 1923, managers from the former LS&WR in the ascendant, the local electrification of the 1930's used the LS&WR favoured 660 volt DC three rail system.

In this period, railways still profitable, their shareholders could expect good returns on their investments and in 1921, the penultimate year of the existence of the SE&CR, the LC&DR chairman, W. Hart-Dyke, stated in his yearly report to his fellow directors that the company had a balance of £436,058-5/-1d after paying it's creditors. The dividend paid on 2nd preference stock £4-10/-0d, this was an increase of 10% over the 1920 dividend.

Its last meeting on the 7th of February 1923, Sir Cosmo Bonsor, the last SE&CR chairman, formally declared the management committee abolished, control having been handed over to the Southern on the 1st of January 1923.

The Southern's inheritance from the SE&CR was considerable and included among other assets: 1,660 miles of standard gauge track, 11 wharves and quays, 729 steam locomotives, 2,769 carriages, 11,345 wagons, trucks and vans, 13 steam ships and 19 shunting horses.

The Southern Railway 1923

The Great War had taught the government some harsh lessons on the problems associated with controlling the nation's fragmented rail network during an emergency, and post-war, the government, wishing to retain the advantages of the more cohesive wartime network and stem the losses caused by the competition between so many small companies, passed the 1922 Railways Act [1] to amalgamate them. Known as "the grouping," on the 1st of January 1923, the many small and medium sized railway companies were amalgamated into just four larger companies.

Locally, public railways were incorporated into the new Southern Railway (SR) to become a part of its eastern division. A conglomerate, the SR consisted of the former major railways companies in southern England :

South Eastern & Chatham Railway
London, Brighton & South Coast Railway
London & South Western Railway

Minor railways on the Isle of Wight and some smaller companies in the South West were also brought into the fold. Other railways were jointly worked, a notable example being the Somerset and Dorset Joint Railway, it was run by a committee composed of officials from both the Southern Railway and the London Midland and Scottish Railway. A few smaller railways such as the Kent & East Sussex Light Railway escaping the net, they were later absorbed into British Railways.

Transfer of ownership from the SE&CR becoming apparent to the travelling public by a change to staff uniforms and more muted liveries, the colourful lined dark Brunswick green and polished brass work of the SE&CR locomotives gave way to Southern lined green. Transformation also coming to carriage liveries, the lustrous purple and gold livery of the former SE&CR changing to SR green, stations and signal boxes were enlivened by a change from SE&CR buff to the Southern's infrastructure colours of green and cream.

Appointed to the post of the Southern's Chief Mechanical Engineer in 1937, O.V.S Bulleid brought another change to express passenger locomotive liveries. A vivid "Malachite" green, this was to remain until 1948. Another Southern introduction were the "target" station signs. Similar in shape to the London Underground's roundels, they showed white lettering on a dark green background.

From the 1930's onward, prefabricated buildings started appearing on the Southern. Built from reinforced concrete components manufactured at a company owned factory at Exmouth Junction, these structures became a distinctive feature of the Southern and were to be seen locally as footbridges, halts, plate-layer's huts and station boundary walling.

It was under the aegis of the Southern Railway that the local railways reached their zenith, the apogee itself coming in 1932 when a spur was constructed to connect the new Allhallows-on-Sea station at Avery Farm to the Hundred of Hoo branch.

Freight handling enhanced in 1928 with the opening of Hoo Junction marshalling yard, passenger services improved in July 1930 with the extension of the 3rd rail 660 volt DC conductor rails from Dartford to Gravesend. Further extended to Gillingham and Maidstone in July 1939, electrification often led to what at the time was called the "Sparks" affect. An increase in passenger numbers, this was largely due to the improvements in journey times, cleanliness and the punctuality brought by electrified services.

Although the smallest of the "Big Four" railway companies, the Southern and its predecessors created what at the time was the world's largest DC third rail electrified

---

[1] *The purpose behind the Act can be summed up from its first paragraph: "With a view to the reorganisation and more efficient and economical working of the railway system of Great Britain, railways shall be formed into groups in accordance with the provisions of this Act, and the principal railway companies in each group shall be amalgamated, and other companies absorbed in the manner provided by this Act".*

passenger railway. Mainly used for passenger workings, it was not widely used for freight services due to the restrictions on availability of traction power during engineering possessions and the dangers of live rails in areas where staff interfaced with rolling stock. Briefly trialled during the 1950's and 60's by BR, this form of freight services were soon discontinued.

Surplus military lorries and their trained drivers beginning to compete with the railways from 1919 onward, this was a major threat to railway revenues. Public road building and repairs being a local authority responsibility, road users enjoyed the almost cost-free use of the highways. Funded by rate-payers, it was a system that had been in use since at least the 16th Century.

The railways, soon beginning to feel the chill wind of competition, were disadvantaged by both the need to pay for the maintenance and upkeep of their infrastructure and the legal requirement to act as a common carrier. Responding by lobbying the government hard for a fairer system, they called for a "square deal".

A partially successful campaign, it resulted in the passing of the Roads Act 1920 and by introducing the road vehicle excise licence, it placed the cost of road upkeep squarely on their users. However, the campaign to remove the obligation on the railways to act as a common carrier was less successful and it was not until the passing of the Transport Act 1962 that this was finally removed.

Under its first general manager, Sir Herbert Walker, the Southern was a progressive company and controlling a large and efficient electrified network, their advertising made the most of this advantage. In charge of the SR's public relations was John Elliot. Now generally accepted as the originator of PR as we know it today, his clever use of colourful posters and publications extolling the advantages and pleasures of rail travel did much to promote the Southern's image.

Their financial situation precarious and in a somewhat run down condition nearly a decade after the end of WWI, the railways were then nearly ruined by the industrial unrest of the 1920's and badly in need of financial assistance, the government recognised this when making over £27 million available for improvements to the nations railways when passing the Railways (Agreement) finance Act 1935. Not a completely benevolent action, part of this money was required to be spent on preparing the nation's transport systems for war.

As would be expected, the Southern used some of this money to continue expansion of 3rd rail electrification, increase the passenger carrying capacity of existing three car units by adding a fourth carriage and bringing new electric multiple units into service. Local road transfer of goods and parcels was also improved by introducing motor vehicles to replace horse drawn carts.

However, all was not expansion, July 1932

Preserved Southern Railway 2BIL electrical multiple unit No. 2090 at Strood station during the Gravesend Edwardian Fair of 29th June 1986. Peter Willis

bringing the end of open civilian access to Milton Range Halt and the downgrading of Rosherville station to halt status.

One bright spot, however, was the 1936 introduction of a new international sleeper service. On its way to France, it passed through Meopham and Sole Street en-route to Dover and known as the "Night Ferry", it's 12 car train, composed of French built, blue liveried "Wagon Lits" carriages, it gave its passengers luxurious overnight accommodation and uninterrupted rail travel from Victoria to Paris via a special rail ferry between Dover and Dunkirk.

With war coming once again in 1939, the government passed into law on the 1st of September 1939 the Emergency Powers (Defence) Act 1939, which among its other measures empowered government to take control of the nations railways and once again, as in the Great War, a Railway Executive Committee sat as the railways overseer.

Largely thanks to the large investments of the 1930's, at the start of hostilities in September 1939 the Southern was in a better position to cope with a conflict than had been its predecessor of August 1914, and with massive casualties imminently expected, air raid shelters were rapidly built and vulnerable assets, such as the lower machine rooms of signal boxes reinforced to resist blast damage. The systems known vulnerable points, identified in advance, these were reinforced and rail diversions put in place.

A notable local example of this preparedness was the reopening of the long closed LC&DR Rochester railway bridge of 1858. Adapted to serve as an emergency bridge for either road or rail use, it was ready to act in place of the other two more modern bridges, should either be put out of action.

Station lighting was reduced to the bare minimum and what remained having its lamps sprayed blue, station entrances in the more threatened areas were sand bagged and by the summer of 1940 even station name boards had been removed to prevent low flying enemy aircraft from identifying their location.

To maintain the blackout, trains had attendants whose job it was to switch off carriage lighting during an air raid and see that window blinds were drawn down. With power saving the order of the day, the unfortunate travellers on electric services shivered in the cold; the electric heating having been turned off as a wartime economy measure, steam passenger services became favoured for their steam heating.

Ambulance trains were once again provided, but this time under the direction of the Ministry of Health, Sevenoaks and Tunbridge Wells stabling those allocated to Kent. Expecting the worst, vulnerable persons living in government designated high risk areas were encouraged to leave, and more than 500,000 people from all over southern England left high risk areas by special trains over the weekend of the 1st of September 1939.

Intended to convey hospital patients or air raid casualties away from areas either threatened or damaged by air attack, a new emergency feature was the casualty evacuation train. Put into use in the late summer of 1940 when an invasion was thought imminent, on the 10th of September 1940 these trains moved 2,352 hospital patients from a 10 mile deep strip around the sea coast.

Travel by train officially discouraged unless absolutely necessary during the WWII period those undertaking rail journeys did so knowing they risked disruption and delay by air raids. Although the local stations escaped damage, the railway lines were not so fortunate and were attacked and damaged on several occasions. Bombed on the 29th of September 1940, the railway at Denton was hit, with further damage was caused by a near miss at Milton Range Halt on 8th October 1940. During the raid on the 16th of August 1940, the railway bridge at Vale Road was strafed by German fighter aircraft. Causing fatalities, the pockmarks left by cannon shells could still be seen until the bridge was demolished in the 1980's.

As the railways telephone systems were considered vulnerable to damage, radios were used to communicate between the Southern Railway's control centres, and to prevent their betrayal to enemy radio location devices, transmitting apparatus was mounted in railway vans and moved to different locations on a random basis.

Fearing that enemy air raids would cause massive disruption to the movement of goods, emergency food stores were set up throughout the railway system and with coal then the predominant heat source, stockpiles were set up at Sidcup among other locations. Military stores also being built up, Meopham sidings still has on site a "Romney" prefabricated building once used for military storage.

Pre-war, it had been assumed that in the first month of a war most of the capital would have been destroyed and with up to one million of the population expected to become casualties, over three million of it's inhabitants it was thought would become refugees.

Preparing for the worst, local sites such as disused chalk pits were identified for use as either morgues, or for mass burial and those identified for the latter purpose would have received their human cargoes by train.

Raw materials having became scarce by 1940, the salvage of waste materials became a national priority and with baskets installed at stations for the reception of waste paper, newspapers, razor blades and cigarette packets, between 1939 and 1945, the Southern alone collected 5,397 tons of paper and 3,290,000 razor blades.

Prior to D-Day, travel to locations near the coast was prohibited and on D-Day itself, the Tilbury ferry vessels were pressed into service to act as tenders to the troopships lying in the Thames.

Somewhat surprisingly, the period saw the introduction of new express locomotives. The "air smoothed" 4-6-2 Light Pacifics, these were the first locomotives of this wheel arrangement

A John Elliot inspired Southern Railway advertising poster.
Courtesy of Southern posters.

to be used locally. However, as the new building of express locomotives was prohibited in wartime, Oliver Bulleid, the CME of the SR used the ruse of describing them as "mixed traffic" types to get the permission needed to build them.

Bulleid's other wartime steam locomotive design with a local connection were the Q1 Class 0-6-0 locomotives. A powerful and robust design, these could be seen locally on most kinds of traffic.

With the ban on leisure travel finally lifted in 1945, and the cross Channel ferries reinstated from 1946, those who could afford the luxury, travelled to holiday destinations mostly by rail.

As public transport was still the main form of travel and with the railways still trying to recover from their wartime deprivations, the Southern were hard put to provide for this extra traffic, and many old and tired locomotives and equally aged carriages were put back into service to give the war weary public their first holiday for six years.

Two years after the cessation of hostilities, the Labour government, elected in 1945 passed into law the Transport Act 1947 in readiness to embark on the nationalisation of Britain's railways, utilities, coalmines, hospitals and some road transport and despite protests from the railway companies, ownership of the railways was soon to be passed to government control. More details on the nationalisation process of 1948 can be found on page 247.

The Southern Railway in 1932

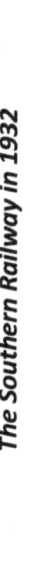

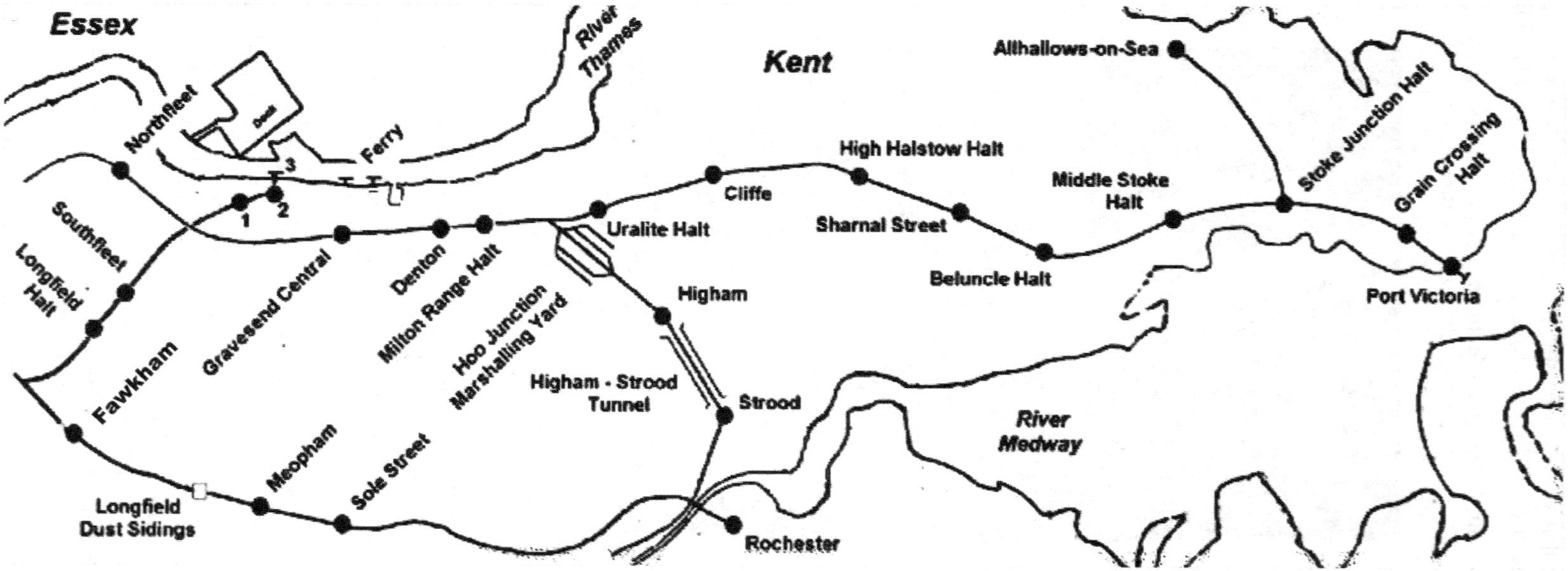

1 Rosherville Station

2 Gravesend West Station

3 West Street LC&DR Pier

Industrial railway connections to the North Kent line at Northfleet circa 1939. The gradient on the 1:40 loop passing under Galley Hill was so severe that if loads exceeded 3 or 4 loaded wagons, two industrial locomotives were required to double head them. Part of the alignment still exists on Northfleet Industrial Estate.

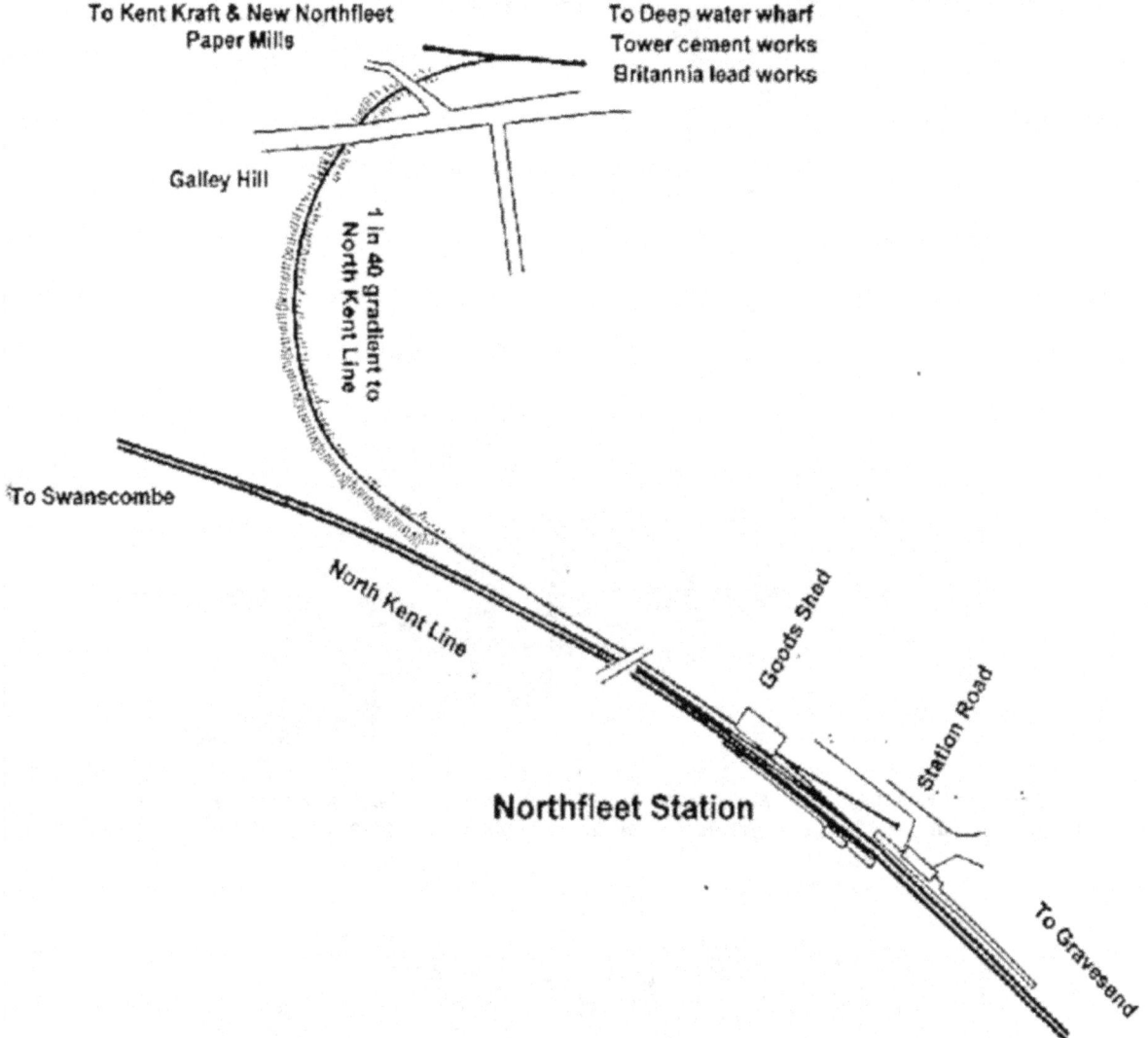

Gravesend Central station Southern Railway "target sign". GRES

An ex-LSWR M7 tank locomotive. A member of this class was briefly trialled on the West Street branch in 1934. Authors collection.

Schools Class 4-4-0 No. 30930 "Radley". Members of the class appeared regularly at Gravesend Central on Kent coast semi-fast workings until the Kent Coast electrification of 1959. Authors collection.

British Railways Southern Region 1948

Early British Railways emblem dating from 1950, it was known affectionately as the "Cycling Lion"

With the turning of the old year into the new, on the 1st of January 1948, the railways of Gravesham and the Hoo peninsular became a part of the nationalised British Railways (BR).

The railways themselves transferred to the eastern division of the new Southern Region, and the Gravesend to Tilbury ferries initially allotted to the London Midland Region, the ferries were reallocated in 1949 along with Tilbury's railways to BR's Eastern Region.

Initially little changed. Locomotive liveries remained in the green or black of the former Southern, with the sunshine yellow "Southern" lettering on locomotives giving way to a white "British Railways" legend and by prefixing their former Southern numbers with the number 3, they became BR Southern Region locomotives.

From the early 1950's, local passenger rolling stock appeared in a slightly darker green livery with an "S" for Southern Region prefixing their serial numbers and pending the appearance of BR designed locomotives and rolling stock, new construction continuing to the designs of the Southern Railway, examples were produced into the early 1950's.

Once BR had got into its stride, change came in several ways. Stamping its mark on passenger rolling stock first, some of the older and newly built Mk I carriages were transformed into a radical new colour scheme; a contrasting carmine and cream livery, it was irreverently called "blood and custard" by some. After a brief experimentation with a blue colour scheme, Southern Region express passenger locomotive liveries settled on a lined green hue reminiscent of the livery of the former Great Western Railway, the lowly goods and mixed traffic were engines repainted into a BR lined black livery.

Standardisation appearing to be the aim of BR in all things, the area was soon to see distinctly foreign looking steam locomotives, the BR "Standards". A range of designs based on the best features of the locomotive designs of the former "Big Four" railway companies. this was a retrograde step, BR having elected to continue with new build coal fired steam traction to save spending foreign exchange on oil when other nations were moving towards more efficient diesel and electric forms of motive power.

Change came close to being very radical indeed for local commuters, two experimental four car double deck trains taking to the rails in 1949 as a unique but failed solution to the overcrowding of suburban trains.

For those who could afford them, holidays in the UK were the norm before cheap air travel and mass car ownership changed holiday patterns and in those more austere times, the more discerning and affluent Kent coast holidaymaker could travel to Margate and Ramsgate on a new luxuriant, all Pullman train, the "Thanet Belle". Inaugurated on the 31st of May 1948, this luxury express passed through Gravesham on the former Chatham main line.

In Gravesham, itself, however, things were not so rosy, the West Street branch passenger services being withdrawn in August 1953.

However, at Hoo Junction there was expansion, 1956 bringing a new halt for rail staff.

Delayed by WWII, the June 1959 extension of electrification to the Kent Coast resorts was one of the fruits of the 1955 Modernisation Plan. A modernised version of the LSWR electrification system, to reduce the problem of perturburance, ¶ the DC electrification voltage was increased to 750 volts. Accelerating journey times by the elimination of steam traction, this was to benefit Gravesham.

The project bringing with it new designs of electric multiple units for the local, express and semi-fast services, the building of 24 electric locomotives was also put in hand for use as motive power on ordinary coaching stock, goods trains and train marshalling. Re-signalling with colour lights completed on the 10th of May 1959, nearly 100 miles of the Chatham main line then dispensed with semaphore signalling.

On Sunday the 14th of June 1959 the finale also came for steam hauled, publicly timetabled passenger services on the Chatham line. In recognition of the line's SE&CR ancestry, an L1 4-4-0 locomotive, No. 31753, passed through both Meopham and Sole Street stations en route to Dover. It's smoke box door adorned with a wreath, it left in its train a poignant trail of coal smoke.

With the Pullman "Kentish Belle" service having been withdrawn the previous year, henceforth, all passenger services on the Chatham line, excepting specials, excursions and the "Night Ferry", were provided by electric multiple units.

Steam-hauled passenger services continuing on the North Kent line until the end of Hoo peninsular passenger services on the 4th of December 1961, steam's last hurrah was on freight services; diesel and electric traction taking over from 1962.

Profitable at nationalisation, the rail network, was in deficit by the early 1950's and after a failed attempt to re-invigorate the system by implementation of the Modernisation Plan of 1955, a rationalisation known colloquially as the Beeching Plan came in 1963, when together with its younger companion, the Development of the Major Railway Trunk Routes report of 1965, they brought about the closure of many miles of track and stations on the national rail network. More change coming in 1965, the British Railways Board became British Rail.

In the following decade, in an attempt to utilise its assets more efficiently and increase revenue, BR inaugurated the "Merrymaker" tourist trains. Essentially sightseeing tours by rail, they were a popular innovation, and a number of these called at Gravesend in the 1970's.

For those who preferred to explore locally, Rail Rover tickets could also be purchased, an example of these being the "Kent Daymaker" which gave a days unlimited travel within the Kent rail network. Inaugurated in the 1980's were the "Golden Rail" package holidays. Inexpensive and popular, they provided door-to-door travel and accommodation to UK destinations.

International rail travel came to an end on the eastern section of BR on the 31st October 1980, when competition from air travel and the run-down condition of its carriages bringing an end to the last of the luxury cross Channel services, the "Night Ferry" sleeper.

1982 brought the introduction of the London and South Eastern sector. Seen by some as an alternative to rail privatisation, it was in fact an attempt to create a more market-focused organisation. With British Rail's passenger services later split into three core sectors, the London and South Eastern sector was re-branded as Network South East in 1986. Bringing with it a change to rolling stock liveries, carriages took on a red, white and blue "toothpaste" colour scheme. Stations acquiring a similar hue, they also sprouted electronic destination screens and clicking digital clocks. Non-railway assets also re-branded, the station buffets became Travellers Fare.

Their introduction requiring a £201 million spend on infrastructure upgrades, the Networker multiple units came into service in 1994. Despite these improvements the railways were still loss making and government started to look to divest itself of the role of railway operator.

¶ *Perturburance is the term used to describe the fluctuations in voltage caused by a large number of trains starting or accelerating on a given traction section.*

Between Downs and Thames - Railways of Gravesend, the Hoo Peninsular and Isle of Grain

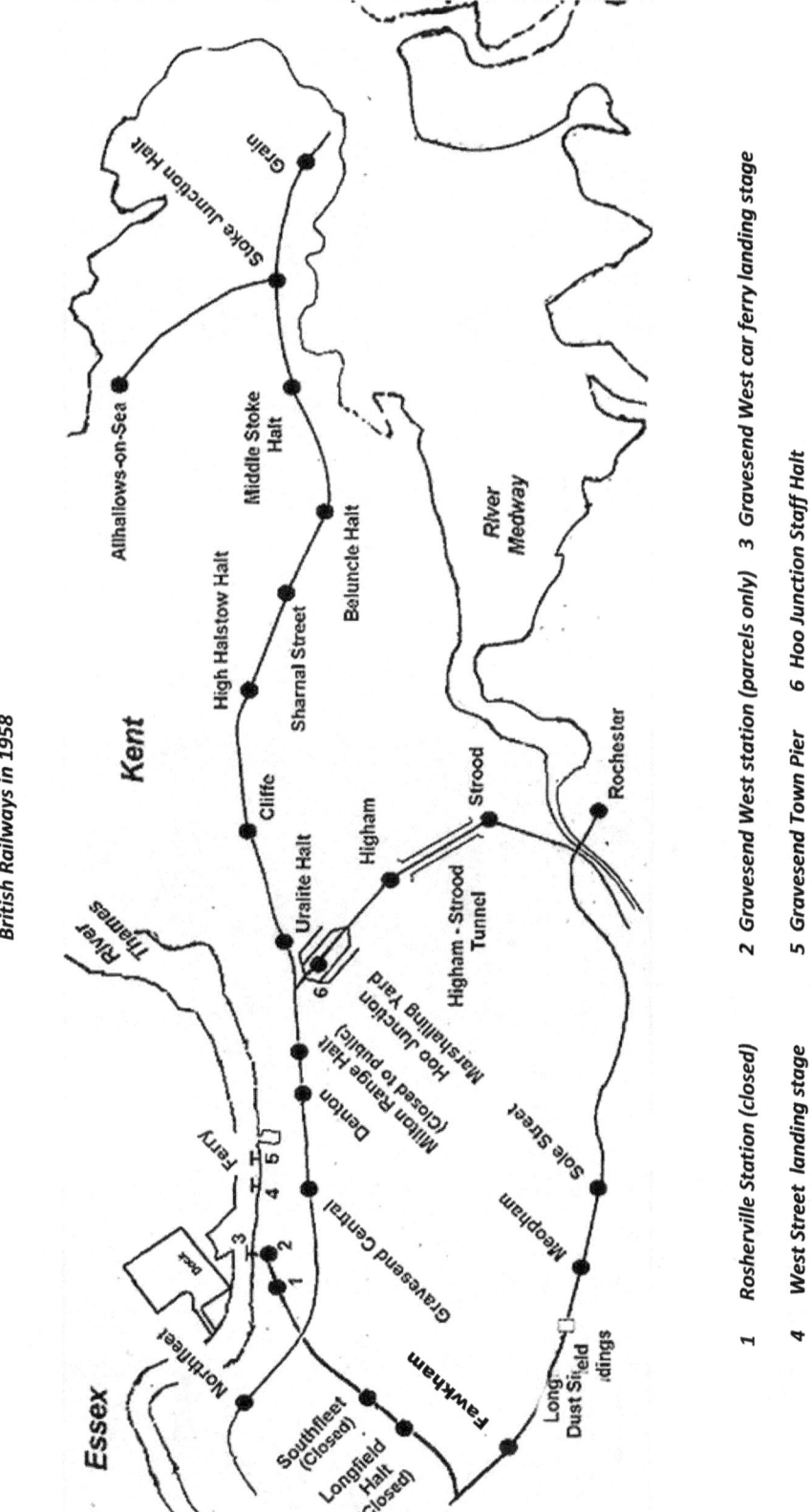

Gravesend Central on the 1st of December 1952. N Class 2-6-0 No. 31181 arrives light engine to take forward the early morning milk van train brought in by an E4 locomotive, No. 32580. Barry Diplock.

Gravesend Central. Q1 0-6-0 No. 33039 coaling in the goods yard circa 1960. Tony Banks collection.

On the 21st of September 1963 Peckett 0-4-0 Saddle tank No. 2080 "Northfleet" is working hard at shunting mineral wagons on the 1:40 graded line to Northfleet Station. The road bridge in the background, now long since gone, once led to the New Northfleet paper mill. Geoff Plumb.

Gravesend West on the 28th of February 1952. C Class 0-6-0 No. 31720 shunts vans. Barry Diplock

A Class 33 diesel locomotive passes Gravesend Central light engine on the 24th of September 1983. The code 5J indicates it has come off a mineral train working within the Southern Region. Dave Fisher.

A Light Pacific rushes past the site of Longfield sidings in the early 1950's. Barry Diplock

Gravesend West station in July 1953, one month before the ending of passenger services. Tony Riley collection

Gravesend Central on a snowy 12th of December 1981, In the foreground on Platform 1 is a Hastings diesel unit. No. 1011, it is on NDSR rail tour while a 4SUB EMU waits on platform 2 with an Up slow train. Dave Fisher

A rare visitor. Class 50 diesel-electric locomotive, No. 50050 "Fearless" enters Gravesend Central on 13th April 1985 with the "Dungeness Pebbledasher" rail tour. Dave Fisher.

Privatisation 1996

The railways continuing to be loss making into the 1970's, politicians of the time saw them as an anachronism. With roads seen as the future for transport, ways were sought to reduce rail subsidies drain on the public purse, and starting in the 1980's, many of BR's non-rail assets were sold off until by the early 1990's, only the railways themselves remained in public ownership. A new Conservative government elected in November 1992, their manifesto was clear that they would complete the rail privatisation process and hopefully relieve the state of its irksome burden.

Passenger Services

Soon realising that before privatisation could begin, the railways needed to be made more attractive to potential purchasers and lessees, the process began with the break-up of the passenger operations of the three Business Sectors into smaller, pseudo businesses, these became known as Train Operating Units (TOU).

South Eastern Passenger Rail Franchise 1996

In October 1996 both of the local TOU's, Kent Coast and Kent Link were transferred into the South Eastern Passenger Rail franchise and thus Gravesham's passenger services entered the brave new world of privately run, publicly subsidised railways.

Connex, their bid asking for an annual public subsidy of £585 million for the first year, tapering off to £2.8 million by 2010 accepted, they **were** awarded the franchise for a fifteen-year period.

Connex South Eastern 1996 - 2003

When taking the ill-starred name of Connex South Eastern, Connex, a subsidiary of Veolia Environment, the French multinational company were the first private company to run trains in the area since December 1947. Also taking over train maintenance as a part of the franchise agreement, this was carried out locally at Slade Green and Gillingham train maintenance depots.

Something that has changed more frequently than ever since the start of the privatisation era is the frequent revisions of train liveries, and Connex being no exception, they replaced Southeastern's "toothpaste" livery with an undistinguished yellow, white and grey livery that did not sit well with some of the older multiple unit classes.

The Connex franchise period originally due to run until 2011, one of the few positive moves made during their tenure of the franchise was the introduction of new rolling stock, the Electrostar Classes 375 and 376. However, the company had a poor financial management record and doubts began to be cast on the company's long-term viability in December 2002 when they had to be given a further £58 million of public subsidy to keep services running.

When Connex requested a further £200 million in 2003, the alarmed Strategic Rail Authority ¶ sent in financial analysts. Soon discovering the company's weak financial position, Connex's lease on the franchise was terminated soon afterwards.

Despite the £700 million they spent on both infrastructure and rolling stock enhancements, Connex were not popular with the travelling public, their policy of reducing train lengths causing misery to their passengers who had to endure severe overcrowding so that Connex could reduce the hire charges it paid to the ROSCO's. Reduction of train lengths, even in peak periods, has continued to be one of the more unpleasant aspects of privatisation.

Connex had also held another franchise, Network South Central. This lease ending in August 2001, with the termination of Connex's lease on the South Eastern Passenger Rail franchise, this brought their exit as a UK railway passenger operating company.

¶ *This body came into existence on 1 February 2001 as a product of the Transport Act 2000 which amended the Railways Act of 1993. The major impact of this legislation on the railways was the abolition of both the role of Director of Passenger Rail Franchising and the British Railways Board, their functions being transferred to the new body. The SRA had a short and ignominious life, being abolished under the Railways Act 2005, it ceased to function from 1st December 2006.*

South Eastern Trains 2003 - 2006

From the 9th of November 2003, the running of those services previously provided by Connex South Eastern were transferred to a subsidiary company of the Strategic Rail Authority, South Eastern Trains. A publicly owned organisation, it was seen as an interim means of operating services until a new franchisee could be found.

Operating from November 2003 to April 2006, the change of organisation brought yet another new livery; the yellow and white of Connex remaining, with subtle livery revisions made by the addition of dark grey tapering bands to the lower panels of carriages.

The returning of services to public ownership was thought by some to herald re-nationalisation, but this was not the intention, and despite a petition organised by trade unions calling for this, services were once again sent out for bid to the private sector.

Integrated Kent Franchise

Superseding the South Eastern Passenger Rail Franchise of 1996, the inception of this much revised franchise was announced by the Department of Transport in November 2005.

The franchise period this time set at eight years, a possible two-year extension was available subject to meeting performance targets. With annual public subsidies set once again at £585 million and following the Connex debacle, it was to be maintained at that level for five years. The High-Speed passenger services from St. Pancras also came under its remit in 2009.

Southeastern 2006 - Present

Southeastern, the trading name of the London & South Eastern Railway Limited, is a part of the Govia group. Operating passenger services in Gravesham from the 1st of April 2006, they are expected to hold the franchise until June 2018. Receiving a three-year extension to their franchise in 2011, a further four year continuation was agreed in 2014.

Southeastern have split the Integrated Kent franchise into three distinct sub-divisions, and in the Gravesham area these are as follows:

Metro - Suburban and local stopping trains originating from the former Southern Region London termini, locally they use the North Kent, Greenwich, Sidcup and Bexley lines as far as Gravesend.

Mainline - Longer distance services from Victoria on the former Chatham main line through Meopham to Gillingham, Thanet, Canterbury and Dover.

High-Speed – The domestic high-speed train services originating from London St. Pancras. Two high-speed routes were originally provided, one route terminating at Dover via Ashford, the other, routed via Gravesend, finished at Faversham. Now expanded, the high speed network takes in services to Ramsgate, Deal, Canterbury West and Maidstone West.

In addition to the Integrated Kent franchise, Govia ¶ currently lease three other franchises, Thameslink, London Midland and Southern. Like their predecessors, Southeastern maintain rolling stock at Slade Green and Gillingham train maintenance depots. Currently leasing a fleet of 367 electric multiple units, these come from both Angel Trains and Eversholt Rail.

Southeastern have been low down the league for passenger satisfaction and punctuality and together with the other Govia franchises, they held the bottom three places in a survey taken in the autumn of 2014. However, nearly 60% of Southeastern's failures to meet performance standards infrastructure-related, only 25% was attributable to the company.

Freight Operations

At the beginning of the privatisation process in 1995, the original six Freight Operating Units (FOU's) being consolidated into three trainload businesses, these were then sold off to the following private companies.

Freightliner 1996 to present

Formed by a management buy-out in May 1996,

¶ *Govia is a company set up by the GoAhead group and Keolis to bid for rail franchises.*

by 2008 Freightliner had been purchased by the Arcapita Bank of Bahrain, only to be sold on again in February 2015 to the current owners, Genesee & Wyoming, the American railway holdings company.

Freightliner is the second largest freight operating company in the UK by revenue after DB Cargo (UK) Ltd and until 2013, they operated some of the Thamesport container services.

English, Welsh & Scottish Railway 1996-2007

In 1996, the lions share of BR's former freight business went to North and South Railways Limited. A consortium headed by a North American railroad business, Wisconsin Central, it changed its name to English Welsh & Scottish Railways Limited (EWS) in October 1996, and it was under this banner that the company handled most local freight.

DB Cargo (UK) Ltd 2007 - Present

On the 13th of November 2007, the German National Railways, Deutsche Bahn, completed the purchase of EWS, and in 2009 re-branded the company as DB Schenker Rail UK, a wholly owned subsidiary of Deutsche Bahn AG.

DB Schenker, now known as DB Cargo (UK) Ltd, currently operate the Hoo Junction marshalling yard. Providing locomotives and rolling stock for the majority of local freight workings, their main customer is the Network Rail infrastructure works trains.

Utilising modified Class 92 electric locomotives, DB also run inter modal freight services on HS1. Operating through the Channel Tunnel to Ripple Lane, these trains utilise flat bed wagons to carry continental gauge road/rail containers, recent cargoes have included automotive parts and drinks.

The other companies operating rail freight and maintenance locally are:

GB Railfreight 1999

Unlike the other FOC's, GB Railfreight was not formed from parts of the former BR holdings at privatisation. A new company formed in 1999, GB Railfreight is owned by Europorte, a subsidiary of Eurotunnel.

Colas Rail 2008

A subsidiary of the French road building company SECO, Colas are a 2008 amalgamation of Amec-Spie and Carillion Rail.

With the end of the Crossrail spoil traffic workings to Northfleet, what local freight remains today is mostly aggregate block trains originating from the Hoo Peninsular and Isle of Grain.

Dollands Moor on 16th December 2015. Class 92 Locomotive No. 92016 arrives from the continent with an inter modal container train. R. Dyke.

DB Cargo (UK) Ltd Class 66 diesel locomotive No. 66134 at Shornemead Crossing with ballast empties on 30th March 2015. Author.

Colas Rail Class 70 locomotive No. 70801 passes Denton with a train of track panels. J. Townsend

Railtrack

In keeping with the rail privatisation policy of fragmenting the national rail system, a separate organisation was set up by BR on the 1st of April 1994 to take over infrastructure maintenance, pathing of trains and control of the signalling.

Known as Railtrack, this was a grouping of small companies that became part of the private sector on the 20th of May 1996 at the dawn of the privatisation era. Financed from charges levied on train operators for track access and the income from leasing stations and depots, it did not receive a public subsidy until 2001.

Railtrack had a troubled history. Acquiring a reputation for bad management, it was this shortcoming that was believed to be behind a series of fatal accidents that were attributed to the poor maintenance of track under its care.

After the fatal rail accident at Hatfield in October 2000, its competency was again put into doubt and Railtrack went into receivership in October 2001.

Network Rail

The successor to Railtrack, this organisation is run on a "not for dividend" basis and lacking shareholders, any profits generated are used for railway improvements. Not initially receiving a subsidy from government, in 2012 it was given £3,989 million and in 2014 the company was effectively re-nationalised as an "arms-length" government body. Unlike Railtrack, Network Rail uses an all in-house labour force for its operations. Locally, Network Rail has depots at both Hoo Junction and Singlewell Infrastructure Maintenance Depot.

With passenger numbers doubling in the last 20 years, and with some 4.5 million people now using the network daily, their numbers continue to grow and to allow for future expansion, Network Rail has been planning an investment programme. Costed at £25 billion, it is the largest spend since Victorian times.

Local Infrastructure Improvements

Increases in passenger numbers during the boom years of the late 1980's led to the decision by the Network Southeast Sector to increase seating capacity on their commuter trains. To be achieved by extending train lengths to twelve cars, it was due to be implemented when the new Networker multiple units came into service.

However, before these longer trains could come into operation, modifications to infrastructure and signalling were required and with the imperative being the lengthening of platforms, work started on extensions at Dartford in the early 1990s, but with rail privatisation imminent, and the economy then in the doldrums, the programme was halted.

Restarted by Southeastern across their franchise in 2013, the twelve car programme has added 95,000 extra seats to their peak hour services. These extended trains running locally from January 2014, this followed completion of platform lengthening works between Stone Crossing and Gravesend. Twelve car trains now running on the North Kent line in peak periods, they are destined to be introduced to the Chatham route, with Sole Street station due extended platforms with the next tranche.

Following the Millennium, when the Westinghouse Company completed the Dartford Area Re-signalling Scheme, this replaced with state of the art colour light multi-aspect signals the 1970's vintage signals that had previously controlled the North Kent line. Local signalling now a thing of the past, it is controlled from a panel in the Integrated Electronic Control Centre (IECC) at Ashford and from 2019, signalling control will pass to the Three Bridges and Gillingham control centres.

A problem associated with conductor rail systems since their inception is icing up in severe weather conditions and a recently introduced solution is the installation of heating tapes directly onto the conductor rails. Connected to the 750 volt DC traction supply, these are fitted where trains are brought to a stand.

Proposed changes to the rail network are published by Network Rail as Rail Utilisation Strategies (RUS). Local changes envisaged by the RUS are the raising of speed limits between Sole Street Bank and Longfield, and increasing the North Kent line speed to 90 mph to accelerate high-speed train journey times.

In the very long-term, 25KV HV overheads may replace 3rd rail DC traction supplies on the Chatham main line.

The Channel Tunnel Rail Link (HS1) 2003

High-speed 1 (HS1) is the current name for what was previously known as the Channel Tunnel Rail Link (CTRL). Originally to be known as either "The Union Railway" or the "The Continental Main Line", HS1 forms the UK's rail link with Europe via the Channel Tunnel.

The Channel Tunnel itself was the first part of the system to be built and with construction beginning in 1986, it utilised in part the 1975 tunnelling works mothballed when severe financial issues halted their progress.

With the link-up between the French and English parts of the tunnel being achieved on the 1st of December 1990, Eurostar services began on the 14th of November 1994 and using the former SER "classic" main line as a part of their route, they ran from the new Waterloo International station to the destinations of Paris and Brussels.

The first new main line built in this country for nearly 100 years, two companies, Union Rail and European Passenger Services were set up by BR in 1990 to manage and oversee the process of its building and operation.

A long time in the making, the CTRL's proposed alignment went through a succession of possible routes. As conceived in the 1970's it was to have taken a route through the Tonbridge area and then go on to London via a tunnel from the M25 at Swanley, but when the Channel Tunnel project was resurrected in the 1980's, the route was switched to a more northerly heading.

Several options being evaluated, one variation considered would have required the building of a large viaduct at Boxley before the line would have passed through Longfield and Darenth to terminate at a new Kings Cross underground station,

By the 1990's, with the government of the day wishing to use the line to regenerate both Thameside and East London, and under pressure from protest groups, the route was finalised on the alignment as we know it today. No doubt the campaigners behind the "Sink the Link" campaign were delighted.

Ironically, some former protesters have come to regret this, their successful campaign to realign the CTRL meaning that Maidstone is without its planned HS1 station.

When the announcement was made that the CTRL would now pass through Gravesham, concerns were raised when part of the revised route showed plans for a high embankment at

The A227 over bridge during construction at Tollgate, Gravesend in January 2002. Author.

Between Downs and Thames - Railways of Gravesend, the Hoo Peninsular and Isle of Grain

High-speed 1

1 - Ebbsfleet High Level Station
2 - North Kent Viaduct
3 - Springhead Junction
4 - Church Path Pit Carriage sidings
5 - Northfleet (SER)

Springhead, or perhaps worse, a tunnel underneath the Pepper Hill housing estate, local anxieties surfaced, and the plan also showing the railway passing through Cobham Woods SSI ¶, environmental concerns were also expressed.

Residents of Pepperhill then banding together to campaign for diversions away from controversial locations, they formed the A2 Rail Action Group and publishing a newsletter called "The RAG" they lobbied BR. Local pressure proving successful, the line was diverted and placed in a cutting to the south side of the A2 road. Unfortunately, part of the Cobham woods SSI area was forfeited.

With the privatisation of BR looming, in 1994 London and Continental Railways (LCR), a consortium of private companies selected by government to build HIS, they were to take over ownership when complete, oversee the UK arm of the Eurostar train services. Now without relevance, the two BR companies created earlier, work was ready to start in October 1998. However LCR running into serious financial difficulties, the starting date of the work was postponed. With the future of the CTRL now looking uncertain, the project was split into two separate phases to reduce the financial risks.

Phase 1, the 46 mile section of the CTRL from the Channel Tunnel portal at Cheriton to Fawkham Junction, was to be built by Union Rail (South). Phase 2, the remaining 24 miles of route between Southfleet Junction and London St. Pancras was unsurprisingly to be constructed by Union Rail (North).

Phase 1 was progressed first to allow the start of a partial 186 mph high-speed service, via a temporary link from Fawkham Junction to Southfleet. Opening to the public in September 2003, Eurostar journey times from London to Paris were reduced by a considerable 20 minutes.

Drivers of Eurostar trains using Phase 1 of

The white line shows the initial proposal for the Channel Tunnel Rail Link at Pepperhill Northfleet.

European Passenger Services and Union Rail, were absorbed into the consortium.

It's terminus now finalised at London St. Pancras and intermediate stations sited at Stratford, Ebbsfleet and Ashford, planning consent was granted for the project by the Channel Tunnel Rail Link Act of 1996 and with Rail Link Engineering appointed project manager, the CTRL sometimes forgot to retract the 750 volt DC supply pickup shoes when entering France. As these were causing considerable damage to the French National Railways line-side infrastructure, an apocryphal tale circulated that a concrete block existed by the Beussingues tunnel exit to shear-off pickup shoes left down!

The construction phases yielding a number of archaeological finds, evidence of a Roman

¶ *Site of Special Scientific Interest.*

villa site and a Saxon mill was found in the Ebbsfleet valley.

Building of the line wasn't without human cost, two deaths occurring locally in August 2005 when a shunter and the driver of a cable train died following a train fire at the Swanscombe end of the Thames tunnel.

Opening throughout on the 19th of November 2007, the final 24 miles of CTRL Phase 2 between Southfleet Junction and St. Pancras allowed uninterrupted high-speed running through the Channel Tunnel and beyond. An expensive project, HS1's final cost was £100 million per mile, a much higher cost than equivalent high speed lines in France and Belgium.

Operating HS1 has seen both difficulties and periods of financial constraint, and when in 2009 LCR became insolvent, ownership of HS1 was transferred to government, LCR then becoming a part of the Department of Transport.

The lessees of HS1 then changing, in June 2010, a consortium of the Canadian Ontario Teachers' Pension Plan and Borealis Infrastructure paid £2.1 billion to hold the HS1 lease until 2040. Divesting itself of its 40% share in HS1 in 2014, LCR passed its holdings to H. M. Treasury, who in March 2015 sold off HS1 assets for £760 million.

The maintenance of HS1 in the hands of HS1 Ltd, the network manager for both the HS1 stations and infrastructure, they use Network Rail for track maintenance only.

An under utilised asset, with the exception of a limited freight service operated by DB Cargo (UK) Ltd, the only current passenger services are run on HS1 by South Eastern High-Speed and Eurostar. A recognised problem occurring throughout Europe, in 2001 EU rail legislation was recast to require member states operating high-speed rail lines to give access to independent operators from the 1st of January 2010.

Taking advantage of this, Deutsche Bahn (DB), were due to run services to the Olympics in 2012. Although these did not materialise, DB is said to be currently looking at proposals for a three times daily service to Amsterdam, Frankfurt, and Rotterdam. Other operators said to have expressed interest in running services are Veolia and the Spanish state railway Renfe Operadora. However, recent major political events may have put these into doubt.

Nevertheless, European travel possibilities should expand in 2017, and Eurostar being still the only international passenger operator on HS1, they plan to use the 199 mph Siemens e320 Velaro train sets to extend services into Germany and Holland, additional services running to further French destinations are a further possibility.

French "La Poste" TGV set No. 951 at Singlewell on 21st March 2012. These sets, carrying up to 120 tonnes of cargo are dedicated to post and parcels duties in France, its presence on HS1 was part of a trial run from Lyon Saint-Exupery to St. Pancras to test the viability of running high-speed postal trains between Europe and the UK. Steve Moor

Between Downs and Thames - Railways of Gravesend, the Hoo Peninsular and Isle of Grain

The North Kent flyover at Ebbsfleet Station seen under construction on 5th June 2004.
Author

Ebbsfleet station on the 18th of November 2007, the day before public opening.
Author

Partially completed carriage sidings at Church Path Pit Northfleet on 4th September 2005. Author

A Networker crosses over the HS1 at Ebbsfleet on the 4th of September 2005. Author

Class 73 electro-diesel No. 73114 in large logo BR livery heads for the HS1 Thames tunnel with a works train on 10th May 2007. Author

Class 66 No. 66552 "Maltby Raider" at Springhead with a ballast train. Author

High-speed Service 2009

Although formal approval for the running of high-speed domestic services on HS1 was given in December 2003, it was to be the 29th of June 2009 before a limited preview service started. A shuttle service only, trains ran between Ashford and St. Pancras, it was to be the 13th of December 2009 before high speed services ran to other destinations.

Originating from St. Pancras, two high-speed routes were originally provided; one route terminating at Dover via Ashford, the other routed via Gravesend, it used the "classic" lines from Springhead Junction to terminate at Faversham. Running up to their maximum speed of 140 mph on HS1, when on the "classic" rail network, the Class 395 units are limited to line speeds of either 75 mph or 90 mph depending on the line.

Recently extended by using the former SER "classic" lines, the Dover route has added a service to Ramsgate via Deal, with a further service now serving Canterbury West and Ramsgate via Ashford. The Faversham route having also been expanded, peak period services now run to Maidstone West via the Medway Valley line and a further extension from Faversham now sees high speed trains running to Ramsgate via Herne Bay.

Provided by the 140 mph Hitachi Class 395 train sets, popularly known as "Javelins" after their association with the 2012 Olympics shuttle services, these are Hitachi's debut rail vehicles for either a UK or European rail operator. Constructed in Japan, the building and maintenance of the Class 395 units was financed by Eversholt Rail, formerly HSBC Rail.

Maintained by Hitachi at a depot at Ashford, the facility includes a carriage washing plant, 25 KV test track and stabling sidings. The introduction of these sleek and comfortable trains has generally been a success, their good reliability and comfort returning high passenger satisfaction figures.

In a modern take on the "Sparks" effect, since their inception on the former SE&CR rail network, ridership has increased markedly wherever the high-speed service is provided.

A Faversham bound Class 395 leaves Ebbsfleet domestic station on the 6th of August 2011 to gain access to the North Kent line via Springhead Junction . Author

A Class 395 unit enters Ebbsfleet domestic High Level station on the 26th of March 2010 with a Faversham service. Author

Detail of the automatic coupling between two Class 395 units. Author

The Hitachi maintenance depot at Ashford seen on the 16th of June 2011. Author

Railways of the Hoo Peninsular & Isle of Grain

Compared to the rest of Kent, public railways came relatively late to the Hoo Peninsular and the line that eventually opened in 1882, the Hundred of Hoo Railway, built during the height of competition between the SER and LC&DR companies could be considered one of the "spoiling" railways.

Now used exclusively for freight, this railway has an interesting history. Before its 1882 opening, a number of other proposals had been mooted to build railways on the Hoo peninsular, a notable example was the North Kent Extension Railway of 1864. Starting from a connection with the SER at Denton, it was then to have run across the peninsular to a pier on the River Medway. As with so many of these schemes, it failed to materialise when insufficient capital was attracted.

The impetus for the Hundred of Hoo Railway came in 1875 when the SER's rival, the LC&DR, opened a short spur from it's Sheerness branch to a new station at Queenborough Pier. Giving the LC&DR access to the deep water of the River Medway's estuary, in the July of 1875, the LC&DR inaugurated a new steamship service to Vlissingen, Holland in conjunction with the Zeeland Shipping Company. Considering this to be a serious contravention of the 1863 Continental Agreement, the SER included the following statement in their Proceedings:

"A most flagrant violation of the meaning and spirit of the Agreement was the establishment by the Chatham board of a New Continental Service by way of Queenborough and Flushing, which has enabled them, by the inducement of lower fares, to divert traffic which would otherwise pass between England and the Continent by the Mail and Tidal services through Dover and Folkestone and be divisible between the two Companies under the Agreement"

The SER believing this was *"unscrupulous competition"* on the part of the LC&DR, they stated that it had *"taken £100,000 out of the pockets of SER shareholders"*! In the era of the "Railway Wars", this deed by the LC&DR was certain to draw a response and after failing to stop the new service by other means, the SER resolved to construct a competing line to the Medway estuary.

Basing their line in part on the intended route of the 1864 North Kent Extension Railway, the SER set the wheels in motion in 1876 by starting to survey the route.

That giant of the 19th century railway world, Edward Watkin, can be seen behind this venture. As Chairman of several railways, the SER, the Metropolitan and the Manchester, Sheffield & Lincolnshire Railways, Watkin had ambitions to establish the Isle of Grain as a major port to compete with that planned for Tilbury.

The Hundred of Hoo Railway

It wasn't just the SER who was interested in building the new railway. The influential Henry Pye ¶ also prominent in supporting the railway, a further measure of support came from a grouping of local businessmen and farmers who could also see the line's potential. Having pretensions beyond local needs, it was hoped that the line would be favoured for boat train passenger traffic, Port Victoria being 40.2 miles distant from London as against the 52 miles of the LC&DR's Queenborough route.

Following the passing of the Act allowing construction of the railway as far as Stoke on the 31st of July 1879, the board of what had become the Hundred of Hoo Railway met for the first time. No SER representatives sitting on the board as yet, only local businessmen and the line's engineer, Francis Brady were present. An arrangement designed to conceal the true intentions of the SER, it gave the impression to the world at large that only a local line to Middle Stoke was to be built.

However, the disguise was blown when later in 1879 a further Bill was presented for permission to extend the railway to Port Victoria. With the truth finally revealed, the LC&DR and other opponents of the railway, the Corporation of Rochester and the General Steam Navigation Company attempted to block the Bill's passage through Parliament.

¶ *Henry Pye is generally credited with improving the economy of the Hoo Peninsular by introducing the growing of different crops by improvements to agricultural techniques. Earning him the title "King of the Hundred", amongst other benefits, this made the peninsular attractive to the railways.*

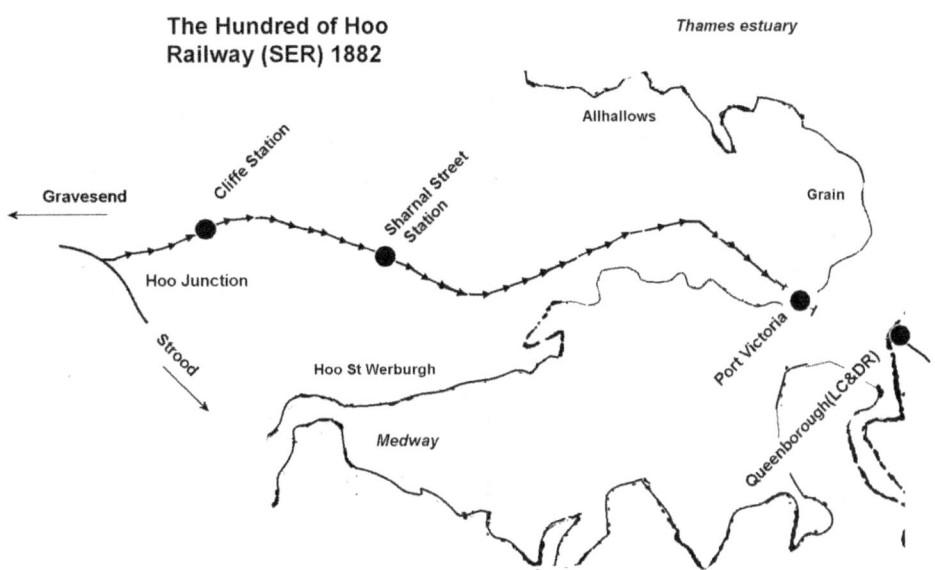

The HOHR June 1883 general timetable. There is a reference in some publications to a twice daily boat train service when the line opened, but a perusal of the timetables for the early years has failed to reveal any boat train workings and probably refers to the Sheerness ferry connecting trains.

HUNDRED OF HOO BRANCH.
WORKED BY TRAIN STAFF.

STATIONS.	DOWN TRAINS—Week Days.												SUNDAYS.				
	Gds.		Goods.				A				S						
	a.m.	a.m.	arr.	dep.	a.m.	p.m.	p.m.	p.m.	p.m.	p.m.	p.m.		a.m.	a.m.	p.m.	p.m.	
Gravesend ... dep.	6 0	7 55	..	9 35	11 7	2 0	3 50	5 6	6 30	7 25	10 0	..	10 38	11 28	2 45	6 27	..
Hoo Junction... pass	6 8	8 5		9 43	11 13	2 6	3 56	5 12	6 36	7 31	10 6	..	10 44	11 34	2 51	6 34	..
Cliffe ... ... dep.	6 18	8 12	9 50	9 55	11 21	2 14	4 4	5 21	6 45	7 39	10 15	..	10 53	11 43	3 0	6 42	..
Sharnal Street { arr.	6 30	8 20	10 5	..	11 27	2 20	4 10	5 26	6 50	7 45	10 20	..	10 59	11 49	3 5	6 47	..
{ dep.	6 50	8 21	..	10 15	11 28	2 21	4 11	5 27	6 51	7 46	10 21	..	11 0	12 5	3 8	6 48	..
Port Victoria... arr.	7 5	8 36	10 30	..	11 43	2 36	4 26	5 42	7 6	8 1	11 36	..	11 15	12 25	3 21	7 2	..

STATIONS.	UP TRAINS—Week Days.								Goods.				SUNDAYS.				
			Eng.&				B		Eng.	p.m.		Emty					
	a.m.	a.m.	m.in.	p.m.	p.m.	p.m.	p.m.	p.m.	p.m.	arr.	dep.	p.m.	p.m.	p.m.	p.m.	p.m.	p.m.
Port Victoria ...dep.	7 35	9 5	10 40	12 45	3 5	5 49	8 5	..	8 5	8 55	10 45	..	12 20	4 10	6 6	7 25	..
Sharnal Street { arr.	7 50	9 20	..	1 0	3 20	6 4	8 20	8 20	..	9 10	..	..	12 35	4 25	6 20	7 40	..
{ dep.	7 51	9 21	..	1 1	3 21	6 5	8 21	..	8 35	9 11	S	..	12 36	4 26	6 21	7 42	..
Cliffe ... ... ,,	7 56	9 26	..	1 6	3 26	6 10	..	8 42	8 50	9 16	..	..	12 40	4 30	6 25	7 46	..
Hoo Junction ...pass	8 4	9 36	11 0	1 16	3 36	6 20	8 24	9 0	..	9 26	11 10	..	12 50	4 39	6 33	7 55	..
Gravesend ... arr.	8 10	9 41	11 5	1 21	3 41	6 25	..	9 5	..	9 31	11 15	..	12 55	4 44	6 40	8 0	..

All Trains 1st, 2nd, and Parly.   A. Runs ten minutes later on Saturdays.   S Saturdays only.
B Attached to 8.5 p.m. Goods between Port Victoria and Sharnal Street.

South Eastern and Chatham Railway.

No. 112.

TIME TABLE OF THE JOURNEY
OF
THEIR IMPERIAL MAJESTIES

The German Emperor and Empress

AND SUITE

FROM

WOLFERTON TO PORT VICTORIA,

Via Liverpool Street (Great Eastern Railway), the East London Line and New Cross,

On TUESDAY, NOVEMBER 28th, 1899.

PILOT FOR ROYAL TRAIN.

A Great Eastern Pilot Engine, accompanied by a Guard who must carry the usual Signals, will run from Wolferton to Port Victoria in advance of the Royal Train as shewn below:—

TIME-TABLE

Miles Distant from Wolferton	STATION or JUNCTION.	G.E.R. Pilot Engine.		G.E.R. Royal Train.		Miles Distant from Wolferton	STATION or JUNCTION.	G.E.R. Pilot Engine.		G.E.R. Royal Train.	
		A.M. arr.	dep.	A.M. arr.	dep.			P.M. arr.	dep.	P.M. arr.	dep.
—	**WOLFERTON (G.E.R.)**	...	9 50	...	10 0	112¼	Eltham	12	40	12	50
103¾	Liverpool Street (G.E.R.) ...	12 15	12 17	12 25	12 27	113¼	New Eltham	12	41	12	51
104	Shoreditch	12	20	12	30	114¾	Sidcup	12	43	12	53
104¼	Whitechapel	12	21	12	31	116¾	Bexley	12	45	12	55
105	Shadwell	12	24	12	34	118¼	Crayford	12	47	12	57
105¼	Wapping	12	26	12	36	120	Dartford (20 miles an hour) ...	12	50	1	0
[illegible]	Rotherhithe	12	28	12	38	122¾	Greenhithe	12	54	1	4
106¼	Deptford Road	12	30	12	40	124½	Northfleet	12	57	1	7
107	Canal Junction	12	32	12	42	126¼	Gravesend (20 miles an hour)	1	0	1	10
107¾	New Cross	12	34	12	44	130	Hoo Junc. (Train Staff Station)	1	5	1	15
108½	St. John's	12	35	12	45	132½	Cliffe	1	10	1	20
109	Park's Bridge Junction ...	12	36	12	46	135½	Sharnal St. (Train Staff Station)	1	15	1	25
110	Hither Green	12	37	12	47	142½	**PORT VICTORIA** ...	1 25	...	1 35	...
110¾	Lee	12	38	12	48						

Speed must be reduced to 4 miles an hour when approaching and passing through the Crossing from the East London Line to the Down Main Line at New Cross, and must also be reduced when passing through the Facing Points at Park's Bridge Junction, Hither Green Junction, Dartford Junction and Station, Gravesend Central, and Hoo Junction. Port Victoria to be entered at walking speed.

REMARKS.

The 5.10 a.m. Down Port Victoria Goods not to run beyond Gravesend but return at once Special from Gravesend to Bricklayers' Arms. Gravesend to run a Special Trip down the Branch with Goods if necessary in the evening. Inspector WATT to travel with this Train.

The 10.35 a.m. Up Dartford Goods Train must not leave New Eltham until after the Royal Special has passed.

The 11.30 a.m. Beadle's Siding to St. John's Coal Train not to leave Beadle's Siding until 12.30 p.m.

The 11.35 a.m. Alexandra Palace to Woolwich Arsenal Train not to pass New Cross No. 1 Signals until the Royal Special has passed. Inspector SETTERFIELD to travel with this Train.

If the 11.35 a.m. Up Angerstein's Wharf Goods Train cannot leave punctually and have a clear run up to Bricklayers' Arms, it must not leave the Angerstein Wharf Branch until the Royal Special has passed St. John's.

The 11.40 a.m. Charing Cross to Chatham Central Train to shunt at Eltham for the Pilot Engine and Royal Train to pass. Inspector WILKES to travel with this Train.

If the 11.43 a.m. Beadle's Siding to Tunbridge Wells Coal Train is run it must be started absolutely to time, and keep good time to Strood.

The 11.45 a.m. Up Port Victoria Goods **will not run.**

The 12.0 noon Down Dartford Train not to leave Erith until the Royal Special has passed Dartford Junction.

The 12.4 p.m. Up Woolwich Train not to leave St. John's until after the Royal Special has passed that Station.

The 12.15 p.m. Up Lower Sydenham Coal Train not to leave Lewisham Junction until after the Royal Special has passed St. John's.

The 12.15 p.m. Down Local Train to leave Charing Cross 12.20 p.m. and follow the 12.35 p.m. Down Loop Line Train from Cannon Street.

The 12.17 p.m. Down Dover Train not to leave London Bridge till 12.38 p.m., and to be held at North Kent East Junction until the Royal Special has passed New Cross. Inspector WALTON to travel with this Train.

The 12.35 p.m. Cannon Street to Dartford Loop Line Train not to leave Cannon Street till 12.40 p.m., and follow the 12.17 p.m. Dover Train from London Bridge.

The Midland Company's Goods Train due to pass London Bridge 12.41 p.m., not to leave Metropolitan Junction until 12.45 p.m.

The 1.3 p.m. Up Hoo Branch Train to be stabled at Sharnal Street and not to start until after the Down Royal Special has passed that Station.

No Goods Train to be started from Bricklayers' Arms or Hither Green Sidings for the Dartford Loop Line between 7.30 a.m. and 1.30 p.m.

No Goods Train, Light Engine, or Empty Train to be allowed to pass Rotherhithe Road for any Station down the Line [illegible]

Nevertheless, despite this opposition, the extension was given the Royal seal of approval on the 2nd of August 1880. One supporter of the new railway being the War Office, they could see it's potential in time of war for quickly moving military stores and equipment from Woolwich Arsenal via the new pier.

Purchasing 500 acres of land for the project on the Isle of Grain, in March 1880, the Hundred of Hoo Railway Company installed new sidings at Hoo Junction for the reception of construction materials. With George Furness, an experienced railway builder and the constructor of the West Somerset Railway of 1862 selected as the lines contractor, work began at Cooling. Carried out in phases, one site housing workers was at Grain, where their lodgings were described by a contemporary as:

"A very dreary and uninviting place, with the huts of the mechanics and navvies employed on the works being of a very crude and temporary nature"

The South Eastern Railway 1881

As was the intention all along, eight months before the April 1882 opening of the line to Sharnal Street, the Hundred of Hoo Railway Company was absorbed into the SER on the 11th of August 1881.

Looking now at the route of this 12 mile long line from its connection with the North Kent line at Hoo Junction, Higham it was built as a single track line, although the track bed and bridges are sufficiently spacious for the provision of a double track railway should this have been required. Running across the Higham Marshes after climbing over the former Thames & Medway Canal, it passes the junction with Brett Aggregates siding's before swinging inland towards Cliffe.

Running then alongside the spine of the Hoo Peninsular, it climbs steadily until the 1:66 Cooling Bank is reached where in the days of steam traction, heavily loaded goods trains often required banking assistance. Reaching the line's summit at 110 feet above sea level in a deep cutting near Cooling Court Farm, it then descends towards the valley of the Medway via Sharnal Street where the line levels out. Heading south, it reaches Stoke, where the site of the former junction to Allhallows is passed at Stoke crossing. Continuing along the north bank of the River Medway, the line currently finishes at the now demolished Grain station where a gate bars access to the remainder of the line to Port Victoria. This part of the line, now private sidings, continues to on to both Thamesport and Hansons aggregate works.

On the 31st of March 1882, the day before the official public opening to Sharnal Street, a special train left Gravesend. Bedecked with flags and bunting, it then proceeded to tour the new line and with the tour concluded, a celebratory banquet was laid on for 250 persons in a marquee The opening ceremony at the completion of the line to Port Victoria on 11th September 1882 was a more restrained affair; in keeping with the parsimony of the SER, this was limited to a celebratory meal at the Port Victoria hotel.

At the public opening of the line throughout, its passenger services were of a somewhat restricted nature and from the timetable of June 1883 on page 67, it can be deduced that with just eight daily passenger workings provided each way, only a solitary daily goods train was timetabled.

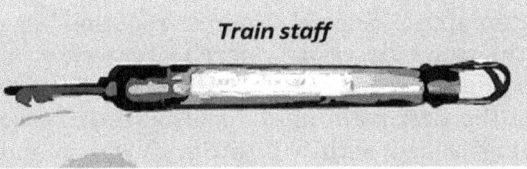

Train staff

Signalling equipment supplied by Stevens & Son, the new line was originally worked on the staff and ticket principle. A system based upon the train staff, a wooden rod, (see above) this was used as the authority to travel the section of line between adjacent signal boxes. A number of staffs being used, each was identified with the section of line between signal boxes it gave authority for.

The driver of a train entering the branch line handed the staff by the signalman, this gave him permission to proceed as far as the next signal box only and, once the signals had been set to protect his train, it proceeded to the signal box in advance, where on arrival the driver handed over the train staff.

Provided that trains alternated in direction, the system worked well, the staff being able to

Ex SE&CR C Class 0-6-0 No. 31233 passes milepost 38 with the 11.50 am Grain departure of the 24th of October 1953. A Gravesend bound train, it has just entered the Kentish mainland by passing over Yantlet Creek which separates the Isle of Grain from the Hoo Peninsular. Tony Riley collection

travel back and forth uninterrupted. Should trains follow each other in the same direction of travel, the system was modified to bring the ticket into use. The driver of the first train to arrive at the signal box being issued with a written ticket, after having been shown the staff to reassure him the section ahead was clear, he then proceeded with the staff following with the next train.

Conversion to Tyer's instrument working coming in 1903, Cliffe's signal box was then switched out. The Tyers system still in use today on other lines, it provides a greater integrity of working. Based upon a metal tablet carried between signal boxes by the engine driver, this tablet can only be given into the drivers possession once the signals and points on the section of line ahead of the train have been set to protect it.

Due to its remoteness from the public gaze, the terminus of the line, Port Victoria was very popular with both British and foreign royalty, Wilhelm II, the German Kaiser, frequently using the line to see his British relatives. Occasionally using Grain parish church, an inscription in its porch records his contribution towards the porch's erection and other notable works.

Having previously been based at Erith, the Royal Corinthian yacht club was also attracted to Port Victoria and thereby using the line to gain access to their yachts, its members provided a steady source of revenue for the railway.

As with many "spoiling lines" the Hundred of Hoo Railway was not as financially successful as has had been hoped. Sparsely populated and unhealthy due to the prevalence of malarial fever, known locally as, "the ague", the Hoo Peninsular initially offered little in the way of traffic. When speaking of the line, James Staats Forbes, the irascible and difficult chairman of the rival LC&DR contemptuously remarked that he did not suppose the line had earned enough money to grease the wheels of the trains running on it!

Marius Wilson, in his work the *"Imperial Gazetteer of England and Wales"* of 1871, states that the entire population of the peninsular in 1851 was just 2,850 souls, and the Isle of Grain itself was scornfully described as "unwholesome" by William Hasted in his 1798 work: *"The History and Topographical Survey of the County of Kent: Volume 4"*.

Before drainage for pasture land was carried out, its stagnant lagoons and ditches were an ideal breeding ground for the malaria carrying Anopheles genus of mosquito, and in 1876, up to 75% of the population were affected with the "ague". Although the last recorded outbreak was in 1918, the local council were still supplying residents with repellent sprays until the 1960's.

Fortunately, at the turn of the 19th and 20th Centuries, the lines fortunes started to improve when it acquired connections with the large military installations then opening on the Hoo peninsular. Notable among these was the 1901 standard gauge Chattenden Naval Tramway (CNT), more of which later.

The South Eastern & Chatham Railway 1899

A reflection of its now diminished status, from the creation of the SE&CR in 1899, the timetables refer to the line as a branch. Now uneconomical, so anxious was the SE&CR to dispose of the loss making section of the line from Sharnal Street to Port Victoria, they offered it to the Admiralty who, however, declined the purchase.

After this rebuff, an attempt was made in 1906 to stimulate more traffic by building a number of halts. Two halts also opening on the North Kent line, one at Milton Road and another at Denton, these had the secondary function of attracting passengers away from the competing Swanscombe to Denton trams.

On the branch itself, halts opening at High Halstow, Beluncle, Middle Stoke and Grain Crossing, the existing private halts at Milton Range and Uralite opened to the public at the same time.

Provided by rail motors, services emanated from both Gravesend Central and Gillingham. The rail motors, composed of a diminutive, vertical boiler steam locomotive permanently attached to a carriage, were built by Kitson & Co of Hunslet to a design of Harry Wainwright.

Steam forerunners of today's diesel multiple units, they also could be driven from either end of the train and it was hoped that their introduction would reduce overheads by cutting fuel and train operating costs. Unfortunately, these 56 seater units proved unsatisfactory at peak times, neither being able to seat enough passengers, nor being sufficiently powerful enough to have more than one small carriage added for extra seating.

As they spent lay-over times at grimy loco sheds, they were disliked for their grubbiness as much as for their lack of seating, and by 1907, the SE&CR accepting that conventional locomotive hauled trains were required, the rail motors were moved away from the branch.

Just before WWI, oil storage tanks were established on the Isle of Grain by the Royal Navy. Built for the storage of warships bunker oil, these were the first appearance of the oil products that later were to become the branch's main freight traffic. Encased in concrete as a protective measure, these tanks were to have long lives, remaining in use well into the period of the BP refinery.

At the start of WWI, both Port Victoria pier and the Royal Corinthian Yacht Club's headquarters were taken over by the Admiralty, the latter building being incorporated into the 1911 Isle of Grain naval seaplane base. However, the navy was not to enjoy the use of Port Victoria's pier for long, as by 1916 it had deteriorated so badly that it had to be closed off at its seaward end. The stations platform then foreshortened, its buildings were turned into offices, and after successive shortenings of the pier's platform, it was closed completely and a timber replacement station, little more than a halt, was constructed in 1932 on the landward side of the pier.

The war, as would be expected, generated much new traffic for the branch, the munitions works, military and naval establishments all requiring transport for both materials and their workforces. Special workman's trains being provided for munitions workers, a daily 7:10 am departure from Gravesend to Port Victoria was one such working.

The Hoo Peninsular and Isle of Grain being heavily defended areas, the railway would doubtless have been used for the deployment of troops if an invasion or a raid had threatened. Armoured trains did not venture onto the Hundred of Hoo branch, the LC&DR Sheerness branch offering greater coverage of the Medway.

Railway reminders. To the left is a 1950's bridge loading warning sign once to seen at High Halstow, to the right is an SE&CR type as used at Beluncle halt. Author's collection.

Gravesend Central October 1953, an experimental A.C.V railcar arrives with a train from Allhallows. A subsidiary of the better known AEC bus manufacturers, in 1953 A.C.V (Associated Commercial Vehicles), produced a lightweight, four wheeled diesel railcar for use on branch lines. Trialled on the Hundred of Hoo branch as well as other branch's around the country, it could be used as a single car unit or in multiple as either a two or three coach set, as seen in the photo. Having bus style mechanical transmission via a gearbox, many bus parts were used to keep costs to a minimum. Known as "The Flying Brick" the set was not popular with drivers and apocryphal stories allude to attempts to sabotage them by putting sand in the fuel oil! Not judged a success, they were later withdrawn. Photo R C Riley

Between Downs and Thames - Railways of Gravesend, the Hoo Peninsular and Isle of Grain

A 1946 Southern Railway Hundred of Hoo passenger service timetable. Peter Willis collection.

Destined for either Gravesend Central, Hoo Junction or inter-branch destinations, by April 1918, the weekly goods traffic having swelled to 19 Down and 31 Up trains, the imbalance between Up an Down workings is explained by the use of special powder barges to import the more volatile explosive materials required for munitions manufacture.

The SE&CR 1918 goods timetable giving the maximum length of goods train that the branch could accept at 35 wagons or vans, this was probably the capacity of the branch's passing loops.

Taking a look at the non-military users of the branch, these had started to develop on the Hoo Peninsular by the end of the nineteenth century. Opening at Higham in 1900 for the manufacture of asbestos drainage pipes was the Uralite works. Using the railway for importing raw materials and exporting completed items, it had its own internal rail network, and from 1902, with the opening of its own private Halt, Uralite began using the railway for special workmen's trains.

Located at Cliffe, other industrial concerns of the time included both the Francis & Co cement works and Curtis & Harveys munitions works, while at the site of the present Hoo Marina was a small private brick works. Having their own internal private rail systems, none of these concerns were connected to the branch. Although Curtis & Harvey had some of its products shipped out in special containers by rail from Cliffe station's goods yard, all these companies normally used barges for both export and import.

When Yantlet artillery range opened in the 1920's, a spur was taken from the branch close by Grain Crossing Halt to connect with the establishment. Used for the test firing of heavy naval guns brought in by barge from the Woolwich Arsenal, Yantlet was chosen as the expended projectiles could be easily retrieved

A 1927 built Berry Wiggins tanker wagon. In addition to Kingsnorth, Berry Wiggins operated from factories in Gloucestershire and Manchester. Mainly using second-hand tank wagons to transport bitumen and refined oil products, one of their better known products was Aquaseal roofing sealant, their wagon fleet was condemned in 1972. Paul Bartlett

The diesel shunter "Kentish Maid" is seen sandwiched between tank wagons at the BP Isle of Grain refinery in April 1983. Kevin Lane collection.

Between Downs and Thames - Railways of Gravesend, the Hoo Peninsular and Isle of Grain

Hundred of Hoo branch - West

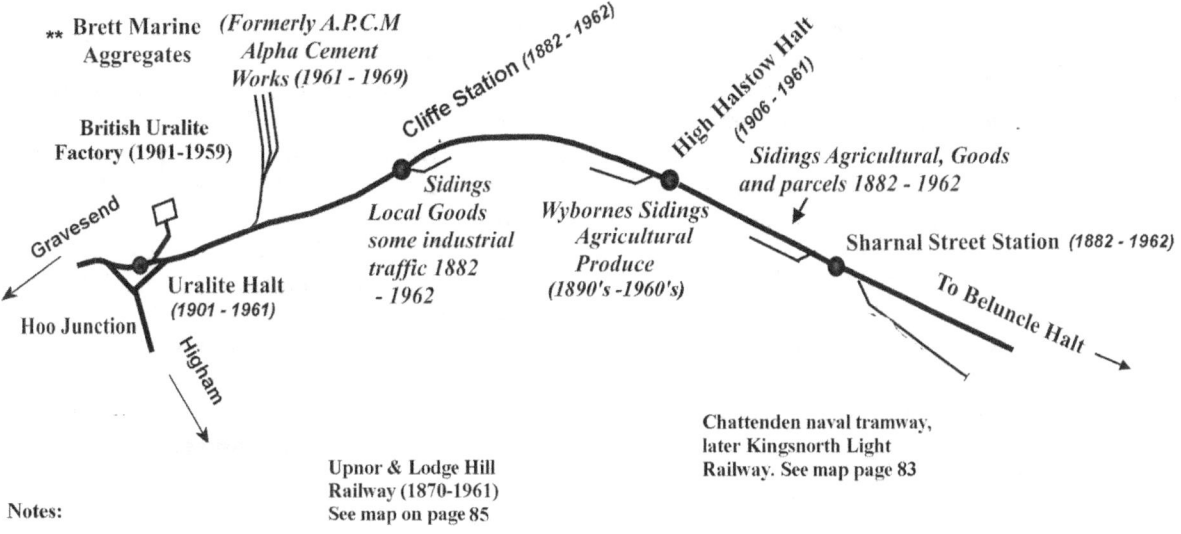

Notes:

Dates shown refer to when a location was rail connected

** Currently (2016) operating

A - Kingsnorth naval airship station 1913 -1920. Premises were taken over by Holmes & Co chemical works in 1922.

Hundred of Hoo branch - East

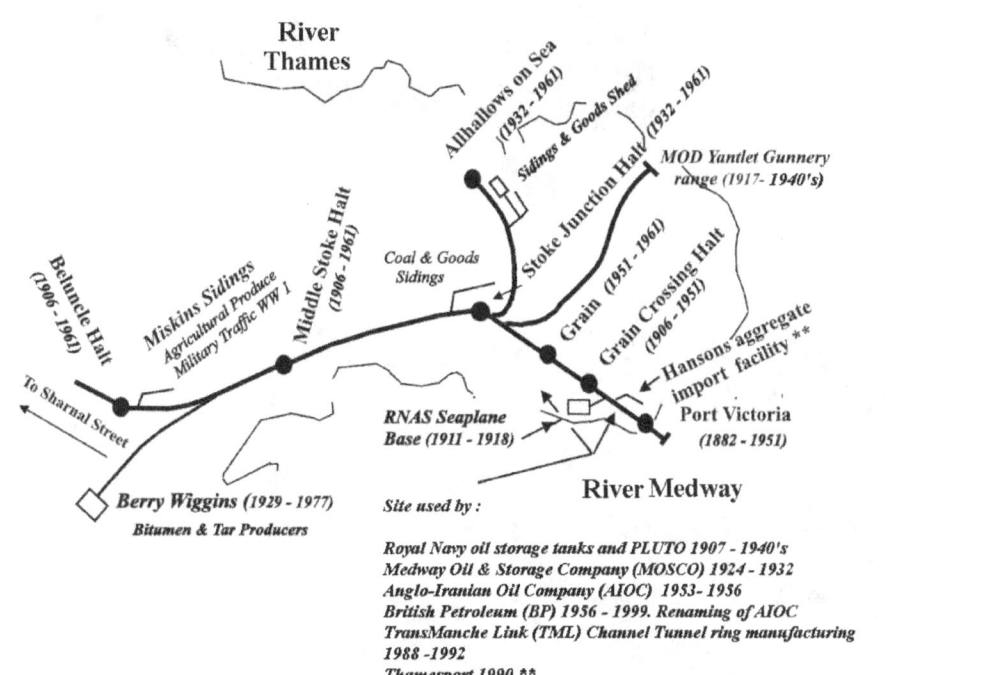

from the target area, the mud flats off the Essex Coast. Coming from Shoeburyness range, here an unfortunate junior officer on a bicycle acted as a "spotter" for the fall of shot!

It's locomotives provided by the Army's Shoeburyness Range in Essex, Yantlet's rail system was working into the late 1940's. Facilities for the test firing of rail mounted guns also being available, archaeological surveys have recently the site of their emplacements[¶].

Southern Railway 1923

The Southern was handed a quiet branch line railway in January 1923. Having few significant prospects, it served only a light passenger traffic plus a few industrial, military and farming concerns.

All was to change however. With the Medway Oil and Storage Company (MOSCO) opening at Grain, as the first refinery in the area it had an appropriate acronym as from 1924 it was refining imported Russian crude. Later acquired by the Power Petroleum Company, its premises were absorbed into the 1948 British Petroleum refinery.

A wood pulp processing factory opening in 1924 on the site of the former Kingsnorth naval air station, it was rail-served by using the section of the CNT between Sharnal Street and Abbots Court pier. Then passing from naval to private use, it became the Kingsnorth Light Railway (KLR).

¶ *Grain Island Firing Point Research report series No.3.*

London Thamesport. The rail container loader in action in 1995. Acquired second-hand this loader came from Stratford, east London.

Brett Aggregates rail loading sidings at Cliffe in 2009. Author

More expansion coming in 1932, a new station, Allhallows-on-Sea, was opened at the end of a short spur taken from the branch via the newly built Stoke Junction. Part of a speculative project backed by the Southern and other developers, it was hoped to promote the Allhallows area as a major holiday resort.

Occupying in part the site of existing coal sidings, and taking advantage of the new junction's position by the Grain Road, Stoke Junction Halt opened later in the same year.

Come WWII, once again the branch was heavily used for both the war effort and the nation's defence, the softly sloping beaches of the peninsular and its proximity to the capital, making it a likely landing place for an enemy invasion.

As a consequence, the peninsular was heavily fortified and a section of the General Headquarters (GHQ) Line, the nations' last ditch defence work, was built across its length in 1940. Pillboxes, tank traps, roadblocks and trenches proliferating, at Chattenden a wide anti-tank ditch was dug across the width of the peninsular.

The Chattenden Naval Tramway was also incorporated into the defences, with rail blocks and pillboxes being hastily erected along part of its formation. By now closed, and with the national drive for scrap metal at its height, the Kingsnorth Light Railway had its rails removed by the military.

Incorporating the existing naval oil storage tanks at Grain, using pipes made at Henley's Northfleet factory, a prototype installation of the Pipe Line Under the Ocean Project (PLUTO) was tested across the River Medway in May 1942.

British Railways 1948

BR should have been reasonably satisfied with the branch they acquired in January 1948.

Already a busy industrial branch and a holidaymaker's line, there was the promise of greater revenues on the horizon from the large new British Petroleum (BP) refinery. Then under construction on the Isle of Grain, this complex was located on the site of the former Power Petroleum Company.

Disaster was to befall the branch in the terrible East Coast floods of 1953, this misfortune occurred when the sea defences were breached between Allhallows and Grain. The partly built BP oil refinery inundated, during the February of 1953, the railway was completely washed away in some places and with its signal wires cut, all public train services on the peninsular were suspended.

The APCM Narrow gauge diesel locomotive "Peldon" seen abandoned at Cliffe cement works in 1969. "Peldon" has since been restored to working order at the Amberley Chalk Pits Museum. D. Willis

With the floodwaters forming a two mile wide shallow lake temporarily joining together the Thames and Medway rivers, the villagers of both Stoke and Grain were totally isolated from the rest of the peninsular and with both the roads and railway impassable, small boats took over as transport.

A small boy at the time, this was all a source of fascination to me, and I can well remember watching as some very damp looking soldiers worked hard at temporarily filling the breaches in the Thames sea wall at Higham with sandbags.

After recovering from the floods, the BP refinery was completed later in 1953, it's formal opening came in the April of 1955 when Her Majesty the Queen visited the new complex by Royal Train.

Providing considerable flows of petro-chemical products loaded into rail tank wagons, the BP refinery traffic flows were a long time staple of the branch. After many years of use, the former BP internal rail system now mostly closed, only a small part is retained by Hanson for their rail borne ballast trade and by Thamesport for rail container traffic.

With it's use as a holiday line diminishing post-war, it was becoming obvious that the Allhallows-on-Sea holiday resort project was now virtually a failure and as a consequence, with all the direct London trains withdrawn, the timetabled passenger services reverted to a steam-powered operation from Gravesend Central only.

However, remaining popular with the day tripper, on three summer days of the week, the branch could be visited by excursion trains full of excited passengers from the London area on their way to Allhallows-on-Sea.

Nevertheless, the growth of private car ownership and road transport in general causing a steady decline in the branch's passenger traffic, most trains travelling beyond Sharnal Street in the winter were almost empty. A journalist from the *Trains Illustrated* magazine visiting the branch in February 1954, confirmed this when reporting that services from Allhallows were carrying only twenty or so passengers. However, despite these light loading's, in 1955 there were still eleven weekday passenger trains in each direction.

In an attempt to stimulate passenger traffic, an experimental ACV 125 HP diesel rail-car was trialled on the branch in 1953. Not deemed as a great success, it was withdrawn in 1954 after a short period in service.

Not considered an important line by BR, the writing was on the wall for the branch's passenger services when it was excluded from the 1955 Kent Coast electrification plans.

In it's penultimate year of operation, the summer of 1960, I was fortunate to travel on the branch to Allhallows-on-Sea. A family outing, the ex-LSWR carriage we travelled in was far from clean. Accompanying us was the family's small white terrier, Bruce, who after insisting on going under the carriages seats, emerged in a grey-black hue. Proceeding then to coat the rest of us with coal dust, all the family spent the rest of the day a somewhat lighter shade of grey, such were the delights of branch line travel in BR steam days. A highlight of the day was an opportunity to see the short lived miniature railway in action that then ran from the "British Pilot" Inn to the resort's beach.

Withdrawal of Passenger Services 1961

In March 1960, when announcing the forthcoming withdrawal of passenger services from the branch, BR stated that thereafter it was to become a freight only line and despite local opposition and a subsequent public enquiry, in September 1960 the South Eastern Area Transport Users Consultative Committee (TUCC) ratified British Railways closure request.

Creating a sudden flurry of interest by the railway enthusiast fraternity in the last days of the branch's passenger operations, on the wet, cold and dark Sunday of the 4th of December 1961, it's passage resonating to the sound of detonators exploding along the line, the last passenger service departed Allhallows-on-Sea.

It's traffic having ceased sometime beforehand, the official closure of the Chattenden Naval Tramway later in the month on the 29th of December 1961 was merely a formality.

When Stoke Parish Council petitioned BR to reopen passenger services in 1974, their plea was rejected by BR. Claiming that operating passenger services intermingled with the branch's freight services would call for re-signalling, this was something they were loath to do, the branch's signalling having recently only been upgraded to colour light control.

Latter Days

With the passenger services now at an end, the branch's main customers now became the peninsular's industrial concerns and refineries.

A new customer coming to the branch in 1961, this was the recently rail connected APCM Alpha cement works at Cliffe. As with many large industrial concerns of the time, this works had its own internal 2'-0" gauge railway system.

Employing small diesel locomotives of the "Resilient" Class to haul chalk wagons from the nearby pits to it's rotary kilns, one member of the Class, Peldon is shown in a disused condition on page 77.

Rail traffic from the Cliffe cement works was normally bulk cement block trains comprised of pressurised "Cemflo" wagons. Destined for

Scotland, it was one of these trains travelling from Cliffe to Uddington that was involved in the terrible Thirsk rail disaster of the 31st of July 1967. Occurring when a cement wagon derailed at Thirsk, North Yorkshire, this caused all but the last wagon and brake van of the train to come off the rails and block the main line. Despite the heroic efforts of the train's guard to protect the derailed cement train, the midday Edinburgh express, headed by the prototype locomotive DP2, slammed into the wagons. A serious collision occurring, it killed seven and injured 45 others.

A subsequent enquiry determining that the accident was due to violent oscillation of the wagons at speed, it's cause was traced to excessive wear in the wagon's suspension mechanism caused by the ingress of cement dust. Heavily damaged in the accident, the locomotive DP2, as railway buffs will know, was an experimental locomotive that was to become the basis of the Class 50 diesel express passenger locomotives.

APCM cement traffic workings ceasing after just eleven years, the rail operations of the Berry Wiggins refinery had ended the previous year when its ageing tanker wagon fleet was condemned. The refinery finally closing in 1977, derelict tanker wagon were to be seen on their disused sidings until late in the decade.

Coming to the area in the early 1970's, another new customer of the branch was Marinex Gravel. Processing marine aggregates at Cliffe on the site of the former APCM Alpha Works, they used the works standard gauge rail sidings for the export of their products. Brett Aggregates, the successor to Marinex, continue to use the sidings.

With BP ending refining on the Isle of Grain in August 1982, BP tanker train traffic reduced significantly and finally ceased in 1999 when the Isle of Grain oil storage facility also closed.

Electrification Proposal 1980

Probably the most revolutionary proposal that the branch has seen, its genesis was a report produced by Medway Council. Concerned at the lack of public transport on the peninsular, in 1979 Medway Council commissioned a feasibility ¶ study from the Transport 2000 advocacy agency.

Their remit to advise on the best way to improve the Hoo Peninsular's and Isle of Grain transport links, there had been increasing concerns on how the lack of transport facilities was affecting both the economy of the peninsular and the quality of life of its less prosperous inhabitants.

With the average bus speeds to Chatham at the time being in the region of 10 mph, this was

---

¶ *Transport 2000 report on passenger trains on the Hundred of Hoo 1980.*

The 1980 Hundred of Hoo branch electrification proposal

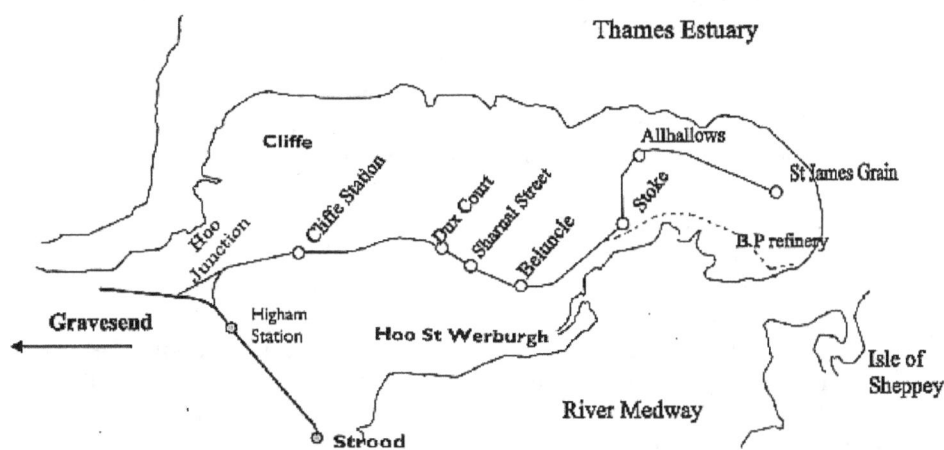

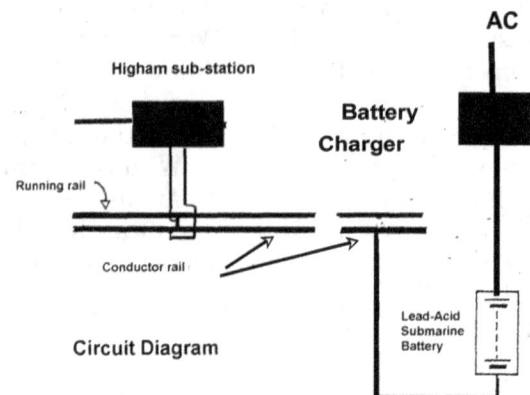

Circuit Diagram

a journey that was considered too lengthy and depressing.

Estimated at £5 million per mile, a road to motorway standards was considered, but was rejected as too costly. A guided bus way was also looked at, but this too was eliminated on the grounds of cost. An increase in bus services being considered, this also was dismissed due to the poor quality of the roads on the peninsular.

The solution they recommended was re-introduction of passenger train services to the existing Hundred of Hoo branch. With a new three mile long single track extension to Grain included, this was to leave the Hoo branch from a junction at Stoke. Then describing a curve to the north across the open farm and marshland, it would have passed through a new station at Allhallows, the site of the former 1932 terminus having been re-developed as a mobile home park.

From the new station, the extension line was then to continue south-eastwards towards it's St James village terminus on the Isle of Grain. Although the existing freight line to the BP refinery was to remain in situ, there does not seem to have been a proposal to reopen the 1951 Grain Station, however, both Cliffe and Sharnal Street stations on the 1882 Hundred of Hoo branch were to be restored and new stations built at Beluncle and Dux Court.

To allow for through workings to the North Kent line, 3rd rail 750 volt DC electrification was proposed for the branch. Accepting that the cost of a traditional substation fed system used elsewhere on the Southern Region would have been prohibitive, a radical solution was offered to keep costs down.

A traction power supply to be taken from the nearest 750 volt DC traction power supply source at Higham substation, it could not, however, power the whole branch as beyond a distance of approximately four miles, the four car electrical multiple units planned for use on the branch would have been unable to start away due to volt drop.

To resolve this, it was proposed to use very large lead-acid battery packs to boost traction power and voltage. Somewhat similar to those used in naval submarines, these would have been located in housings at each station to boost the voltage during traffic hours up to levels sufficient for train working.

Recharging during non-traffic hours, the supply would presumably have been taken from the cheaper surplus night-time generating capacity at Kingsnorth and Grain power stations. A battery being more efficient than an equivalent transformer due to lower electrical losses, more cost savings were expected.

There were, however, drawbacks as lead-acid batteries need more frequent maintenance and careful control of their operating environment. Moreover, dependent on usage, a lead-acid battery has a life cycle of only 10 years or so, whereas the life of an oil cooled high voltage transformer is some 50/60 years.

With signalling to be under the control of the Dartford signalling control centre, the cost of re-opening was put at £3.5 million with a further expenditure of £750,000 expected on new rolling stock.

Since the closure of passenger services in December 1961, the population of the peninsular had more than doubled and it was hoped that the revenue needed to operate the re-opened branch would come from two main sources, e.g. those inhabitants without access to car travel and the estimated 1,260 persons who commuted to London daily.

Furthermore, the survey showing that there were another 3,000 persons who travelled to the peninsula's industries and power stations, some of these could be expected to take advantage of the new service. However, the survey method used for this group did not differentiate between those persons who were working temporarily on the construction of the Grain power station and the permanent staff employed at these places, whose numbers were considerably less.

With the operating method decided, all that was needed now was funding. Medway Council agreeing to provide some financial support, as did both central government and Kent County Council, it was hoped that further investment would be provided by British Rail. However, with British Rail not being prepared to contribute to the fund, there the scheme foundered,

Transmanche Link

Transmanche Link, a consortium of British and French companies responsible for building the Channel Tunnel, they brought a new source of revenue to the branch in 1988 by opening a factory at Grain for the manufacture of concrete lining segments for the Channel Tunnel. After a spectacular opening event using the West Country Pacific locomotive No. 34016 *Bodmin* for the occasion, they used the branch both for the import of raw materials and the export of finished tunnel segments to Cheriton.

Thamesport

Thamesport, actually on the River Medway, opened in 1990; a major project for its owner Thamesport Ltd and possibly too big for the original developers, the losses incurred in developing the site caused them to go into administration in the latter half of 1990. By 1998, after several changes of ownership, it was bought by the ports current owner, the Hong Kong based shipping company, Hutchison Whampoa. The UK's third largest container port, up until 2014 Thamesport was the weekly host to ten inward bound and eleven outward bound container trains.

With traffic arriving from or destined for Southampton, Trafford Park and Bristol, at its peak, rail transport accounted for something over 25% of Thamesport's total traffic movements. Upgrading of the national network taking place to allow modern containers to access the port, this included track lowering at some road bridges on the North Kent Line.

Since the 2013 opening of the Dubai Ports Thames Gateway container terminal on the Thames estuary, Freightliner having shifted their operations to there, rail container traffic to Thamesport has virtually ceased. With over 2 million tons of aggregate delivered annually by sea from Glensanda quarry, the branch's main customer today is Hanson's Isle of Grain stone processing plant. The last concern on the branch to have a privately owned shunting locomotive, Hanson use the appropriately named, *"Isle of Grain"* Class 08 diesel shunter to make up the 29 block train movements diagrammed weekly for the plant. One of two sources of aggregate traffic or the branch, the other being the Brett Aggregates facility at Cliffe, in 2014 this plant was seeing four weekly departures for Tolworth, Purley and Crawley. Railway enthusiasts trains occasionally visiting the branch, the most recent was the aptly named "Dr. Hoo" of the 8th of November 2014. Colour light signalled, the branch is controlled from Ashford signalling centre with the exception of the approaches to Grain level crossing. Retaining semaphore signalling, this is controlled from Grain Crossing signal box. After a number of fatal and serious accidents on the difficult approach to the level crossing at Stoke, this was replaced in 2011 by a flyover bridge.

No stranger to grandiose schemes, the Hoo Peninsular was proposed in 2011 as the site for a large international airport whose transport connections were to include a high-speed railway.

Coming up to date, rail freight operators said to be keen to expand their business on the branch, the upgrading of the ageing rail infrastructure is badly needed to allow this. Thamesport said to be hoping to expand rail operations, possibly this will be undertaken.

Chattenden Naval Tramway and Kingsnorth Light Railway

Expansion of the peninsular's naval facilities being considered in the early 20th century, a new dockyard was planned at Grain, and hoping to sell off the loss making portion of the Hundred of Hoo branch between Sharnal Street and Port Victoria, the SE&CR offered the Admiralty this section of the branch for a connection with their new dockyard. However, the Navy decided to build elsewhere, but as with so many other schemes, this was not proceeded with either.

Using a Light Railway Order, in 1901 the Royal Engineers constructed the 2½ mile long Chattenden Naval Tramway (CNT) as an alternative means of transporting naval stores. Connecting with the Hundred of Hoo branch, this standard gauge line ran from the Lodge Hill munitions complex to cargo transfer exchange sidings at Sharnal Street.

Extended in 1915 to Abbots Court pier on the River Medway for the provisioning of warships, the cargoes carried on the CNT consisting mostly of naval stores, shell cases and gun cotton, the

"Lord Fisher" an Andrew Barclay & Co 0-4-0 saddle tank locomotive of 1915, it was used on both the Chattenden Naval Tramway and the standard gauge sidings of the naval airship station. "Lord Fisher" is now preserved at the Yeovil Railway Centre after a period at the Air Ministry establishment at Farnborough.

Similar to No. 3 of 1929 that worked the Kingsnorth Light Railway, shown below is a Kerr Stuart 0-4-0 saddle tank locomotive. Transferred away from the KLR in 1939, No. 3 was scrapped circa 1954.

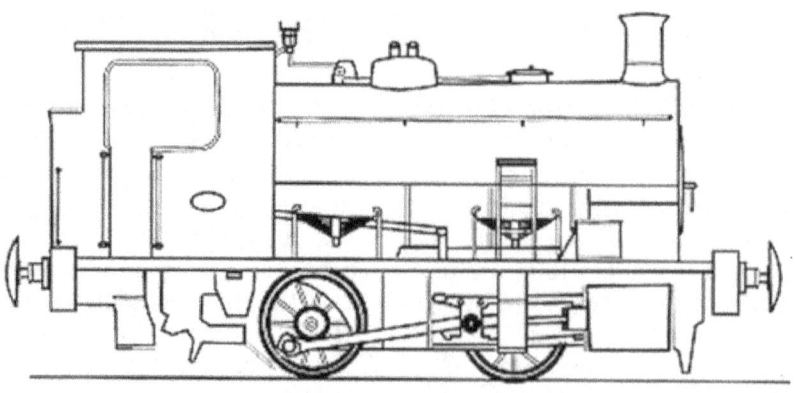

more volatile ammunition and explosives were delivered to the Lodge Hill and Upnor Railway via river transport.

Originally worked by the Royal Engineers, the CNT's initial motive power was supplied by War Department locomotives. Probably three Manning Wardle saddle tanks, all dating from 1885, these were *Burgoyne, Thor* and *Pioneer*.

Worked by the Navy from 1906, one of it's locomotives was an Andrew Barclay & Co. 0-4-0 saddle tank, *Lord Fisher*. Heavily used during WWI, the CNT conveyed both workers and stores from Lodge Hill and in 1915, to the Kingsnorth naval airship base.

Brush 0-4-0 saddle tank No. 314 once used on the Berry Wiggins internal railway. Snibston

By 1944, the motive power for the CNT was being provided by small diesel-mechanical locomotives and post-war it was actually used more extensively than the narrow gauge U&LR. However, unlike its narrow gauge neighbour, the CNT's traffic had largely ceased by the late 1950's.

Closing on the 29th of December 1961, the last of its locomotives, Yard Nos 43 and 71, were then sent away to other Royal Naval depots in January of the succeeding year.

Opening in 1915, the Kingsnorth naval airship station also used a rail spur from Sharnal Street to connect with the air ship bases's internal 2'-6" gauge railway's transfer sidings. An extensive narrow gauge network, it also had a short branch to Abbots Court pier.

Several locomotives were brought in from the Hoo Ness Railway to work the bases's 2'-6" gauge system and one engine known to have worked on the system was *Nipper*. A Bagnall 0-4-0 saddle tank of 1909, with its duties finished at Kingsnorth, it returned to it's home at Hoo Ness.

Opening a timber processing plant in the former naval air station in 1923, Holmes and Co, chemical manufacturers, re-used the former base's rail spur from Sharnal Street to connect with their works.

When in 1929 a Light Railway Order was granted to allow civilian use of both the spur and a part of the CNT, this became known as the Kingsnorth Light Railway (KLR). It's Light Railway Order giving it the authority to carry passengers, but not public merchandise, as far as is known, it carried neither.

A Kerr Stuart 0-4-0 saddle tank of 1929, known to have worked on the KLR, it was later joined by two petrol locomotives. Probably Simplex types, one arrived in 1930, the other in 1936.

When Berry Wiggins opened a new Kingsnorth refinery in 1932, they stopped using the KLR, and opened a private spur line from a junction close to Beluncle Halt.

Developing a fairly extensive private standard gauge system at their Kingsnorth site, this included a short branch to Damhead Creek.

Worked by both steam and petrol locos, two are preserved. No. 4217, a Simplex petrol locomotive is at Shildon, while No. 314, a Brush 0-4-0 saddle tank was until recently at Snibston.

After languishing for a time in a disused condition, in 1940 the KLR was dismantled by the military, the KLR then suing the War Office for removing it!

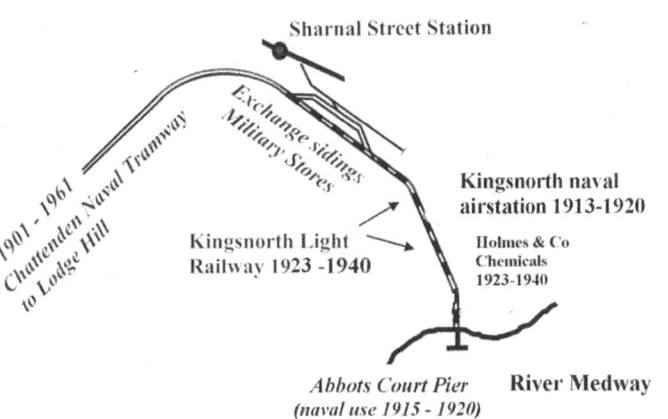

The Chattenden & Upnor (later the Upnor & Lodge Hill) Railway

No history of the Hoo Peninsular's railways would be complete without including the Chattenden & Upnor Railway (C&U). Initially a standard gauge system using convict labour to construct it's earthworks, the C&U opened in 1870 for the training of sappers of the Corps of Royal Engineers (RE). An unusual locomotive type claimed to have been used on this early system was the "Steam Sapper". Basically an Aveling & Porter traction road engine, these vehicles were equipped with power take-offs which allowed them to operate as an early form of Multi Purpose Vehicle. One or more of these supplied to the RE with a set of flanged ¶ railway wheels, several examples are believed to have worked on the early C&U.

Opening a new barracks at Chattenden in 1872, the RE shortly afterwards built an experimental 1'-6" gauge railway from there to connect with their depot on the Medway at Upnor. It's construction largely carried out by men of the RE as part of their training, it is thought that the unit concerned were elements of the 8th Company RE.

Chosen by the military for its ease of portability and adaptability to most types of terrain while on campaign, the Chattenden site was said to offer an ideal testing ground for experiments with a 1'-6" railway as it's topography was considered similar to the North West Frontier of India. This small gauge not finding wide acceptance outside of military circles, its use was mainly confined to defence establishments such as the Woolwich Arsenal and a few railway works such as Horwich on the Lancashire & Yorkshire Railway. A 1'-6" gauge branch running from Chattenden to Hoo St Werburgh at one time, this closed in 1895.

The 1'-6" system re-gauged to 2'-6" in 1885 and a railway depot built at Chattenden for the servicing of both locomotives and rolling stock, transportation then became the railways primary purpose. It's loads including explosives, ammunition, military stores and personnel, these were mainly transported from either Pontoon Hard or the RE pier on the Medway to the Lodge Hill and Chattenden enclosures (bunkers). While in army control, the C&U was worked by two RE companies under the command of a captain.

A powder train and a passenger train colliding on 22nd June 1891 and fatally injuring a Corporal A. H. Lockwood, R E he was to die later at Fort Pitt military hospital.

By late 1891 daily traffic consisted of six ordnance and nine passenger train workings in each direction, each passenger train carrying over one hundred persons. An intensively used system, in 1893 over 60,000 personnel and 21,000 tons of munitions were carried.

Having assumed responsibility from the army for the supply of ammunition to the fleet in 1891, the Admiralty taking over running of the railway after the RE Railway School moved to Longmoor in 1906, they renamed the 2'-6" system as the "Upnor and Lodge Hill Railway" (U&LR).

Mostly carrying ammunition and torpedoes discharged from warships under repair in Chatham Dockyard, the railway was expanded until the 1940's. Starting with a spur leading from Church Crossing to the Upnor Depot of the Royal Engineers, the locations of other extensions are listed below:

1891- Lodge Hill enclosure armament depot.
1892 - Further extended to a point just inside the west of the Lodge Hill enclosure, other sites rail connected were stores buildings and a rifle range.
1899 - A Branch to cordite and cartridge store.
1902 - Spur to a new armament producing facility.
1905 - Track added to the east of Lodge Hill enclosure.
1906 - Further magazines, examining rooms and a laboratory for cartridge filling built.
1909 - A signal box controlling both home and distant signals erected at Lodge Hill to replace the existing ground-frame.
1912 - Further various extensions.
1940 - Extensions to new support structures and stores.

A somewhat humorous incident occurred in 1907 when the commanding officer, wishing to

---

¶ D.Yeatman, Industrial Railway Record December 1966.

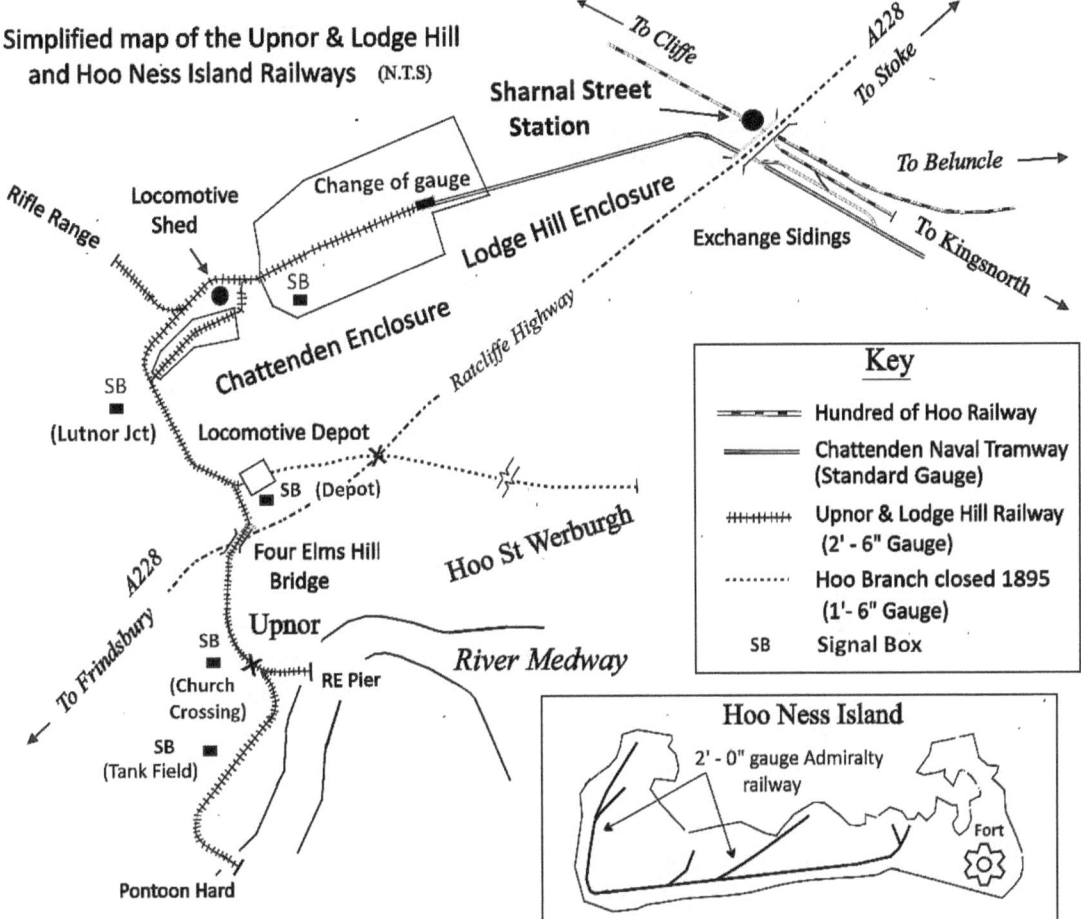

have a group photo taken of the railways' staff, he duly assembled the workforce. As all were about to pose, they could only watch in horror as an unattended engine started off on its own accord.

Just missing a policemen by the security gate, the loco careered down the incline towards Upnor. It's speed increasing, it fell off the track at the curve by the Chattenden Enclosure! Tackle and ropes then being brought from Chatham Dockyard, after much effort the loco was recovered.

With platforms provided for the use of naval personnel travelling within the complex, it's passenger workings running to a timetable in compliance with the U&LR's rule book, it was worked by train staff and token. Originally worked from ground frames, by 1912 there were five signal boxes on the system with Saxby and Farmer interlocking frames in use on what was a semaphore signalled system. Several items of signalling having survived, an example of an interlocking frame from the C&U, dating from 1871, along with other interesting U&LR artefacts can be seen at the Narrow Gauge Railway Museum at Tywyn, Wales.

It's functionality increasing circa 1905, the U&LR was integrated with the standard gauge Chattenden Naval Tramway via a transfer facility at the Lodge Hill enclosure.

With a fully developed railway facility in operation by the beginning of WWI, the railway was to see intensive use during the conflict. Not escaping damage by the enemy, the railway depots roof was wrecked in a Zeppelin raid during the course of the war. Amazingly, this damage was not repaired until the 1950's.

By 1931, the U&LR's rolling stock comprising of 91 powder trucks, 16 ammunition vans, 17 assorted trucks for ballast and

The "Busy Bee" 0-4-0 saddle tank was one of the 1'- 6" gauge locomotives used on the Chattenden & Upnor Railway(C&U) by the Royal Engineers. Built by Manning Wardle, she was one of nine locomotives originally supplied to Chatham Dockyard that was later transferred to the C&U.

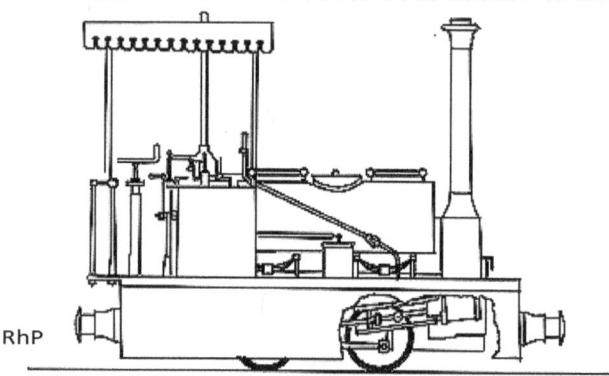

An Aveling & Porter standard gauge "Steam Sapper" of the 1870's, it is similar to the type used or trialled at Chattenden. Described as 2-2-0 tank locomotives, they were basically road traction engines adapted to rail use for the Royal Engineers. As well as being used for traction, these engines could power ancillary machinery such as lathes, circular saws and pumps via belt drives. In road-going form they accompanied the army on its campaigns in Africa.

The last surviving U&LR working steam locomotive is "Chevalier". Seen at the Sittingbourne & Kemsley Light Railway in 2005, "Chevalier" is now based on the Great Whipsnade Railway. Liz Fuller SKLR

engineering trains, plus an officers' coach, seven workmen's coaches, three brake vans and a breakdown van, motive power for this stock was provided by light green liveried steam and electric locomotives, six of the latter being supplied by either the Battley or Brush companies. Restricted to maximum loads of two tons, 16 hundredweight, eight self-propelled electric trucks were also used for the shunting of light loads.

The U&LR system incorporating gradients as steep as 1:30, neither the Battley nor Brush electric locomotives were sufficiently powerful to handle the systems heaviest trains, these continued to be steam hauled until the first modern diesel locomotives arrived post WWII. Four of the systems steam locomotives withdrawn in 1932, these were taken to Strood for breaking.

During WWII the site was again extended to provide additional stores buildings, support structures, anti-aircraft gun sites and air raid shelters. In constant use throughout WWII, the railway was worked on a 24 hour, three shift system. With traffic on the system intensive, the tank locomotives "Burnett Hall" of 1933, and "Norbury" of 1934, bore the brunt of wartime traffic.

With a timetabled service of up to nine trains running daily each way immediately post-war, additional workings ran "as required". Updated in the post-war period, the systems motive power stable was increased when three diesel locomotives were newly purchased. A Hunslet coming in 1947, and a Drewry appearing in 1949, a Hibberd came in 1954.

However, with the system in decline post war, following some railway enthusiasts visits, on the 29th of May 1961, the last scheduled train ran from Upnor to Lodge Hill although some non-timetabled workings carried on until December 1961. In a return to the ownership situation of pre-1906, the line was then taken over by the War Department who in December 1965 lifted the track and in the 1970's, the Royal Engineers built over part of the former track formation for re-use as the Upchat Road.

Of the locomotives, the Drewry diesel locomotive was transferred in 1960 to an armaments depot in the Plymouth area and the other two locos, the Hibberd and Hunslet, were put up for sale. Some of the former railways passenger coaches were also sold, and these can now be seen on both the Sittingbourne & Kemsley Light Railway and the Welshpool & Llanfair Railway. Fortuitously, the 0-6-2 tank locomotive "Chevalier" escaped scrapping and after many years on the Bowaters Kemsley mill railway, it is now owned by a private individual as a resident of the Great Whipsnade Railway.

Two of the diesel locomotives have also survived, the Planet locomotive "Yard No 44" of 1954, since re-named "Upnor Castle" is at the Welsh Highland Railway, whilst the Drewry locomotive of 1949, now known as "Chattenden", is based at the Welshpool & Llanfair Light Railway. Little now remaining of the railway, some narrow gauge rails are to be seen set in concrete at Upnor, on the Upnor RSME pier and in derelict buildings at Chattenden.

The Hoo Ness Railway

Built on the Medway island of Hoo Ness, this was the last of the ex-naval narrow gauge lines to remain in service. Originally 2' 6" gauge, it was re-gauged to 2'-0" in 1952. Initially a military railway, it was used for conveyance of ordnance and stores to Hoo Ness island's fortification, Fort Hoo. Opening in 1871 following fears of a French invasion, the fort never fired a shot in anger. Closed in the early 20th Century, it was re-opened in the 1920's for experiments with explosives.

In the 19th Century, as part of an upgrade to the system, the Admiralty started building a bridge to link the island's railway system with that on the mainland. Never completed, its pilings can be seen in the Medway's mud flats. A purchase in 1904 by the Admiralty of a locomotive with a salinometer cock fitted boiler, it would suggest that salt water was used to raise steam. Other locomotives known to have worked on the island are: *Avonside* an 0-4-2T of 1909, *Nipper* a Bagnall 0-4-0ST of 1895, *Ness*, a Bagnall 0-4-0T of 1911 and *Sirdar*, a Kerr Stuart 0-4-0T of 1903. Simplex petrol locomotives also found work on the system, some survived long enough to be re-gauged. It's last new motive power came in 1962 when two "Planet" 2¼ ton diesel locomotives were purchased.

With its defence role gone and ownership of the island and its railway passing to the Department of the Environment, it was put work on the dispersal of dredgings from the Medway. Going out of use in the early 1990's, its last use was on sea wall maintenance, I am informed that the loco shed and other parts of the system survive, as does the 1962 built diesel locomotive, Works No. 3982. Renamed *Planet,* she now resides at the Yaxham Light Railway.

Four Elms bridge seen in 1963 after closure. Built by the navy, it was constructed using steel from a scrapped light cruiser. Superseding an earlier level crossing, the bridge itself was removed in the 1970's.
David Willis

Church Crossing signal box. Note the pillbox in front of the crossing. A stopping place for passenger trains, a platform was located just to the right of the signal box. H. Townley

Ex U&LR workmen's coaches. Built in 1941, these are now preserved on the Sittingbourne & Kemsley Light Railway.
Author

The Planet diesel, Yard No. 44 at the U&LR in its working days. It's train having two intrinsically safe explosives wagons next to the locomotive, the 1949 built officers' carriage is at the rear, this locomotive is now preserved as "Upnor Castle" on the Welsh Highland Railway. *H Townley.*

Disused passenger rolling stock seen on the closed U&LR in the 1960's. The boy is standing on the 1949 "Officers" carriage", it should be more correctly described as a 1st and 2nd Class carriage, as anyone with clean clothing could ride in it. *David Willis.*

Photos taken of the working Hoo Ness Railway during an Industrial Railways Society visit of April 1983. In the background of the lower photo can be seen the "Medway Queen'"paddle steamer which has recently been partially restored. *Kevin Lane*

Stations and Halts

Canterbury West station. A close contemporary of Gravesend, it opened on the 6th of February 1846 as part of the SER line to Ashford. Typical of the ostentatious station buildings of the early railways, it is architecturally a single storey building of Classical design with a stucco facade and a recessed central portion supported by two Greek Doric columns and two pilasters.

While the stage coaching system relied upon inns to provide its requirements, this would not suffice for the railways. Although locomotives, like their equine predecessors required replenishment, water and occasionally fuel on their journeys, there the similarities ended. Railways, the new wonder of the age were more space hungry, their passenger interfaces needing platforms hundreds of feet long and spaces able to handle multitudes.

The architecture of the earliest railway stations, whilst often reflecting the local vernacular building styles, had to incorporate those fundamentals of the railway station layout, the ticket office, platforms and booking hall, all still with us today.

In its heyday a railway station was often the social hub for town or village life before the age of mass road travel. Their buildings, providing each Class with its own segregated space, saw the comings and goings of travellers from the noblest to the humblest.

Here too, was where parcels were brought and newspapers collected, and at some stations, such as Sole Street, postal orders and stamps could be purchased and pensions drawn, the station also housing the village's post office.

Liquid refreshment was also usually close at hand; landlords seeing station sites as ideal for the location of both public houses and hotels, they often incorporated the word "Railway" in the name of their premises to indicate their location next to the new marvel.

Livestock was another commodity transported to market or farm from the station's livestock pens. Conveyed in dawdling goods trains, these arrived and departed to the once familiar sounds of wagons and vans being rough shunted in goods yards and sidings.

If the station was the railways showpiece, the halt was very much the poor relative, their lowly platforms having more in common with the modern bus stop. Usually situated in isolated locations, these often badly lit and sometimes unsheltered stops were initially known as platforms, the term Halt only coming later when steam rail motors made

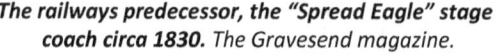

The railways predecessor, the "Spread Eagle" stage coach circa 1830. The Gravesend magazine.

a brief appearance in the early 20th century. Mostly built in rural locations where passenger numbers could not support a station, they could also be found in urban locations, their purpose then to compete with trams. Typical of these were those at Milton and Denton, they appeared when competition from the new Gravesend electric trams forced the SE&CR to provide better passenger connections. Station colour schemes changing with ownership then as now, by the time of the SE&CR, stations were decorated in a plain buff colour with their signage in black characters on a enamelled white background.

Stations and halts could also be promoted and demoted as the need arose and both Rosherville and Southfleet stations were downgraded to un-staffed halts before their final closure. In fact, most stations in Gravesham today would qualify for halt status.

Local Stations

The stations of the Gravesend & Rochester Railway were utilitarian wooden structures and little is currently known of what facilities they offered. Those of the later SER were built in a more exuberant and robust manner, Higham excepted, which retained the buildings inherited from the former canal's towing contractor.

When in 1861 the LC&DR arrived at Sole Street, the station was built using stock bricks in what was then a contemporary, if domestic architectural style. Meopham station on the other hand, being something of an afterthought, it's passenger accommodation was constructed in less expensive timber, only the stationmaster having the luxury of a brick dwelling.

The architectural style of the 1882 Hundred of Hoo Railway's stations was more muted, its stations were built in the South Eastern Railways later and more functional timber clapboard style usually reserved for its lesser wayside stations. Although a single track line, it had been built in a manner that allowed for a later conversion to double tracks.

Perhaps, if traffic had increased, as indeed the SER desired, the line would have been converted to twin track and Port Victoria station and its pier rebuilt in a more substantial style.

The arrival of the Gravesend Railway at West Street in April 1886 brought a more flamboyant building style to the local railways. Not for the LC&DR were the utilitarian timber structures of the SER, Gravesend West and Rosherville stations ornate and substantial masonry styles betraying the ambitions of this new railway.

Unlike the earlier SER and LC&DR stations, those of the Gravesend Railway were built with island platforms. An arrangement similar to that of Ebbsfleet station's platform layout today, this economical arrangement achieves savings in both staffing and building costs while giving access to trains in both directions from a common platform and station building.

The Allhallows-on-Sea station of 1932 was a more functional, composite style of building. Partially built in pre-fabricated concrete, it also incorporated steel girders, asbestos and masonry in its construction.

Ebbsfleet Station of 2007 is an attractive and architecturally pleasing edifice of brushed steel, glass and concrete. However, passenger comfort is not a priority here, the platforms in particular providing very little in the way of shelter or conveniences.

Local Halts

Apart from Uralite and Milton Range Halts which had been built at an earlier date for industrial and military purposes, the area's other halts, dating from 1906 or later, were introduced in an attempt to encourage more passenger traffic.

With financial prudence as ever always in mind, frugally built from time-served timber sleepers, some of the 1906 built SE&CR halts also had a passenger shelter. A few additionally sporting a small ticket office, these fell out of use when tickets started to be issued by the train's guard. Updated in the 1930's and the 1950's, all the surviving halts apart from Longfield, were then rebuilt in reinforced concrete.

Dependent on their location, their lighting provided by either electric, oil or Tilley ¶ pressure lamps, one of the guard's duties was to light these lamps at dusk and extinguish them with the last train of the day.

¶ *A pressurised form of paraffin lamp where the paraffin is turned to gas to give a brighter light.*

Rochester G&RR Station

Its name something of a deceit, Rochester G&RR station actually stood on the west bank of the Medway at Strood. With partial honesty coming with the opening of the SER North Kent Railway in July 1849, it was renamed to the catch-all "Strood, Rochester and Chatham".

Finally coming clean in June 1852, the former G&RR station was renamed to plain "Strood" and just to confuse everyone even further, their rival, the London, Chatham & Dover Railway, when arriving on the west bank of the River Medway in 1860, also took the name of "Strood" for its new station. Fortunately, it was later renamed as "Rochester Bridge".

Strood's G&RR's terminus, similar in style to its Gravesend relative, was an insubstantial timber building. Built as a single span train shed, it's overall roof covered both its single platform and the three tracks that entered the structure. Sharing the station's site was a separate engine shed, carriage sheds and a coke manufacturing facility.

On arrival here, rail passengers could continue their journey either by steam ferry to Rochester, Chatham or Sheerness via a pier adjacent to the station, or alternatively, cross the river by Rochester's medieval bridge to board stage coaches at that city. Having splendid names such as the "Wonder Omnibus", horse-drawn omnibuses could also be used for onward travel; the regal sounding, "Victoria Omnibus" taking four hours for it's journey to Canterbury.

The opening of the railway must have been an exciting event, as on the day itself, the vicar of Strood and his congregation all rushed excitedly from the church after divine service to the station to see the spectacle.

Becoming something of a railway town with the arrival of the SER in 1849; a number of railway employees are recorded as living at Strood in the 1851 census. Their occupations including engine driver, porter, clerk, labourer and the long lost post of "railway timekeeper" held by Henry Jennings, that of "switchman" occupied the time of a Joseph Welby.

A rail guard by the name of William Price is also recorded as living in the High Street in 1851. William must have had a successful career as he re-appears as the station master for Strood's North Kent Railway station in 1865 and again in 1877.

A notable event in the life of the station was the arrival in January 1855 of wounded soldiers from the Crimea. These men, the recuperating amputees and more severely injured casualties from the Battles of the Alma and Inkerman, were then conveyed to Fort Pitt military hospital to be attended to by a Dr. Grey and his medical team ¶.

Smethams History of Strood also relates stories concerning the first railway steamer pier of 1845. A rather flimsy affair, it had been constructed as a pontoon from redundant canal barges (known as dummies) from the Thames & Medway Canal. Arriving aboard HMS *Adder* in 1855, this short pier was used to disembark Russian prisoners-of-war on their way to London by train.

Becoming somewhat decrepit in its latter years, this was to have a hilarious if dampening consequence for the spectators of an illegal prize fight. After enjoying one of these pugilistic contests, it's lookers-on retired to the now very rickety pier to await a river steamer. So many were there that their combined weight causing the structure to partially collapse, the assembled multitude was unceremoniously deposited into the river! Fortunately escaping with nothing worse than a ducking, a stream of top hats were to be seen floating down the Medway!

Closing on the 18th of June 1856 after the opening of the SER Strood Medway Valley line station, a map of 1863, shows the former G&RR station of 1845 as still extant, it is referred to the as "The Old Terminus". After demolition, the site was in use as sidings until 1990.

¶ *The Era newspaper Sunday 21st January 1855*

2016 Status: Demolished, the site is now covered by housing and commercial premises.

Location map grid reference: 2C

Opened: 8th February 1845 by G&RR
Closed: November 1856 by the SER.
Operating Companies: G&RR, SER

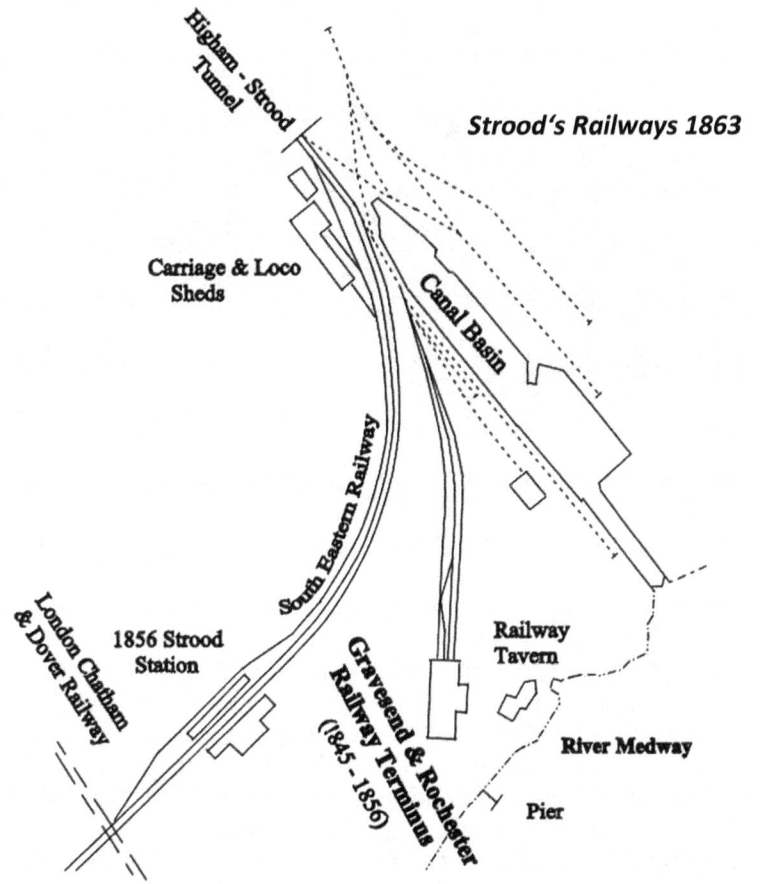

The Rochester G&RR stations engine and carriage sheds in 1845.

Gravesend G&RR Station

This, the short-lived Gravesend terminus station of the Gravesend & Rochester Railway, it was actually located in Denton. Situated 30 yards to the south side of the Gravesend Canal Basin, a timber constructed building, it was similar to the G&RR's Strood station, also having an overall roof covering two platform faces and three access tracks. First used by the public on the 31st of January 1845, the company offered free travel on that day and again on the trial runs of the 8th of February. It's official public opening coming on Monday the 10th of February 1845, the inaugural train was described in *Lloyds Weekly Newspaper* of February 16th 1845 thus:

"The carriages, consisting of two of each Class being completely filled with passengers, to and fro on every trip. The carriage or truck for luggage being also well freighted on each occasion"

Eager to sample the new wonder, on the opening day itself over 600 passengers, mostly local inhabitants, travelled on the railway. A very popular novelty, all four carriages were filled within 15 minutes of each trains arrival.

With fares of 6d for 2nd class and 9d for 1st class passengers, any intending travellers were advised to be at the station five minutes before departure time as the train, we are told, left promptly.

Only passengers were carried initially and in the March of 1845, the railways receipts amounted to £377 for carrying 12,096 passengers. It's popularity increasing, by May of the same year, passenger journeys had risen dramatically to 32,818. Many of these arriving by river steamers, as the railway's main source of revenue, its timetable was carefully compiled to ensure connections to pleasure boats. With passengers allowed thirty minutes for interchange, ships arrived at either the Town or Terrace Piers depending on the river steamer company. A day out on the G&RR for Londoners was not without its risks, as should a fog descend on the Thames, a not unusual occurrence when coal was the universal fuel, the river travel part of the journey could be suspended.

Train control arrangements very basic, when *Frazers Magazine* visited, they observed:

"Everything is done on the Rochester railway in the primitive style of travelling".

Their reporter observing that the station staff consisted of two railway policemen and several youths dressed in cast-off servants' livery, his concerns grew when he was locked into his carriage. Upon enquiry was told:

"On the first week of operation a whole string of carriage doors had been smashed in the tunnel, when curious travellers had opened the doors"

The new railway proving very popular, on the Good Friday of 1845, in excess of 2,000 persons used the line. With over 1,500 of these visitors coming by river steamer from London, their return fare was inclusive of not just the delights of the G&RR, a voyage to Chatham by steamboat also to be enjoyed, all of this was to be had for the very reasonable sum of 1/-3d.

After sale to the SER, the G&RR and its

stations closing for conversion to double track in 1846, they reopened on the 23rd of August 1847 with the re-launch of the Strood services. Closing to passengers in July 1849 with the opening of the present Gravesend SER station, after a short period of use as a goods only station, the Gravesend G&RR station closed completely. Later demolished, no trace of it appears on an OS map of 1866, the site then being covered by the towns gasworks.

2016 Status: Demolished, the site is now a coach and bus storage area, no traces remain.

Location map grid reference : A2

Opened: 8th February 1845. **Closed:** November 1846
Reopened: 23rd August 1847 **Finally closed** 1849-50

Operating Companies: G&RR, SER

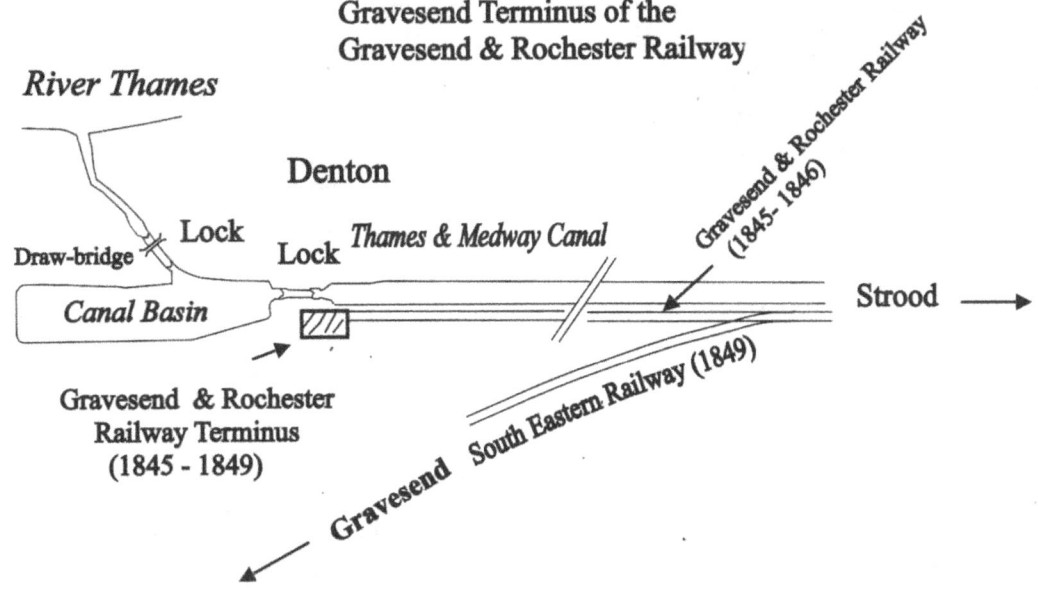

Opening of the Gravesend and Rochester Railway.

Higham Station

Higham Station seen in 1933. The view shown is looking west in the direction of Gravesend. Bell photo Co

Higham is composed of two habitations, Higham Upshire and Lower Higham. A steepish slope separating the two, it is in the village of Lower Higham that the station is located.

Opening on 8th of February 1845 as a single platform station, Higham was the only intermediate station and passing place on the Gravesend & Rochester Railway. Closing temporarily in November 1846 with the rest of the G&RR when the line was widened and rebuilt as a double track railway, upon re-opening on the 23rd of August 1847, Higham had acquired a second platform.

Continuously open since then, not only is Higham the areas oldest surviving station, albeit extensively remodelled, it also holds the title of being the longest in continuous operation.

The first station buildings a re-use of the canal towing contractor's premises, these were later replaced by timber buildings. Also used for the housing of railway staff they were demolished in 1909 to be replaced by the current booking office and waiting room.

Equipped to handle the transshipment of general merchandise, horses, livestock and goods, a small goods shed once existed here, which provided with a 1 ton, 2 cwt capacity goods crane, was able to cope with the heavier loads of the district. Closing in September 1961, the goods shed was later demolished. A typical SER timber signal box once sitting on the Down platform it also was removed after the North Kent line converted to colour light signalling in 1971.

Near to the portal of the Higham to Strood tunnel was once a ballast pit. Used as a source of permanent way ballast, the sidings to serve it were listed as being open in the SE&CR working timetable of 1904.

One of a number of fatal accidents occurring in the Higham to Strood tunnel was that of a platelayer in the August of 1846 [1]. Struck by a train and killed, at the subsequent inquest, the railways representative stated that the accepted practice for men working in the tunnel was for them to stand clear when hearing an approaching trains whistle, this being sounded when the loco crew saw the workers' red lamps.

In this case, the engine driver claimed not to have seen the deceased's red lamp and proceeding then through the tunnel at the normal speed of 15 mph, he attested that he was

[1] *London Morning Post 31 August 1846.*

not aware of any impact, only being informed of the incident later.

When coming to a decision, the Coroner's jury returned the following obsequious verdict:

"The deceased was killed by being run over by the railway train; and the jury express their full conviction that the accident did not occur through the negligence of the management of the superintendent or any other person connected with the management of the line, but purely by accident"

The tunnel has been the scene of several other accidents since then, and a tunnel watchman, upon retiring in 1958 after 41 years in post, recalled that one of his less pleasant duties was recovering people who had fallen from trains into its Stygian gloom. Two of these unfortunates having died, in WWII several individuals are reputed to have become lost in the tunnel during the wartime blackout. A more recent misfortune to occur in the tunnel came on the night of 25th November 1962; a watchman being struck by an empty stock train close to the Higham portal, he later died of his injuries.

An early Higham stationmaster identified in the 1851 census is a George Lloyd. Living at the station with his family, George may well have

Dating from 1889 this pencil sketch by the artist Smith-Niemann shows the Higham portal of the Higham-Strood tunnel. The signal shown at the bottom of the sketch appears to be of the slotted type, and in 1876 a similar type of signal had been the cause of the Abbots Ripton disaster when the signal arm froze into its post. The long vanished windmill that was once above the tunnel can also to be seen. Courtesy of the Victorian web.

A 1933 map of Higham Station showing the goods shed still in situ. The direction of travel is Gravesend to the left with Strood to the right, the Higham to Strood tunnel starting just by the Old Limekiln. Crown copyright.

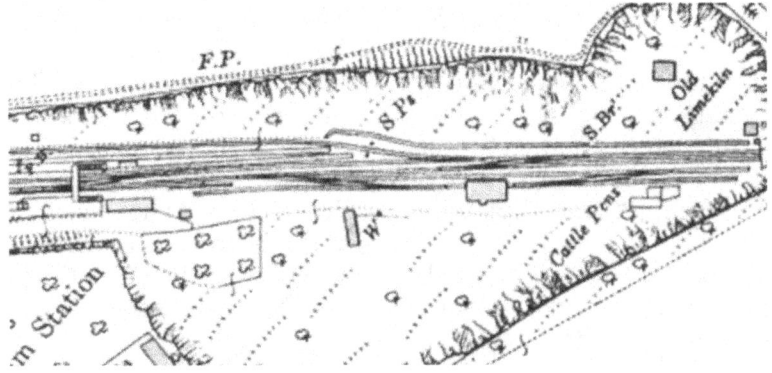

still been the incumbent in 1856 when Higham station first played host to Charles Dickens when he moved into the nearby Gads Hill Place.

A gift from a friend, several of his books were written in a Swiss chalet he used as a study. Arriving at the station in 1864 in crates, this early form of flat-pack was then delivered to his home for erection.

A number of Dicken's literary friends using Higham station to visit him, one such was Hans Christian Anderson. Staying at Gads Hill for five weeks, this was three weeks beyond his invitation.

Much used by the Dickens family, the station was the starting point for the special train that the doting Charles provided for his daughter Kate's marriage in 1860. More mournfully, in June 1870, Higham was also the start of Dickens last rail journey to London for interment at Westminster Abbey.

Sir Arthur Conan Doyle weaving the station into his 1894 Sherlock Holmes short story, *The Adventure of the Golden Pince Nez,* he has Holmes alight at Higham on his way to the fictitious Yoxley Old Place to see Professor Coram.

The station's main goods traffic being agrarian produce and livestock, in season, extra goods porters were brought in to help with the loading of wagons and vans with either farm produce or livestock from the stations pens. Used to handle sheep or bullocks, these animals are still raised today on the areas marshy pasturelands.

For the next 45 years little was to change at Higham and retaining its archaic oil lighting into the mid 1930's, Higham was to acquire the name of "Paraffin Junction". However, all was to change in July 1939 when the 660 volt DC 3rd rail brought the first electric train services to the station.

Spelling the end of the local steam hauled trains that had served the station for over 90 years, only some early morning Cannon Street trains continuing with steam haulage, these too bid farewell after the completion of the 1959 Kent Coast Electrification.

As a child I would cycle to Higham to watch the few remaining steam engines, normally ex SE&CR H Class 0-4-4 tank locomotives. Usually provisioned with corned beef sandwiches, one way of disposing of them was to wait on the former cast iron road bridge, drop them into a passing locomotive's chimney and then watch them rise with the exhaust blast and disintegrate in a form of aerial ballet.

In 1981 the disused goods yard became home to the North Downs Steam Railway Society (NDSR). Staying at Higham until 1983, they then moved away to Chatham Dockyard.

Seen as an occasionally waterlogged shallow ditch behind the back wall of the Down platform are traces of the railways transport predecessor, the Thames & Medway Canal. Now in private hands, situated on Chequers Street a survivor of the early SER is the former stationmaster's house.

The area still shows evidence of the canals construction, and behind the station house, the spoil from the canal tunnels excavation can be seen as a large raised field.

It's style betraying its SER origin unlike many other stations in the area, Higham still retains it's cast iron and steel lattice footbridge. Another survivor is the cast iron mile post on the Down platform. Giving the distance to London as 28 ½ miles, these are often thought to be provided for the sole use of engine men to indicate distances. While admirably fulfilling this function, it was not their original purpose. An obligation of the Railways Clauses Consolidation Act of 1845, these were installed to give passengers a means of determining the length of their journeys in the era when railway fares were set by mileage. A system remaining unchanged throughout the 19th century, until 1914 3rd class fares were charged at 1d per mile

Not too heavily fortified against the fare dodger, Higham still retains it's Southern Railway and BR era re-inforced concrete panel walls supplied from Exmouth Junction.

In 2016 Higham has a seven-day a week off peak service providing twice hourly services in each direction. All trains being semi-fast, Down services terminating at Gillingham, Up trains call at the major intermediate stations to Charing Cross. The ticket office now mostly closed, it is only staffed during the weekday peak periods.

The distance marker referred to in the text. This showing rail miles to Charing Cross, each dot signifies a 1/4 mile. Author.

2016 Status: Open, operated by Southeastern.

Location grid map reference : 2B

Opened: 8th February 1845. **Closed** November 1846
Reopened: 23rd August 1847

Operating companies:G&RR,SER,SE&CR,SR, BR, Connex, South East Trains, Southeastern.

Higham goods yard circa 1930. Local farmer Ed Darby loads vans with soft fruit destined for London. Sheelagh Darby

Higham signal box as seen on 19th April 1969 shortly before its closure in 1971. Tony Riley

The "Granville Express" steam rail tour of 25th February 2006 rushes through Higham pulled by ex LMS Black Five locomotive No. 45407 en route to Thanet. Author.

Gravesend Station

Gravesend Station in the 1850's. Note the overall track canopies. Gravesend library

Now the only station in Gravesend, this is one of the grander stations of the former South Eastern Company's North Kent Railway (NKR).

A map of 1844 showing the land before the arrival of the railway to be semi-rural, it was home to both market gardens and an orchard. The land bought for its building, an area of seven acres and thirty-five perches, purchased from a Miss Swinney ¶ for £6,000, it was described as inferior, presumably by the railway!

The building of the new station requiring some excavations, properties in that part of Stone Street that is now Railway Place were demolished. Before the coming of the railway, Railway Place the site of timber buildings, these included a row of cottages known as Teapot Row,§ and a Mr. Edwards's livery stables where visitors to the town's attractions such as Windmill Hill could hire donkey carts.

Nearby to the south is an interesting survivor, the former Gravesend parish workhouse. Dating from 1797 it is now used as commercial premises.

The station's design the work of the architect Samuel Beazley, he was also responsible for the design of the 1845 Northfleet and Erith stations, other notable structures attributed to him are the London Lyceum and the Royalty Theatre. Not only was Samuel an architect, he was also a playwright and novelist, his literary output including the novel, *"The Boarding House"*.

Once completed, the station was inspected on behalf of the Board of Trade by Captain R. M. Laffan, Royal Engineers and before allowing the opening of this four track station, one of the conditions he specified was the locking of the points levers controlling the centre sidings to prevent their use until re-positioned.

On the 3rd of March 1849, after the line had been declared practically complete and before opening to the public, an engineers' inspection train hauled by an ex G&RR locomotive, *St Vincent*, travelled the line to Gravesend. Arriving at 3:00 pm, upon the completion of their duties, they retired to the Waites hotel, Gravesend, where we are told they:

"sat down for a splendid entertainment"

¶ *Kentish Gazette August 1847*

§*The Gravesend Magazine*

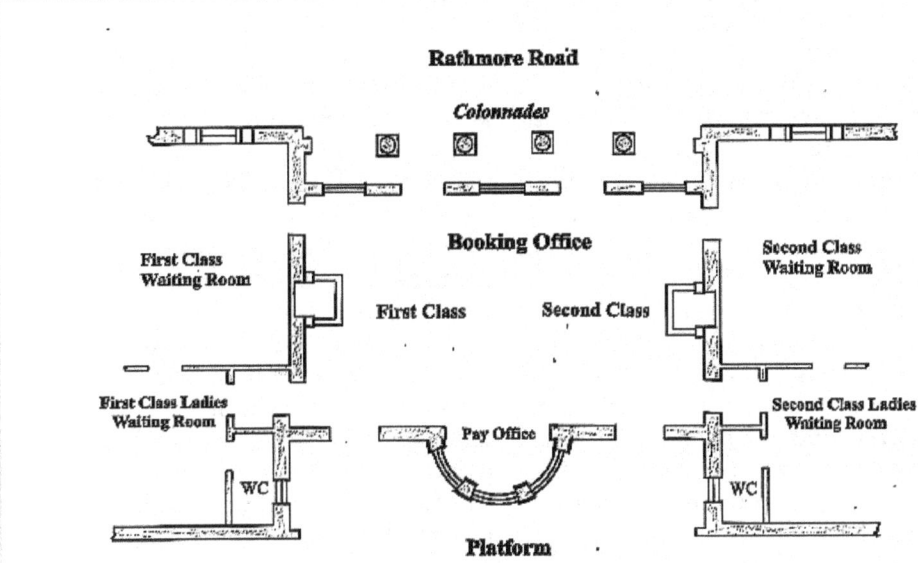

A 1849 plan of Gravesend Station main buildings ground floor. Note the lack of facilities for 3rd Class travellers.

Something of a joint celebration, the line's navvies were not forgotten either, being:

"regaled during the day, at the expense of the contractors with good Old English fayre". ¶

Looking now at the station as it appeared on its July 1849 opening. In architectural style the 1849 Rathmore Road building has a classical frontage with a colonnade of four rendered brick columns, the central portion comprising one storey, it is flanked on either side by two storey pavilions with sash windows to the frontage. Structurally, it is built from stock bricks with stuccoed cornices and frescoed stone linings.

The Barrack Row building on the Down side platform is of a more mundane nature. Comprising a one storey brick structure with a hipped slate roof and sash windows, once reflecting the social mores of the day, its interior space was originally divided into a general waiting room, a ladies toilet, a booking hall, ticket and parcels offices.

Returning now to the main Rathmore Road building, the intending traveller of 1849, when entering the building, would have been presented with a segregated space as laid out on the plan above. With a ticket purchased and stepping onto the Up platform, our traveller would notice that the station, having a four track layout, this was arranged as two platform roads and two centre siding. With no footbridge provided, its omission making passing over to the Down platform by a timber foot crossing a risky undertaking, this was particularly so if both platforms were occupied by trains.

Originally, ornate overall roofs were provided over both platform roads, these were considered of sufficient interest to be mentioned in *Measoms Guide to The South Eastern Railway*:

"Handsome glazed sheds cover each side line of way, and are sustained by iron columns, and the roofs are supported by ornamental iron girders, the centre line of rail being open"

Surviving until the early 20th century, they were removed at the time a steel lattice footbridge was erected.

The station presenting what was cutting-edge communications for the time, a public telegraph office and GPO postbox were provided. Although the telegraph is long gone, the Victorian postbox is still in situ and was in daily use until fairly recently.

The entertainment of passengers not being

¶*Dartford Chronicle March 1849*

neglected, this was provided for by a book-stall. For years the premises of W. H Smith, this is now occupied by the Pumpkin franchise.

In the October of 1849 ¶ the travelling public experienced the dangers of railways when a passenger train struck a carriage shed located near to Stone Street's over-bridge. Demolishing the shed and blocking the line for over an hour, when reversed from the wreckage, ineptitude was then piled on calamity, the train colliding with the platform overall glazed roof, it partially demolished that also!

The culprit was a train formed of carriages described as "larger than usual". Reported to be forty feet long, these vehicles were viewed with suspicion by local passengers, who believed them to be both unstable and prone to de-railing. Described as being gang-way connected, these vehicles may have been the eight wheeled articulated carriages described on page 211.

A complaint was received from a Mr. Heald in late 1849. Aggrieved at the overcrowding of carriages, he protested to the SER that twenty-two passengers were being squeezed into a space measuring 10 foot by 9 foot. The usual width of carriages on the NKR at the time being eight foot or less, the reference to a nine foot wide carriage may indicate that the stock referred to by Mr Heald is possibly the very same unpopular 40 feet long carriages mentioned above.

Another particular concern of Gravesend's passengers was a continuation of the G&RR practice of locking passengers into their barred window carriages. Petitioning the SER to have this practice stopped, a visit by the Board of Trade's inspector followed. However, some two years later, the petitioners were still waiting for a response from the SER.

For all the complaints received concerning the discomfort and primitive design of early SER carriages, they must have been sturdy vehicles, several carriages from the 1850's still being in use on the NKR into the 1890's.

In January 1850, six months after the station's opening, the *Kentish Independent* newspaper reported on complaints from the public concerning the state of the roads adjacent to the station. Left in an un-made state by the railways contractors, the Commissioners responsible for the upkeep of local roads decided to serve 21 days notice on the railway company to make good the defects and, if not completed by then, a penalty of £5 per day would be levied.

The coming of the railway was a mixed blessing for some. The Corporation of Gravesend issued licenses to porters who paid for the privilege, and until the arrival of the railway they had mostly worked from the riverside piers, where they held a monopoly. With the arrival of the railway in 1849 and its own porters, the licensed porters were barred by the SER from working from the station.

The licensed porters became aggrieved at the loss of income, particularly as some of the railway's porters were carrying passengers luggage into areas where only the licensed porters could legally operate. Matters coming to a head in 1850, the *Kentish Independent* newspaper reported on litigation brought by a William Smith, borough licensed porter, over a dispute with a railway porter, John Alexander. It was alleged that Alexander was seen to be carrying a bag for a gentleman as far as Bath Street, whereupon he asked for 6d for the service.

Claiming this contravened the local bye laws, the borough licensed porters asserted that only they were allowed to charge. However, the railway's solicitor retorted that it was *"the extortionate and violent manner of the licensed porters"* that lead the public to prefer the services of the railway's men.

The courts verdict, however, went in favour of the licensed porters, the borough byelaws and the Town Quay Act 1800 being considered by the court as superior legislation. The SER then being ordered to allow the licensed porters to work from the station, this no doubt lead to more tense scenes.

The Charing Cross Extension Railway not opening until 1864, in 1851 the railway terminated at London Bridge, a timetable from that year shows a hourly service in both directions. With Up trains calling at eleven intermediate stops to London Bridge, the first train of the day left for London at 7:20 am. Taking one hour 10 minutes to reach its London terminus, the last Down train to Strood departed at 11:05 pm.

As with today, arrival and departure times of trains were not guaranteed and in 1851, the company was careful to avoid potential claims.

¶ *Kentish Independent 3 November 1849*

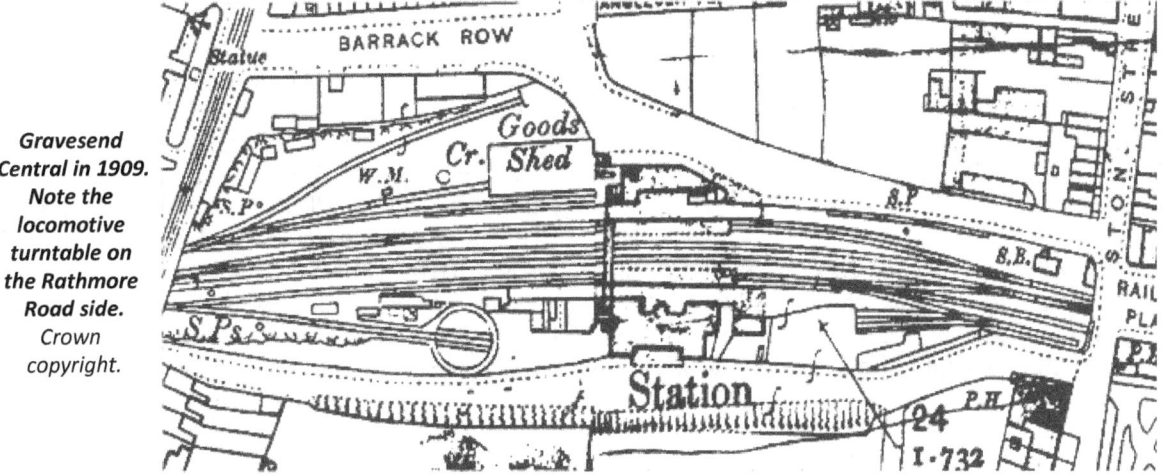

Gravesend Central in 1909. Note the locomotive turntable on the Rathmore Road side. Crown copyright.

A Q Class 0-4-4 tank locomotive departs Gravesend in the 1890's. Tony Riley collection.

E4 Class No. 32578 waits with an empty milk van train in the centre roads on 9th February 1952. Barry Diplock

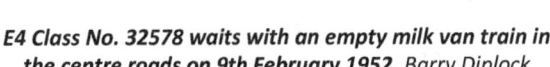

Ex SE&CR 4-4-0 Class L1 No. 31782 arrives with the summer Saturdays only 9:36 Ramsgate service in the early 1950's. Barry Diplock

To quote the statement in small print at the bottom of the 1851 timetable:

"The Company do not pledge themselves for the arrival of Trains at the exact time notified in these Tables, which are intended to show the approximate times only"

The 1851 census, the first taken since the opening of the station, it shows the station master as a George Anderson living in the first floor accommodation in Rathmore Road with his wife and family.

In 1854, during the Crimean War, wounded soldiers were landed at both the Town and Terrace Piers for onward travel by train from Gravesend. One such vessel was the *Sultana*. Landing wounded from Scutari at the Terrace Pier, these were conveyed by a special train to the Fort Pitt military hospital at Rochester.

Assuming that some of the casualties were stretcher cases, this may have been an early example of an ambulance train. Also during the Crimean war, Queen Victoria together with Prince Albert and the Prince of Wales passed through the station on their way to Chatham to visit the wounded at Fort Pitt.

Wounded heroes were not the only military travellers, deserters too were something of a problem, especially during the Crimean war period. With some two to three attempts made weekly by absconders to escape via the railway, the station had a "lookout sergeant" in attendance in 1856.

Gravesend was a rapidly expanding tourist spot by the 1860's and when the inspector for Bradshaw's Guide visited Gravesend in 1861 he had this to say on the delights of the town:

"Shrimps and water-cresses tempt the visitor in every possible variety of supply and places where both are obtainable, with 'Tea at 9d. per head' are in wonderful numerical strength".

The shrimps doubtless coming from the Thames, they were netted by the sailing bawleys which once populated Bawley Bay; the cress was sourced from the Ebbsfleet River watercress beds at Springhead.

Travel possibilities expanded considerably when the extension to Charing Cross opened in 1864. Followed in 1866 by a connection to Cannon Street, this finally gave direct rail access from Gravesham to the City of London.

A further improvement to services came in 1877 when the disused link to the LC&DR at Strood re-opened. Giving SER passengers direct rail access to the "Chatham", Gravesend was to benefit significantly from these changes, the June 1878 timetable showing Gravesend services to have increased to twenty Charing Cross and twenty-one Strood trains.

Before the 1882 opening of the Hundred of Hoo Railway to Port Victoria, Gravesend was frequently the destination chosen by Royalty to board ships in the Thames. Notable visitors included the Grand Duke and Duchess of Russia who travelled to Gravesend from London in 1861 to board a Russian man-of-war that was lying off-shore awaiting them.

Princess Alexandria of Denmark also took the train from Gravesend to London in 1863. After disembarking at the Terrace Pier, she was on her way to marry the Prince of Wales, the future King Edward VII.

Another Royal visitor to the town was Alfred, Duke of Edinburgh, Queen Victoria's second son. Quite an event for the town, the newspapers reported that £300 was to be spent on the Terrace Pier for decorations.

A journey undertaken following his marriage in St. Petersburg to the Grand Duchess Marie, the daughter of Tsar Alexander II of Russia, the couple arrived at Gravesend on March 7th 1874. Processing then to the station via Harmer Street, Milton Road, King Street, New Road and Somerset Street, on arrival they would have observed that the station had been specially cleaned and decorated for the occasion. With seats installed for the excited spectators, a guard of honour was provided by the local Yeomanry and Volunteers, plus a battalion of infantry soldiers from Chatham.

The German Kaiser, Wilhelm II, "Kaiser Bill" of WWI fame, also passed through Gravesend station on 14th August 1894 when making his way to the Terrace Pier where he was to take ship on the imperial yacht, the *Hohenzollern*. Arriving at midnight when returning from a visit to Aldershot, he was nevertheless greeted by a crowd of well-wishers who cheered both him and his party.

The imperial yacht departing Gravesend shortly after 8:00 am the next day, it was saluted by the guns of Tilbury Fort, after which its band played *God save the Queen*.

Not all travellers could expect to be treated with such deference and even 1st class travellers could be inconvenienced; a letter appearing in the *London Times* of Tuesday the 30th of July 1878, it complained of the treatment received at the hands of a clumsy lamp man at Gravesend. To quote the correspondent:

"Sir - I wish, with your permission, to point out a danger and annoyance the travelling public are quite unnecessarily exposed to. I left the Charing Cross station yesterday afternoon by the 5.32 train for Strood (Rochester), in a 1st class carriage of the South Eastern Railway, with my wife, and infant of five weeks and a nurse. At Gravesend we were startled by an explosion through the roof, like a bursting shell, accompanied with falling glass and a deluge of dirty oil. The lamp man, in the way usual with these functionaries, had dashed down the lamp through the circular opening in the roof with such force as to smash it to pieces; two thick pieces of glass falling close to the child's head, cut my wife's mantle and silk dress, and bruised her foot, and the oil completed the destruction. I have sent in a claim on the company for the value of the dress. It was a narrow escape from serious personal injury to my wife and child. Until the lamp men do their work quietly travellers would do well to avoid seats directly under lamps in railway carriages"

No record can be found of a reply.

The SER preferred their customers to pay for their journeys and a Special Traffic Notice for the 3rd of March 1894 instructs ticket collectors to be extra vigilant and to examine carefully all season tickets presented to them.

Some expired season tickets having not be surrendered, this was an offence against the railway byelaws of the time, and a list accompanying the notice shows that two of the suspect ticket holders were using Gravesend station. If apprehended, the suspects were to be detained and the names and addresses of persons using the tickets taken. Little changes then.

A curious omission for such an important station was that of a restaurant or bar, although it appears that in 1888 beer could be purchased on the station, a newspaper article referring to *"two gentlemen consuming a half-pint in the refreshment room"* wherever that establishment was.

By 1897 the station's facilities having increased significantly since it's opening, it now had a locomotive turntable, two signal boxes, a goods shed and sidings and located at the eastern end of platform one was a short siding leading to a small coal yard.

A short bay platform being provided for stabling of the Port Victoria passenger trains, the centre

Royal Trains

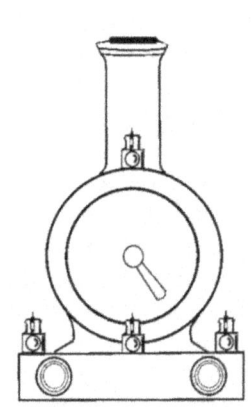

Shown to the left is the locomotive head code for the SER royal train. Trains with this head code would have been a common sight in Gravesham in the Victorian era. The code showing four oil lamps by night or four white discs by day on the front of the locomotive, this would indicate to signalmen and other railway staff the presence of a royal train Specially timetabled to ensure non stop running, it would have been been preceded by a pilot engine to check that the line was clear.

Signalmen used special bell codes to alert other signalmen of the trains status, and the train would normally be under the control of an onboard superintendent with other officials also present. All other train movements would be suspended until the special had passed and level crossings, station entrances and vulnerable points would be guarded The Gravesend Central and Port Victoria Station masters were required to send a telegram to the lines general manager once the train had either passed or arrived as the case may be.

When Queen Victoria travelled from Windsor to Port Victoria she would use a special line through Waterloo station which required part of the platform to be moved to access a special bridge connecting the London & South Western Railway with the SER at Waterloo East station. The bridge is still in existence although it is no longer used for trains.

sidings by this time having been converted to through roads, a speed limit of 30 mph was imposed on the trains using them. Always a cramped location for goods handling, at the formation of the SE&CR in 1899, some goods workings were moved away to the more capacious and accessible Gravesend West station goods yard.

The station was to see high drama on the 4th of May 1899 when a serious incident occurred. Involving a train and signal box, a local newspaper carried the following story:

"An accident occurred at Gravesend Station on the South-Eastern Railway, shortly after nine this morning. As a train was being shunted from the main line it ran into and smashed No. 2 signal box. The signalman, seeing an accident was inevitable, jumped from the box and thus escaped injury. The mishap occasioned some delay."

Having been known as "Gravesend SER" since 1886, at the formation of the SE&CR in 1899, the station was re-named "Gravesend Central" to differentiate the station from the former LC&DR station at West Street. After the closure of Gravesend West station in 1968, the former SER station reverted to its 1849 name of Gravesend. Interestingly, the electronic platform train departure screens at London Bridge were still showing the station as "Gravesend Ctrl" well into the 1990's.

Since the opening of Milton barracks in 1862, troop trains had been a regular feature of the station and in October 1899, at the start of the Boer War, the regiments stationed at Milton Barracks, the 2nd battalions of both the Scots Fusiliers and the Scots Guards, were marched to the station with bands playing and flags flying to the applause of the patriotic locals who thronged the station to bid them farewell. Once departing from Gravesend, the battalions were conveyed to Southampton to board troop ships.

In 1902 the station master was a Herbert Jasper Head; the goods yard coming under the control of the station agent, a Mr. A.M. Cooper. A station agent responsible for the running of the goods and freight side of the railways business, this should not be confused with the United States term which describes the UK equivalent of station master. These gentlemen's office address in 1902 listed as Stone Street, Gravesend, this would indicate that the business offices had moved away from the station itself.

It is likely Herbert would have had to deal with the fatal accident that occurred on the 20th of October 1903 when Joseph Britton, a locomotive fitter, was tragically killed when struck by a passing train while oiling the motion of a locomotive.

The renewal of assets is a constant requirement on the railways and a special notice of 29th November 1902 refers to the replacement of the old No. 1 and No. 2 signal boxes and their associated signalling. Requiring a capital expenditure of £593-5/-6d, the work was carried out by the SE&CR's Engineers' Department.

1904 saw a partial modernisation of the station, the convenience of a footbridge at last being provided. A typical SE&CR lattice steel type, it also incorporated the convenience of a corrugated iron roof. No doubt an improvement for passengers, the price paid aesthetically was the removal of the overall glazed roofs. I wonder if this provoked a protest? Significantly damaged in the 1990's when struck by an engineer's train, one of the footbridge's cast iron support columns required replacement. Removed in 2013, the footbridge now awaits re-erection at Shepherdswell on the East Kent Light Railway.

Other 1904 additions were the timber platform canopies. Still extant, they are supported by ornate cast iron brackets and columns. A large water tank building added at the western end of the Up platform for supplying this vital liquid to thirsty steam locomotives, three new water cranes were also acquired; one provided on each platform, the third was located in the centre roads.

By now well equipped, the station and its goods yard could now handle a wide range of loads including furniture vans, carriages, portable engines, machines on wheels, small horse boxes and cattle vans.

The handling of large loads amply provided for by a large 10 ton crane, this was probably steam powered. Reported as being out of action in October 1913, any items requiring heavy lifting were then temporarily redirected to Gravesend West station until further notice.

Bunkering of the Hundred of Hoo branch locomotives being an essential requirement, a

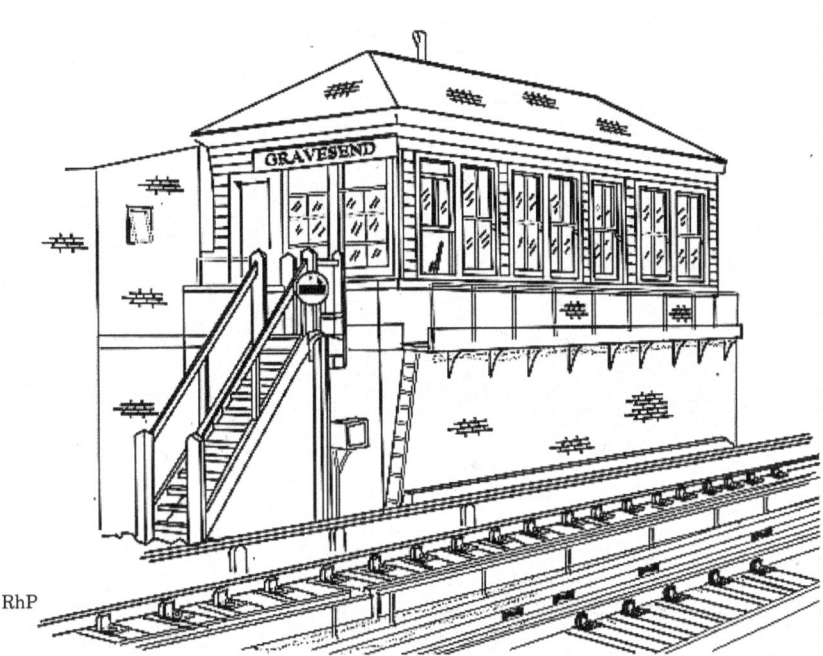

The No. 4 signal box which was once located just to the west of the station by the Darnley Road over bridge. Opening in 1928 shortly before electrification in 1930, it replaced two smaller signal boxes and was itself superseded in 1971 when the Dartford power signal box was opened.

small coaling stage was situated in the goods yard as was a lobby for the accommodation of the yard shunter.

Concern for animal welfare is a fairly recent phenomena and in earlier times the interest would have been more for the commercial loss to the farmer than an animals suffering. This seems to be what was behind the sacking in May 1905 of the head porter at Gravesend when the railway company incurred a £10 fine from the local magistrates after he allowed the overloading of livestock wagons that caused the deaths of five sheep.

Goods trains were a frequent sight, the SE&CR 1910 working timetable showing the following daily weekday workings:

12:45 am – ex Bricklayers Arms terminating.
2:15 am – ex Strood pickup goods calling as required.
3:57 am – ex Holborn mail train. #
4:45 am – ex Bricklayers Arms goods.
4:51 am - ex Blackfriars Goods depot
5:45 am – ex Strood pickup goods calling as required.
9:19 am – ex Southwark newspapers.#
2:10 pm – ex Port Victoria terminating.
2:50 pm - ex Bricklayers Arms calling as as required.
5:00 pm – ex Yalding.
7:50 pm – ex Port Victoria terminating.
11:00 pm – ex Maidstone mail train.#

Newspapers and mail were usually conveyed in vans attached to passenger trains.

Oddly, newspapers and mail for Northfleet were unloaded at Gravesend and taken forward by road. Coal was brought in up to four times daily, dedicated coal trains dropping off loaded wagons and collecting empties.

Following the onset of WWI, the station became a destination for much military traffic and between the June and August of 1915 Belgian soldiers and recruits were entrained here for travel to Folkestone presumably after having been billeted in the Gravesham area following their evacuation from their home country. A special wartime responsibility of Gravesend Central's station master was to inform Milton Range when a Down train was

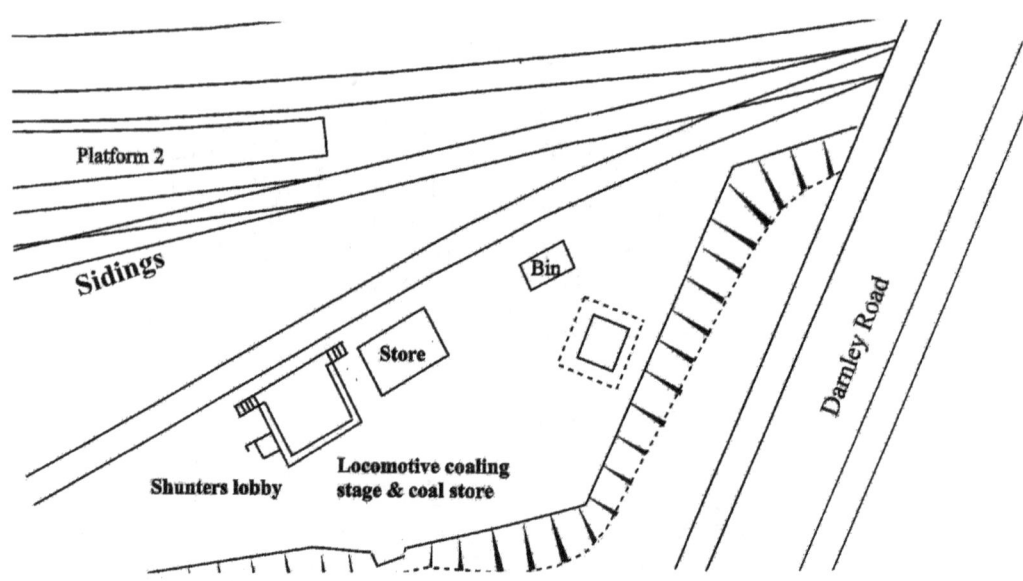

The goods yard and locomotive servicing area, now part of the station car park. Controlled by the shunter, his lobby is next to the coaling stage. The yard being of a very restricted nature, it was unable to accept certain special vehicles such as the SE&CR Class E 16'-6" wheelbase horse-boxes.

due to arrive with troops going for firing practice at the butts. These were not the only special trains run for military traffic, another example was a working of the 24th of April of 1918. Consisting of 22 cattle trucks and two brake vans, it was diagrammed to transport horses and mules between Maidstone West and Guildford. After calling at Gravesend at 4:58 am to collect horses, on departure it was loaded to 106 horses and 65 mules. Upon arrival at Guildford, a London & South Western Railway locomotive was to take charge of the train for onward travel to the South West of England.

Before the era of the "talkie" cinema, Gravesend had several theatres. Their shows usually put on by touring companies, in the days before long distance road transport these artistes used the railways to travel around the country. Requiring special vehicles known as "scenery vans" for transport of their sets and props, these could be hired from the railway companies.

After finishing their tour at a local theatre, the 30 performers of the "Six Brothers Luck" theatrical company were timetabled to depart at 9:00 am from Gravesend Central on Sunday 6th of October 1918. Travelling separately from the two scenery vans containing their props, they were to connect with the 12:00 pm Euston departure for Blackburn, Lancashire.

No scenery vehicles were included in the make-up of the train listed in a Special Notice of October 1st 1918, just a reserved coach being provided for the "Hula Maid" company of 23 troupers travelling to Faversham on that day.

At the grouping in 1923, apart from a change of uniform to the style of the Southern, and a change of colour scheme for the station itself, it was business as usual for the station master Walter Penn Capon and the goods agent, Edwin Walkey.

Major change came once again on the 24th of June 1928 with the opening of the new No. 4 signal box. Replacing both the Nos 1 and 2 boxes of 1902, this was a precursor of the next change wrought by the Southern. One of the most significant events in the station's history, this was the 2nd of July 1930 extension of the 660 volt DC 3rd rail from Dartford.

Henceforth, all suburban passenger services from Gravesend to London were in the hands of the cleaner and faster electric trains, journey times tumbled as result. Now without a daily purpose, the stations locomotive turntable was removed around this time. Steam power, however, still held its dominion over passenger services to the Hoo Peninsular, Maidstone, the Medway Towns and the longer distance services to Faversham and beyond.

With the May 1932 opening of the spur to Allhallows-on-Sea, excursion trains serving this terminus station on the Thames marshes also began to call at Gravesend to pick up local excursionists. When in July 1939 the 660 volt DC 3rd rail was extended once again to both Gillingham and Maidstone West, the steam locomotive hauled passenger services were reduced again and only those destined for the Hundred of Hoo branch or the Kent coast continued to call.

In September 1939, with another World war again putting a great strain on the railways, in the early September of 1939, an emergency passenger timetable was immediately put into effect. This conflict bringing with it the added threat of mass aerial attack to vulnerable towns and villages, the railway's evacuation plans were dusted down, and during the first weekend of September 1939, 500,000 people, some from Gravesham, were moved by the Southern to safer locations in the UK.

The predicted heavy air raids not manifesting themselves during the "Phoney War" period, many evacuees drifted back home. However, with the start of the Battle of Britain in July 1940, Gravesham was brought into the firing line and once again, special trains ran to evacuate those wishing to leave from what was now a war zone.

One such working was on the 7th of July 1940. Run exclusively for evacuees, this special starting from Gravesend and calling at Dartford and Crayford en route, it discharged it's 582 passengers at Victoria.

Had the Germans invaded, plans existed for the complete evacuation of 250,000 people from east Kent. To be transported by special trains over a two-day period, many of these would have passed through Gravesham.

The station was very fortunate to avoid any bomb damage, the nearest bombs falling some distance away at Pelham Road. With the tide of war now turning, the special travel restrictions put in place shortly before the June 1944 D-Day landings prohibited unauthorised rail travel to locations within ten miles of the coast.

With the flowering of peace in 1945 came a new government. An administration bringing with it the philosophy of nationalisation, this came to the railways on the 1st of January 1948 when Gravesend Central found itself answering to yet another new master, the Southern Region of British Railways.

By 1952, Gravesend Central's stationmaster was a Mr. Hayden; his business address now being given as Rathmore Road, Gravesend, this indicates that the offices in Stone Street had now closed, and the post of goods agent no longer listed for the station, this official had now moved away to the Gravesend West. In the early BR period, the former Gravesend goods shed saw a change of use when it was converted into a cold store on becoming the premises of Messrs W.Weddel & Co. Ltd, meat importers.

A herald of the future came in 1953 in the form of an experimental ACV diesel rail-car. Sarcastically known as "The Flying Brick", it was for a brief period trialled on the Hundred of Hoo services, but proving unpopular with passengers due to rough riding characteristics, it was withdrawn after a short trial period of operation.

Gravesend did not have milk delivered by rail tanker as the area had sufficient dairy farms to meet local needs, but to fulfil the demand for more choice of dairy products, until 1956, a daily working delivered milk in churns to Gravesend from the West Country. Brought in by vans from both the Southern and Western regions, the working was routed via Woking, Guildford, Redhill, Tonbridge and Maidstone West. Arriving at Gravesend sometime after 5:00 am, somewhat exotic motive power was used on these trains, the ex-London, Brighton & South Coast Railway Class E4 0-6-2 tank engines usually providing their motive power.

In the early BR era various small businesses operated from the station and one of these being the newspaper wholesaler and confectioner, A. E. Bondi, he had premises in the Barrack Row building and the lease on a small kiosk in the Rathmore Road booking hall. The kiosk being a somewhat primitive affair, it used the sliding bow window of the former pay office that looked onto Platform 1 as a shop front.

Newspapers, the main source of news in the days before radio, television and the Internet, these were delivered at least twice daily by rail, especially sought after was the last page of the evening newspaper, the "stop press" section of its "final extra" edition providing the most recent news. Delivery of newspapers by rail ended in the 1980's when road transport took over.

Domestic fuel was also delivered to Gravesend daily with Beadle Brothers, the coal merchants, later Hardys, using the short siding at the eastern end of the station's Up side for it's wagon load reception. Here, in a small yard, the coal and coke products were weighed and after transfer into hessian sacks, they were then ready for local distribution by cart or lorry.

Then still a busy facility, the main goods yard provided the spectacle of carmine and cream liveried Scammel three wheeled "mechanical horses" bustling around the goods yard with their articulated trailers.

As was mentioned earlier, the bookseller W. H Smith had a shop on the station and as their only outlet in the Gravesham area, it could be accessed from either Platform 1 or via a public entrance from Rathmore Road.

Then places of great interest, stations were a veritable hive of activity and a magnet for those who enjoyed the sights and sounds of railways. With little having changed since the Edwardian heyday of railways, in the 1950's, as had been the norm for many years, the ringing of the platform bell by the signalman still announcing the arrival of trains, the guard's shrill whistle signified their departure.

There were no electronic train indicators then, the destination of the next train was shown on wooden "finger boards" slotted into place prior to each arrival and departure. Waiting rooms then welcoming places, they were warmed by coal fires glowing in their cast iron grates.

The station amply supplied with vending machines, these providing cigarettes and confectionery, a set of "penny in the slot" mechanically operated scales was provided for the weight conscious. My personal favourite was the machine that for the expenditure of a penny, would allow you to punch letters and numbers into an aluminium strip. Turning a pointer to the desired digit and then pulling a lever, your choice of character was impressed into the metal.

1961 was a significant year of change for the station. A harbinger of change and decline for the local railways as a whole, this degeneration continued almost unabated until the 1980's. First to go was the station's goods yard. Closing in that fateful year when its daily goods trip workings ended, what goods business remained was transferred to Gravesend West.

The Allhallows and Grain passenger services, were the next loss and after having provided passenger services to the Hundred of Hoo since 1882, the last passenger working to Grain station was to depart on the 2nd of December 1961. When the red tail light of the last Allhallows train disappeared into the gloom of the 4th of December 1961, Wainwright's H Class 0-4-4 tank locomotives and ancient wooden bodied carriages, both features of the station for over 50 years, departed for ever.

With the centre roads now no longer needed by the Allhallows trains, these had a change of use to provide overnight stabling for 4EPB electric multiple units.

March 1971 bringing the removal of the station's semaphore signals, the squeaking wires, rods, pulleys and rattling chains of their mechanisms were to be heard no more. Now without a use, No. 4 signal box closed, and control of the new, silent colour light signalling passed to the new Dartford signalling centre.

When the *Gravesend Reporter* of the 28th of December 1973 was published, it revealed the biggest threat yet to the 1849 station building. A plan hatched by the property developer, London and Overseas Investments, it included the demolition of the 1845 Rathmore Road building and its replacement by a four-storey office block. Enjoying backing from both British Rail and Gravesend Council, it was hoped the development would lure London businesses to the town.

Fortunately for the station, some determined local historians and activists mounted a very successful campaign to prevent the station's demolition, and Grade II listing was secured for the main station buildings in 1975.

1977 bringing the end for regular timetabled services to the Kent coast, they were probably axed due to the journey times to the Thanet area via Gravesend being significantly longer than by changing at Rochester and continuing on a Chatham main line service. Now run as part of the high speed services, these services have now been re-introduced. In the 1970's, with extra public car parking now being required, the former goods shed was demolished to make room for this, and the disused bay platform on the Up side was filled in for re-use as staff car parking.

After over twenty years of stagnation, growth finally came to Gravesend in 1984 when the Rathmore Road booking hall was altered to incorporate a bright, shiny new travel centre. More change coming in 2010, both booking halls were remodelled for the installation of passenger operated ticket barriers. Uncovered during the course of the works, the sash-cord bow window of the 1849 pay office has again been revealed.

The Networker Class 465 and 466 trains taking over passenger services from the venerable EPB multiple units from 1994 onward, their last public duties ended in March 1995. With their passing, the guard and the familiar sound of his whistle going, so too did the sound of the starting buzzer, the ticking of the brake systems air compressor and the smell of ozone on wet days.

Visiting the class's former haunts in South London and Kent, a "Farewell to the EPB" special was run from Gravesend on the 31st of March 1995. Arriving late, and clutching my ticket for this train tightly, I found the special sitting in the centre roads and unable to board, I could only watch as it departed.

Privatisation coming to Gravesend on the 13th of October 1996, the operation of Gravesend station was then transferred from BR to the first holder of the South Eastern Passenger Rail Franchise, Connex South Eastern. Following their departure in 2003, the modified franchise has changed hands twice since. Managed by South East Trains from 2003 to 2006, it is now held by Southeastern. The station enjoying a direct service to London St. Pancras from the 13th of December 2009, these services, provided by the Hitachi Class 395 multiple units also call at intermediate stations to Faversham, Maidstone and Ramsgate.

Calling at Gravesend hourly, in 2012 the Class 395 multiple units, re-branded as the "Javelin", provided a high-speed shuttle service to the London Olympic Games. As part of Gravesend's Transport Quarter project, the most extensive changes to the stations layout since 1849 took place in 2013-14. The centre roads, the 1904 footbridge and the water tank building being removed, a new footbridge, platform extensions for 12 car trains and a new island platform were added. Although the Urban Gravesend Society campaigned to retain both the 1904 footbridge and water tank building, as neither had listed status, their demolition went ahead.

Gravesend station closed during these works, the London services terminated at Northfleet with buses replacing trains between Northfleet and Higham. The station reopening in the January of 2014, 12 car trains services have since been inaugurated at peak periods. This re-modelling has brought changes to train workings and the Down slow services now terminating at Platform Zero,Up through services use the island Platform 1, while Down through trains continue to use Platform 2.

With Phase 3 of Gravesend's Transport Quarter project now in progress, a new public footbridge, access road, multi-storey car park and bus station will be provided when complete. In 2016 Gravesend provides direct services terminating at three London termini and Ramsgate. An important rail centre and interchange, Gravesend is certain to host more passenger journeys than the 2.65 million seen in 2012.

The Down side Barrack Row building in 2009. Author

A three wheeled Scammel "mechanical horse" tractor unit with its articulated trailer. These vehicles were favoured by the railways from the 1930's to the 1950's for local deliveries.

Then in use as a meat cold store, Gravesend goods shed is seen on the 19th of April 1969. The shed was demolished in the 1970's.
Tony Riley.

Starting to appear in Gravesham from 1951, the SR design EPB electric multiple unit standing at Platform 2 does not show the small yellow warning panels on the driving cab end introduced from 1962.
Dave Fisher collection.

A "Networker" stands at Gravesend Station on 30th of December 2006. Some years before the 2013 remodelling, the SE&CR lattice steel footbridge can be seen in the mid distance. *Author*

The remodelled Gravesend Station seen on a wet 14th of January 2014. A Class 395 Javelin stands at platform 2 with a Faversham service, while a Networker is seen at the new island platform 1 on a Charing Cross semi-fast. In the distance is the new footbridge and to the left is the re-named platform Zero, now a bay road. *Author.*

Push-pull fitted H Class 0-4-4 tank locomotive No. 31512 awaits departure at Gravesend Central from Platform 2 with a Hundred of Hoo service circa 1961. J. Thorpe collection.

Gravesend Station as remodelled in 2013-14 to accommodate a 3rd platform, new footbridge and lifts.

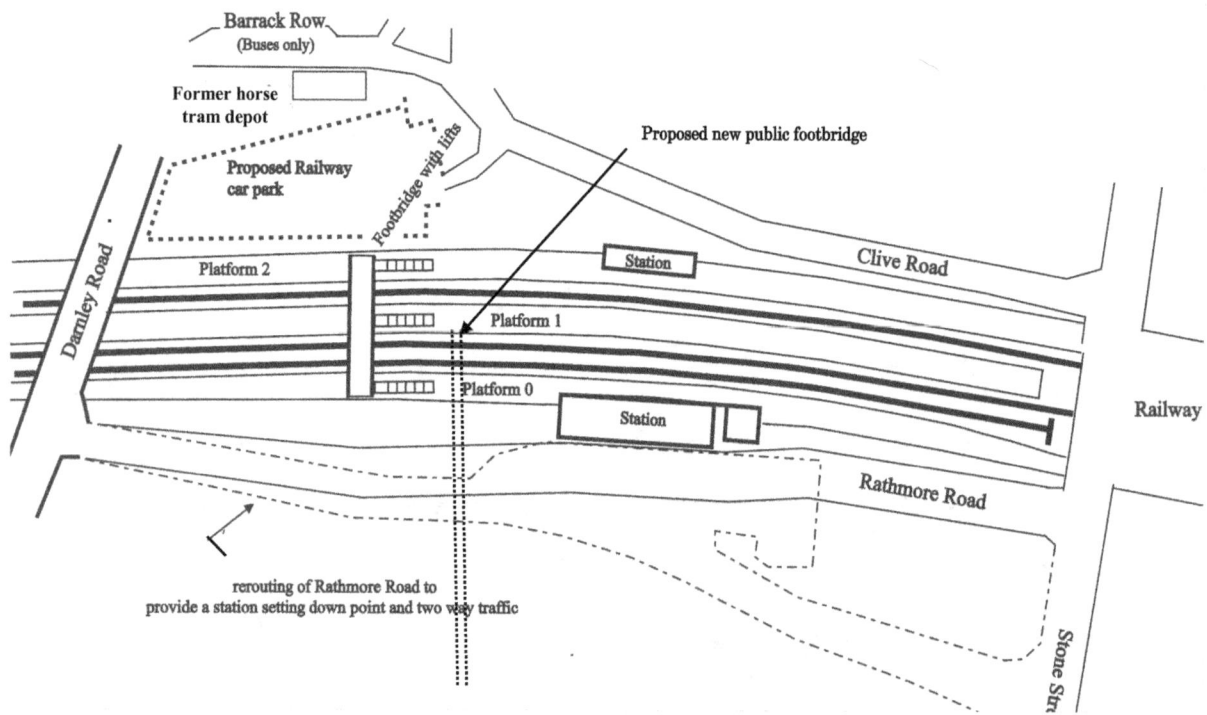

2016 Status: Open, operated by Southeastern.

Grid reference on location map: 1B

Opened: 30th July 1849.

Operating Companies: SER, SE&CR, SR, BR, Connex. South East Trains, Southeastern.

Northfleet Station

Northfleet station seen from Rose Street in 1919.

A tithe map of 1838 shows a mill near the site of Northfleet Station; probably a windmill, this was an ideal spot for a sail powered mill. Situated on an exposed south-west facing ridge it would be able to benefit from the prevailing westerly winds. Otherwise, the site was then open fields.

In architectural style said to be somewhat similar to a miniature of Greenwich station, the original two storey masonry station building, situated on the Down platform, was the work of Samuel Beazley, the architect whom we met at Gravesend. A goods shed, also situated on the Up side was another original feature. Now long since demolished, its site is occupied by a motor repair business.

As we saw earlier, disputes with landowners while building railways were almost inevitable. Mr. Sylvester, the owner of watercress beds at Northfleet took a case to the Vice Chancellor's court in the August of 1849 when claiming that the new railway had cut through an "ancient footpath" which he used to access his beds. Somewhat unusually, he won his case and the Court ordered the SER to build a wooden footbridge to restore his access. Perusing an OS map of the 1860's, a footbridge is shown at the bottom of what later became South Kent Avenue. A path then leading on to the Ebbsfleet River, it would suggest that this humble wooden bridge is the ancestor of the present modern steel footbridge.

Northfleet's first stationmaster was James Weeks and after ending his career on the railways, he took up a management post in the local cement industry. Becoming prominent in December 1894, he was the first chairman of Northfleet Urban District Council.

James may have been in office on the 27th of July 1855 when a Kent coast excursion train called at Northfleet destined for the resorts of Ramsgate, Margate, Dover and Folkestone. It's route taking it by way of Canterbury, it was advertised as having "covered carriages". Indicating that the train's make up included "Parliamentary" 3rd Class carriages, doubtless its 3rd Class passengers would have been grateful to have a roof over their heads, as in the fairly recent past their accommodation would have been in breezy open trucks. For an impression of a "Parliamentary" 3rd carriage, see page 211.

Bradshaw's 1863 guide mentions a public telegraph at Northfleet and as the sole means of fast communication in the 1860's, its cost was astronomical; messages of no more than 20 words, transmitted over less than 50 miles being charged at two shillings each.

Its staggered platforms overlapping each other at their ends, Northfleet's platform arrangement is unique in Gravesham. An arrangement favoured by railways before the advent of underpasses and footbridges, this allowed passengers to cross to the opposite platform should both be occupied by trains.

Presumably still the arrangement in 1874, an article in the *Dover Express* reported the gruesome details of "*A shocking accident*" that befell a passenger at Northfleet on the 16th of November of that year.

A commuter, 22 year old Mr Becker, was described as being "cut to pieces in full view of the other passengers" by the 9:10 am Charing Cross express train. An awful event, this happened when he was crossing over the line.

Perhaps it was this incident that prompted the construction of the present underpass. Built before 1885, it can be seen on page 117 on a photo of that date, together with the 1849 station building. When next you use the underpass, you may notice a blocked-off doorway below Platform 1. Once leading to both Ebbsfleet Park and the APCM sports grounds pavilion, these sites are now buried under later railway construction and the A2260 road.

Ebbsfleet Park has fond memories for me. As a child in the late 1950's, I would often visit my grandfather here. Sitting in a small wooden hut close by the now closed underpass entrance, he hired out putters and golf balls for the Park's pitch and putt course.

On the railway embankment in the vicinity of the station were allotments, one of which was shared between my father and grandfather.

When fire damaged the 1849 station building

Map showing Northfleet station in 1863. Crown copyright

in 1891, it was later demolished and replaced at a more easterly location by the present SER wooden station building. Other buildings to appear around this time were a waiting shelter on the Up Platform and a small timber built signal box. Situated on the Down side platform, this box replaced an earlier ground frame.

Northfleet station was where the North Kent line had its junction with the spur that connected with the local industrial railways to the north of the town. A short line, it curved in through what is now a housing estate.

Skirting the site of the former Robinsons Paper Sacks factory, a small part of this line's former track bed can still be seen beside the private road that passes under Galley Hill.

Northfleet could well have become a junction station, had a scheme of 1881 to build a Northfleet to Snodland Railway gone ahead. Intended to be a freight line, its purpose was to relieve rail congestion in the Strood area. It's route taking it to the Medway via Cobham and Luddesdown, it was intended to carry cement coming from factories on the Medway and Thames rivers.

On the 1st of February 1885, a serious incident occurred at Northfleet station. A Jonathan Hills attempting suicide, his wife and daughters desperately tried to stop him from throwing himself in front of a train.

Northfleet's station master in 1902 is listed as a Mr. William K. Thomas and by 1904, his station being shown as having a five ton crane, this is indicative of the industrial loads likely to be offered to the station, as for its size, the station was relatively well appointed and was capable of accepting nearly all the variety of traffic that the larger Gravesend Station could handle.

Served by five daily goods services in 1910, beginning with a pick-up goods originating from Bricklayers Arms at 3:45 am, the last working

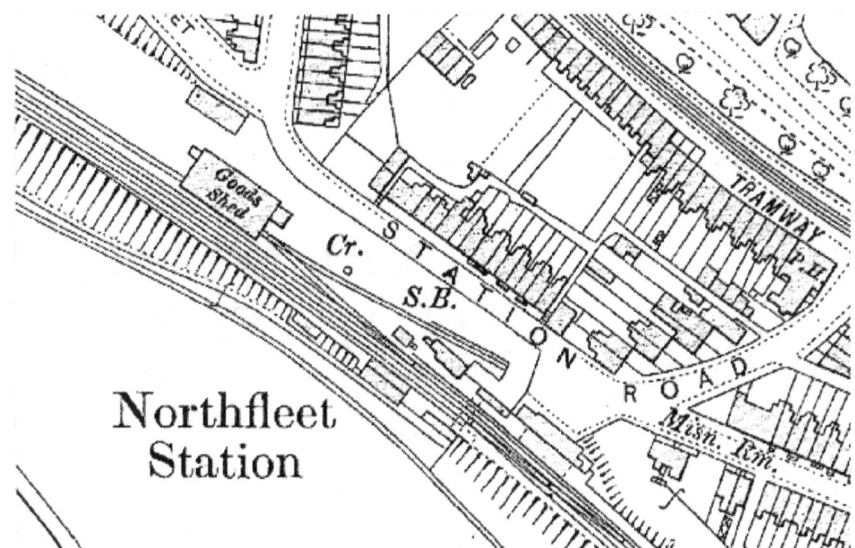

A 1909 plan of Northfleet station. A tramway shown at the top right hand corner, this would have been the electric tramway that ran from Denton to Swanscombe. Crown copyright

Northfleet in 1885. The photo showing the original 1849 Down side station building, a wealth of detail including the staggered platform's, original ground frame, the goods shed and underpass can also be seen. Tonbridge Historical Society

The station's Up platform in the early 1960's seen before the removal of its buildings.

was the Northfleet to Slades Green mixed goods at 9:35 pm.

Something resembling a theatrical farce took place on the 12th of December 1913 when yet another bad tempered bovine, "an infuriated bull", strayed onto the railway at Northfleet. Although it was knocked down by a light engine, the beast rose once again to its feet and continued it's rampage. Bringing an Up express to a squealing halt, it was finally chased off by the combined efforts of a police constable and some railway staff who broke down fencing to allow it to escape into a field.

Electrification was finally to come to Northfleet on the 2nd of July 1930, the 660 Volt DC 3rd rail being then extended to all the stations and halts between Gravesend and Dartford.

Northfleet was in the news again in June 1964, the *Gravesend & Dartford Reporter* informing its readers of a request made to Kent County Council by the local Council to include an extension of the Bakerloo line to Dartford in the South East Study & Review Development Plan of that year. Perhaps the Council had hopes it would be extended to Northfleet at a later date.

The intention to extend the Tube to Dartford was a genuine proposal of the time as I myself have seen plans held by London Underground for a Bakerloo line station at Woolwich.

Northfleet stations goods handling ended in 1968, and with the installation of colour light signalling three years later removing the need for Northfleet's signal box, it closed in 1971.

There was however, some rail expansion. As mentioned earlier, in 1970 a new junction was installed to the south side of the station, this connected to a "Merry-Go-Round" loop line for the import of coal and gypsum and the export of finished cement products from the APCM New Bevans cement works. A small marshalling yard also forming part of the system, it was used for the handling and storage of wagons. Motive power normally provided by Class 33 or Class 47 diesel locomotives, these were specially fitted for slow running to allow discharge of cargoes while on the move. The line remaining open until 1993, it was then severed from the North Kent line when the cement works changed over to oil firing.

Seeing a rebirth in 2012, the formation of the loop was partly re-used for a new line for the transshipment of spoil from Crossrail's tunnelling works. Only the easterly part of the former "Merry-Go-Round" rail loop being reused, it lead to a new riverside rail-head. Comprised of storage sidings, stockpile bases and conveyor systems, a cripple siding was also built in Church Path Pit. Part of a unified transport system, after arrival by rail at Northfleet, small sea-going bulk carriers took the spoil to Wallasea island in Essex, where it was used to enlarge the islands wildlife sanctuary.

It had been hoped that Northfleet would also become the site for a tunnel segment manufacturing factory for Crossrail, this, however, was located elsewhere.

The official opening of the spoil line coming in June 2012, trains started to bring in tunnelling waste from Royal Oak, Paddington. Crossrail spoil import operations having now ended, the line awaits use for the shipment of aggregates and bulk cement powders by the successors to Lafarge.

There are also hopes that the line may attract industrial and commercial concerns to the area. Marks & Spencer said at one time to be interested in siting warehousing here, they withdrew when stating that the site was not suitable for their requirements.

When major works were undertaken at Gravesend station in the winter of 2013-14,

Head Codes

Introduced with electrification were train head codes. These were alpha or numeric displays on the front of the train to identify the trains route for signalmen and staff, and the more knowledgeable traveller. Typical 1930's head codes to be seen at Northfleet were as below:-

L - Blackfriars to Gravesend via Sidcup.
N - Gravesend to Holborn Viaduct via Charlton.
P - Cannon Street to Maidstone West via Blackheath.

By the 1950's these codes had been changed to numerals, and a typical head code to be seen would be 75 indicating a Gravesend Central service from Cannon Street via Bexleyheath These codes were perpetuated in a dot matrix form on the current multiple units, and have only recently been discontinued.

Northfleet station had a brief moment of glory. Becoming the temporary terminus of the North Kent line, a barricade was put in place, as was a crossover for train movements.

Like other smaller stations in Gravesham, Northfleet is now a shadow of its former self. The station windows boarded up against vandalism, the platforms are protected by high security fencing, cameras and gates.

Now a basic, mostly un-staffed stop on the North Kent line, its ticket office only open at peak times, an automatic ticket machine provides these when the ticket office is closed. Off-peak services now comprising two trains each hour, these call at intermediate stations to Charing Cross while the Down services terminate at Gravesend.

When the proposal for Ebbsfleet HS1 station was announced, Northfleet residents, asked to vote on either to retain the SER station or have services relocated to Ebbsfleet, they chose the former.

Northfleet and Ebbsfleet stations being only 350 yards apart, no foot passenger link exists for interchange between the two, and with the landowner reputed to have objected to its building, this begs the question of Northfleet stations long term future. However, with the developments planned for the area in the future including new housing, hopefully this will bring a better level of custom to the station.

Happy looking rail man Geoff Jewiss celebrates with a platform scrub up after receiving the runner-up prize for the 1979 "best kept station award". Geoff told me that in fact the award belonged to a colleague who was on holiday and he just stood in for the photo. GBL.

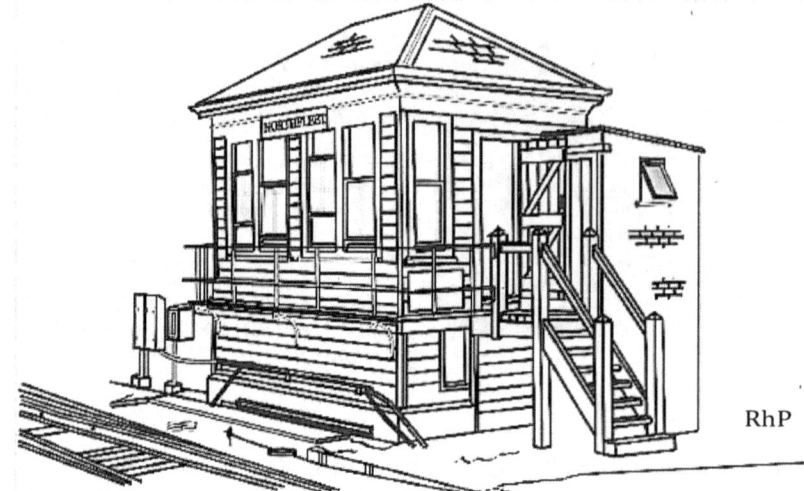

Northfleet signal box in 1969. Opening in the late 19th century, the box closed in 1971 after the area's signalling control passed to Dartford power signalling centre.

In the late 1970's, a coal train arrives at the APCM Northfleet "Merry-Go-Round'" sidings with a train of Nottinghamshire coal behind Class 47 No. 47355 . Dave Fisher

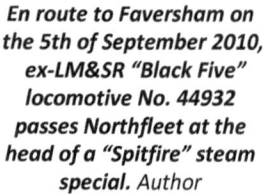

En route to Faversham on the 5th of September 2010, ex-LM&SR "Black Five" locomotive No. 44932 passes Northfleet at the head of a "Spitfire" steam special. Author

Headboard from the inaugural Crossrail spoil train. Courtesy of Lafarge

The Crossrail spoil line seen on the 4th of October 2012, the Gilbert Scott designed Northfleet Catholic church looms over the railway. Author

Class 66 No. 66718 "Gwyneth Dunwoody" awaits the road at Northfleet with a train of empty spoil wagons on the 6th of February 2013. David Ward

2016 Status: Open, operated by Southeastern.

Grid reference on location map: A1

Open: 30th July 1849.

Operating Companies: SER, SE&CR, SR, BR, Connex. South East Trains, Southeastern.

Sole Street Station

Two steam services meet at Sole Street in August 1923. Note the porter with his barrow at the lower right, this is a sight now long gone at railway stations. Tony Riley collection.

Sole Street viewed initially as being a more important location than Meopham, this was presumably as it is closer to Cobham, then the largest habitation on the line between Strood and St. Mary Cray. Another factor for siting the station here was the proximity of Cobham Hall. The residence of the Earl of Darnley, the Earl had an unusual privilege at Sole Street, i.e. the right to stop an express train once daily. Whether this privilege extends to the current Earl is a matter for conjecture.

The station sitting at the summit of the five mile long Sole Street bank, as the steepest main line gradient on the former LC&DR system, its ascent was a challenge for the crews of steam locomotives and called for skilful locomotive handling.

Banking assistance does not appear to have been a normal provision, the perusal of a 1920 track diagram for the foot of the bank failing to show any release sidings for locomotives. Should a train come to a stand, banking assistance could be summoned from either Chatham or Gillingham. Heavier trains often piloted, this is the most likely method of assistance used.

The loose coupled goods train was the predominant type of goods service prior to the 1950's and composed of wagons and vans without automatic brakes, these trains relied on the locomotive's steam brake and the guards hand brake for their stopping power. Before descending the bank, this type of goods train was required to stop at Sole Street station where the guard applied the goods wagons' hand brakes before setting off. Probably carried out in Sole Street's goods passing loop, this was capable of holding 39 wagons. After descending the bank, upon arrival at Strood distant signal box, goods trains came to a halt while the wagon brakes were released before proceeding.

A primitive arrangement, this could be the cause of accidents. A coupling parting on a goods train at Sole Street on the 5th of March 1864, *Diomede*, the train's locomotive then proceeding unaware of the calamity, it was struck by the runaway train when stopping at Strood signal box and many of it's train's wagons were destroyed.

Both Sole Street bank and the winding route of the LC&DR through the Medway Towns made working the line difficult, and in 1895 an alternative route was proposed. Had this been built, Sole Street would have become a junction station on what would have been the Chatham Loop Railway. Routed south of the Medway Towns, it was to have rejoined the LC&DR main line at Newington. However, as the Medway Towns were an important revenue source for the LC&DR, it is difficult to see how the line could have paid its way and this was probably the reason why it was not built.

Sole Street signal box in 1902 with the signalman and box-boy posing for the camera. The block section then shorter than today, there was also a signal box on Sole Street bank known as Cobham Park. SE&CR Society

Sole Street station in August 1923 before the addition of the footbridge. Tony Riley collection.

The LC&DR, as we have seen was always close to penury and their staff were expected to be capable of fulfilling several roles, one of these was to provide first aid. Railway staff being instructed not to summon professional medical aid lightly, the LC&DR General Instructions of 31st of December 1871 advises stationmasters that if a doctor was called, he was to inform the medico that the company would not authorise any payment.

Perhaps it was the limited medical diagnostic skills of rail staff that contributed to the death in 1866 of 39 year old James Rowell. A once popular tenor vocalist, he expired at Sole Street station from "ruptured lungs", maybe while singing? The *Era* newspaper of the 18th of February 1866 lists a number of donations for his funeral, so it appears unlikely that he could have paid for professional medical assistance anyway.

The village, its pub, orchards and station were subject to an invasion of an unusual kind in August 1897, when a derailment further down the line at Lower Bush caused a train carrying a party of soldiers and sailors to be held at the station for some hours. Becoming frustrated they left the train, drank the Railway Inn dry and raided the local orchards, carrying their haul of fruit back to the waiting train.

In the days before the internal combustion engine became dominant, communities such as Sole Street relied for the most part on the railway for deliveries from the outside world of life's essentials and little luxuries. Largely transported by the pick-up goods train composed of a collection of wagons and vans, they slowly made their way between stations. Dropping off and picking up wagons and vans on they went, the train's locomotives usually shunted rolling stock into a station's goods yard or shed.

After residents of the London boroughs had campaigned for relocating the storage of this fetid material away from suburban stations, Sole Street was selected by the SE&CR in 1903 for the storage of London's horse manure.

Fortunately for Sole Street, when the SE&CR sought to purchase land for this purpose, the vendor, on getting wind of the company's intentions (pardon the pun) insisted on a clause banning the unloading of manure.

In 1904 the station was well appointed, and having facilities for most traffic, its trade in livestock was considerable with both prize cattle and horses being imported each autumn.

A goods crane capable of lifting a maximum of one ton 15 hundredweight available, so was a goods shed and carriage stabling sidings.

Acquiring a high-level signal box in 1876, circa 1924, the station's current footbridge was built for a cost of £820-12/-11d. The scene of a major fire in 1928, Sole Street station was lucky to escape with minor damage when the rupture and bursting into flames of a 1,000 gallon tank of white spirit at the nearby varnish factory of Messrs Leemings set alight the railway's sleepers. Buckling the rails of the main line, it took four hours to get the fire under control and trains were diverted for a few days whilst repairs were effected.

The line through Sole Street and Meopham was electrified later than the North Kent line, the 3rd rail not arriving here until July 1939. Although providing the power for local and London bound passenger trains, all goods services and most passenger services for destinations beyond Gillingham remained steam hauled until the completion of the Kent Coast Electrification scheme in 1959.

On the night of September 17th 1940, the Sole Street signalman was responsible for a false invasion scare. Upon receiving a message that parachute mines had been dropped across the tracks in the Chatham area, he mistakenly transmitted the following message:

"Germans landing by parachute, also dropping magnetic mines eight foot by two"

Army units then being rapidly dispatched to the area, they discover no sign of invaders. This error by the signalman would have been regarded by the railway authorities as a cardinal sin, the Railway Rule Book being emphatic that all safety messages received are to be repeated back to the sender to ensure correct transmission.

A former stationmaster of the early 1950's was Hubert Browning. Also the stationmaster for Meopham and the supervisor of Longfield Dust sidings, should that not be enough he also fulfilled the role of postmaster at Sole Street station. Hubert recalling the goods traffic handled at Sole Street as largely being agricultural produce plus horses and foals from

JUNE, 1897.

PIC-NIC OR PLEASURE PARTIES.

DURING THE SUMMER MONTHS
(BANK HOLIDAYS AND PRECEDING SATURDAYS EXCEPTED)

FIRST, SECOND AND THIRD CLASS

RETURN TICKETS AT SPECIAL REDUCED FARES

WILL BE ISSUED AT ALL THE PRINCIPAL STATIONS ON THE LONDON, CHATHAM, AND DOVER RAILWAY

To parties of not less than TEN 1st Class, FIFTEEN 2nd Class, or TWENTY 3rd Class Passengers, desirous of having pleasure Excursions to the undermentioned places, viz.:

ST. MARY CRAY, SWANLEY JUNCTION, SOUTHFLEET (for SPRINGHEAD), **ROSHERVILLE & GRAVESEND**

(FOR THE ROSHERVILLE GARDENS),

EYNSFORD, SHOREHAM, OTFORD, WROTHAM, MALLING, SEVENOAKS, MAIDSTONE, ASHFORD

FARNINGHAM ROAD, SOLE STREET,
(FOR THE ROMAN VILLA)

ROCHESTER BRIDGE (STROOD), ROCHESTER, CHATHAM, SITTINGBOURNE, SHEERNESS-ON-SEA, FAVERSHAM; WHITSTABLE-ON-SEA,

HERNE BAY, BIRCHINGTON-ON-SEA, MARGATE, BROADSTAIRS, RAMSGATE,

CANTERBURY, WALMER, DEAL, DOVER,

And other Places of Attraction upon this Line of Railway.

Map of Sole Street station dating from 1939. Crown copyright.

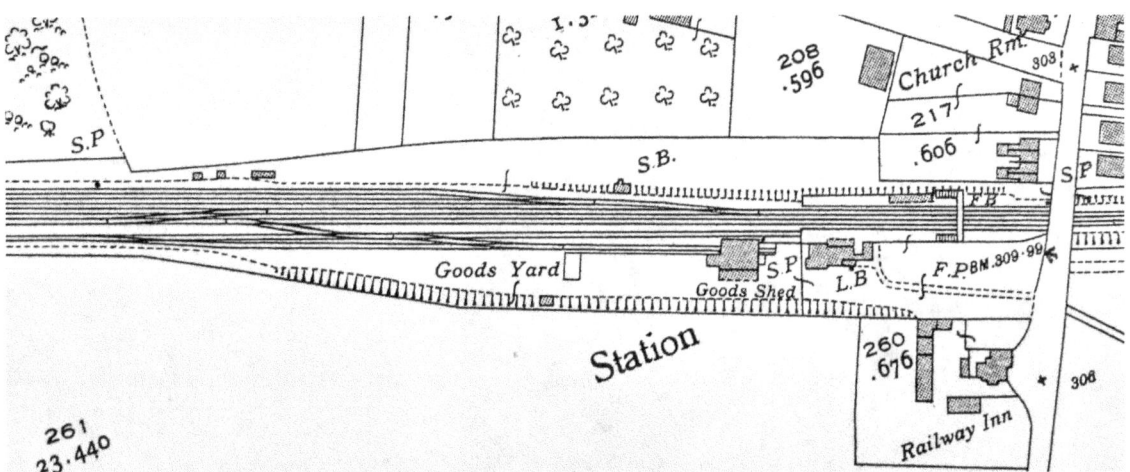

stud at Cobham Hall, paint and varnish from the nearby Leemings factory was another cargo.

The goods shed having closed by then, parcels traffic was sent to Gravesend by road; the station buildings then still in use as staff accommodation, Hubert and his family lived in these.

One hilarious event recalled by Hubert was winning a local raffle and upon being presented with the prize, he discovered it to be a live piglet! Sole Street being fully staffed in those days, it was manned by three signalmen, two leading porters and a junior porter, all of whom worked on a shift system.

Although both the goods shed and signal box are now demolished, Sole Street still retains much of its LC&DR character, the original station buildings, Down side platform timber shelter and spiked steel fencing are still extant. The stations goods traffic ending in the 1960's, Leemings paint factory is also now long gone.

North Kent line high-speed services having siphoned away commuters to Strood and Gravesend, passenger numbers have recently declined here. With additional peak hour workings including the recent addition of an early morning Blackfriars service, in 2016 the off-peak services provide hourly trains to Faversham and Victoria, A shadow of its former self, the accommodation now disused and the ticket office staffed part-time, Sole Street still occasionally reverberates to past glories when steam specials hurry past.

2016 Status: Open, operated by Southeastern.
Location map grid reference : C1

Opened: 1st February 1861
Operating companies: LC&DR, SE&CR, SR, BR, Connex. South East Trains, Southeastern.

BR Standard Class 5MT 4-6-0 No. 73096 passes Sole Street with the Down Shepherd & Neame "Spitfire" special on the 31st of August 2003. Dave Fisher.

On 6th February 2004, Class 465 Networker EMU No. 465908 enters Sole Street with a Victoria bound service. Author.

Meopham Station

Meopham station basking in the sunshine on a summer's day in 1926. The station still has its full range of facilities and the signal box can just be seen peeking from behind the foliage on the Down platform, the signalman having set the starting signal to "off" for the Down service, it can be seen departing. Tony Riley collection.

The decision to provide Meopham with a station was something of an afterthought, it was only agreed upon in the March of 1861, nearly four months after the LC&DR opened on 3rd December 1860. Initially to be called "Meopham Road" as it was situated 1½ miles from the main village centre of that time, this was a stratagem the early railways used if a station was some distance from its named habitation, and the wary traveller would be conscious of the possibility that a station having the suffix "Road" could be some miles from their final destination.

Meopham, at first considered inferior to Sole Street, reflected this in the timber construction of it's 1861 station buildings. However, its importance soon beginning to grow, the arrival of the railway stimulating growth in the area, it soon generated sufficient passenger traffic for the provision of a horse bus to connect Meopham with Gravesend and Cobham.

A 1st Class return by ordinary train to Victoria in the station's opening year costing 6/-0d, to take your horse would be an extra 10/- 0d. Should you wish for your pets to accompany you, a pet monkey, suitably crated would cost 1/-0d.

The first train of the day to Victoria being at 7:38 am, and you could expect the next one at 8:30 am. A further five Victoria services calling thereafter, the last of these was at 9:43 pm.

On the 7th of September 1869 a felony occurred at Meopham when Charles Smith, a pickpocket, stole a purse from a Mrs. Hutton while on her way home from the races. Apprehended by a Detective PC Sheen, Smith then begging forgiveness for his actions, this was to no avail. Tried at the County Magistrate's Court for his crime, he was sentenced to three months hard labour.

One year later in 1870, the first recorded prosecution for the improper use of the emergency communication cord occurred. An act carried out between Meopham and Farningham Road stations (Fawkham station not opening until 1872), the culprit, a passenger, missing his Rochester stop, used the communication cord to stop the train at Farningham Road. Convicted at Dartford's magistrates court, the misdemeanour cost him a huge 15 shillings fine.

Meopham must have been a good vantage point for the train spotters of the 19th and early 20th centuries as several non-stop expresses could be seen rushing through Meopham. Including the Flushing boat trains heading for Victoria from Queenborough Pier, the "Granville

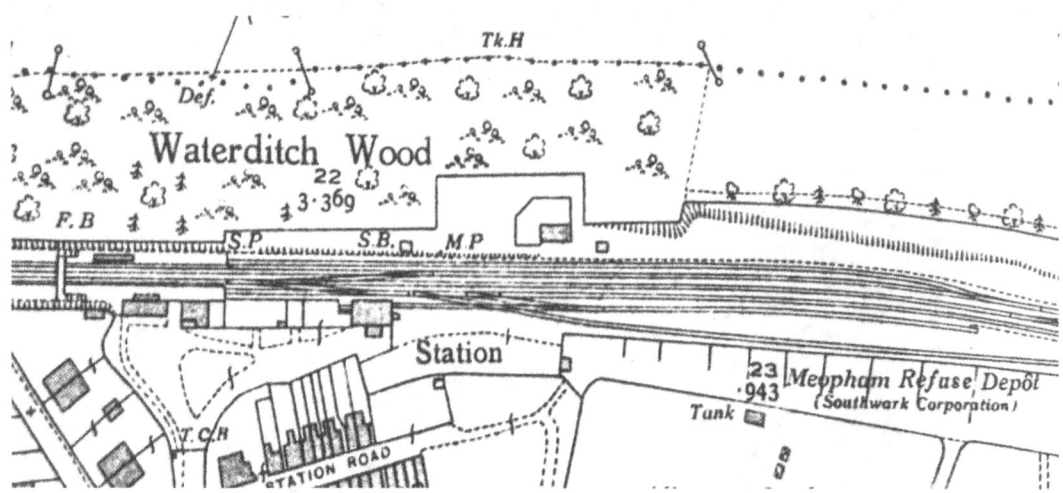

A map of Meopham station dating from 1933. Shown to the right are the reception siding for the Meopham refuse depot; in 1893 a train called daily at the depot on its way to Longfield dust sidings. Crown copyright.

Express", the heaviest of the express services on the LC&DR would also have passed. Timed to take two hours for its non-stop 80 mile journey from Victoria to the stations of Westgate and Ramsgate Sands. Deriving its name from the Pugin designed Granville Hotel at Ramsgate, it was the hotels wealthy customers who provided most of the trains clientele.

This trains importance was such that in 1897 it was the first LC&DR service to feature carriage steam heating. Not for the impecunious, the fare was 15/-0d for a return ticket on this 1st Class only Pullman train. No doubt intended to keep it's clientele select in the days of rigid class division, it also ensured the maximum revenue for the railway company.

Other trains of note including the "Cliftonville Express", the "City Express" and the "Thanet Express", carriages in the liveries of other railway companies could also be seen in the make-up of LC&DR express trains. Carrying passengers from other railways on their uninterrupted, direct journeys from other parts of the UK, an example was an 1897 working from the London & North Western Railway. Comprising a through carriage from this railway, it departed Wolverhampton at 7:00 am, due to arrive at Dover for 12:50 pm.

Before 1899, the locomotives heading these express's resplendent in the lined black livery of the LC&DR, this turned to a lustrous and elaborately lined Brunswick green on the formation of the SE&CR.

Passengers weren't the only live traffic to Meopham. In 1893, Meopham having an occasional weekly delivery of cattle, the trucks with these beasts arrived on some Mondays by the 11:25 am ex Stewarts Lane "as required" goods working. After unloading these cattle trucks, the train's locomotive was then diagrammed to carry out shunting duties in the station yard.

Meopham's signal box opening in 1876, in 1910 the signalman being a J. P. Rowland, he can be seen in the photo on page 129. A signal box such as Meopham on the busy main line employing a "box boy"; usually a teenager, his main duty was to record all train movements and signalling related actions in a large book. Known as the Train Register, all train movements and every communication made between the signalman and adjacent signal boxes via bell codes was religiously logged in its lined pages.

The well being and safety of the public and railway staff always being a priority for the railways, following a series of accidents in the 19th century, these Registers had been brought into use to record signalling related actions, and with safety in mind, the LC&DR Rule Book was quite unequivocal on who could operate signalling controls when stating:

"if they (the signalman) permit any boy, unless specially authorised, or any other person, to touch the Levers or Electrical Plungers and that they and the boys also subject themselves to instant dismissal and prosecution before a magistrate"

After winning a trophy in 1910, stationmaster Walter Kift (seated left) poses proudly with St. Johns ambulance men and station staff, signalman J. Rowland is seen extreme left J.Trevethey , Meopham Historical Society.

Lit by the autumn sunshine, Meopham signal box is seen on the 13th of October 1956. PHT 95

Doyen of the BR Britannia Class Pacific locomotives, No. 70000 "Britannia" passes Meopham in the evening sunlight of 28th July 2011 with the Victoria bound "Cathedrals Express" rail tour. Author

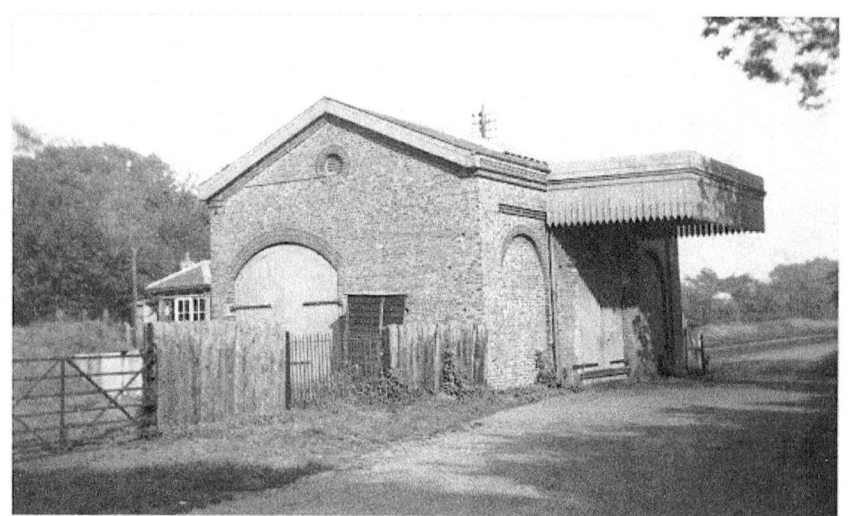

Meopham's good shed as it appeared on the 13th of October 1956, along with the sidings, it closed sometime before 1962.
PHT 95

The original Meopham Station buildings of 1861 seen here in 1972 shortly before they were swept away and replaced with the current CLASP building.
Bayliss

The 1861 station frontage seen on the same windy day in 1972. Bayliss

The "Night Ferry" passing Meopham circa 1963. The train is hauled by one of the E5000, later Class 71, electric locomotives. The service had started on the 5th of October 1936 featuring sleeping coaches provided by the French "Compagnie Internationale des Wagons-Lits" to fit the smaller British loading gauge. Initially it ran from Victoria and Paris via Dover, departing Victoria at 9.05 pm and arriving at Paris for 9.10 am. The carriages together with their 1st Class only sleeping occupants were loaded on to specially adapted ferries with 2nd class passengers having to disembark. The service was later extended to Brussels and ran until the 31st of October 1980. The vehicle closest to the locomotive is a French luggage van, known as a fougon.

Harsh words indeed. Railway servants, as their employees were then called, could be treated severely and punishments could be grim. When in 1862 Meopham was the scene of a derailment caused by the negligence of a porter, the miscreant was sentenced to six months hard labour for the misdemeanour.

Their duties minutely specified and the strict adherence to the Railway Rule Book being mandatory, one of the less onerous of the duties of the Meopham stationmaster was that of having to wind all the clocks on the station and the signal box on a Monday morning, another duty was ensuring that passenger's foot warmers (metal containers containing chemicals) were not placed in front of the fire in case the solder melted.

Although probably not on the LC&DR, an apocryphal story relating to foot warmers involves the odd actions of a Russian nobleman whilst travelling in the UK for the first time. Having been a target for anarchists in his own country, when seeing foot warmers in his compartment, he believed them to be bombs and promptly threw them out of the carriage window!

The census of 1901 recording him as living at nearby Hook Green, Meopham's stationmaster of 1910, Walter John James Kift, is to be seen in the photo on page 129. Loath to dispose of anything that still had some use left in it, life-expired rolling stock, particularly carriage and van bodies, were re-used as static grounded bodies after having their wheels removed. Their most common use being as stores, offices or staff accommodation, they were also occasionally used for yard shunters or locomotive crews mess rooms. Meopham having such a grounded vehicle in its goods yard in 1922; an ex SER 1st class carriage of 1866, it was in use as a bicycle store.

Despite pleas from the Parish Council to the LC&DR to provide a footbridge, Meopham station was not to have this facility until a fatal accident in 1923 forced the Southern to finally install this important convenience.

One of the sights of the line in both the inter-war and early post-war periods, was the "Night Ferry" express. Bound for Dover for a Channel crossing to Dunkirk, it was timed to pass through Meopham at 10:35 pm. Few photos exist of the Down "Night Ferry" it being difficult to photograph after dark with the cameras of the day. It's Wagon-Lit carriages stranded on the continent during WWII, they were used as accommodation for German officers. Another luxury express train to pass by was the all-Pullman "Thanet Belle". In service post-war from 1948 until 1958, it ran from London Victoria to the Thanet resorts. Later including a connection to Canterbury by a through carriage from Faversham, it was renamed the "Kentish Belle".

Still having a functioning signal box in the early 1950's, the station building was then occupied by the signalman, Jim Cadwell. A fully staffed establishment, in 1953 the station staff composed of a stationmaster shared with Sole Street, a signalman, a lamp cleaner and a part-time signalman for Longfield sidings.

Major decline beginning in 1959, the stations signal box closed that year together with it's neighbour at Sole Street. Meopham's goods traffic having declined significantly by the early 1960's, it was to cease completely in April 1962, its goods shed having closed sometime previously.

The original LC&DR timber station buildings removed in the early 1970's, they were replaced by uninspiring prefabricated CLASP ¶ buildings. The SR steel footbridge also removed, it too was replaced by a contemporary concrete structure.

Some reminders of the station's past still existing, the abandoned West Brothers coal yard and the derelict Southwark Corporation refuse storage bays are still to be seen in the station car park. Once the stations main goods reception area, the nearby Railway Sidings Industrial Estate, approached by a cobbled road, is home to a WWII "Romney" prefabricated building. Now in private hands, it was used post-war for scrapping surplus army vehicles delivered by train.

Its station house today the premises of an Indian restaurant, Meopham, now only staffed at peak periods, it provides a weekday off-peak service of three trains each hour to London Victoria or Faversham.

¶ *Consortium of Local Authorities Special Programme system.*

2016 Status: Open operated by Southeastern

Location map grid reference : C1

Opened: 6 May 1861.

Operating companies: LC&DR, SE&CR, SR, BR, Connex, South East Trains, Southeastern.

Gravesend West Station

The frontage of Gravesend (C&D) platform accommodation building as built in 1885.

Originally opened as Gravesend C&D (Chatham & Dover) station in May 1886, the station went through several changes of name during its life. Becoming Gravesend West Street in 1899 on the formation of the SE&CR to differentiate it from the Gravesend SER station, in 1949 the terminus became simply Gravesend West. To avoid confusion, it's last title has been used in the text.

The terminus of the Gravesend Railway, Gravesend West's platform was constructed as a "vee" shape. Boat trains using the west facing platform side on the pier, the platform side for local and other services faced towards the station yard. After the ending of boat train services, the local passenger services were relocated to the pier platform.

Constructed from stock bricks, the station buildings were situated at the widest part of the platform where the station's street entrance opened onto a vee shaped approach drive connecting with Stuart Road.

A drawing dating from 1885 (see above) shows a brick structure approximately 40 foot long with a roof of slate construction, this had finials on the front gables and at the roof ends. The station canopies being of daggeted timber construction, they were supported by ornate cast iron wall brackets and vertical columns.

Living accommodation for the stationmaster being in a fine detached house, with cottages provided for other essential railway employees, these buildings have unfortunately now gone. Gravesend West's station master in 1891 a Thomas Holt-Shepherd; he chose to live away from the station at 43 Darnley Terrace, Gravesend where he shared his home with his wife, aunt, daughter, a general servant and his eldest son, also employed by the railway as a clerk.

By 1912 the stationmaster having become William Tatnall, the goods agent was an Edward T. Wood. Gravesend West had its own link of drivers and firemen and in 1898, ten drivers were based here and their wages ranging between 4/-6d and 7/-6d per day, this was dependant on their seniority.

In 1904 the station had a full range of facilities and the site could offer services for passengers, parcels, goods and horse boxes plus carriages, portable engines, furniture vans, cattle vans and machines on wheels. A goods shed and a locomotive turntable also provided so were both steam and hand powered goods cranes and a weighing machine.

Goods traffic was always important to the station and in 1897 a daily goods service arrived at Gravesend West from Herne Hill at 6:50 am

Gravesend West Street in 1930 showing the station and SR Pier. The stations surrounding shows a heavily industrialised area. Crown copyright

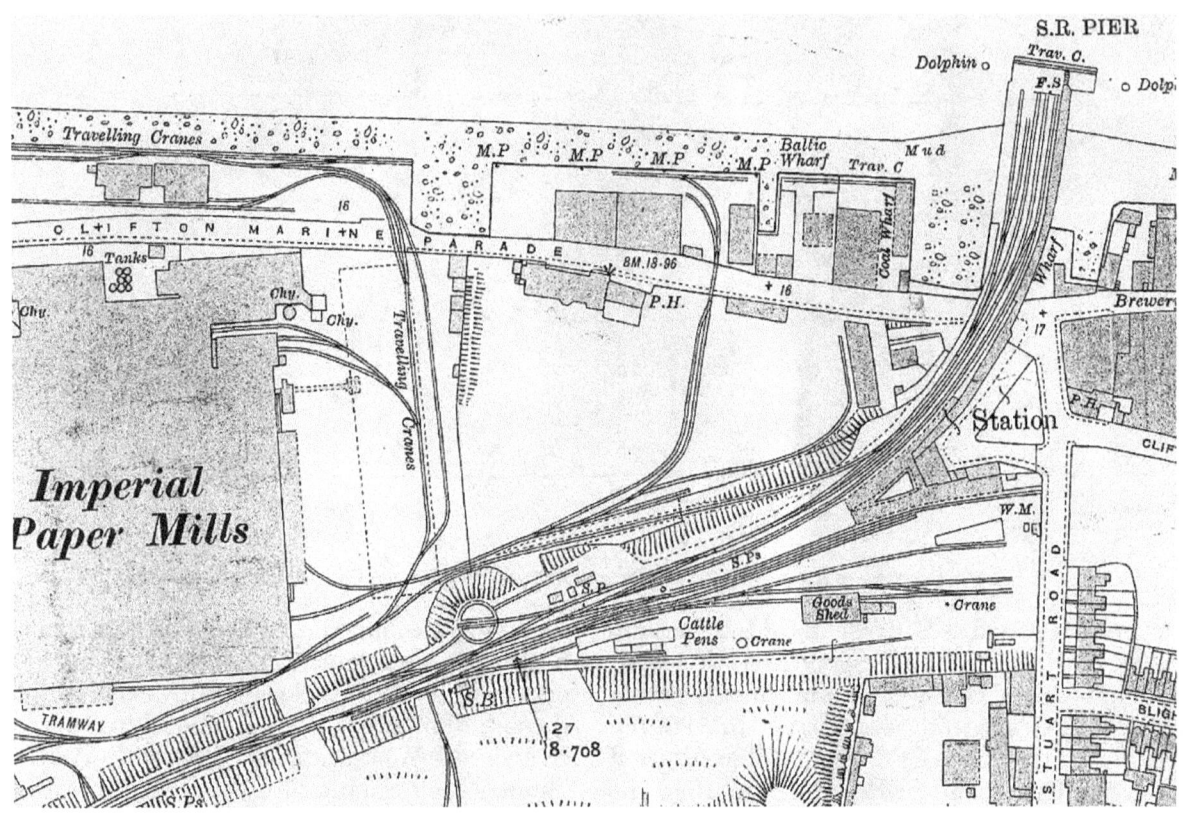

after calling at Southfleet for 6:18 am. Much of the goods offered for shipment by rail being small consignments, a traffic often presented here was fruit and vegetables, and one such consignment offered to the railway on the 12th February of 1915 comprising of four and a half pounds of cucumbers, it was transported for the sum of 1/-0d.

Another cargo being livestock, an essential fixture in the days when animals moved mostly on the hoof were drinking water troughs. With one provided here, another was available at Gravesend Central station.

During WWI a large number of troop trains ran from Gravesend West. Conveying soldiers from Milton barracks and other local military depots, workings occurred between the 14th and 16th August 1914 when 1,200 men of the 2nd Battalion of The Royal Dublin Fusiliers were entrained here. More following on the 31st of August 191, 450 men of a Royal Marines reserve unit also boarded trains here after recall at midnight by bugle calls around the town. The barracks were, however, not to remain empty for long; the Royal West Surrey Regiment moving in upon mobilisation, on the 7th and 8th of September 1914, they too marched to Gravesend West for entraining.

Goods traffic mushroomed during the war and by April 1918 the station was dealing with sixty-one weekly goods train workings to the destinations of Faversham, Stewarts Lane, Bricklayers Arms, Herne Hill, Chislehurst and Farningham Road.

The Batavier steamer service starting to use the railway pier as a port of call on their London to Rotterdam steamer service, a new connecting boat train service from Victoria was inaugurated on the 15th of June 1922,

Kelly's Directory of 1929 showing William Kean Thomas as stationmaster, although no mention is made of a goods agent, the post had presumably by now been transferred to the West Street car ferry landing stage.

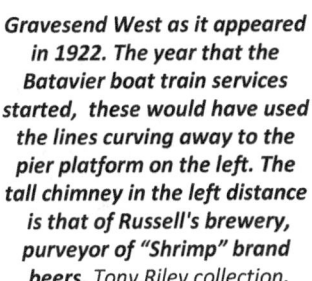

Gravesend West as it appeared in 1922. The year that the Batavier boat train services started, these would have used the lines curving away to the pier platform on the left. The tall chimney in the left distance is that of Russell's brewery, purveyor of "Shrimp" brand beers. Tony Riley collection.

The station on 2nd February 1952. Note the white bands around the water tank column, these are a left-over from the wartime black-out precautions. Lens of Sutton.

The Stuart Road entrance to Gravesend West goods yard on 30th April 1969. Tony Riley

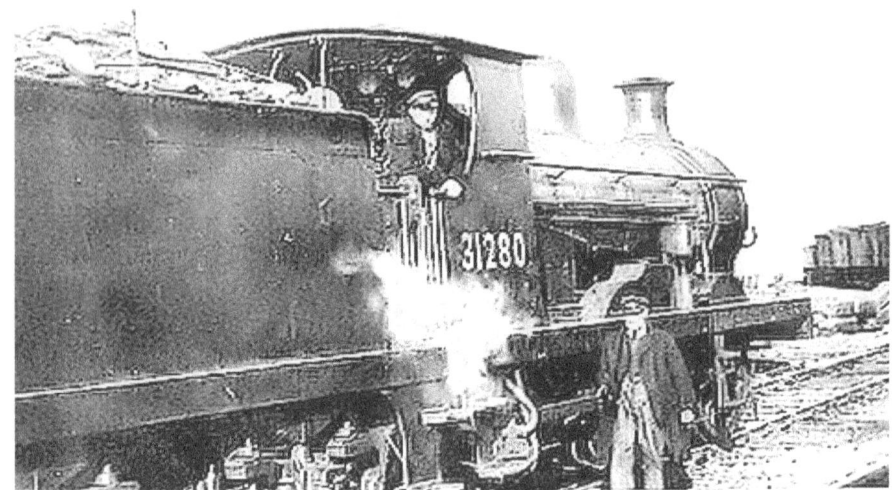

Gravesend West in the early 1950's. Fred and Maurice, the crew of C class locomotive No. 31280 appear to be enjoying a tea break.
Barry Diplock

R1 Class No. 31697 departs for Farningham Road on the 25th of February 1952.
Barry Diplock

A derelict West Street station entrance on the 1st of September 1979. Dave Fisher.

WWII bringing the end of the Rotterdam steamer services, these were destined never to return to Gravesend West. Gravesend West having some near misses from enemy air raids during the war, a particularly close shave came on the 6th of November 1940 when the nearby Imperial Paper Mills, heavily damaged by incendiary bombs, it's paper production was halted for some time.

Much of the munitions and war materials manufactured at local factories passed through the station's goods yard and perhaps the staff employed to handle this additional traffic were accommodated in a former London, Brighton & South Coast Railway grounded carriage body that is recorded as being here in 1946.

elephants made a run for it down the platforms! These circuses also travelling on the Gravesend-Tilbury car ferry, a 1957 schedule of charges for the ferry shows the fare for an elephant at £2-11/-0d. Touring seasonally, these entertainments retired to winter quarters when the summer was done, and one of these fairs having its winter quarters on a patch of land in Gravesend known as the Fair Field, it was conveniently close to the station in Stuart Road.

The military still using the station for the occasional troop train movement until as late as 1952, these servicemen probably came by the ferry from troopships docking at Tilbury. By 1952, the year before the ending of passenger services, a station agent, an F.E. Farley, having

Gravesend West Street station platforms under demolition on 1st September 1979. Dave Fisher

Before the mass take up of television, much entertainment provided locally, this included travelling circuses and fairs. Most of these making their way around the UK by rail, as with the theatrical companies mentioned earlier, special vans could be hired for transporting these shows. These vehicles including "elephant vans", a late friend of mine, "Noddy" Forbes, then a steam locomotive driver, when recalling the antics needed to get circus animals into these vans said that sometimes animals as large as

returned to Gravesend West station, he was also responsible for the goods business at the West Street car ferry landing stage.

The ending of the West Street branch's passenger services coming in 1953, the area's railway management was then rationalised and Gravesend West then coming under the control of the stationmaster at Gravesend Central, so did the London Tilbury & Southend section (Steam Ferries) at Gravesend Town Pier.

Gravesend West's permanent way staff and

lengths-men must have taken pride in their work as in 1950 the station won an award for the areas best maintained track, so to the ordinary railway man in the post war period, it must have seemed like business as usual for the West Street branch. However, things began to look ominous in 1952 when a passenger survey revealed that the busiest train of the week was the Saturdays only Farningham Road 1:08 pm service. Hardly overloaded, it had only 14 passengers aboard.

A further survey confirming the earlier results, in March 1953, BR asked the Transport Users Consultative Committee for a closure notice. This being granted, after a short working life of 67 years the station closed its doors to rail passengers for the last time on the 3rd of August 1953. With the population of the area by then growing rapidly, the loss of Gravesend's direct rail link to the Chatham main line removed a valuable transport link from the town.

Goods and freight services continuing, the award winning double line track of 1950 was singled in 1959 and somewhat ironically, the station yard was used for the overflow parking of its competitor, buses and coaches from the nearby Maidstone & District bus garage. Once located at the top of Stuart Road, the garages site and the former bus station buildings are now the premises of the retailers, Iceland.

2016 Status: Demolished, few traces remain.

Location map grid reference: A1

Some local industrial concerns remained major customers of the branch, particularly the local paper mills and with items going astray on the rail network, a letter from Bowater Scott of the 17th of October 1966 queries the loss of items in transit between Gravesend West and St. Marys Goods depot, Derby.

The last passengers to use the station did so in September 1966. Not boarding trains, they

Gravesend West station approach in 1979. Dave Fisher

were embarking on a Thames pleasure steamer from Gravesend for the last time, the General Steam Navigation Company ships ceasing to call after that month. Gravesend West's grand finale came on Sunday the 3rd of March 1968 when the *"Invicta"* rail enthusiast's special visited the station as part of a tour of Kent and Sussex railway bye-ways.

My own visits to the station in the 1970's revealing the platforms and station buildings to be largely extant, the corrugated iron goods shed then still retained it's loading platform and hand operated crane.

In 1991 what remained of the station was levelled to become an outlet of the Great Mills chain. Most of its fabric now destroyed, some of the stations cast iron canopy supports live on in use in their intended role at Groombridge station on the Spa Valley Railway.

Opened: 10 May 1886
Closed to Passengers: 3 August 1953
Closed to Freight : 25 March 1968
Operating Companies: LC&DR, SE&CR, Southern Railway, British Railways

Rosherville Station

A view of Rosherville Station in 1922 looking towards Gravesend West, its signal box can just be seen nestling in the chalk cutting to the left. Also evident are the ornate gas lighting standards and the wide staircase and footbridge provided for the large numbers of passengers expected to visit the Rosherville Gardens. The tunnel seen in the far background has now been converted to road use. Tony Riley collection.

The tourist attraction of the Rosherville Gardens was one of the main reasons for opening the Gravesend Railway, and a station to serve these Gardens was inevitably to be a prime feature of the line. Like the gardens themselves, the station derived it's name from the local land owners, the Rosher family.

Originally opened as the "Kent Zoological and Botanical Gardens" in 1837, this genteel attraction was originally intended to appeal to the more wealthy visitor with high-brow cultural tastes. When just too few visitors of that ilk were attracted, the gardens were re-packaged in 1842 to appeal to the common man as the Rosherville Gardens. Then promoted more for their pleasure activities, they reached their peak popularity in 1880.

Another driver for locating a station here was the prestigious Rosherville housing development. Including a hotel and yacht club, it was financed by the Rosher's with the prime intention of attracting wealthy Londoners to reside in North Kent.

Returning to the station, this was built as a single island platform situated in a cutting in the local chalk strata. With the needs of the large parties of trippers to the Gardens in mind, access to the booking hall from the platform was made via a wide covered footbridge to the undistinguished, single storey booking hall.

A solid brick and masonry structure, it was made a little more architecturally appealing by the addition of contrasting orange brick banding in its walls. The platform canopies, as at Gravesend West of a daggeted edge timber construction, they were also supported by ornate cast iron wall brackets and columns. As with Southfleet and Gravesend West, lighting was provided by glass encased gas lanterns atop of ornate spiraled cast iron lamp standards.

The first Bank Holiday after the opening of the station being the Whitsun of June 1886, the *Gravesend Reporter* newspaper informed its readers that 1,802 persons, the main rail borne part of the tripper traffic to the Gardens, passed through the station on Whit Sunday after having been brought

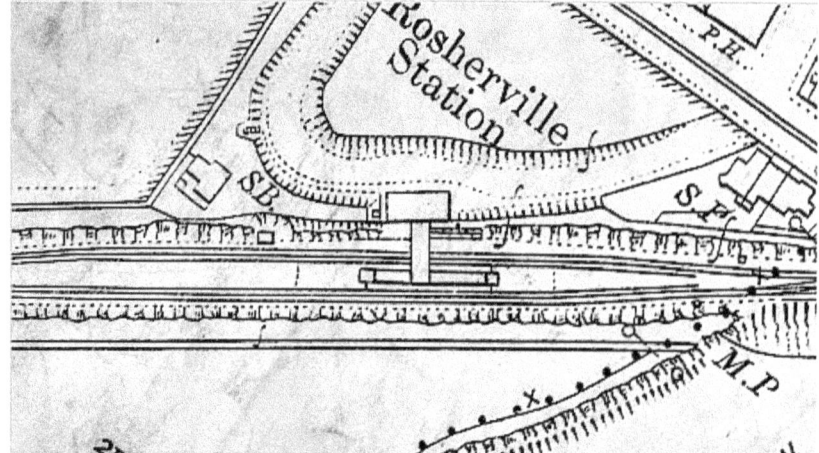

A plan of Rosherville station dating from 1909.
Crown copyright

An abandoned Rosherville seen in April 1953 some twenty years after its closure and shortly before the ending of passenger services on the branch. R C Riley

The rosery at the Rosherville Gardens in Victorian times.
Tony Larkin collection.

July, August and September, 1899.

ROSHERVILLE GARDENS.

PLEASURE TRIP TICKETS

to

GRAVESEND and including admission to ROSHERVILLE GARDENS

Are issued, available by Trains shown on page early,

EVERY WEEK-DAY

AT THE FOLLOWING REDUCED FARES:—

FROM		FARES FOR THE DOUBLE JOURNEY, THIRD CLASS	
		TO GRAVESEND.	INCLUDING ADMISSION to ROSHERVILLE GARDENS
		1st Class / 2nd Class / 3rd Class	1st Class / 2nd Class / 3rd Class
CHARING CROSS / CANNON STREET / BLACKHEATH / CHARLTON / DEPTFORD / GREENWICH / LEWISHAM / MAIDSTONE / MAIDSTONE BARRACKS / MAZE HILL	WATERLOO / LONDON BRIDGE / NEW CROSS / PLUMSTEAD / ST. JOHN'S / SPA ROAD / WESTCOMBE PARK / WOOLWICH ARSENAL / WOOLWICH DOCKYARD / HITHER GREEN	2:6 2:- 1:6	2:9 2:3 1:9
STROOD, ROCHESTER and CHATHAM CENTRAL		2:- 1:6 1:-	2:3 1:9 1:3

Cheap Tickets are also issued from the following Stations:—

Victoria, Battersea Park Road, Wandsworth Road, Clapham Road, Brixton, Loughborough Junction, Camberwell New Road, Walworth Road, Elephant and Castle, Borough Road, St. Paul's, Ludgate Hill, Holborn Viaduct, and Herne Hill.

To Rosherville Station and Back,

INCLUDING ADMISSION TO THE GARDENS,

AT ONE SHILLING & NINEPENCE EACH

(Until September 30th, 1899).

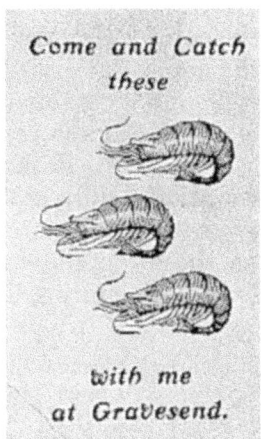

A Gravesend delicacy, the brown shrimp, these were caught in the Thames in multitudes before pollution ended the fishery. Gravesend library.

in on eleven special trains. Snugly fitting into a niche in the chalk cutting, situated on the west side of the station, was a small signal box. Controlling the signalling of both the station, nearby engine shed and private sidings, in March 1898 a signalman was rostered here both mornings and evenings to allow engines to access the nearby Perry Street locomotive shed.

An important station on the LC&DR system in the early 20th Century, Rosherville required its own stationmaster, and the incumbent in 1902 a William K. Thomas, he resided in his company house just a short distance away.

The attractions local to Rosherville station were widely advertised, particularly at London's large main line stations where large placards proclaimed:

"ROSHERVILLE GARDENS GRAVESEND THE PLACE TO SPEND A HAPPY DAY FARE RETURN TO GRAVESEND 1/-6D"

On opening in 1886, 14 services ran each weekday to Victoria. Some of these offering special cheap fares, on most Sundays and Bank Holidays excursions were also run for the day tripper traffic.

However, with traffic volumes not developing as was hoped, by 1900 these services had been cut back to just five weekday trains.

One fast service, however, was to remain. Departing from Holborn Viaduct at 2:25 pm on Saturdays only and arriving at Rosherville for 3:35 pm, this was a saving of 26 minute on the normal timetabled stopping trains.

The trains referred to on the London station placards being Sunday trains, they were unaffected by these changes. Travel on these priced at "1/6d there and back", this was a response to the LT&SR's attempt to undercut the LC&DR fares.

While goods facilities were not listed for Rosherville, some goods trains, however, did call here. The 1897 LC&DR working timetable showing a goods train terminating here for 6:48 am, it probably brought in newspapers, goods and provisions for the Gardens and hotel.

Rosherville and its surroundings becoming unattractive when the Thames became polluted by sewerage, and the increase in local industries also making the air unwholesome, the larger Kent coast resorts drew visitors away. It's halcyon days ending when going bankrupt in 1900, after a brief re-opening in 1903, Rosherville finally shut its gates to visitors for the last time in 1913. Not to completely die for some years, the last use of the gardens was for local fetes in the 1930's.

With the demise of the gardens, the direct London services ended, and by the March of 1919 the station was served by just nine local trains a day, all of which terminated at Swanley.

With its pivotal trade gone, in 1928 the by now little used Rosherville was reduced in status to an unstaffed halt. It was in this period my father used the halt to travel to Swanley to see my great aunt who was employed at a large orphanage there. A large establishment, this home was of sufficient importance to have its own private halt.

Rosherville Halt finally closing on the 16th of July 1933, its buildings were put to non-railway use. After demolition in the 1960's the last trace of the station, it's platform mound, was removed during the building of Thames Way.

The site of Rosherville station in the process of being buried in preparation for the building of the Thames Way road, the tunnel has been reused as part of the road. Dave Fisher

2016 Status: Demolished, nothing remains.

Location map grid map reference : A1

Opened: 10th May 1886
Closed: 16th July 1933

Operating Companies: LC&DR, SE&CR, SR.

Southfleet Station

Showing the steep staircase leading to Station Road, Southfleet Station is seen from the largely abandoned goods yard on 21st February 1950. G. Hookham

Known of since antiquity, the springs in this area attracted those Latin invaders, the Romans to the site. Here, they were to build temples to the local water genii and eventually the site was to become a way station of their Imperial post.

The source of the small River Ebbsfleet, these cool and chalky natural springs also used to irrigate the local watercress beds, it was this rich, green, peppery produce that the official from Bradshaws guide savoured on his Gravesend visit.

Watercress grown here since circa 1808 by William Bradbury, he became the first cultivator of water-cress on a large scale in the UK when setting up a plantation here. Mainly bound for the London markets, large quantities also finding their way to local outlets, it was this produce, plus fruit from the fertile local orchards and the revenue from visitors to the now vanished Springhead Pleasure Gardens that provided the impetus for the LC&DR to site a station here.

Opening in the mid 1840's, by the 1880's the Gardens offered rail borne visitors the attractions of a refreshment room, a smallish zoo, a museum, amusements for children and a plant nursery.

Considerably enlarged in size, the nursery still exists. The doors to the Springhead Gardens finally closing in 1936, the only survivor is the house shown on the poster above. No longer grown here, watercress is occasionally to be found growing wild in the Ebbsfleet.

A poster advertising Springhead Gardens. Closing in in 1936, they were located where Springhead Nursery and the National Grid switching yard are in 2016. Tony Larkin collection.

As at Rosherville, Southfleet station was located in a cutting, access to the station's island platform gained via a steep stone staircase leading down from Station Road.

The plainest in style of the branch's stations, Southfleet, constructed from plain brick with a slate roof, was accompanied by an archetypical LC&DR timber and brick built signal box.

It's locking frame made by the LC&DR at its Longhedge works, the box controlled the stations points and signals. A four road goods yard sited to the east side of the station, cattle pens were also provided for livestock handling.

Southfleet boasting its own stationmaster, he dwelt in a detached house facing onto Station Road, housing for other railway staff was provided in the still extant terraced cottages near to the junction of Station and Dale Roads.

Orchards once abounding here, it was once n important area for soft fruit growing and the station was heavily used for the transshipment of this and other agricultural produce. Appearing on a waybill of the 6th of September 1900, a typical load delivered to the station was a consignment of ten crates of blackberries. Destined for West Hartlepool via Kings Cross, they were delivered for a price of £1-5/-9d.

Once manufactured in a small factory located nearby on the B259 Southfleet Road, another traffic was jam and preserves,. Not all produce was delivered to the station, some other farm produce was collected from the nearby Chambers sidings. Adjacent to Hook Green Road, rail access to these sidings was controlled from a ground frame, it's Annets key being held at Farningham Road signal box.

The quantity of fruit delivered to the station warranted its own special train. Known as the "Southfleet & Maidstone Fruit Special" this left Southfleet at 6:25 am each day during the fruit harvesting season. Due to arrive at Blackfriars for 7:45 am, the train's journey time is shown as equal to that allowed for passenger trains. A must for the transporting of perishable loads before the days of chillers, these timings were achieved by the use of specially built fruit vans and being fitted with automatic braking systems, these vans could run to passenger train timings.

Surprisingly, for such a small station, a crane of five tons lifting capacity was on site. Probably provided for the handling of the equipment associated with steam traction engines and their ploughing engines, these were used for cultivating the soil as an alternative to horse plough teams. Too expensive for farmers to own, they were hired from contractors by farmers as required. Southfleet being listed in the Railway Stations handbook of 1904, it could also provide facilities for parcels and goods, furniture vans, carriages, horse boxes and prize cattle vans.

Passenger fares from Southfleet now seem ridiculously low, a 1913 3rd Class fare to the nearby Longfield Halt being priced at 1½ d single. Looking to increase passenger revenues, a commercial ploy of the Southern Railway was the renaming of the station to "Southfleet & Springhead" in the 1920's to capitalise on the nearby pleasure gardens.

Served by nine trains daily in each direction, by 1923, these were destined for either Gravesend West or Swanley, direct London trains having been withdrawn in 1913.

By 1952, four years after becoming a part of British Railways, the branch was in financial difficulties, and suspected to be operating at a significant loss, a passenger survey was conducted on the branch and at Southfleet this

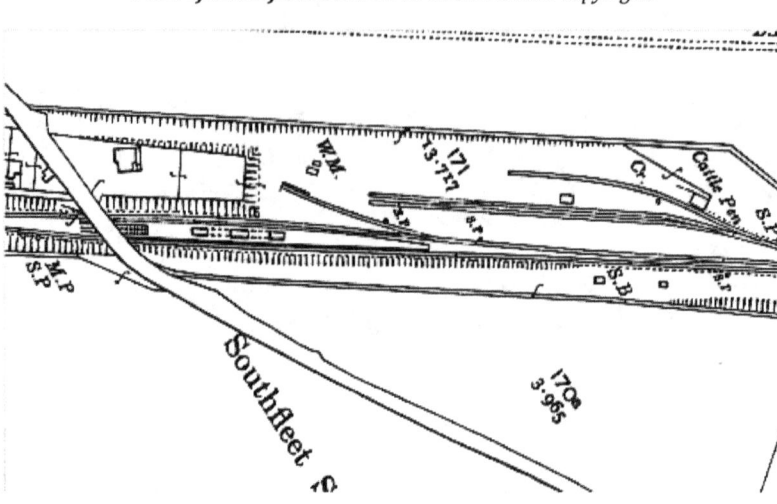

Plan of Southfleet Station in 1933. Crown copyright.

This Class 45 locomotive has just arrived from the London Midland Region with what may have been the first coal train to use the new APCM Coal Terminal. © David Morgan

The wagon tippler in action with a 16 ton vacuum braked mineral wagon being rotated for discharge. © David Morgan

A view of the coal handling facility after closure in 1976. The wagon tippler can be seen in the distance with the loco shed in the left foreground.
Dave Fisher

revealed that in the year as a whole, just 1,563 passengers had used the station. Following this revelation, in the spring of 1953, as with Rosherville before it, Southfleet was reduced to the status of an un-staffed halt. However, even this wasn't to last, the branch's passenger services completely withdrawn from the 3rd of August 1953, the infant halt then closed. Left to decay for the next six years, its buildings were removed in 1959 when the line was reduced to single line status.

Requiring coal to fire the rotary kilns of its newly built Northfleet cement works, in 1969 APCM took over Southfleet as a reception centre for coal brought in by rail from the Midlands. The platform removed and Station Road's over bridge reinforced, a coal handling and storage centre, composed of a wagon tippler, conveyor and a large storage silo was constructed here, so was a small concrete locomotive shed for stabling the site's 0-4-0 Sentinel diesel shunter.

Coming from the Nottinghamshire coalfields, this mineral was brought in by a variety of London Midland Region diesel locomotives. With Classes 45, 25 and 31 predominant, a Class 20 made an occasional appearance. By 1974 there were two arrivals per day: a 10:00 pm Toton departure, arriving Southfleet for 6:10 am, a 10:55 pm Thoresby working arrived at 11:29 am. Propelled to the tippler by the sites shunting locomotive after arrival, individual wagons were then inverted and discharged their cargo of coal to the storage silo via conveyors.

Brought in by 16 ton steel mineral wagons, once emptied of coal, these wagons were removed twice daily by Southern Region Class 33 locomotives to either Ashford yard or Shepherdswell colliery. Using a private road, now a public highway, Fox Hounds Way, the final part of the coal's journey to the cement works was by lorry. Closing in 1976, Southfleet's coal unloading duties were transferred to the 1970 Northfleet "merry-go-round" line. It's role ended, Southfleet was demolished in 1982.

The former Southfleet station site now privately owned, it's platform mound now a tennis court, in 2014, Southfleet's station house, the last on the Gravesend Railway, was demolished and replaced with a new luxury home.

2016 Status: Dismantled, only the former railway cottages remain, now in private hands.

Location map grid reference : B1

Opened: 10th May 1886
Closed: 3rd August 1953
Operating Companies: LC&DR, SE&CR, SR, BR.

Longfield Halt

Longfield halt seen sometime in the 1920's. SE&CR Society

Also located in a chalk cutting, ¾ mile north of Fawkham Junction, adjacent to where Whitehill Road now crosses over the HS1 Waterloo link line was Longfield Halt. Unlike the 1906 SE&CR halts on the North Kent line, it's twin timber platforms were not rebuilt in concrete, these and their shelters remaining in situ until closure.

Platform access being provided by staircases from either side of the road, this halt's platforms were very short. Just 100 feet long, they were only capable of taking two carriages.

The branch's trains usually composed of non-corridor type stock, getting into the right carriage was essential to alight here should the train's length exceed two coaches.

With train services never frequent, by 1946 they had been reduced to four trains daily. The halt not appearing to have been staffed, tickets were purchased on the train. In 1913, its year of opening, a range of fares published in a SE&CR passenger waybill show the halts's 3rd class single fares as:

West Street	4d
Swanley Junction	8d
Rosherville	3 ½ d
St Mary Cray	8 ½ d
Southfleet	1 ½ d
Bromley	11 ½ d
Farningham Road	3d

Longfield Halt in 1933. Crown copyright

Longfield, like nearby Southfleet, was also a fruit and hop growing area and with temporary camps built in the area for casual workers employed during the fruit and hop picking seasons, special trains were run for these folk.

A little used and quiet corner of the branch, Longfield Halt opened in an attempt to increase traffic receipts, it seems to have met little success despite fares from the halt being less than the comparable bus fare.

The passenger survey taken on the branch in 1952 showing Longfield Halt to be used by just 323 passengers yearly, just six of these being regular travellers, they all bought their tickets at Longfield Station. Closing with the branch in August 1953, the halt was removed in 1959 when the branch was reduced to a single track.

2016 Status: Dismantled, no traces remain. The site is now part of the Waterloo HS1 link.
Location map grid reference: B1

Opened: June 1913
Closed: 3rd August 1953
Operating Companies: SE&CR, SR, BR

The site of Longfield Halt in 2010. When in use as part of HS1, Eurostar trains changed power supplies from 750 volt DC to 25 KV AC here. Author.

Milton Road Halt

A typical SE&CR timber platform waiting shelter, this is similar to that provided at Milton Road and the other 1906 built halts. Jim Greaves SE&CR Society

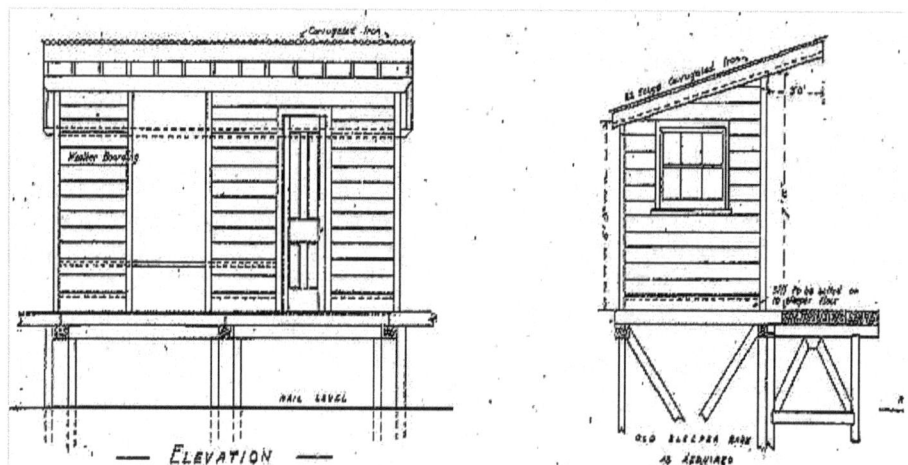

Unfortunately, despite much searching, I cannot locate a photograph of this halt, so the drawing above will have to suffice as an impression of its probable appearance. Located just ½ mile from Gravesend Central station, this short-lived timber halt, situated to the north of the SE&CR North Kent line, it was near to the bridge that carries the A226 road over the railway at Milton.

As with all the 1906 built public halts on the North Kent line itself, only the Hundred of Hoo branch passenger trains stopped here. In 1911, poorly served in comparison with the other local halts, it had a service of just three trains each way daily and no Sunday service. Built to compete with local trams it was not a success.

It's closure coming in 1915, just nine years after its opening, Milton Road Halt became one of a number of little used SE&CR stations and halts that closed in WWI to release staff and materials for the war effort.

A near miss occurred at Milton on the 6th of June 1863. A gang of plate layers working on the track using a rail trolley were surprised by a non-timetabled train as it rounded the bend just 60 feet away. Whistling furiously with its wheels spinning in the reverse direction and its brakes full-on, the ten men jumped out of the way just in time to avoid certain death. The locomotive, derailing on hitting the trolley, narrowly avoided plunging down an embankment.

Map of Milton Road Halt in 1906, its year of opening. Crown copyright

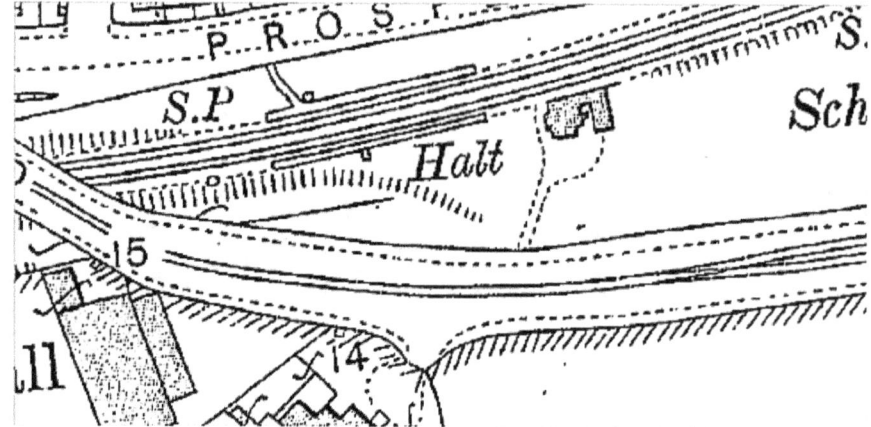

The location of Milton Road Halt as seen in January 2010. Author

Prior to the 1875 building of the bridge that now carries the A226 road over the railway, the railway crossed this road via a level crossing as this map of 1869 reveals. Crown copyright.

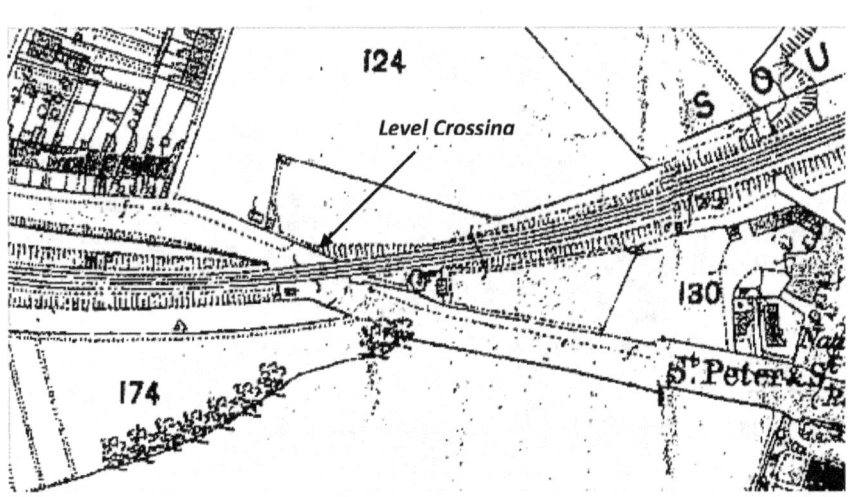

Status: Dismantled, no traces remain.

Location map grid reference : 2B

Opened: 1st July 1906
Closed: 1st May 1915
Operating Company: SE&CR.

Denton Halt

Denton Halt circa 1960 with the Port of London Authority Denton isolation hospital in the background. Dave Fisher

Another victim of multiple naming, this halt opened as Denton in 1906. Suffering a brief name change to Denton Road in 1914, it finally settled on Denton Halt in 1919. One of the five local halts to have a signal box continuously manned in traffic hours, it was situated immediately to the west of the halt at a signal protected level crossing. Remaining open until December 1971, the signal box closed when the crossing was replaced by a footbridge.

Besides operating the crossings semaphore signalling, the signalman's other duty was turning a large wheel inside his box to provide the power to the machine which operated the crossing gates. An SER built signal box, its locking frame was made at the SER's Angerstein signalling works.

My memories of Denton as a boy are of the crossing gates closing with a loud clang, this making both the gates netting and circular warning targets reverberate.

Predating its successors was a reminder of the North Kent Railway of 1849, an 1840's crossing keeper's cottage. Standing here until 1971, it was swept away with the demolition the crossing, signal box and halt.

Penalties for trespass on the railway were stiff and the consequences and fine for doing so were displayed prominently on the once commonplace SE&CR cast iron trespass notices and with Denton Halt having several of these signs, each gave notice to would be trespassers of the 40/- penalty risked for venturing uninvited onto the railway.

Listed in the 1922 SE&CR timetable as part of the Hundred of Hoo branch services, Denton Halt enjoyed a weekday service of five trains in each direction. With an extra two services being provided at weekends, a special service was furnished for workmen going to Uralite halt.

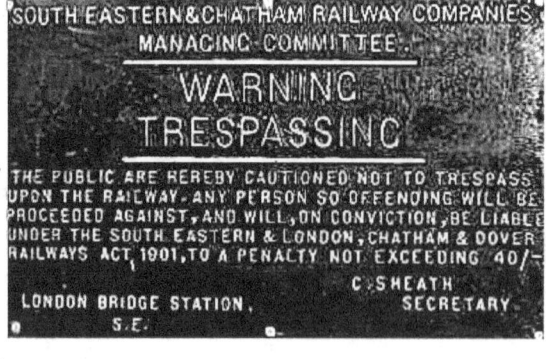

A cast iron SE&CR trespass warning notice similar to those to be seen at Denton Halt. GRES.

With Denton Halt serving local industries and the communities of Milton and Denton, another reason for siting a halt here was the nearby Denton Isolation Hospital. Used to quarantine patients with infectious diseases from inbound ships, it was the only one of its kind in the UK.

By 1960, Denton providing four Up and five Down weekday services to Allhallows plus two extra trains for Grain, the Sunday service of six trains to Allhallows reflected the resorts popularity with local day trippers. Seeing its last passengers on 4th December 1961, Denton Halt closed to be later demolished.

Denton Crossing signal box in 1968.

A 1963 plan of Denton Halt shortly after closure. Crown copyright

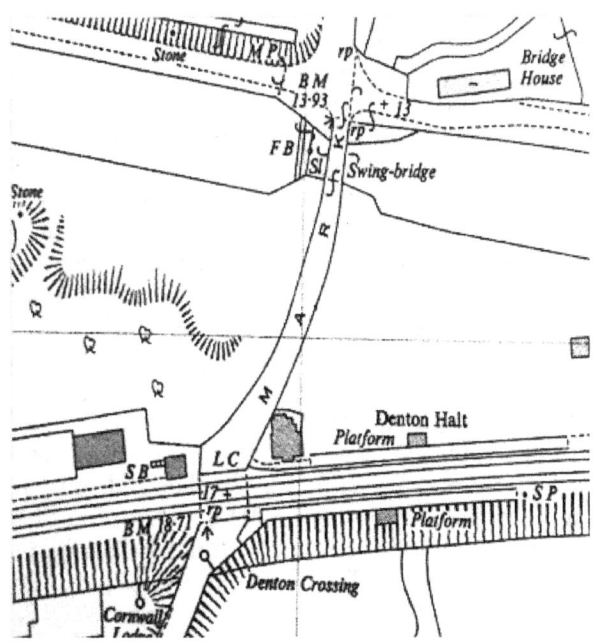

2016 Status: Dismantled, no traces remain.

Opened: 1st July 1906
Closed: 4th December 1961

Location map grid reference : 2B

Operating Companies: SE&CR, SR, BR

Milton Range Halt

Milton Range Halt in 1995. The last halt to retain its platforms, they were not finally removed until 2009. Author

Opening in the 19th century as a single platform halt, it was initially used exclusively by the military for accessing the nearby Milton firing range. Referred to as "Milton Rifle Range Platform" in an SER Special Traffic Notice of the 3rd of February 1894, this makes Milton Range Halt the oldest of the local halts. Well used by the military, this Notice goes on to advise that two troop trains, one from Charing Cross and another from Cannon Street, were to set down soldiers here, return workings calling later in the day to pick-up.

The choice of Milton marshes as the location for a firing range was made in 1859. Selected for its remoteness from habitation, it was still close enough to Gravesend to give the troops access to the town's facilities. With no platform showing on an OS map of 1866, it would appear the range was not rail served at opening.

It's civilian visitors seemingly mostly wild fowlers, when opened to the public in 1906, the halt was providing just four weekday and three Sunday stopping services in each direction. The original timber island platform replaced by what were then the longest twin platforms on the branch in 1914, it's intensive WWI use is indicated by the weekly visits of up to six military trains from each direction in May 1915.

With the one time presence of an engineer's siding to the rear of the Down platform, a permanent way maintenance function is also indicated. Notorious in local railway history as the scene of the areas worst railway accident, a multiple collision here caused several fatalities in August 1922. See page 239 for more information on this tragedy.

Later rebuilt in prefabricated reinforced concrete, unlike the other local halts and perhaps indicative of its primary military role, Milton Range Halt did not have passenger shelters. Shown in the public timetable as a regular scheduled stop until the 17th of July 1932, after this date any public access to Milton Range was by special arrangement only, from 1956, all public access had been withdrawn.

Normally the command of a Royal Marine officer, the range and its halt was see heavy use by the military both during WWII and in the immediate post-war period.

Its disposal being in the hands of the Ministry of Defence, unlike the other halts on the branch, it did not officially close with the ending of the Allhallows services in December 1961 and as a consequence, Milton Range was to retain its platforms into the 21st Century. The Down platform remaining in situ until 2008, the Up platform went in 2009.

Now only accessible by road, the firing range is currently used by the Metropolitan Police for training purposes.

This map of Milton Range Halt dating from 1912, it shows the original island platform. Crown copyright.

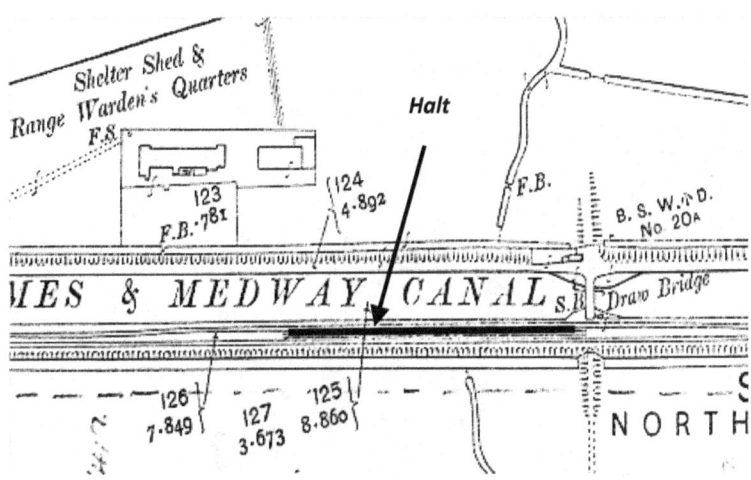

2016 Status: Dismantled, the Up was platform removed in 2009.

Opened: Uncertain. Certainly open in 1894 as Milton Rifle Range Platform.

Closed: Request stop only from July 1932. In use by the military from 1956, it was then closed to the public.

Location map grid reference : 2B

Operating Companies: SER , SE&CR, SR, BR

Hoo Junction Staff Halt

Built in 1956, it's two staggered platform a considerable distance apart, as its name implies, its purpose was to give rail staff access to the Hoo Junction marshalling yard.

Built in concrete from its inception, its appearance is similar to the concrete built halts of the Hundred of Hoo branch. Semi-derelict in 2016, it is now almost certainly out of use and no longer has any regular scheduled services as the local Freight Operating Companies prefer to use taxis to position their staff rather than use the railway.

Now one of only three railway staff platforms left in Britain with the suffix "Halt", this isolated and lowly, halt deserves better recognition.

Hoo Junction Staff Halt Down platform. David Glasspool

2016 Status: Still extant but out of use.
Location map grid reference : 2B

Opened: 1956
Operating Companies: BR, Railtrack, Network Rail

Uralite Halt

The halt seen in its later ferro-concrete form, the rail connection to the Uralite factory can be seen diverging off to the left just past the platform end where the branch starts to rise at 1:120 to climb over the Thames and Medway Canal. Lens of Sutton

Restricted at its opening to the use of employees of the nearby British Uralite factory, the 1902 SE&CR working timetable showing two 3rd Class carriages attached at Gravesend Central to the 3:45 am weekdays only Blackfriars to Port Victoria service, these were for the exclusive conveyance of workers to Uralite Halt.

The name Uralite indicating the source of the factory's original raw material, asbestos rock from the Russian Ural Mountains, after the 1917 Russian Revolution, this material was sourced from Canada.

Opened to the public from the 1st of July 1906, a workman's ticket to Gravesend in 1928 then costing 6 ½ d, the halt also saw extensive use by railway employees travelling to the nearby Hoo Junction marshalling yard. As with most other halt's on the branch, the original single wooden platform was later rebuilt in reinforced concrete and a waiting shelter added.

This halt was to have a close shave in 1942 when a damaged German FW190 fighter aircraft just missed the factory and halt. Crashing into the lake alongside them, the aircraft's wreckage and pilots remains were not recovered until the 1980's, the pilot's spectre was then reputed to haunt the factory.

The factory possessing extensive sidings up until the 1960's, it's wagon traffic entered the factory's internal rail system via a short reception siding to the south of the halt. Further sidings extending to the west parallel with the North Kent line as far as Shornemead Crossing, in the 1950's and 60's these were the scene of a health and safety officers worst nightmare, extensive amounts of waste asbestos littering the site.

Loaded onto well wagons in the factory's private sidings until their closure circa 1958, the company's asbestos products, including cement smoke hoods destined for railway locomotive depots in South Wales were moved around the works by a petrol engine powered wagon pusher. Similar in design to the "Locopulsor" unit shown opposite, final marshalling was carried out by the train's locomotive.

Uralite works was visited by unwelcome guests in 1964, when the offices were raided by safecrackers who took £22,500 held in one of the safes for paying the wages of the 520 strong workforce. Finally ceasing production in 1988 the former factory buildings, recently damaged by fire, are now known as Canal Road Industrial Estate.

With access to its site restricted, no trace can be seen of Uralite Halt. However, I was informed by an employee of Railtrack that the halt had been comprehensively removed and it is believed that parts of this halt were re-used for the repair of the nearby Hoo Junction Staff Halt.

Between Downs and Thames - Railways of Gravesend, the Hoo Peninsular and Isle of Grain

Dating from 1961, this map shows Uralite Halt in its last year of passenger operations. Crown copyright

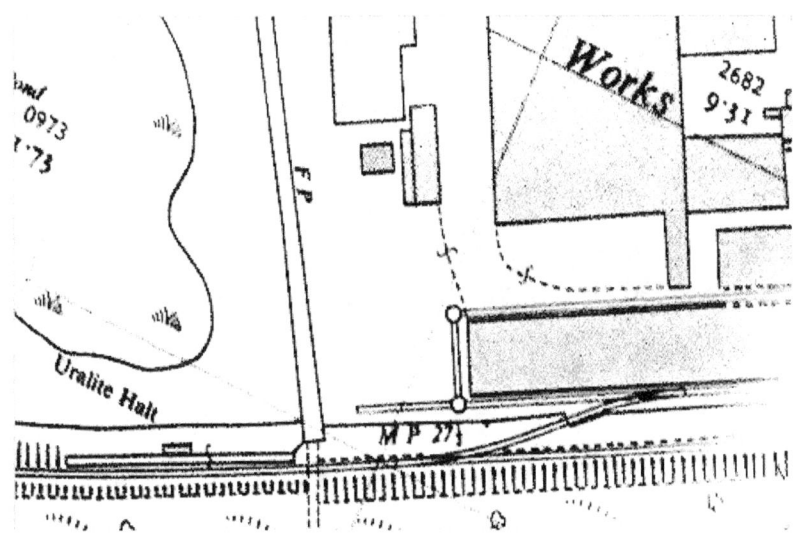

Where the use of a shunting locomotive would be uneconomic, a "Locopulsor" motorised shunting unit could be used for the movement of wagons on industrial premises such as Uralite. Pushing against the wagon to propel it, the "Locopulsor" was powered by a petrol engine that gained traction via a rubber tyred wheel gripping the factory floor. SRPS

Driving wheel

2016 Status: Dismantled, no traces remain.

Location map grid reference : 2B

Opened: 1901 for Uralite employees, 1906 to the public.
Closed: 4th December 1961.

Operating Companies: SE&CR, SR, BR

Cliffe Station

Cliffe Station approach road and frontage as it appeared in 1902. Tony Harden collection.

Railway construction works at Cliffe uncovering a Saxon burial site, the bones were reputedly carted away by the wagon load to fertilise local fields. As elsewhere, not everyone welcomed the coming of the railway and with its arrival imminent, the parish's rector warned his flock on the perils of rail travel, advising them:

"Not to become a self-seeking, money loving, God forgetting population"

In an astute piece of PR, the railway allowed the children of Cliffe to be given free rides to Gravesend on its opening day thereby encouraging their parents to accompany them. At the time, much of rural England's inhabitants having strayed no more than a few miles from their homes, the railways gave them the chance to venture further and not a few of the peninsular's population saw Gravesend for the first time that day. Hopefully they heeded the rector's warning and were not tempted by the charms of Gravesend!

A humorous story relating to Cliffe station concerns a local farmer and his faithful goose. Related to me by his granddaughter, the farmer, from Cliffe Woods, used the railway for business trips and with the trains then not as punctual as they could have been, his time of return was uncertain. The goose, it appears, was unerringly accurate on the train's arrival time, and long before any one else was aware of the trains approach, this clever goose would set off for Cliffe station to greet his master! A typical SER clapboard wayside station, provided with toilets, a porter's room, a parcels room and ticket office, it was situated one mile from the centre of the village it served.

Originally provided with just the one platform, a second platform and passing loop were added in 1934 as part of the stations upgrades after the advent of the Allhallows services in 1932. Cliffe's signal box the most important on the branch, it housed the master or "king "lever for switching out the branch's other signal boxes when worked as a long section during engineering works. Closing in December 1926 after the start of the Allhallows-on-Sea services, the box re-opened in May 1934.

A solid brick construction station house being provided for the stationmaster and his family, the first stationmaster recorded here is a Charles Wood. The position of stationmaster was much respected in the communities of the time, and with many rising to high office on the railways, the job included welcome perks such as free housing, rail travel and gas and coal for domestic fires and cooking. Coal and gas were, however, rationed, only half the quantity of coal allotted for the winter period being provided during the summer months.

Provided with ample sidings, apart from lacking a crane and goods shed, Cliffe could accept the same range of traffic as Higham. It's loads including milk, brewers' grain, farm produce, coal, fertiliser and some additional freight came from both nearby industrial concerns and Curtis & Harveys explosive works. Stationary engines could also be unloaded at Cliffe, and brought in by flat-bed or well wagons, this is probably how Henry Pye, "King of the Hundred", received his steam-ploughs.

The controller for the whole of the branch during the middle part of the 20th century was Cliffe's stationmaster, and when offered promotion, he declined, preferring the rural charms of the Hoo Peninsular.

Post-war, passenger traffic declining rapidly, services finally came to an end on the 4th of December 1961. Parcels traffic, continuing for a brief time until ending in August 1962, the station buildings were demolished in 1966. The signal box going in 1973, the platforms having a longer life, they survived until as late as 1988.

Plan of Cliffe Station in 1912

Cliffe Station seen in the 1950's looking towards Hoo Junction. Tony Riley collection.

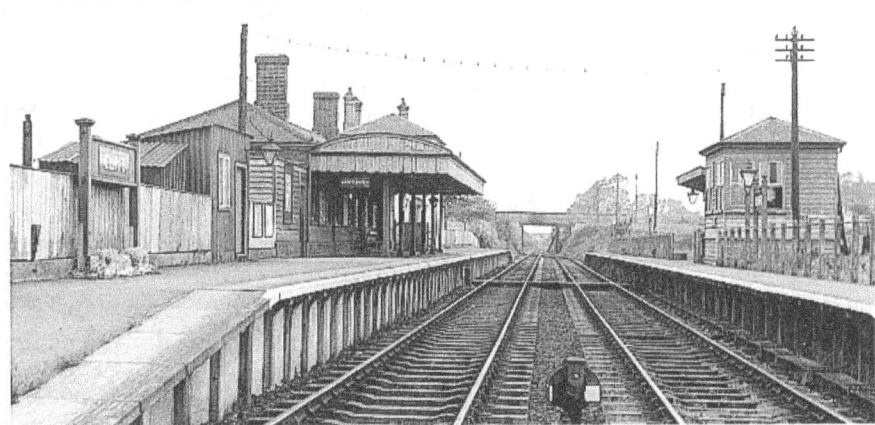

A dilapidated Cliffe signal box in 1967. The box was to remain open for a further four years. Terry Tracey.

2016 Status: Demolished, now partially covered by a small housing development.

Location map grid reference : 2A

Opened: 1st April 1882
Closed: To passengers 4th December 1961. Remained open until 20th August 1962 for parcels only.
Operating Companies: SER, SE&CR, SR, BR

High Halstow Halt

High Halstow Halt sometime in the 1950's. The bicycle leaning against the signal box indicates the signalman is in residence. Tony Harden collection.

A modern signalling room being built on the site of this now vanished single platform halt, all that now remains is the concrete base of the former halts waiting shelter. Situated to the west of the halt and providing access to nearby Wyborne Farm and some local housing is an automatic level crossing.

A small railway complex, High Halstow was also home to the Wyborne sidings, which together with the level crossing and its signal box, predated the halt. Given its remote location, somewhat surprisingly, the SER Rule Book of 1894 stated that the signal box was to be kept open between 6:00 am and 9:30 pm.

Additionally instructing that the crossing gates, both here and at Stoke and Grain, were to be shut to rail traffic at night, the humble gate-men were also given a reminder on their duties:

"They are to be held responsible for the lamps to be well and properly trimmed, so they may burn brightly during the night"

Serving the local farming community, Wyborne sidings were reasonably active and in the April of 1918 being visited by 12 trains weekly, these workings included the six times weekly 8:45 pm Gravesend Market train.

Should any shunting be required here in the absence of a signal man, it was to be done under the control of the train's guard after he had obtained the section's train staff from the signalman at Sharnal Street station.

Post-war passenger services remaining quite frequent, the 1946 SR timetable shows a weekday service of ten trains daily. The first train of the day, a 6:55 am Allhallows service, the last train was the 9:58 pm service to Gravesend Central.

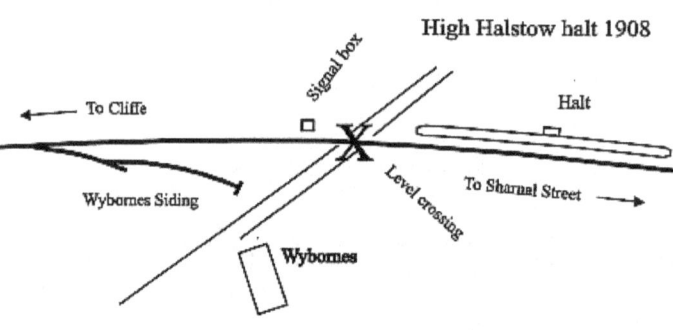

From the 1960 timetable onward, passenger services reducing to just eight trains in either direction, Gravesend Central continued to be the destination for Up trains, with all Down trains now terminating at either Grain or Allhallows since the closure of Port Victoria station in 1951.

High Halstow closing on the 4th of December 1961, Wyborne siding's boarded-up signal box lingered on until 1973.

Wyborne sidings' signal box at High Halstow in 1967. In the foreground is what looks suspiciously like a single line tablet catching device. Terry Tracey

2016 status: Demolished, site now occupied by an automatic signalling control housing.

Location map reference: 3B

Opened : 1st July 1906.
Closed: 4th December 1961.
Operating Companies: SER (sidings), SE&CR, SR, BR

Sharnal Street Station

Sharnal Street complete with passengers sometime in the 1950's. Tony Harden collection

Sharnal Street station was inconveniently sited for the local population, the nearest village, High Halstow, being some 1¼ miles distant, Hoo St. Werburgh, the largest habitation in the area, and the main population which the station was intended to serve was two miles away.

Sharnal Street being the temporary terminus station of the line prior to its opening throughout to Port Victoria, Sharnal Street was to serve that function once again between 1895 and 1900 when the winter passenger services to Port Victoria were withdrawn after the ending

Between Downs and Thames - Railways of Gravesend, the Hoo Peninsular and Isle of Grain

1936 Sharnal Street Station plan

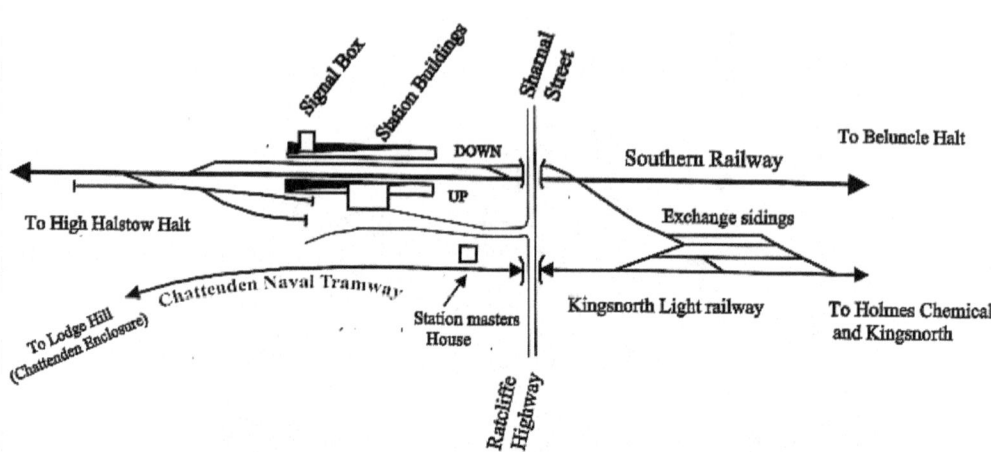

of the Sheerness ferry service. The "Crewe" of the branch, Sharnal Street had quite extensive facilities. Mainly sidings, these were split into either public or military usage this being the location of the line's junction with the private standard gauge Chattenden Naval Tramway (CNT), from 1915 a spur to the Kingsnorth naval airship station also came in here.

Aside from military traffic, the civilian goods loads that could be received here were similar in scope to Cliffe station. The station house being the one substantial building, this overlooked the timber structures of the remainder of the station. As with Cliffe, Sharnal Street had its own signal box and in 1902 this was kept open between the hours of 5:30 am and 10:30 pm.

The appendix to the 1922 SE&CR Rule Book placing a special restriction of 443 feet on the length of trains that could be run round at Sharnal Street, this was removed when the passing loop was extended to accommodate the Allhallows-on-Sea excursion trains in 1935.

On 26th May 1960 H Class No. 31553 waits at Sharnal Street with a Gravesend train, the signalman about to pass the single line token to the driver. Joanes Publications.

The station opening in March 1882, it's first stationmaster is listed as a Mr. Day and by 1891 the holder of the post, living in the station house with his wife and two children, was Henry. J. Bowles.

In 1902, the branch's senior manager was a Mr J. M Moore. Based at East Croydon station. he held the position of the Superintendent of the Western and the Central District of the SE&CR.

As did the additional wartime only workmen's trains, all goods services originated from and terminated at Gravesend Central. During WWI Sharnal Street was a busy station and it's goods traffic considerable, the 1918 SE&CR working timetable shows weekday workings alone of a minimum of three daily arrivals and departures. Mostly military traffic, starting with a 6:40 am arrival, they finished with an 11:05 pm departure.

Originally having just one platform, after the opening of Allhallows-on-Sea in 1932, a Down platform was added in 1935. As would be expected for what was the branch's principal intermediate station, a good passenger service was provided and in 1946 there was a weekday service of 17 Down and 18 Up trains. Starting with the 5:49 am Allhallows departure, the last train of the day was the 9:54 pm Up working for Gravesend Central.

After attempts at economies in the 1950's such as singling the track from Stoke Junction to Allhallows and the trial running of a diesel rail-car, Sharnal Street, along with the rest of the branch closed to passengers in December 1961.

Parcels traffic continuing until August 1962, the signal box stayed in operation up to 1964. When the line was colour light signalled in 1973 both the box and the passing loop were removed.

When the station buildings were demolished in 1966, the intention had been to spare the station house. Regrettably being partially demolished in error, it lingered on into the 1990's until the building of a new road bridge finally brought its removal.

2016 status: Demolished, now covered by a 1990's built over bridge on the A228 road.

Location map grid reference: 3B

Opened : 31st March 1882

Closed : To passengers 4th December 1961. Remained open until 20th August 1962 for parcels only.

Operating companies: SER , SE&CR, SR, BR

The alignment of the Chattenden Naval Tramway, later the Kingsnorth Light Railway, it is seen in 1995 with Kingsnorth power station in the far distance. Author

"Black Five" steam locomotive No. 45407 "Lancashire Fusilier" approaches the site of Sharnal Street station with the "Granville Express" steam rail tour of 25th February 2006. Author

Beluncle Halt

Beluncle seen before rebuilding in the 1930's. The wagons behind the platform are occupying Miskins sidings.

The curiously named Beluncle Halt is now the site of commercial buildings. A single platform halt, it acquired its name from Beluncle Farm which is still extant some 1/4 mile to the south. As with most of the other halts that opened in 1906, it was rebuilt in concrete form sometime in the mid-1930's. At one time railway cottages and a ticket office being on site; this was the only one of the halts to be provided with both.

Originally opened as a rail loading point for agricultural produce, pre-dating the halt were Miskin's private sidings and its signal box. Acquiring their name from a local farmer, William Miskin, in addition to farm traffic they were later used for the reception of building materials and probably military stores.

William's son, Walter, in possession of Beluncle Farm among other properties in 1906, it was he who sold land at Bartons Farm to the Admiralty for the site of a torpedo testing station. By 1913, after further land had been purchased from the Miskin family, this had become the Kingsnorth naval airship station.

During the construction of the naval air station, traffic to Beluncle Halt significantly increased and to cater for this, an additional siding was installed in 1913. This proved to be a prudent move as the proximity of later naval, military and munitions establishments called for a much greater goods handling capacity.

By April 1918 the sidings had become host to a considerable weekly traffic. Consisting of 13 Down and eight Up goods trains, this imbalance in workings suggests that the sidings were in use for other than farm produce. Also a calling point for the Gravesend Market train, this was timetabled to arrive at Beluncle for 8:02 pm on six days of the week and after arrival it was allowed ten minutes for shunting and making up of trains at Miskins sidings.

The 1922 SE&CR passenger timetable showing six trains calling here on weekday, four being workings to London, two trains also called here on Sundays. A short distance to the east of Beluncle Halt was the junction with the 1932 built Berry Wiggins refinery sidings and the disused and rusty steel bridge that once carried Stoke Road over the Berry Wiggins line remained in situ here until quite recently.

Curiously, at the nearby road junction of the Stoke and Eshcol Roads, a plausible road sign directs one to Beluncle Halt. However disappointment awaits; the halt having not re-appeared, trains call no more.

The closed Miskins sidings signal box looking very much the worse for wear in November 1967. Terry Tracey.

A plan of Beluncle Halt as it appeared in 1920, Miskins sidings shows behind the halt platform, the small waiting room and booking office were added in later days.

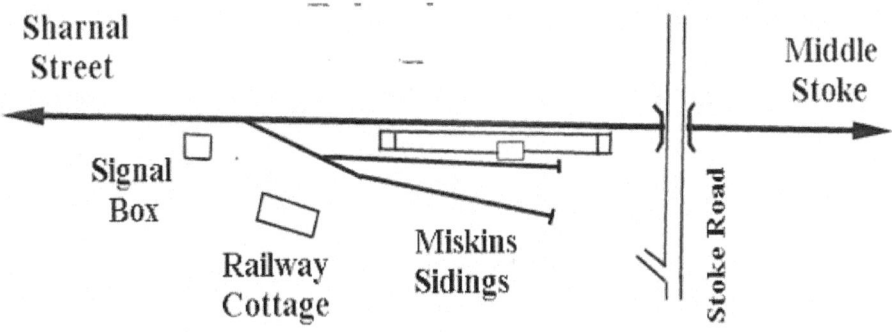

Beluncle halt in 1961. Terry Tracey

The now demolished road bridge which once carried Stoke Road over the rail spur to Berry Wiggins refinery. Author.

2016 Status: Dismantled, no traces remain.

Location map grid reference: 3B

Opened: 1st July 1906.
Closed: 4th December 1961.

Operating companies: SE&CR, SR, BR

Middle Stoke Halt

An isolated Middle Stoke Halt as it appeared in May 1928. Tony Riley collection.

Situated between Stoke Junction and Beluncle Halts, this somewhat windswept and isolated halt was the closest of the halts to habitation, the village of Stoke being a ¼ mile to the south.

If the original plans for the Hundred of Hoo Railway had been followed, Middle Stoke rather than Sharnal Street would have been the line's temporary terminus prior to the extension of the

Line to Port Victoria. At it's opening, the Hundred of Hoo branch was only meagrely provided with stations, and the footsore inhabitants of Stoke, Grain and Allhallows, facing a walk of several miles to reach the nearest station, approached the SER in 1897 for an additional station to give them greater access to the railway.

As the SER was at the time trying to sell off the Sharnal Street to Port Victoria portion of the branch to the Admiralty, the villagers' hopes were to remain unfulfilled until the coming of the 1906 SE&CR rail motor halts. Middle Stoke once enjoyed a considerable traffic in milk, and with churns often outnumbering passengers, in 1912 a wooden platform was built to handle these. Like most of the other wooden platform 1906 halts, Middle Stoke was rebuilt in concrete in the 1930's. Closing with the branch's other halts and stations on 4th December 1961, all that now remains to be seen is the concrete base support for the passenger shelter and one of the former entrance gate posts.

Closing in 1929, a small crossing box was once sited at Lower Stoke near to the occupation crossing that now leads to a Microlite airfield. Once controlling access to Medway Wharf, the remains of a partly demolished SER crossing keeper's cottage also precariously stands here.

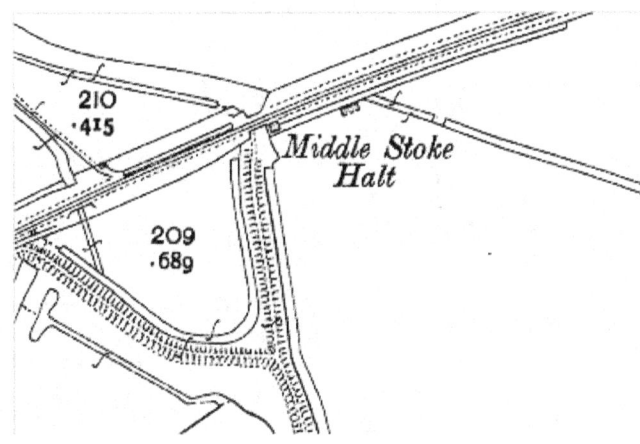

Map of Middle Stoke Halt in 1909. Lower Stoke crossing, leading to the former Medway Wharf is off the map to the left. Crown copyright.

Middle Stoke Halt in 1962. The signal post in the background, less its arm, still survives in 2016. Terry Tracey

The forerunner of the railway, a sailing barge unloads at Medway Wharf, Lower Stoke circa 1900. Loading alluvial mud, this was used in the manufacture of cement.

The site of Middle Stoke Halt on 7th October 2014. Author

This sign outlasting the halt by nearly 40 years, it was not removed until a by-pass road was built. Author.

2016 Status: Demolished, only the platform shelter base remains

Location map grid reference: 3B

Opened: 1st July 1906
Closed : 4th December 1961.

Operating Companies: SE&CR, SR, BR

Stoke Junction Halt

Stoke Junction Halt seen sometime in the 1950's when it was still a fairly substantial railway establishment. Coal is obviously still being delivered and the parcels office is to be seen at the middle right distance. To the right of the picture can be seen a typical SR corrugated iron lamp hut and grounded van bodies. Authors collection.

The last of the branch's halts to be built, Stoke Junction Halt took its name from the nearby rail connection to the delights of Allhallows-on-Sea. Opening in July 1932 on the north side of the A228 road, it married into both pre-existing sidings and a level crossing. The sidings, mainly used by a local coal merchant, were also visited thrice weekly by a mixed goods service to drop off general merchandise.

Unlike the branch's other halts, Stoke Junction Halt was built in stark concrete from new. A fairly large rail complex by the branch's standards, passengers using the eleven weekday and six Sunday passenger trains calling here in 1946 enjoyed the benefits of both a timber waiting shelter and the ticket office situated in the wooden crossing keepers box that also acted as a ground frame and parcels office.

Closing to passengers on the 4th of December 1961, coal was to continue to be was delivered here for some time afterwards. Although the crossing box itself closed in 1966, the crossing's elderly wooden gates were to remain manually operated until they too were replaced by an automatic half barrier crossing (AHBC) on the 28th of September 1972.

Now closed to the public following a number of fatal and serious accidents on its approach, the crossing itself has been bypassed by a flyover bridge since 2012.

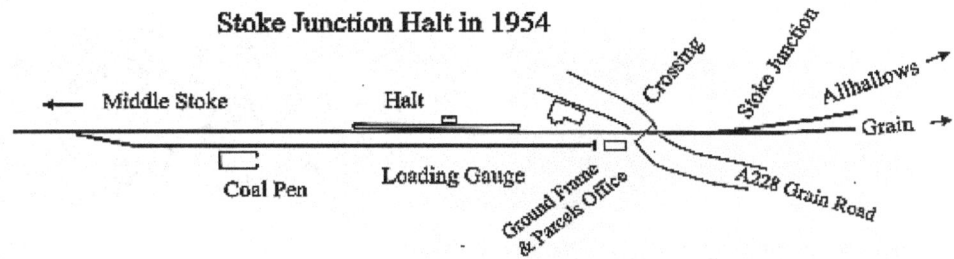

Stoke Junction ground frame and parcels office in 1967. Following the closure of Port Victoria in 1951, the halt had an unusual timetable arrangement with the same service, the 4.44 pm arrival from Gravesend calling again at 4.59 pm and then once more at 5.45 pm, this very frequent service was a product of certain branch line trains having to reverse after calling at both Grain and Allhallows-on-Sea stations.
Photo Terry Tracey

Site of Stoke Junction Halt on 14th November 2011. Author.

The 2012 over-bridge which has now replaced the former level crossing.
Author

2016 Status: Demolished, now the location of the automatic control housings of the now superseded crossing.

Location map grid reference: 4A

Opened: 17th July 1932
Closed: 4th December 1961

Operating companies: SER & SE&CR (sidings only) SR, BR

Allhallows-on-Sea Station

Allhallows-on-Sea in the Southern Railway era. Seen on the advertisement holding a lantern is "Sunny South Sam", his was an image used to advertise the SR slogan "South for Sunshine". Tony Harden

Located at the end of a spur diverging from the branch at Stoke Junction, in its heyday this station was once a popular destination for holiday makers and excursionists alike. As a part of a failed scheme to develop this isolated location into a major tourist resort, nowadays only the former water tower, now a listed structure, reminds us that a substantial railway terminus once stood here.

Opening on the 16th of May 1932, the station saw a considerable summer tripper traffic and over a three-month period in the summer of 1934, 72,000 passengers passed through Allhallows-on-Sea on Sundays alone. With UK holiday resorts expanding to meet the demand created by the 1936 Annual Holiday Bill that made a one week annual paid holiday a statutory right for all workers, perhaps it was both in anticipation of this need and the recognition of Allhallows' growing popularity that the SR, in partnership with the Kent and London County Councils hatched a scheme to develop Allhallows as a holiday location.

Somewhat over optimistically, it was hoped to eventually turn Allhallows into one of Europe's premiere holiday destinations and had Allhallows attracted sufficient interest, its major attraction was to have been the UK's largest swimming pool incorporating the country's first artificial wave machine. With an amusement park even larger than Blackpool's pleasure beach also planned, it was hoped that the promise of these delights would tempt large numbers of visitors away from its Thames estuary rival, the Essex resort of Southend.

In 1935, concurrent with the building of extra sidings, a locomotive turntable and a goods shed, the single track spur from Stoke Junction was doubled and with the single platform remodelled to an island platform layout, the station of 1932 could provide the additional platform face needed for the anticipated increase in passenger numbers. Additional to the station and railways upgrading, other developments included a large public house, flats and a row of shops. Some of these buildings still surviving, they are a mute testament to what was to become a failed dream.

The developers plans didn't stop with just a holiday resort, however, Allhallows also being perceived and promoted as the site for a new commuter town. Buying up land for building plots, the SR encouraged people to settle here by pasting up posters advertising Allhallows advantages at London stations.

With reduced fares offered as an inducement, and additional services planned, two direct services to London were provided daily for a return fare of 6/-6d and with visitor figures continuing to increase, electrification of the branch was considered, as was the doubling of

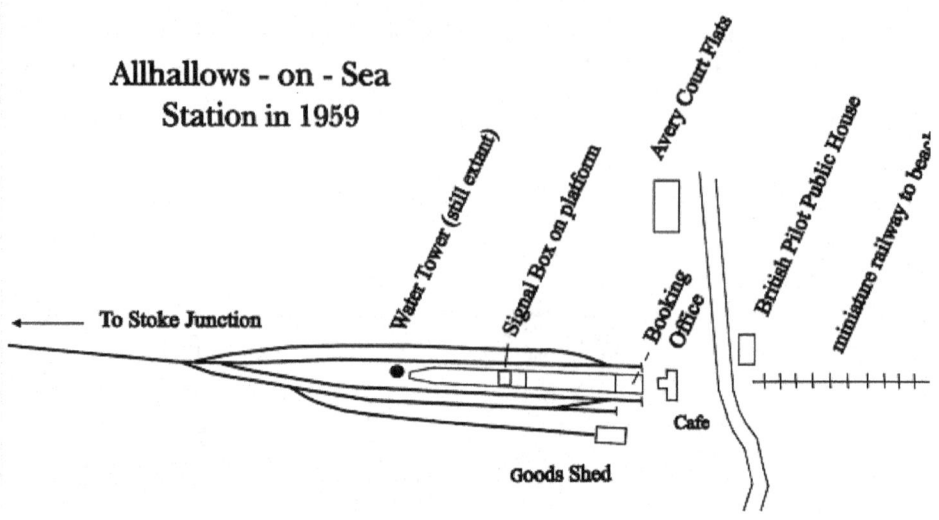

Allhallows - on - Sea Station in 1959

Posters from the 1930's advertising the new resort. Courtesy of Southern Posters

the single line branch from Hoo Junction.

With all this activity stimulating demand, and facilities rapidly increasing around the station, passengers alighting at Allhallows on summer weekends could refresh themselves at the station cafe, and then continue their journey to the beach by a steam operated miniature railway, should they not want to undertake the short walk to its attractions of a fun fair, restaurants and scenic railway.

However, by the late 1930's it was becoming apparent the resort was not developing as hoped and with the September 1939 outbreak of war putting plans on hold for the duration, its attractions were left unused and untended.

In 1946 Allhallows was still listed as one of the SR's principal stations with an ordinary 3rd class single fare from Allhallows to London being priced at 6/-0d. However, in the late 1940's with the end of its Southern Railway backing, it was becoming blatantly apparent that the Allhallows development had failed, neither commuters nor businesses having taken up building plots and with both mass car ownership and the lure of bigger resorts factors in the dwindling of Allhallows passenger numbers, its fate was sealed.

The failure of the dream having been finally acknowledged, in 1957 the spur between Stoke Junction and Allhallows was returned to single track and with the branch excluded from the Kent Coast Electrification scheme, it was clear that the branch was of only minor importance to BR.

Excursion traffic was, however, still sufficient to run special trains to the resort, an excursion timetable from Easter 1960 showing up to four trains visiting daily. Originating from Charing Cross, a 2nd Class return on these services was priced at 7/-6d. These excursions bringing a variety of motive power to the branch, visiting locomotives included BR Standard 2-6-2 tanks and ex-SE&CR 4-4-0 types. Leaving their trains at Allhallows, locos travelled back light engine to Hoo Junction, returning in the evening.

The fall of passenger revenues continuing, closure of the branch's passenger service was inevitable, and on the 4th of December 1961, the last passenger train departed for Gravesend. After closure, the spur between Stoke Junction and Allhallows was used to store condemned wagons with 189 being stored there in 1962.

After a period of use as a shop, the station was demolished in the 1970's, and its site is now a mobile home park. Although not fulfilling the hopes of the 1930's developers, on a more modest scale Allhallows now has the Haven Holiday Park.

The beach in the Edwardian period. No sign of golden sands however. Real Photo postcards

H Class Tank No. 31548 at Allhallows in 1960 with a Gravesend train. Exmoor Heritage postcards

Allhallows abandoned signal box and platform in 1967. Terry Tracey

Allhallows in September 2015. The water tower marks the eastern end of the former platform. Author

2016 Status: Demolished, now the site of a mobile home park.

Opened: 16th May 1932
Closed: 4th December 1961

Location map grid reference : 4A

Operating Companies: SR, BR

Grain Crossing Halt

Grain Crossing Halt in its timber form with a train approaching from Port Victoria. Lens of Sutton.

Giving much needed road access to the railway, this single platform halt was situated alongside the Grain Road and prior to it's opening, the villagers of Grain would have been faced with a long trek to Sharnal Street by road, or a tramp over fields and marshland to Port Victoria station.

The halt must have been a hive of activity on Sunday August 9th 1914 at the start of WWI when the 7th Battalion of the Middlesex Regiment entrained here on their way to Sittingbourne. Their train, made up of nine carriages, two horse boxes and two brake vans, it was scheduled to stop at Stoke to pick up the Battalion's 1st Company, a further stop timetabled at Sharnal Street to pick up horses.

For the loading of troop trains the SE&CR Rule Book stipulated that soldiers wearing full kit in passenger carriages were to be allocated extra seating, and an eight seater compartment was to be provided for six soldiers.

Again, as with the other halts the wooden structure of Grain Crossing Halt was replaced by prefabricated concrete in the 1930's. Close to the site of Grain Crossing Halt is the 1882 vintage Grain Crossing signal box. Supplied by Stevens & Son, it is the last operational signal box on the branch, and now has grade II listed status. Now sadly gone, a crossing keepers cottage also once stood here. After closure of the halt in June 1951 a shuttle bus service was provided to Sharnal Street until the new Grain station opened on the 3rd of September. The last crossing on the branch to retain manually operated gates, the installation of automatic barriers has been considered due to the high number of road users ignoring the crossing's traffic signals.

The plan of Grain Crossing Halt in 1920, it is very different to today. The line to the Yantlet Creek ordnance testing ground can be seen diverging off to the top of the map. Crown copyright.

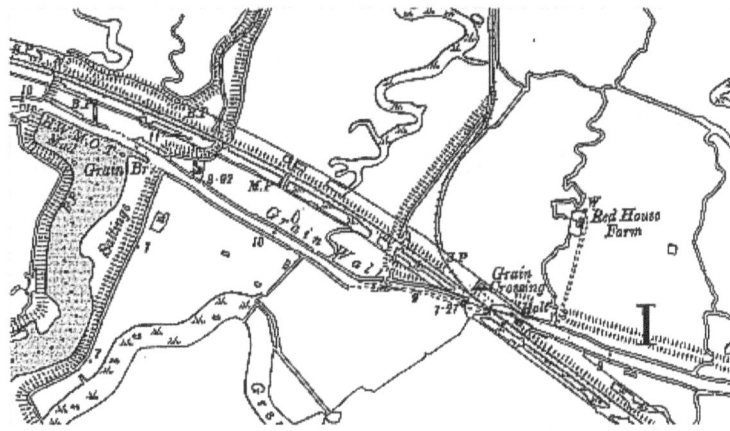

The site of Grain Crossing Halt on 23rd of April 2010. This small signal box is still occasionally used to operate the semaphore signals protecting the crossing. Grain Crossing Halt itself stood on the scrub land in the fore ground. Author

Also seen on 23rd April 2010, is one of the stop signals protecting Grain Crossing. With economy in mind, the signal posts have been constructed from life expired rail. Author

2016 Status : Demolished, no trace remains

Location map grid reference: 4B

Opened: 1st July 1906.
Closed: 11th June 1951.

Operating companies: SE&CR, SR, BR

Grain Station

A view of Grain Station taken on 19th July 1958. A. E Bennett/transporttreasury.co.uk

Although British Petroleum (BP) subsidised the building of this short-lived and utilitarian station primarily for the use of the employees of their nearby refinery, it was also open to the travelling public in recompense for the loss of Grain Crossing Halt. A single island platform station built from preformed concrete, it made little attempt at alleviating the greyness of its construction, only the brick accommodation buildings and signal box giving relief to the eye. Surprisingly, in view of its windswept and often inhospitable location, no provision was made for the shelter of potential passengers.

Grain, possessing the longest platform on the branch, was capable of taking the full-length trains anticipated to be required by the number of refinery workers expected to use it.

Unfortunately for BR, the anticipated passenger numbers never materialised, the refineries' workers preferring to travel by road. Its full capacity put to use only once, this came on the 5th of April 1955 when, after a break of nearly 50 years, an Isle of Grain station was visited by a Royal Train. Carrying H.M the Queen Elizabeth II, she arrived at Grain for the official opening of the new Grain Refinery. An embarrassment for someone, the Royal Train was too long for the platform and it had to be pulled forward to allow all of the Royal party to alight. The stations unsheltered and uninviting design contributing to its commercial failure, by 1959 the station was being served by just two trains on weekdays and three on Saturdays. BP's internal rail system connecting to the branch at Grain, their small diesel shunting locomotives could often be seen marshalling oil tank trains by the station.

After saying farewell to its last passenger service train on the 2nd of December 1961, the station was closed to the public. Partially taken over by BP for use as a part of their internal rail system, following a 1980's derailment, damaged ballast wagons were for long stored here.

Transmanche Link (TML), a British-French consortium responsible for building the Channel Tunnel opening a factory at Grain in the early 1990's for the manufacture of concrete segments, for lining the Channel Tunnel, they brought further traffic to the branch by using it both for the import of raw materials and export of completed linings to the Channel Tunnel work site at Cheriton. This factory's site now absorbed into the Thamesport complex, incomplete tunnel linings can be seen at Grain today in use as bollards.

Largely demolished in 1986, in 2016 the last remaining station structure is the former staff accommodation building. Now signed as "The Old Station" and used for train crew accommodation by D.B Schenker, what remains of the station's track work is now used for Hanson's ballast trains and Thamesport rail traffic.

Between Downs and Thames - Railways of Gravesend, the Hoo Peninsular and Isle of Grain

The diesel shunter "Man of Kent" at the Isle of Grain refinery in April 1983. This loco worked at the refinery until 1992 when it was moved to Hamble where it was renamed "Hamble-le-Rice". The locomotive since moved, it is reputed to have gone to another BP site. Kevin Lane.

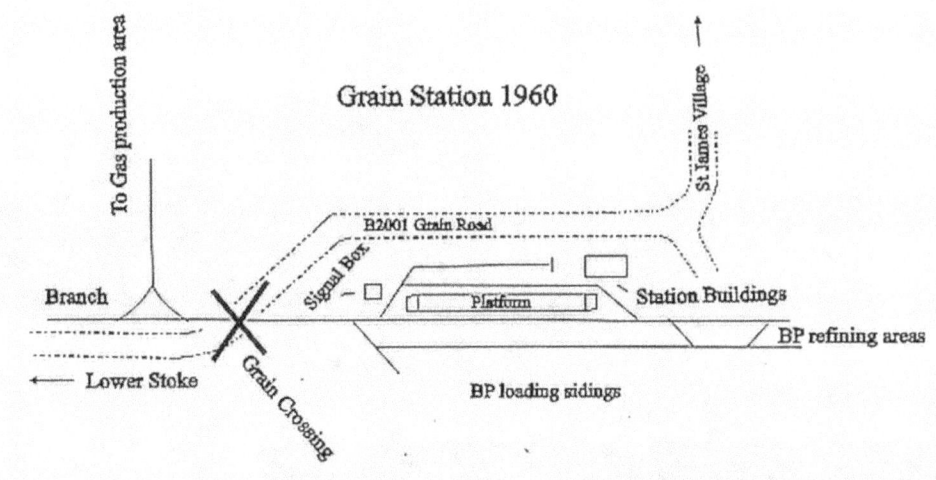

Also seen in April 1983 are BP tanker wagons at the Isle of Grain refinery. Note the warning sign that prohibits the Barclay locomotive from going any further. Kevin Lane.

Class 56 No. 56006 seen at Thamesport on 30th November 1992. The first coal empties train to call here, it is about to receive the first load of coal landed at the terminal. © *David Morgan*

With Damhead Creek gas fired power station seen in the distance, Class 66 No. 66147 sits at the Hanson's sidings at Grain. Author.

A container train at Thamesport. Courtesy of London Thamesport

2016 Status : The platforms and signal box are now demolished, the former staff buildings remaining in use by D B Schenker.

Opened: 3rd September 1951
Closed: 2nd December 1961

Location map grid reference : 4B

Operating company: BR

Port Victoria

Port Victoria pier and station in 1905. Supported on some 600 oak piles, the pier could accommodate ships of up to 20 feet draught these including warships, at any state of tide. Tony Riley collection

The site chosen for the terminus of the Hundred of Hoo Railway was where the estuaries of the Rivers Medway and Thames meet to form the Nore. Given a grand title and situated on a 400 foot long wooden pier, it was a basic and disappointing clapboard timber structure. However, Port Victoria's pier was a useful landing point for either cross river ferries or North Sea steamers.

Only a miserly £4,000 having been allocated for the railway associated buildings and facilities at Port Victoria, these severe financial constraints predicated the architectural style of this terminus station. Without road access, this was a source of annoyance to both the local populace and a visiting Lord Lieutenant of Kent. When travelling to Port Victoria station, he foolishly arrived by road and was forced to walk the tracks to the station in full regalia. Upon arrival at the station he would have discovered a single platform provided with just two tracks, one being the platform road, the other was for locomotive release. An already sparse layout, this was reduced to just a single platform road sometime after 1904. It's infrastructure supplying only the bare minimum required for a terminus, Port Victoria had just a turntable and signal box.

Surprisingly, given the grandiose ambitions by the SER to attract mail steamers here, there was not a floating pontoon at the pier head and depending on the state of the tide, one of the two levels provided on the pier head was used to board ships.

A separate timber built hotel located nearby on *terra firma;* having cost a paltry £1,900 to erect this establishment offered basic and somewhat Spartan accommodation.

To be fair, these structures were intended to be only temporary and were to be replaced with something more substantial once the lines fortunes improved. Had this occurred, a large dock with seven acres of water surface area, having a depth of 25 feet of water maintained by lock gates would have been added plus a 780 foot long riverside wharf. The cost of building these expansive facilities estimated at £150,000 in 1882, the SER had purchased 150 acres of nearby land in anticipation.

To bring short sea shipping to the new pier, in 1884 the SER chairman, Edward Watkins, entered into clandestine negotiations with the Zeeland Steamship company. Hoping to lure their ships away from the rival LC&DR pier at Queenborough, the negotiations foundered when the Zeeland company preferred the terms agreed with the LC&DR to use Queenborough. Watkins next approaching the Admiralty in the hope they could be enticed to bring their warships to an expanded Port Victoria, this initiative was also unsuccessful, the Admiralty deciding that any new facilities they might require would be built elsewhere on the estuary of the Medway.

Despite these setbacks, the station opened with an inaugural service of eight passenger trains daily. Two of these connecting with the Sheerness cross river ferry, the other six local services to Gravesend, by 1890, local services increased to eight trains on weekdays.

servicing of the Royal Yacht. With the opening of the line throughout, she used Port Victoria as the favoured location for boarding the Royal Yacht, the *Royal Albert,* for the remainder of her reign. Usually starting her journeys from Charing Cross, so popular was Port Victoria with the Queen, it was said by some that the station was built at the end of a line leading directly to Windsor!

In her later years, when the landing stages were out of commission, the Queen, an inveterate traveller, is reputed to have been lowered by crane in a basket chair onto the Royal Yacht. No record exists, however, of her state of amusement!

The popularity of Port Victoria also extended to other heads of state such as the German Kaiser,

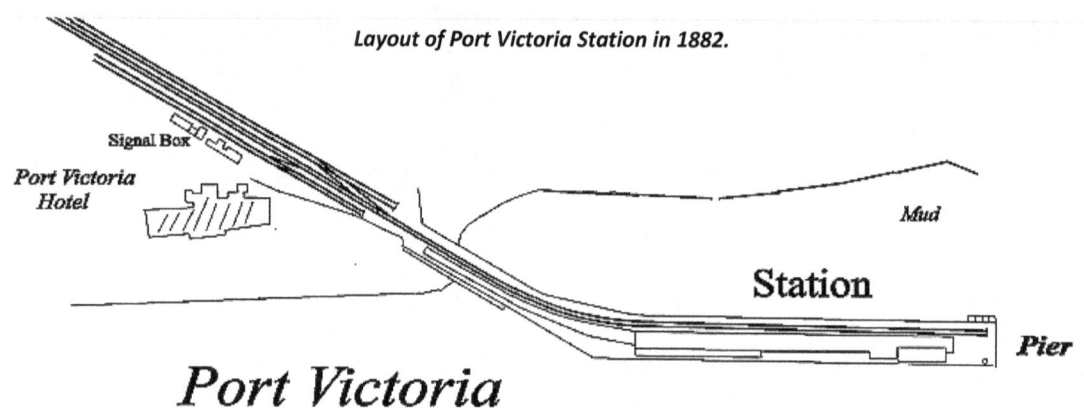

Layout of Port Victoria Station in 1882.

Another service inaugurated with the opening of the railway to the new pier, was a ferry to Sheerness. Diverted here from Strood, the vessel inaugurating this service was the paddle steamer *"Napoleon III"*. Not hugely successful, the Sheerness to Port Victoria ferry service was withdrawn in 1901.

Port Victoria, however, appears to have had a flourishing social life, the Port Victoria & Hundred of Hoo Railway cricket club holding their meetings at the hotel, in 1889, the "veteran umpire", Mr. L. Miskin, a name that is well known on the peninsular, was awarded a silver mounted pipe and tobacco at a social gathering.

Port Victoria was popular with its namesake, Queen Victoria, its remoteness from the public gaze being appreciated by the Queen, especially after the death of her beloved Prince Albert. Close to Sheerness naval dockyard, the pier was conveniently situated for the victualling and

and his arrival here seen in a print of 1891, he appears again in a photograph of 1911 when on his way to attend his cousin George's coronation. On these occasions, should docking occur after dark, all 50 of the pier's Duplex oil lamps would be lit by station staff.

King George V also used the station up until the start of WWI, a Special Operating Notice relating to the running of the Royal Train testifying to him travelling here from the more grandiose London Victoria on May 19th 1913.

The public, however, weren't excluded from the station and as detailed on the poster reproduced on page 180, the SER ran excursions to the Thanet resorts via Port Victoria during the summer months of the late 1890's. Originating from Charing Cross, these excursions offered both a bracing sea voyage and a rail journey under the huge skies of the Kentish marshlands.

Before the building of modern sea defences,

Grain was no stranger to flooding. After a great gale in November 1897, the inhabitants of the station and hotel on awaking to find themselves surrounded by a lagoon created by a breach in the sea defences, made their escape by small boat.

Despite the primitive nature of the site, few accidents occurred here, except for when one in 1901, this is the same HMS *Gannet,* which recently restored to its former glory, is now open to the public at Chatham Dockyard.

Departing at 5:15 pm, in 1902, a daily goods service was running from Port Victoria destined for Bricklayers Arms. Calling at Sharnal Street, Cliffe and Uralite to pick up trucks and vans, it

The SER Paddle steamer "Myleta", built at Poplar in 1891. With her sister ship "Edward William'" she ran the SER Port Victoria to Sheerness ferry services for a short period until both vessels were transferred to Folkestone in 1897. Ceasing to run regularly from 1901, in 1904 the Sheerness ferry was re-introduced for one day only on Sunday 6th November, the event was occasioned when Kingsferry Bridge was closed for alterations. Interestingly, the vessel used the LT&SR owned vessel 'Carlotta', she was temporarily diverted from her duties on the Gravesend -Tilbury ferry.

person was injured in a derailment in 1883.

With the formation of the working union between the SER and the LC&DR in 1899, the importance of Port Victoria declined, the Flushing continental steamer and boat train services then being concentrated at Queenborough Pier, Port Victoria was left without a maritime role except for the Sheerness ferries.

The station and pier were, however, to have one brief period of importance. Following a fire at Queenborough Pier station, the prestigious "Flushing Night Mail" express was diverted to Port Victoria between the years of 1900 and 1904. Leaving Holborn Viaduct station at 8:45 pm, with an intermediate stop at Gravesend Central, the express arrived at Port Victoria at 10:10 pm.

With 50 "tide" porters then temporarily employed here to handle the additional workload, perhaps some of these were accommodated in the rusting hulk of the ex-Royal Navy gunboat, the *Gannet*. Recorded as being moored by the pier then ran non-stop to Bexleyheath where its locomotive was detached to shunt wagons as required. Bricklayers Arms, in south London, was the SER's major centre for goods handling.

Port Victoria being listed as suitable for passengers and parcels only, in 1904 just a 15 hundredweight crane, perhaps that used to convey Queen Victoria on her earlier aerial journey, was provided here for handling this traffic.

With the 1912 opening of the Grain naval air station, a rail connection was inserted on the landward approaches to the pier.

Famous as the location for the 1918 trials leading to the world's first successful landing of an aircraft onto a ship, it was at Grain naval air station that some of the earlier trials were witnessed by Winston Churchill when First Lord of the Admiralty.

During WWI, the pier was commandeered by the Admiralty as an anti-aircraft gun position. Neither station nor pier escaped lightly during the conflict. Both suffering considerable damage on two occasions, the first event coming in November 1914 when HMS *Bulwark* blew up while moored in nearby Kethole Reach, the second and worst incident was the explosion of HMS *Princess Irene* in May 1915 while anchored off Port Victoria. Both pier and station badly damaged, at St. James, a girl of nine was killed by flying debris, a farmhand also died from shock.

The Achilles Heel of the pier was its timbers. Suffering badly from attacks by marine worms and badly damaged by storms in 1897 and frequently requiring repairs to its pilings, a cost of £75 for this work is recorded in the 1900 SER Proceedings. Declared unsafe in 1916, the pier head was closed to rail traffic and the platform was shortened by increments until its eventual closure.

When the Kingsferry bridge leading to the Isle of Sheppey was hit by a ship in 1922, thus putting it out of action, Port Victoria pier was used by a temporary Sheerness ferry between December 1922 and March 1923.

A new smaller replacement station being built in 1932 on *terra firma,* nemesis came to the 1882 station and pier in 1941 when it was demolished by the Royal Navy. The Port Victoria Hotel escaping this fate until 1951, in 1938 it's manager was William Mc Leod.

When Grain station opened in June 1951, Port Victoria closed and Steve Hills, stationmaster, signalman, *et al,* employed at Port Victoria since 1900, retired on a railway pension of 8/-0d. By its closure, passenger services to this once prestigious location were a twice daily, weekdays only shuttle to Grain Crossing Halt. After closure the site became BP's No. 8 Jetty and today Port Victoria is buried under Hanson's aggregate handling works. Not all has gone, however, the pier's timber stumps are still visible at low tide.

1899 advertisement for daily excursions by sea from Charing Cross via Port Victoria to the Thanet resorts.

2016 Status : Demolished, now partially covered by the site of a stone and aggregate processing facility.

Location map grid reference: 4B

Opened: 11th September 1882.
Closed: 11th June 1951

Operating companies: SER, SE&CR, SR, BR

The Port Victoria Hotel in 1950. Once a remote outpost of the Spier & Ponds catering firm, for 1/-0d a luncheon basket could be had here containing a pot of tea, rolls and a slice of cake. The hotel was still open in 1947 when its bar was quenching the thirsts of the crews of tanker vessels. HJPR

Seen in 1950 shortly before closure is the 1932 Port Victoria station that replaced the 1882 pier station. HJPR

Class 08 diesel shunting locomotive No. 08660. Appropriately named "Isle of Grain", the loco rests between duties on the 8th August 2015. Author

Ebbsfleet Station

The entrance to Ebbsfleet Station on 22nd July 2009. Author

Ebbsfleet station, located just inside the Parish of Swanscombe, and part of the Dartford Local Authority, it cannot be justifiably claimed by Gravesham. However, it has been included for completeness.

One of the names suggested for the new station was the rather misleading title of "Dartford International". The station being nearly five miles from Dartford town centre it was wisely rejected in favour of "Ebbsfleet International" after pressure from the Gravesham Local Authority.

Located in a valley, the station takes its name from the River Ebbsfleet which flows sluggishly along a waterlogged and swampy valley bottom. Now no longer to be seen, natural springs once abounded in the area. Disappearing after chalk extraction disturbed their waters, in a form of revenge they flooded the exhausted chalk pits, thereby creating man-made lakes.

At nearby Springhead, partially covered by an embankment of the former Gravesend Railway, is what remains of *Vagniacae*. A Roman Imperial way station mentioned in the 3rd century *Antonine Itinerary,* the historical significance of this and other sites in the area prompted archaeologists to work with the contractor's teams both before and during the construction period.

A number of significant finds being made, these included the skeleton of a 400,000 year old elephant and a brooch in the shape of a hare. An exquisite object, it's outline has been used as an emblem on the footbridges crossing the A2 road at Pepper Hill and Singlewell.

Ebbsfleet was not the only site considered for an intermediate station between Stratford and Ashford; the other locations examined including Rainham and Nashenden, these were eventually ruled out as they were unable to offer Ebbsfleet's connections to major road transport links.

So it was that in 1995 Ebbsfleet became the preferred location for an HS1 intermediate station. Expected to become the transport hub for a large commercial and housing property development, the Thames Gateway project, the proximity of Bluewater shopping centre was an added enticement.

When Ebbsfleet was announced as one the intermediate station sites, residents were given to believe that the station's environs would be populated with retail and leisure facilities. As with so much promised with the coming of the CTRL, these have yet to appear.

After the area had been stabilised and toxic waste in the form of flue dust from the nearby cement works removed, building work started on the concrete, steel and glass complex in July 2001. Construction work at both Ebbsfleet and the nearby rolling stock berthing sidings in

Church Path Pit being formally declared complete on the 12th of September 2006, following the enlivening of the 25,000 volt overhead power supplies between Ebbsfleet and St. Pancras in January 2007, the station opened to the public on the 19th of November 2007 after a further commissioning period. Something of a white elephant, the Church Path Pit sidings have yet to find a purpose.

The station owned by London & Continental Railways, they use Southeastern and Network-Rail (High-Speed) to manage Ebbsfleet on behalf of the lines leaseholders, HS1 Ltd. Ebbsfleet, together with Ashford International, is now one of two medial UK stops regularly used by Eurostar services, as Stratford now rarely sees Eurostar stopping services.

Split into two discrete stations, there is a multi-level international station catering for Eurostar and Southeastern's HS1 high-speed services, and dedicated purely to the domestic high-speed services, is the high level station.

Neither of these stations are particularly welcoming. Purely utilitarian, architectural appeal and functionality has been put above passenger needs. This is particularly so on the platforms, which without full-length canopies, offer only a small glass fronted waiting room with hard seating. For those unable to enter on a cold January morning, just unheated bus-stop style shelters are provided.

Eurostar's international travellers better catered for, they enjoy transit lounges leading to customs and passport control areas. However, once on the international platforms, Nos 1 & 4, their comfort levels descend to those of the domestic traveller. Hopefully, London & Continental Railways will improve matters for their often travel-worn long-distance passengers.

Eurostar services having then been running for nearly two years, on the 29th of June 2009 came the domestic high-speed "Preview" services. Limited to shuttle services between Ashford and St. Pancras, a fully timetabled high-speed service, including services to Gravesend and Faversham, started on the 13th of December 2009.

During the 2012 London Olympics, Ebbsfleet was the primary park-and-ride rail centre for those visitors travelling from Kent to the Olympic park at Stratford. Using Hitachi Class 395 units branded as "Javelins", embellished with Olympic logos, up to eight trains an hour worked between Ebbsfleet and Stratford.

With some services calling at Calais and the French metropolitan destinations of Avignon, Lyon and Marseille, in 2016 Eurostar services provide six Paris and five Brussels services on each weekday. All trains calling at Lille for interchange with the SNCF, Disney World is also served by a dedicated daily return service to Marne-Le-Vallee station.

The Southeastern domestic services are much more frequent; nearly 70 services calling here daily they are either shuttles to St Pancras or longer distance services for Faversham, Ashford, Dover, Canterbury Ramsgate and Rye.

The concourse of the International station on 22nd July 2009 with the mock-up Hitachi Class 395 on display. Author

Between Downs and Thames - Railways of Gravesend, the Hoo Peninsular and Isle of Grain

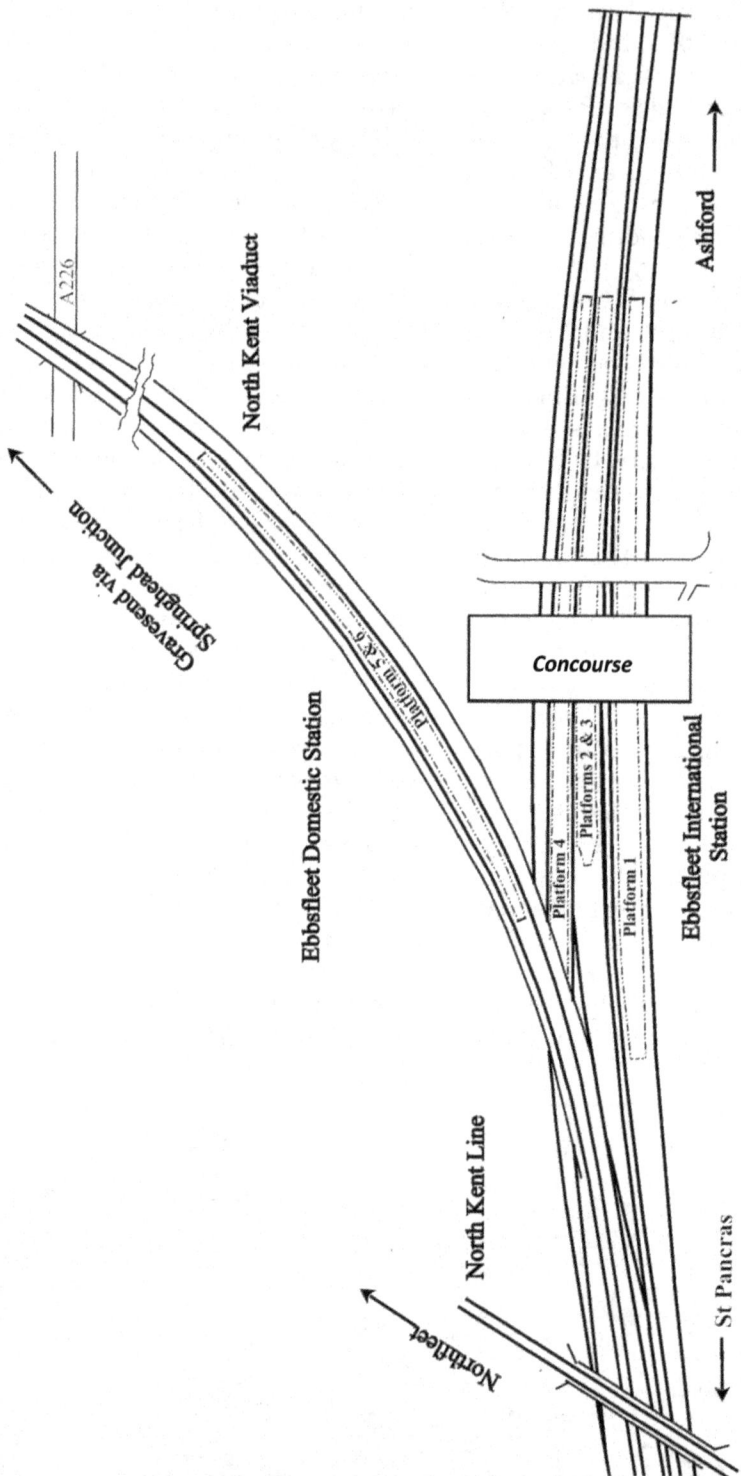

2016 Status: Open, serving Eurostar and Southeastern high-speed trains   **Opened:** 19th November 2007

Location map grid reference: 1A

Operating companies: Network Rail (High-Speed) and Southeastern.

The domestic station's platforms looking towards the north on 26th February 2010. Author

A Paris bound Eurostar service departs Ebbsfleet International on 22nd July 2009. Author

View of the International station platforms looking south on 26th February 2010. Author

Depots, Works and Marshalling Yards

These have fluctuated over the years, and now only Hoo Junction marshalling yard and the Singlewell IMD remain open.

Little endures of the other locations, nearly all traces of their existence having gone.

Horlocks Iron Works Northfleet

"Fire Queen" seen at Penrhyn Castle museum after preservation. Eric Lander

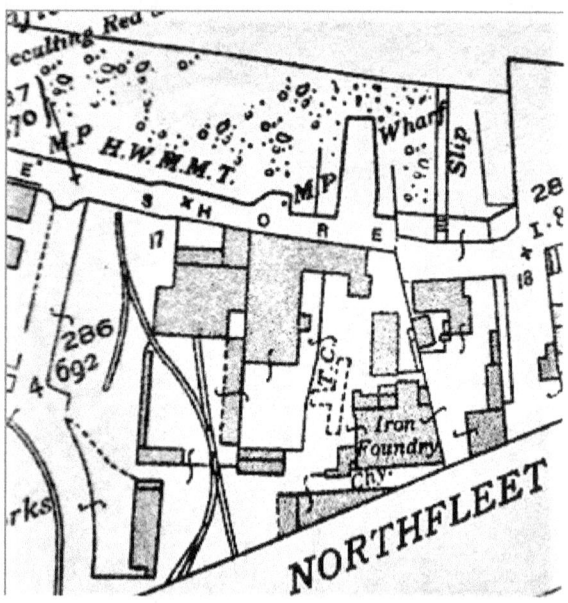

The location of Northfleet Iron Works, shown on the map as "Iron Foundry". Crown copyright.

The first mention of a local railway industry comes in 1830 when a William Marshall is reputed to have built three locomotives of the Stephenson "Planet" type at Gravesend. The next, and more reliable manifestation comes with the manufacture of two small steam locomotives in 1848 at the Northfleet Iron Works. The only railway locomotives built at the works, one survives to this day.

When buying the Iron Works in 1847 from Poynder and Medlicott, Alfred Horlock, their builder and part designer was probably helped to set up in business by his uncle Thomas Horlock. An already established engineer, he owned a nearby engineering works.

Specialising in building marine and quarrying equipment, Alfred soon became a sub-contractor to a number of Thames-side shipyards and mining businesses, and it was one of the latter, the 4'-0" gauge Padarn Railway in North Wales, then replacing draught horses with locomotives to transport slate products from Dinorwic quarry to Port Dinorwic who placed an order with Horlock for two small 0-4-0 locomotives.

An unusual move, normally this work would have gone to a more established locomotive builder, but in what was the era of "Railway Mania", all had full order books. Although recorded in the late 1830's as a maker and designer of marine steam engines for the local shipbuilders Messrs Cullen & Jackson, Alfred's venture into railway locomotive building was a move in a new direction. Seeking advice on the construction of locomotives, it is thought he may have acquired this from the nearest locomotive builders, G.& J. Rennie of Millwall.

Rennie's at the time retaining a Thomas Crampton as their designer, this was the same engineer who was later to be involved with construction of the LC&DR. Although these locomotives display some of Crampton's design principles such as trailing wheels behind the firebox, there is little else that conforms to his patent. Supplied as No. 1, *Fire Queen* and No. 2, *Jenny Lind,* the completed locos were sold for the price of £1,200 each, with delivery by sea an extra £80. Alfred, becoming bankrupt in 1853, worked for a local shipbuilder following a spell in Maidstone debtors prison and his health declining, he died of tuberculosis in 1866.

Although *No. 2 Jenny Lind,* was scrapped in 1886, her more fortunate sister, *No. 1 Fire Queen,* managed to survive by being stored away at the Padarn company's Llanberis workshops.

Seen then only by a few privileged visitors, *Fire Queen* was to remain there for the next 85 years. However, thanks to the efforts of Sir John Smith, MP, *Fire Queen* was eventually moved in 1970 to the Industrial Railway Museum at Penrhyn Castle where today *Fire Queen* can be seen in her original form.

Having remained un-dismantled since the mid 19th Century, *Fire Queen,* one of the world's oldest non-standard gauge industrial locomotives, is an important example of Victorian engineering.

Perry Street Locomotive Shed

Peeking from behind the right hand side of the cutting wall, Perry Street locomotive shed is seen from Rosherville station in 1922.

The only main line locomotive shed in Gravesham, Perry Street was to have a short working life. Opening in 1886, it had closed by 1916. Given its location out of the public eye and its workaday function, the shed was in keeping with the Gravesend Railway's over elaborate architectural style. A brick and timber building, an outline drawing of it can be seen on page 188.

Provided with a slate roof which incorporated timber smoke ventilators, being glazed over the workshop area, the shed had two covered roads for locomotive servicing. A siding for loco coal wagons located to its west side and a disposal area with ash pits incorporated to the rear, it was used only for stabling and minor servicing of the branch's locomotives, all major repairs and overhauls being undertaken at Battersea shed.

Built for a cost of £1,764-9/-0d in 1885, a general arrangement drawing bearing the company stamp of Head Wrightson & Co, a Thornaby-on-Tees heavy engineering firm, confirms this.

In 1887, members of the J Class 0-6-0's, Nos 128,130&132, all rebuilds from the *Adrian* Class of 1866, then working on the Gravesend goods services, they would have occasionally been serviced here. Built as *Ampherite* of the *Acis* Class in 1862, No. 119 of the LC&DR's powerful 0-6-0 H Class was also recorded as being at Perry Street in 1895. Normally used on goods workings, the class were sometimes to be seen on slower passenger duties.

By 1891 the branch's passenger services were in the hands of R Class 0-4-4 tank locomotives, and it would be reasonable to assume these also used the shed. 1916 bringing the introduction of push-pull passenger working to the branch, and motive power for the branch then being supplied by Gillingham and Stewarts Lane, the shed was closed. The shed demolished sometime before 1939, its site was later used as coal sidings.

Current status: Demolished, no traces remain.
Opened: 1885 Closed: 1916

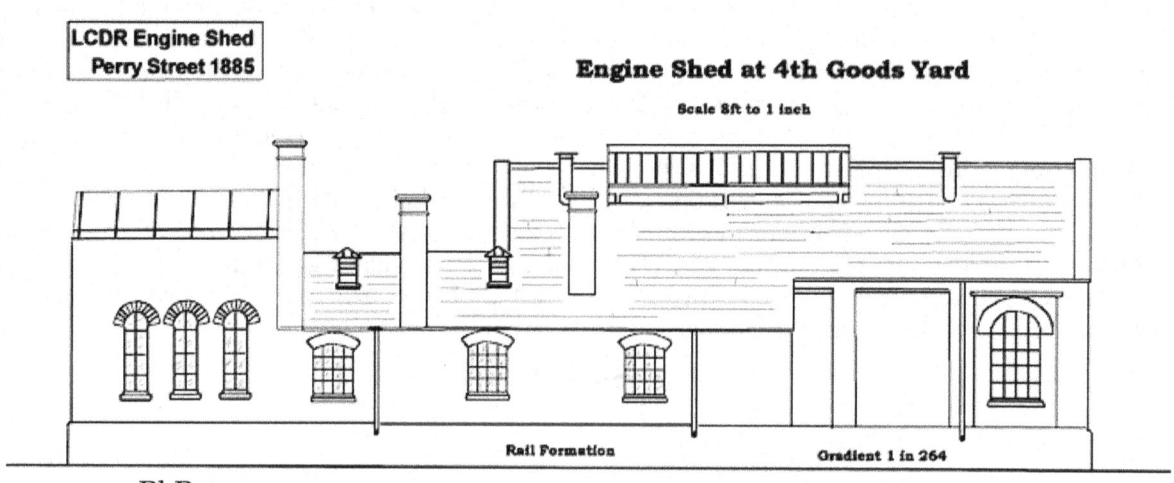

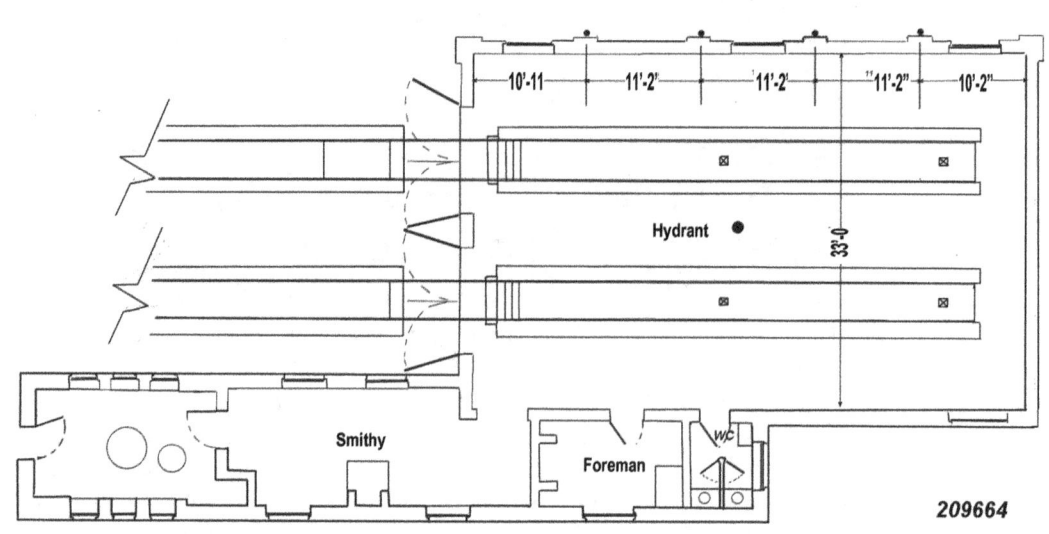

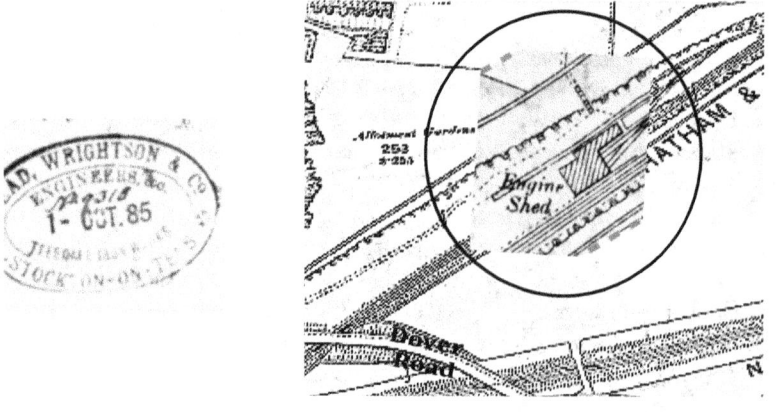

Location of Perry Street Locomotive shed shown on a map of 1897, the site is now covered by housing.

Longfield Dust Sidings

Also known as Newington Vestry ¶ dust sidings after their Newington, south London source of traffic, these were part of a rail served refuse tip. Situated at Longfield Hill just outside of the Gravesham borough boundary, they were a mile or so west of Meopham station from where the tip's main line rail operations were controlled.

Before opening in 1874 as a refuse tip, an Ordnance Survey map from the 1860's shows the site as open fields. Sourced from the now closed Walworth dust sidings located in what is now Newington, much of the refuse ashes from coal fires, it was made more fragrant by the inclusion of manure from London's streets. Newington in 2016 a part of the London Borough of Southwark, refuse from Wandsworth was also brought to Longfield sidings; Newington council charged Wandsworth 9d per ton for delivery to Longfield.

Requiring a fairly substantial workforce, housing was provided for the tip's employees in a nearby small row of terraced houses. Then known as Sidings Cottages; today in private hands, they still bear the plaque commemorating their completion in 1899.

In 1893, wagons loaded with rubbish destined for Longfield sidings departed from Walworth on six days of the week at 12:29 am. Initially bound for the Herne Hill sorting sidings, the assembled trains departed Herne Hill at 4:45 am. Mondays excepted, they arrived at Longfield for 7:34 am.

On arrival the loaded wagons were taken to reception sidings where they were weighed before their journey to the rubbish disposal area. A train arriving at 11:00 am on the same day, the empties were then returned to Walworth.

Kelvin Curtis, who lived in the area as a child during the 1950's was familiar with the site recalls being told that up until 1939, shire horses were used for on-site wagon movements. The siding's stables regularly winning Southwark's prize for the best kept horses, post-war a tank locomotive was used for wagon movements.

¶ *A vestry was the term once used for a committee that would now be known as a Parish Council.*

Sold as "Newington Mixture", processed horse manure could be bought here as fertiliser. The tip and its produce was not approved of by all, particularly by Archibald Dobbs of Hartley Manor who in 1899 was to describe the contents of the refuse trucks with the words: *"every foul and fetid matter"*

During the ghastly 1914-18 conflict, Longfield sidings became the location of Messrs E. C. Powders munitions works. Their workers also housed here in temporary hutting, the works volatile products were shipped out by rail and an SE&CR working timetable of 1918 confirms this when instructing freight charges were to be billed to Meopham station.

Shortly before WWII, when London's air raid casualties were expected to be in their millions, Longfield tip, along with other sites, is reputed to have been earmarked for the macabre purpose of the mass burial of the capital's air raid fatalities.

When recalling BR operations in the early 1950's, Hubert Browning, supervisor of the sidings rail operations at the time, said that refuse trains arrived almost every day at Meopham station's Down platform for 11:00 am. Made up of sheeted wagons, their passage through London's suburbs often gave rise to complaints over their rich bouquet.

Running round its train on arrival, the train locomotive, usually a C Class 0-6-0, after taking the loaded wagons across to the Up line, proceeded to the sidings. A signalman, brought in "as required" controlling train movements at the sidings from a now vanished sidings signal box, a return working later on the same day collected the empty wagons. Trains occasionally arriving on fire, if prompt action was not taken by Meopham's rail staff to extinguish the blaze, fire brigade assistance was sometimes needed.

Rail operations ending in 1964, lorries were used until closure in 1974. In 2016, what remains are the cottages, a partially demolished 20th Century transit shed, ruins of the 19th century admin building and overgrown cobbled roads.

2016 Status: Closed and ruinous.

Headed by D1 4-4-0 No. 502, an SE&CR express passes Longfield dust sidings sometime after 1903. G. Cramp collection

Two draught horses with their driver at Longfield dust sidings. Note the loaded refuse wagons in the background. G.Cramp collection.

Commemorative plaque on "The Sidings" cottages. Kelvin Curtis

Between Downs and Thames - Railways of Gravesend, the Hoo Peninsular and Isle of Grain

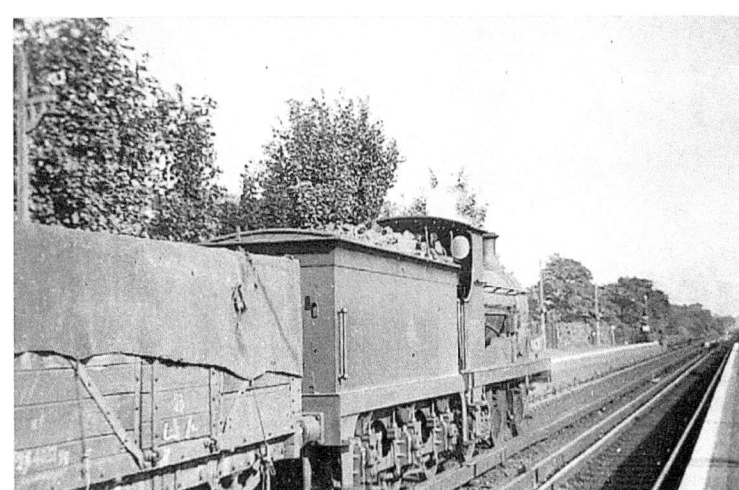

In the early 1950's a loaded refuse train bound for Longfield Dust Sidings stands at Meopham station's Down platform.
Barry Diplock.

The ruinous administration building in 1990. Neil Knowlden

Longfield Dust sidings shown on a 1909 map. Crown copyright.

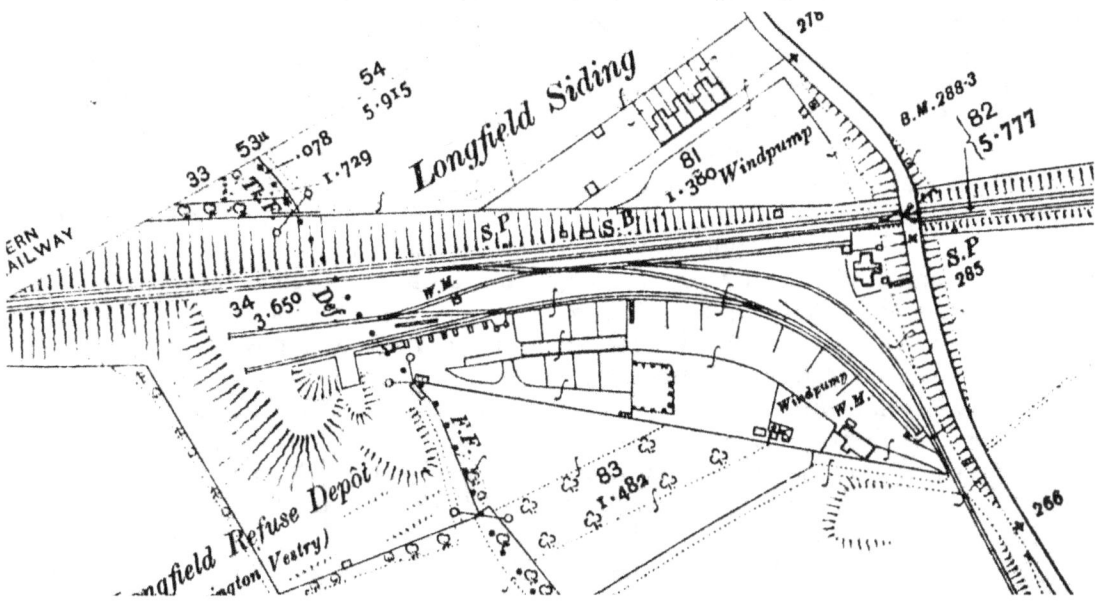

Hoo Junction Marshalling Yard

Hoo Junction Marshalling Yard seen in April 2006. A varied assortment of rolling stock on view, a civil engineer's crane is seen nearest the camera. Author.

At the time of the opening Hoo Junction itself in 1882, the rail connection between the North Kent and Hundred of Hoo Railways, the few railway facilities at this location consisted of the junction's signal box and sidings remaining from the construction of the Hundred of Hoo Railway.

Incorporating the sidings of 1882, all was to change in February 1928 when the Southern Railway opened a new marshalling yard here to re-marshal freight loads from the North Kent line, the Hundred of Hoo branch and the Chatham main line. It's loads coal, cement, petrochemical products and general goods, these remained the yards staple traffic until post-WWII.

Until the 1960 arrival of the Class E5000 electric locomotives, shunting duties at the yard had been the domain of steam tank locomotives supplied from Gillingham shed.

A distinctively Southern Region design, the E5000 Class, when used for shunting picked up power from the yard's 750 volt DC catenary system. Thus avoiding the need for either diesel or steam shunters, the system also removed the hazard of live conductor rails in the yard. However, despite this precaution, some serious accidents were to occur when steam locomotive firemen accidentally touched the catenary cables with their fire irons. The catenaries a source of speculation amongst local railway enthusiasts fraternity, their installation was to give rise to rumours, and hopes, that electrification was also to be extended to the Hundred of Hoo branch.

Looking at a snapshot of the yard in 1960, we find that in addition to train marshalling, the yard was also home to a wagon repair facility. Gainfully employing 31 men in the repair of 30 to 35 wagons a week, this was mainly damage to floors and axle boxes. The yard then handling 1,800 wagon movements daily, these were occasioned by the arrival and departure of eight inward and thirteen outward trains.

Steam locomotives then still much in evidence, the locomotives in charge of goods and freight services were mainly ex SE&CR C Class 0-6-0's, the N & U Class moguls and Q1 Class 0-6-0's. A turntable not being provided here, locomotive turning was achieved by using the rail triangle formed by Hoo Junction itself and a freight only chord east of the yard that linked the North Kent line to the Hundred of Hoo branch.

In August 1960, with shunting mainly a steam diagram, a powerful Class Z 0-8-0 tank locomotive was provided daily by Gillingham locomotive shed for these duties. 1963 seeing the arrival of Bulleid's Class 12 diesel shunters with their distinctive "box pox" wheels, by the mid 1960's, the type JA, later the Class 73 electro-diesel locomotives, came into service at Hoo. Versatile locomotives, able to take power from the DC conductor rail or from their internal diesel engines, they are still in service today.

With their arrival, the need for the Class E5000 electric locomotives, later the TOPS Class 71, and the Class 12 diesel shunters disappearing, both classes moved away.

The electro-diesels displaced in their turn by BR diesel shunters, a BR Class 08 is active here in 2016. The disused catenary systems removed in 1975 after becoming surplus to requirements with the withdrawal of the Class 71 locomotives, some of its support poles survive at the yard's eastern entrance.

A long time feature of Hoo Junction were the Type 3, later TOPS Class 33 diesel-electric locomotives. Known to enthusiasts as the "Cromptons", they were to become synonymous with the yard and indeed the Southern Region as a whole. Regularly used on most workings, one duty for the class was as the motive power for the APCM block cement trains to Uddington in south Scotland. Originating from Cliffe cement works, the Class 33's were to be seen on these working as far north as Scotland on the East Coast Main Line.

Retirement for the Class 33's starting in 1985, they lingered on as part of the EWS fleet until 1998, and after the running of farewell specials, some as far away as Scotland, the "Cromptons" finally departing Hoo Junction in December 1998, their final duties on engineering trains were then handed over to Brush Class 31 locomotives.

The yard has been visited by a variety of diesel locomotives since BR days, causing much excitement to enthusiasts was the 1977 visit by a an exotic Western Region Class 52 diesel-hydraulic locomotive, *"Western Venturer"*. Now mostly the domain of North American designs, particularly the General Motors Class 66 locomotives, some ex-BR locomotives, the Classes 47, 57, and 60 of Freightliner, Colas Rail and GBRF can occasionally be seen here. The General Motors Class 70 heavy haul diesel locomotives, latest in a long line of freight locos to work here, are often to be seen laying over at the yard after working engineer's trains.

The yard also used for the breaking of life expired rolling stock, the 1980's saw the wholesale slaughter of ex-SR 4SUB multiple units here. Accidents could also occur and rail staff were injured in chemical spillages from container wagons in October 1986 and May 1987.

Training now an important function for the yard, UKRS Training Ltd provide instruction for rail staff here. The scene in December 1990 of a major training exercise, with the emergency services taking part, a collision between a car and train at a mock level crossing was simulated here.

In 2016, the yard now operated by DB Schenker Rail UK, their Class 08 diesel shunter is used for the re-marshalling of trains and together with light engine movements, the yard now sees up to 55 weekly train movements.

Engineers train stabled at Hoo Junction on 7th April 2011. Author

Now mostly aggregate trains, these workings are bound for Whitemoor yard, Eastleigh works or Hither Green.

Network Rail another user of Hoo Junction, it is now the main centre for their Southern area's engineering operations; their yellow liveried Class 73 electro-diesel locomotives and engineering trains are often seen here waiting at the engineer's sidings to collect plant and repair materials from storage compounds.

Looking into the future, should Crossrail extend into Kent, land has been safeguarded at Hoo Junction for the franchise's train maintenance depot.

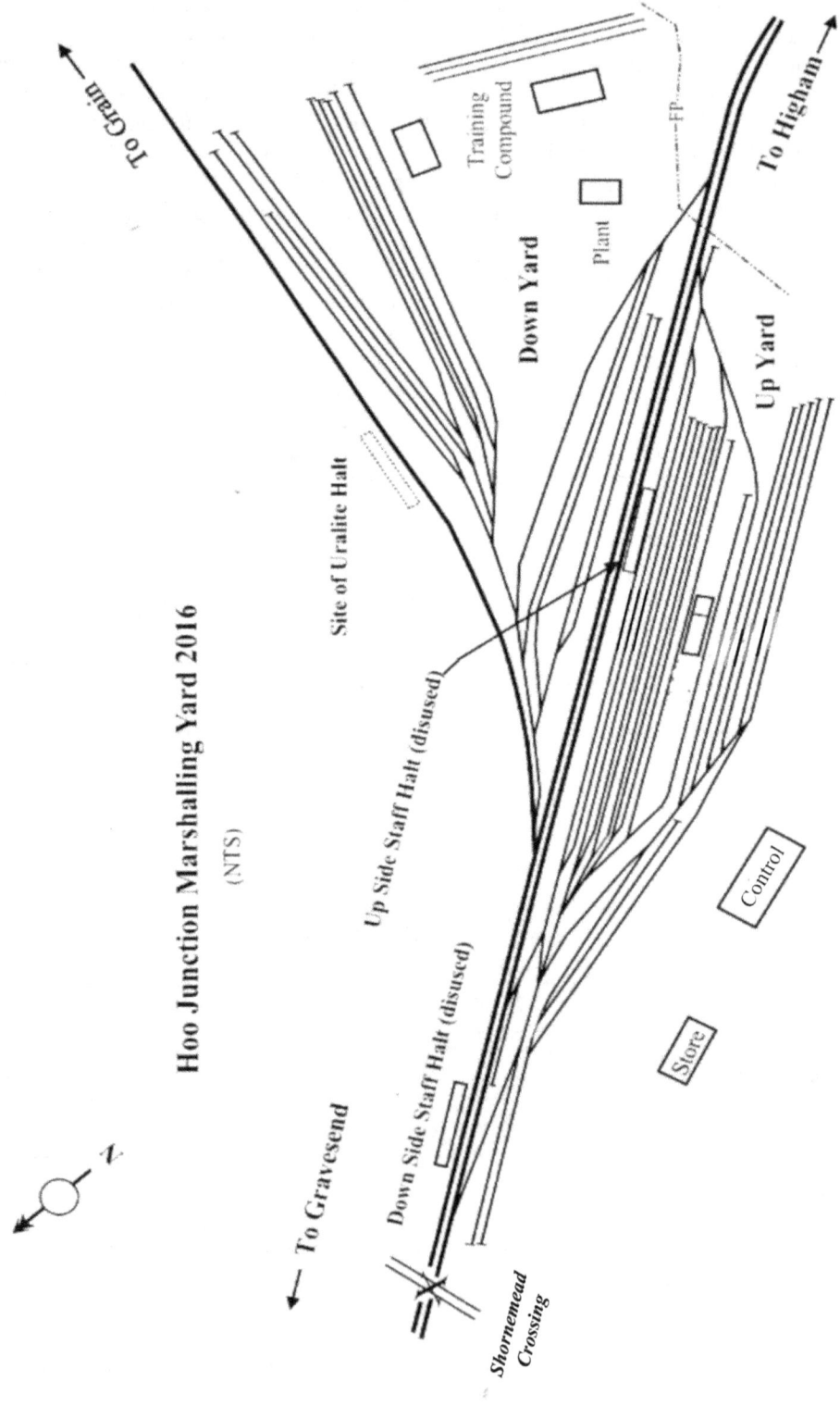

Class 73 electro-diesel No. 73139 passes Hoo Junction control room with a train of Grampus wagons on 3rd October 1982. Paul Bartlett.

A Z Class 0-8-0 tank locomotive. Examples of the type were used at Hoo Junction for shunting before the arrival of diesel locomotives. G.J Morris

The yard's Class 09 diesel shunter No. 09024 marshall's a Foster Yeoman aggregate hopper wagon train in 1996. The Class 09 are higher geared than their Class 08 brethren, this enabling them to undertake goods trip workings, the gantry for the former DC overhead catenary can be seen above the loco. Author.

Between Downs and Thames - Railways of Gravesend, the Hoo Peninsular and Isle of Grain

Class 33/2 "The Burma Star" leaves Hoo Junction in 1993 with a ballast train. Narrower than other locomotives of the type, the Class 33/2 locomotives were designed to work through the restricted width tunnels on the Hastings line. Author

PQA MAT car transporter wagon at the yard on 28th November 1987. Paul Bartlett.

Coal hopper wagon seen on the 19th of June 1983. Paul Bartlett

Plasser-Thurer Universal tamping machine at Hoo Junction on 6th February 1988. Paul Bartlett.

Hoo Junction training compound in 2006. The short platform name board displays the word "Hoo". Author.

Status 2016 : Open, operated by DB Schenker Rail UK

Location map reference : 1C

Opened: February 1928

Operating companies: SR, BR, EWS, D.B Schenker

Singlewell Infrastructure Maintenance Depot (IMD)

Singlewell IMD on 21st April 2009 looking west towards Ebbsfleet. Author

Operated by a subsidiary of Network Rail, Network Rail (High-Speed), the Integrated Maintenance Depot (IMD), opened in May 2007, carries out maintenance operations here on behalf of HS1 Ltd, the lines leaseholders.

Situated to the south of the A2 trunk road, this one kilometre long complex at Singlewell provides a 24 hour maintenance facility for the whole of HS1 and is home to the following departments:

Track and signalling
Control and communications systems
Power supply systems (UK Power Networks also have facilities here.)
Civil Engineering
Staff Training

Comprised of two buildings providing 3,600 square metres of accommodation, each has a discrete function. The smaller of the two, a maintenance shed, it is used by track repair vehicles while accommodation for offices and workshops is provided by the larger of the two buildings. Berthing sidings for materials unloading and plant refuelling are located towards the eastern end of the Down Singlewell freight loop.

When the CTRL Act was passed in 1996, the need for a CTRL IMD was accepted and with eight potential sites identified, three of which being local, these were Singlewell, Church Path Pit at Northfleet and the Swanscombe Peninsular. With the last two having the advantage of being close to Ebbsfleet, Swanscombe was considered the most likely site as it was then in use for the stabling and minor servicing of the CTRL Phase 2 rail construction vehicles.

However, the line's freehold owner, London & Continental Railways, favoured the Singlewell site as it could be accessed by rail from the freight sidings there. When Railtrack became involved in the CTRL project, the requirement for a separate IMD was deleted. Later, when realising that the German built Multi Purpose Vehicles (MPV) were over-size for the British C1 loading gauge and therefore limited to operating on HS1, the IMD was re-instated.

Although the IMD site includes an area for the laying out of new points and turnouts, permanent way maintenance not coming under its remit, this is dealt with from Hoo Junction. Neither does train maintenance or servicing take place here, Eurostars being maintained at Temple Mills depot in east London, the Class 395 Javelins are maintained and serviced at Ashford.

Construction costs for the IMD being in the order of £10 million, they included relocation of an electrical substation and parkland restitution.

The maintenance building as seen on 1st February 2011 with MPV vehicles in the berthing sidings. Author.

A view across the track maintenance yard on the 1st of February 2011. Author.

Also seen on 1st February 2011 is the office and workshop building. Author.

Locomotives, Carriages and Multiple Units

What follows is an overview of the locomotives, carriages and electric multiple units that have worked at one time or another on either the railways of Gravesham or the Hoo peninsular. Intended as a sampling of the more common motive power and rolling stock that the local railways have seen, for more detailed information on locomotives and items of rolling stock, a number of very good and informative publications are listed in the bibliography.

Background

Most of the early railway companies had little or no manufacturing facilities, their locomotives and rolling stock usually being purchased from contractors, this was also true of the G&RR, who did, however, undertake their own maintenance and servicing at Strood. Absorption of the G&RR by the SER and its later integration into the NKR brought new locomotives to the area. Amongst these were some Nasmyth long boiler 4-2-0 locomotives and No. 92, a member of this Class, later converted to a Crampton type, is known to have worked locally.

With the coming of the SER in 1846, their first Locomotive Superintendent, James l'Anson Cudworth, took control of locomotive affairs. Notable for inventing a fire box which enabled coal to be burned instead of coke, it was under his supervision that the SER opened Ashford Works in 1847.

Although the "Coffee Pot" of 1850, a diminutive locomotive partially constructed at Bricklayers Arms could technically lay claim to the title, officially locomotive construction began with the "Hastings" Class of 1853, Ashford's manufacturing facilities became complete when wagon and carriage building were transferred from Bricklayers Arms.

Considered sufficient for the SER's relatively short distance passenger services, early carriages of either of four or six fixed wheeled design were a type built here for many years. Some of this stock having long lives, an SER built van of 1845 was in service until 1929.

The first bogie coaches appearing in 1878, they were only used on the boat train services, the long suffering suburban passenger having to wait until 1880 for this advance when Richard Mansell introduced an experimental "close coupled" nine carriage set for the North and Mid Kent lines. Achieving his aim of increasing seating capacity by squeezing a nine car train within the length of its eight car predecessor, comfort wasn't the priority with this stock and it was the lowly 3rd class passengers who paid the price, these unfortunates being compressed into compartments of just 5 foot 3 inches wide. Long-lived, some of this stock came to a dramatic end when destroyed in a train wreck sequence in the 1928 film, "The Wrecker".

Up until its absorption into the SE&CR in 1899, the SER went on to produce a range of competent, if small locomotives, some prominent examples being Cudworth's 2-2-2 "Mail" engines of 1861 and Stirling's long lived 1881 O Class 0-6-0.

The LC&DR, also starting with a rather mixed bag of motive power purchased secondhand locomotives when required, this was true of *Æolus,* the locomotive that hauled the first LC&DR train through Gravesham on the 3rd of December 1860. A 4-4-0 Stephenson design, *Æolus* was originally built for the Turkish Smyrna-Aidan Railway.

By 1862 the LC&DR had opened a locomotive works at Longhedge, Battersea and with a carriage works soon following, William Martley, then at the helm as Locomotive Superintendent, the first locomotives built here to his design were the *Enigma* Class, of 1869. Some fine designs were produced by both companies, and a significant LC&DR express passenger type to regularly work trains through Gravesham was the Class M 4-4-0 locomotives. Originally supplied in 1877 by Neilson of Glasgow, the design was perpetuated until 1901. Later examples, the Class's M1, 2 and 3, incorporating progressive improvements, were built at Longhedge works.

The LC&DR's precarious financial position precluded building numerous bogie coaches, and like the SER, the first of the type appeared on the prestigious boat train services. However, four and six wheeled carriages were to continue in use on local, main line and suburban services well into the period of the SR in the 20th century.

Large scale rationalisation of locomotive and carriage manufacturing beginning with the formation of the SE&CR, manufacturing was centred on Ashford while Longhedge Works was relegated to undertaking light repairs.

Despite a difficult personal life, Harry Wainwright, the SE&CR's first Locomotive and Carriage Superintendent, went on to produce a range of designs that are amongst the most elegant steam locomotives built in this country. Two class's of these handsome locomotives, the C Class 0-6-0 goods engines and the H Class 0-4-4 passenger tanks had long local associations and remained in service until the end of steam in North Kent.

A major carriage upgrade undertaken by the SE&CR being the fitting of electric lighting to the older SER carriages and most LC&DR carriage stock, the brilliance of the tungsten lamp replaced the dim glow of gas and kerosene lamps. Half of all carriages having been fitted electric lighting by 1910, nevertheless, in 1930 the SR still had over 1,000 vehicles lit by oil lamps.

Another advance, first introduced by the SER in 1897 and a major improvement to the comfort of SE&CR passengers was the provision of carriage steam heating.

SE&CR carriage building methods, however, continued to be traditional. Differing little from the methods of road carriage construction, they continued to use wooden panelling fixed to hardwood frames, thus making them both fragile and flammable. Also perpetuated was the primitive chain coupling, it's continuing use allowing trains to separate in accidents.

With the inception of the Southern Railway in 1923, Richard Maunsell, then the SE&CR's Locomotive and Carriage Superintendent, was appointed as the role of the Southern's Chief Mechanical Engineer. During his reign a step forward in safety was taken, when the Buckeye semi-automatic coupling, a design that inhibits carriage overriding in accidents, was introduced to boat train stock.

All of these being regular local visitors, Maunsell's competent locomotive designs included the N and U Classes 2-6-0 mixed traffic engines and the superb Schools Class 4-4-0 express passenger locomotives. Electrification in the 1930's bringing new trains, calling them new, was however, a misnomer. Mostly rebuilds of ex-steam stock wooden carriages bodies, it wasn't until the 1938 introduction of the 2HAL multiple units that a purpose designed electric multiple-unit appeared. The work of O.V.S. Bulleid, successor to Richard Maunsell, Bulleid was to bring revolution to the Southern Railways locomotive and carriage designs. One of his groundbreaking locomotive designs with local connections the Light Pacifics, they appeared on the Chatham line's express and semi-fast services from the late 1940's. Another Bulleid design seen locally on more mundane workings were the powerful austerity Q1 0-6-0 freight locomotives of 1942.

With the 1948 nationalisation came a movement towards more standardisation, and introducing the faster acting electro pneumatic brake into carriage stock, came the new EPB electric multiple units of 1951. Remaining the mainstay of local and suburban passenger services, this class lasted into the 1990's. Another radical design, was Bulleid's 1949 unique, if experimental double deck electric multiple units.

With electrification of the Kent Coast lines completed by 1959, new electric multiple units came into service. Configured on the 1951 BR Mk I carriage, these, together with the introduction of electric and diesel locomotives, ended steam traction locally in 1962. With the failure of the 1955 modernisation plan, a dearth of new motive power and rolling stock provision was inevitable and it was to be 1993 before a new design of suburban passenger stock appeared, the 1980's designed Networkers.

The rail privatisation's of 1996 bringing a flow of cash into the railways, the local TOC, Connex South Eastern capitalised by purchasing new multiple units, the Electrostar Classes 375 and 376. Together with the Networkers, these classes now form the backbone of local and medium distance services on the "classic" lines. With freight services also privatised, North American General Motors diesel locomotives have now largely displaced homegrown designs.

Opening in November 2007, Ebbsfleet International station has brought Paris and Brussels only four hours away by using the 186 mph Class 373 Eurostars. The latest in a long line of multiple units, the revolutionary Hitachi Class 395 units have since November 2009 provided Gravesend with high-speed services to St Pancras via Ebbsfleet.

The G&RR's locomotive works and carriage shed was at Strood, and here, both repairs and servicing took place. Coke was also produced here, which along with anthracite, was the only fuel meeting the requirements of legislation that stated a steam locomotive was to "consume its own smoke".

G&RR long boiler Stephenson "patentee" locomotive of 1844

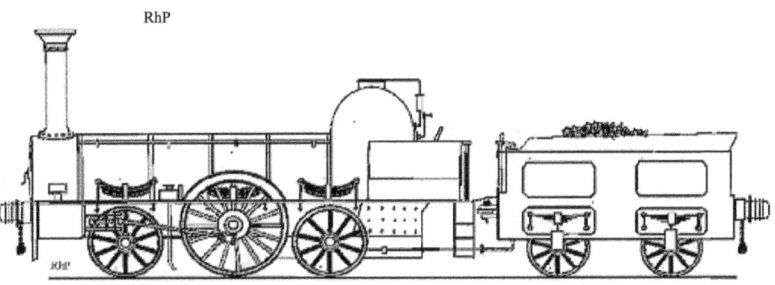

Three new steam locomotives were ordered by the G&RR from Robert Stevenson & Co on 26th February 1844 and before entering service, all were given names recalling British naval victories and those bestowed by the Admiral commanding Chatham Dockyard *Trafalgar, St Vincent* and *Camperdown,* by March 1845 they had been joined by *Van Tromp,* a Fossick-Hackworth outside cylinder variant.

Supplied as 2-2-2 locomotives, all of the examples were later rebuilt as 4-2-0's, excessive oscillation having made the original wheel arrangement unsatisfactory. All of long boiler design, this was a response to firebox and chimney overheating problems encountered during the longer journeys then being undertaken with the success of railway travel.

Ending their careers on the G&RR and North Kent Railway, all except for the locomotive sold to the Leopold Railway were moved away to the Ashford and Hastings local services. None surviving, *Van Tromp* finishing its days in 1862 at Maidstone as a stationary boiler, *St Vincent*, withdrawn in November 1878 was the last in service. A similar although later design of long boiler locomotive, the North Eastern Railway Class 1001 of 1852, has been preserved and can be seen at the NRM.

Appearing in 1869, the *Enigma* Class were the first in a long line of locomotives and carriages built at the Longhedge works of the LC&DR.

LC&DR *Enigma* Class of 1869.

Constructed to a design of William Martley, it had been the intention to call these the *Premier* Class. However, as their building coincided with the period of financial difficulties that followed the collapse of the LC&DR's bank, Overend, Gurney and Co, there was considerable difficulty in raising the funds to complete them.

Martley being reputed to have said to the LC&DR's Chairman, George Watson Milles, that *"it was an enigma to him how they had been built at all"* it was this remark that resulted in the name of *Enigma* being bestowed on the class.

As was the practice of the early LC&DR, all three of the class were given names, the other two being called *Mermaid* and *Lothair* after the naming of *Enigma* itself. With its smaller driving wheels *Enigma* was used on express goods workings whilst her younger sisters, both having larger diameter driving wheels, were normally used for passenger duties. When William Kirtley became the LC&DR's Locomotive Superintendent in 1874, all of the company's locomotives traded their names for numbers, the *Enigmas* became numbered as 50/51/52 of the L Class.

Regular performers on the Chatham main line, they occasionally worked the Flushing boat trains. A long lived design, when becoming extinct in 1906, the first two members of the class had each recorded over a million miles of service.

A familiar sight in Gravesham at the turn of the 19th and 20th centuries, this design by James Stirling was the SER's first significant class of standard passenger tank locomotives. Not the first of their type, they were preceded by the short-lived Class M "Gunboat" 0-4-4 tanks of 1877. A class of nine locomotives, these were normally restricted to working in the London suburbs.

SER Q Class of 1881

Previously placing little reliance on tank engines, the Q Class established the type as reliable performers across the SER. Favoured by most UK railways for suburban and local passenger work, the 0-4-4 side tank design was both safe and practical, the combination of a trailing bogie and four large driving wheels making them stable at relatively high-speeds, water tanks above the driving wheels gave extra adhesion.

By dispensing with a tender, tank engines could easily run in either direction, an advantage at busy termini. Based on a type Stirling had built for the Glasgow and South Western Railway, they were perpetuated over a period of 16 years with the last example appearing in 1897. Acquiring a reputation as indifferent steam producers, some were rebuilt by the SE&CR as the improved Q1 Class of 1902. Based at Slades Green depot, those Q & Q1 locomotives working local passenger services from there were well thought of and were consequently kept in immaculate condition.

In April 1917 some of the class went to foreign parts when lent to the GWR to relieve motive power shortages there. Gradually withdrawn during the 1920's, the last survivor of the Q Class went in March 1929, the Q1 Class becoming extinct in June 1930.

The LC&DR adopted 0-4-4 tank locomotives for their stopping passenger trains earlier than the SER, the first of the type into service being the A Class of 1875. Designed by Kirtley as an improved version of the A Class, the R Class were better able to maintain speed on the LC&DR's heavily loaded suburban and local passenger workings. Popular with railway enthusiasts, they were known as the "Bobtails".

Performing both competently and unsung on the LC&DR and later the SE&CR's local and suburban passenger trains, these were to be their main duties until electrification of these services in the inter-war years relegated them to branch line and secondary duties.

Push-pull fitted examples of these locos were to be seen working local passenger trains on both the Hundred of Hoo and West Street branches well into the 1950's, and an example of the R Class holds the distinction of inaugurating push-pull

LC&DR R Class of 1888

No. 31658 takes water at Farningham Road in 1951. Barry Diplock

operation on the Hundred of Hoo branch in 1914. By the early years of the 20th century, an increase in performance again needed, the SE&CR rebuilding some of the R Class with H Class boilers, these became the R1 Class of 1910.

When withdrawn in 1955, R Class No. 207 (BR No. 31666) was the last surviving locomotive of purely LC&DR origin in service and by 1956, all examples of both the R and R1 Classes had succumbed to the cutters torch.

Synonymous with local goods services until the end of steam traction, the genesis of the 0-6-0 C Class came with the formation of the SE&CR. Partly based on the LC&DR B2 Class, they provided the greater motive power needed for the railways increasing goods business, as their ability to maintain timetabled goods trains speeds with ease avoided disruption of the system's intensive passenger services by slow moving goods workings.

Although primarily goods engines, their excellent acceleration and free steaming characteristics allowed them to work local passenger trains, excursions to Allhallows, hop-picker specials and occasionally grander duties such as the "Continental" boat trains to Gravesend West. In company with the N, U and Q1 Class's, they provided the staple motive power for the area's goods workings for over sixty years.

Their particular duties being on the West Street and Longfield dust sidings workings, they were not supplanted locally until the arrival of the "Crompton" diesel locomotives in the early 1960's. One of the class having the misfortune to fall into a bomb crater at Abbey Wood in February 1944, after retrieval, it was able to proceed under its own

SE&CR C Class of 1900

No. 592 at the Bluebell Railway 30th May 2015 Author.

steam such was the robustness of the type. However, by 1962, the class was all but extinct and the last example, No. 31592, being taken out of traffic in 1966, she is now happily preserved at the Bluebell Railway where with her copper and bright work now highly burnished, as No. 592 she is painted in the magnificent Wainwright livery of gleaming lined Brunswick green. Achieving fame in 1999, No. 592 appeared as the *"The Green Dragon"* in the television film, "The Railway Children".

Another elegant design from the Wainwright stable, the H Class was a more powerful successor to the SER Q Class. Made distinctive by their "pagoda" style cab roofs, a style unique to SE&CR locomotives, their first duties, like those of their predecessors, were on suburban and stopping passenger train workings.

Their boiler design in particular was very successful, so much so that it was fitted to some older locomotives of both constituents of the SE&CR to improve their performance. The electrification's of the 1920's and 30's seeing their transfer to secondary and branch line duties, a greater versatility came with their fitment for "push-pull" or auto train passenger workings, and it was in this mode of operation on the Hundred of Hoo and West Street branches that they are remembered by local enthusiasts.

Another indication of their abilities came during the 1930's, when, like the C class 0-6-0's, they occasionally provided the motive power for the Batavier Line "Continental" boat train services from Victoria to Gravesend West.

An unusual duty for the class during WWII being as temporary air raid shelters at both

SE&CR H Class of 1904

H Class No. 31522 at Ashford in the early 1950's. Barry Diplock

Dover and Ramsgate loco sheds, it was during this conflict that two examples were transferred to Scotland, their immaculate condition showing the local crews affection for the class.

With the 1960's rundown of steam services all had gone locally by December 1961 and by January 1964 just one example, No. 31263 remained in service. After a spell at the ill-fated Ashford Steam Centre, this loco is now preserved in full Wainwright livery on the Bluebell Railway.

As the first of the locomotive designs of Richard Maunsell's SE&CR standardisation programme, these two cylinder locomotives used those principles for improved efficiency in their design laid down by the foremost British locomotive designer of the day, J. G. Churchward, of the GWR.

Introduced to replace the ageing 0-6-0 locomotive types that were by then struggling with the railway's increasing heavy goods loads, on steep gradients such as Sole Street Bank, these mixed traffic locomotives could also be used on passenger trains should the need arise.

Ready for construction in 1915, WWI delayed their first deliveries until 1917. Adopted by the SR as their standard mixed traffic engine, examples of this 2-6-0 continued to be built until 1934. Giving greater route availability, higher running speeds and better fuel economy a three cylinder variant, the N1 Class, was introduced in 1922. Both types more than fulfilling their design remit, they were equally at home on goods trains at Hoo Junction or on summer weekend North Kent line excursion trains to the Kent Coast.

Work for the class declined following completion of the 1959 Kent Coast Electrification

SE&CR N Class of 1917

No. 819 temporarily fitted with a stovepipe chimney due to a shortage of normal types in the 1920's. Authors collection

and after moving away from the Chatham main line, the last example was withdrawn by BR in 1966.

Just one locomotive, No. 1874 escaped the scrap man and now undergoing restoration on the Swanage Railway, No. 1874 previously saw service on the Mid Hants Railway from 1977.

Using an inherently unstable mixture of pebbles and flints as ballast, this was a formation, that combined with weak bridges, restricted locomotive axle loading's to 17½ tons on the LC&DR main line, thus making it unable to accept the most powerful of the SE&CR's express engines, the L1 4-4-0 Class.

With the SE&CR's decision of 1917 to concentrate the Dover and Folkestone boat trains at Victoria post-war making an increase in express passenger locomotive power imperative for the Chatham route; with major civil engineering works to strengthen bridges unacceptable in wartime, a solution was found by modifying some of the existing E Class 4-4-0's. Then the largest locomotive class allowed on the route, an improvement in performance was achieved by fitting larger cylinders, boiler and firebox. Also undergoing weight reductions as part of their modifications, they were-classified as the E1 Class. Prone to slipping on banks, this disastrous occurrence sometimes threw the contents of the firebox out of the chimney.

SE&CR E1 Class of 1920.

No. 179 shown above was first of class, and in November 1920, the loco was specially prepared to work the train carrying the Unknown Warrior to London. However, due to an unfortunate breakdown, another locomotive had to be substituted. Settling into their work, the E1 Class became the usual allocation for working the route's most prestigious trains, the "Granville Express" and the Royal Train.

The upgrading of the Chatham route in the 1920's seeing 4-6-0 types take over the route's principal express workings, the E1's were relegated to weight restricted routes such as the Sheerness branch. Surviving intact into the BR era, they worked summer specials locally until 1958. Relegated to secondary duties they bowed out in November 1961. None survive.

Not a native design, the N15 Class 4-6-0 *King Arthurs* were the largest of the Southern Railway's express engines before arrival of the 1926 *Lord Nelson* Class. A product of Robert Urie, the Chief Mechanical Engineer of the London & South Western Railway, a batch was sent to the Chatham main line in 1925 to remove the need for piloting the small 4-4-0 locomotives then used on the increasingly heavy passenger trains.

Fitted with modified cabs and smaller fixed wheel tenders to meet the eastern division's loading gauge, they were put to work on the Chatham route's principal expresses. After initially returning some indifferent performances, modified to improve both steaming and reliability, they then gave sterling service.

In 1926 they were the first locomotives in the UK to receive smoke deflectors. Vertical plates fitted to the locomotive's smoke-box sides, these lifted smoke above the loco cab to improve the crew's vision. An odd experiment, carried out in November 1940, was the fitting of three small "stovepipe" chimneys to No. 783 *Sir Gillimere*. Set

N15 King Arthur Class of 1919

"Sir Bors De Ganis". ELC Postcards

in a triangular formation, these were supposed to reduce the exhausts visibility from the air, but being found unsuccessful, the experiment ended.

Introduction of the Light Pacifics to the Chatham line's express workings in the late 1940's seeing their move to lesser duties, they would, however, often deputise should a Pacific be unavailable. After electrification of the Chatham route, all moved away and the last example, No. 30777 *Sir Lamiel*, withdrawn in 1962, is now preserved at the Great Central Railway.

SR U Class of 1928

The U Class was in part a rebuild of the ill-starred SE&CR K Class of 2-6-4 express passenger tank locomotives. Known to posterity as the "Rolling Rivers" due to their poor riding characteristics, these tank engines took their names from rivers in the SE&CR's territory. Comprising twenty members, it was imperfections in their suspension design that was thought to be the main contributory cause of the Sevenoaks rail disaster of the 24th of August 1927. A terrible accident, 13 people were killed and many injured when *River Cray* derailed at speed near Dunton Green.

Then withdrawn, the entire class were re-constructed as two cylinder 2-6-0 tender locomotives to cure their riding problems and re-classified as the U Class, they were eventually increased to 50 examples by new builds.

A further development the twenty-one strong three cylinder U1 Class, this was Maunsell's last mogul design. Working on the Chatham main line's semi-fast passenger services until WWII, the conflict saw their transfer to the Central Section of the SR where their additional power was urgently needed on goods workings. Returned to

U Class No. 31616 awaits it's fate at Wards scrap yard at Grays in 1964. Jack Willis

the Chatham route immediately post-war, they were set to work on heavy de-mobilisation troop trains and Kent coast passenger workings. Often appearing at Gravesend, both classes saw service on North Kent line express goods workings and Kent coast excursions. Leaving the area in 1962 at the end of local steam, all had gone by 1964. Two survive, No. 31618 on the Bluebell Railway and No. 31625 on the Mid Hants Railway.

Primarily a passenger railway, the massive increase in freight workings precipitated by WWII put a great pressure on the SR. Possessing few specialised goods engines, more goods locomotives urgently required, the Southern's CME, Oliver Bulleid, elected to produce a a new class of locomotive rather than build more examples of existing designs.

Reflecting the compromises needed in wartime to minimise the use of scarce raw materials and save labour, his response, the no-frills Q1 design of 1942 was loosely based on Maunsell's Q Class 0-6-0 locomotive of 1938. Perhaps not the most handsome of his steam locomotive designs, these 0-6-0 locomotives were, however, the most powerful of their kind to work in the UK, delivering a respectable tractive effort of 30,080 lbf.

As a wartime austerity design, they were not intended to last beyond the end of hostilities, but such was their usefulness they remained in service until 1966. Locally undertaking duties on tank trains to the Isle of Grain and the Hoo Peninsular

SR O1 Class of 1942. *Argo photo store*

No. 33040 at an un-identified British Railways Goods depot. Authors collection

and goods working at Hoo Junction, they could also be seen deputising for the H Class tanks on the Hundred of Hoo branch line passenger services. Occasionally straying outside the Southern Region, they appeared amongst other places at Tilbury on inter-regional freights and in 1962, it was a Q1 in charge of a tank train at Milton that was the last steam locomotive I saw in BR service in Gravesham. Now preserved, residing on static display at the National Railway Museum, York after a long period of service on the Bluebell Railway, is the first of class, No. 33001.

This was the last class of conventional steam locomotive built by the Southern Railway. With a lower axle loading than their larger sisters, the Merchant Navy Class, the Light Pacifics could be used on a wider variety of routes, these included the Chatham and North Kent lines. Although identical in design, depending on subclass, they were named after Battle of Britain airfields, personalities, squadrons or picturesque West Country locations.

Well liked by their crews, they provided the motive power for the principal express passenger workings on the Chatham main line until 1959.

Another unorthodox design from the Bulleid stable; conceived during WWII to save on precious raw materials, improve efficiency and reduce maintenance they had a number of novel features including chain driven valve gear, an all welded steel firebox and a steam reverser.

Also sporting an "air smoothed" casing which gave rise to their nickname, the "Spam Cans", this allowed cleaning by mechanical carriage washers. These idiosyncratic features, however led to problems in service and many of the class were

SR Light Pacific Class of 1945.

No. 34007 'Wadebridge' seen at Alton on 26th June 2010. Author

rebuilt in the 1950's to a more conventional form. Transferred away following the Kent Coast electrification, the class remained in service until 1967 on duties both in the southwest and on main line expresses from London Waterloo. On 30th January 1965, No. 34051 *Winston Churchill,* performed the classes' most famous duty when heading the funeral train of its namesake.

Several have been preserved and examples such as No. 34067 *Tangmere* and No. 34036 *Braunton* are active on local rail tours.

A mixed-traffic type, these small Bo-Bo locomotives were equally at home on passenger or freight duties and with a power output of 2,300 hp, they were able to handle the heaviest duties with ease. Able to climb Sole Street Bank with scarcely a drop in speed, they were the motive power of choice for prestigious trains such as the *Night Ferry* and *Golden Arrow* at the end of steam traction.

Operating exclusively from the Southern Region's 750 volt DC traction supply, the rostering of their duties could be problematical, any engineering works requiring traction supply isolation meaning that they were unable to use that route. Also used for shunting duties at Hoo Junction marshalling yard and other Southern Region yards, they collected power from 750 volt DC catenaries by use of their pantographs. The risk of electrocution ever present when on the main line, their brake pipes and jumper cables, nicknamed "bagpipes" were placed at high level.

When the introduction of the Class 73 electro-diesel locomotives in 1962 began to displace them from their duties, ten of the class, the short lived Class 74 were converted to electro-diesels in an

British Railways E5000, later Class 71 electric locomotives of 1958

No. E5011 at a Selhurst depot open day, 16th September 1973. Authors collection.

effort to improve route availability. However, as more of the Southern Region lines' converted to electrical multiple unit operation, little work was left for the class and in 1977, after brief working lives, all 14 surviving members were withdrawn *en bloc*.

The lone survivor, the first of class No. E5001, now part of the National Collection, it is currently on loan to the Barrow Hill Engine Shed Society.

The workhorse of the Southern Region, the Birmingham Railway & Carriage Wagon Type 3 diesel-electrics could be seen on virtually all of the regions duties. Known to railway enthusiasts as the "Cromptons" in an allusion to their Crompton-Parkinson electrical system, with the introduction of the TOPS rolling stock management scheme of the late 1960's, they became the Class 33. Produced as three major variants, these were the Class 33/0 standard locomotives, Class 33/1, a push-pull fitted variant and a narrow bodied version, the Class 33/2 "Slim Jims" designed for working the restricted gauge Hastings line.

Used locally on a variety of workings, their duties on the Hundred of Hoo branch included tank trains, container trains, aggregate and cement trains, and up until December 1961 they could be seen on the branch's passenger services.

In Gravesham, as well as working gypsum and coal trains to Northfleet cement works, they were also to be seen on general freight and engineering duties. After a working life of nearly 40 years, before they were phased out in 1998 by the new

British Railways Type 3, later Class 33 diesel-electric locomotives of 1960

Class 33/2 No. 33208 at Ashford on 10th September 1994. Authors Collection.

EWS General Motors Class 66 locomotives, a number of farewell rail-tours were run by this popular class for rail enthusiast's. Fortunate to be a passenger on one of these, the "Robin Reliant" tour of 15th February 1997, Nos. 33051 and 33116 ran double-headed from Kings Cross to Scarborough via York. Thirty surviving into preservation, two are operated on the national network by the West Coast Railway Company.

British Railways Type JA later Class 73 Electro-Diesel locomotives of 1962

Class 73/2 No. 73210 "Selhurst" on the Mid Norfolk Railway. Author

Able to run as either electric locomotives powered from the DC 3rd rail or as diesel locomotives using their internal 600 HP engine, the class were originally intended for working parcels, freight or passenger duties on rail routes with non-electrified sections such as sidings and docks.

Once used extensively at Hoo Junction for train marshalling, Eurostar formerly retained two of these locomotives to rescue failed cross-channel Class 373 trains when these ran on the 3rd rail DC "classic" lines.

Allocated over the years to many duties, these have included hauling the Gatwick Express, use as rescue locomotives for failed trains on the former LS&WR main line and BR engineers trains. Some having now passed into preservation, a number are still operating on the national network for Network Rail and FOC's such as GB Railfreight, FM Rail and a charter company, Transmart Trains.

The class has seen a renaissance in recent years, three locomotives being fitted in 2013 with upgraded 1,600 HP engines for passenger duties. With a further batch to follow, such is the demand for these versatile locomotives, one of the class was bought back from preservation for main line duties.

With their high route availability an advantage, and in a far cry from their original mundane duties on the Southern Region of 1962, three of the re-engined locomotives have broken new ground by being assigned to the Caledonian Sleeper trains to Fort William.

British Railways Type 4, later Class 47 diesel-electric locomotives of 1962

Class 47/3 No. 47361 Peterborough 21st July 1997. Authors collection

With the end of steam traction planned for 1968, BR were in urgent need of a large fleet of powerful, lightweight Type 4 diesel-electric locomotives as replacements, and to evaluate the best design, two prototypes were built, *Lion* by AEI and *Falcon* by Brush.

However, with the end of steam looming and the new type 4 urgently needed, neither of these prototypes was selected for production. Retaining only a few features of the prototypes, the future Class 47 was quickly rushed into production.

Soon becoming regular visitors to Hoo Junction, with more than 500 of these 2,580 HP Co-Co locos built between 1962 and 1968, they were to become the largest class of BR built diesel locomotives. Soon proliferating into a number of sub-classes, the class 47/3, a variant fitted for slow speed working, was frequently rostered for the Northfleet cement works MGR coal and gypsum trains.

Introduced in 1998 were the up-engined Class 57. Occasionally visiting Hoo Junction, these more powerful rebuilds from Class 47 locos have the capability to rescue failed trains, and as such are fitted with a variety of couplings for use when acting as the so called Thunderbird" locomotives. Reflecting these duties, some have taken names from characters from the TV series such as *Brains* and *Parker*.

With eighty examples surviving and thirty still having mainline operational status, their operators include Colas Rail and Direct Rail Services.

Since 1996 there having been a seismic shift away from UK built locomotives to the products of North America, the seminal event starting this trend was Foster Yeoman's exasperation with the pitiful 69% availability of the Class 56 locomotives then rostered by BR for their aggregate trains. Unable to find a manufacturer in the UK who could offer a better locomotive, they turned to the US.

So it was in 1986 that Foster Yeoman imported four General Motors diesel locomotives modified to work on the UK rail network. Known as the Class 59, they were a revelation and when they achieved an availability of 99% in service, some of BR's other customers took note and acquired Class 59 locomotives for themselves.

EWS taking control of most of the UK rail freight business in 1996, they found the locomotive fleet they inherited from BR wanting. Most of it over 30 years old, its backbone, the 1960's built Class 47, they were struggling to achieve 65% availability were failing every 16 days on average.Following the success of the Class 59, EWS also purchased North American products. Ordering 250 Class 66 locomotives from General

General Motors Class 66 diesel-electric locomotives of 1998

Class 66/0 No. 66155 in DBS livery at Tilbury Town. Author

Motors in 1998, this was the largest UK locomotive purchase since the 1960's. Known as "Sheds" by enthusiasts, these 127 ton locomotives were a success from the start. A twelve powered axle, diesel-electric design, they are capable of a 95% availability with an average of 180 days between failures. Built as a number of variants including low geared heavy haulage and low emissions types, they undertake the majority of local freight workings.

Bringing locomotive matters up-to-date are the Power Haul Class 70 freight locomotives. Manufactured at the General Electric's, Erie, Pennsylvania plant and designed in collaboration with the North American owned Freightliner Group, these 135 ton, 3,690 HP diesel locomotives will eventually replace the last of the BR era heavy-haul locomotives.

Similar in appearance to the now extinct BR Class 58 locomotives, their unique cab shaped has been designed with input from train crews to achieve improvements in crash worthiness. Also a twelve powered axle design, they feature both regenerative braking and crew-cab air conditioning. More efficient and powerful than the Class 66, the extra 400 HP they enjoy over the latter achieves savings in fuel and crewing costs by allowing increases in train lengths.

Not without teething troubles, locomotive fires, seemingly caused by leaking fuel lines have been an issue. Currently operated by Colas Rail and Freightliner, twenty-one locomotives are in service

General Motors Class 70 heavy haul diesel-electric locomotives of 2009

No. 70008 in Freightliner livery at Tilbury east Junction. Author

and with a further nineteen ordered by the latter, they will join the solitary example previously on trial with the Turkish railways. Now delivered to the UK, this locomotive is allocated to the private owners pool.

Becoming frequent visitors to Hoo Junction, they are to be seen on aggregate block trains and engineers track panel workings.

It's outline taken from a contemporary poster advertising the railway's 1845 opening, a somewhat speculative drawing of a G&RR 2nd Class carriage is shown opposite.

A newspaper report of the time stating G&RR rains consisted of: *"four double ones, (carriages) two of each Class"* indicates the provision of 1st and 2nd Class accommodation only at opening, 3rd Class passenger trucks did not appear until later in the history of the G&RR, Herepath listing an income from 3rd class in 1846. Primarily a passenger railway, the provision of wagons for heavier items of luggage is evidenced by a newspaper report of 1845 that stated: *"The carriage or truck for luggage being also well freighted on each occasion"*

Early G&RR passengers enjoying covered carriages; journalists of the time referring to carriages with barred windows and lockable doors, this was something that would not have been feasible with open trucks. The hiring of carriages being a common practice for many early railways, there is no evidence for this on the G&RR.

A reflection of the dominance of road coach styles in railway carriages designs of 1845, the

Conjectural G&RR carriage of 1845

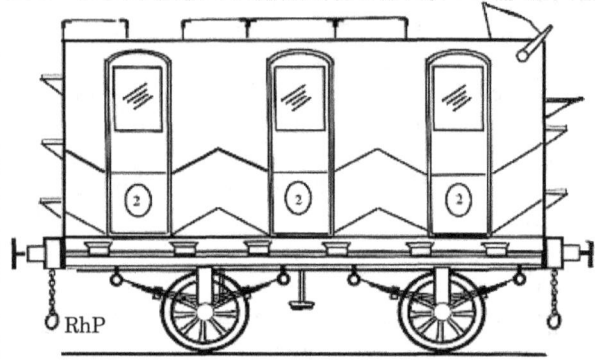

guards position echoed contemporary road coaching practice. Seated outside at roof height, in addition to his duties to passengers, the guard acted as a brakes-man in conjunction with the engine crew to stop the train. An indifferent system, it caused an accident on the Railways opening day.

Some G&RR carriages had long lives and in 1874, an ex G&RR 1st class, 24 seater carriage built by Wright, was still in service on the Canterbury & Whitstable Railway.

The early railway companies were not usually interested in catering for 3rd Class passengers, by and large preferring to convey the more affluent members of society and lucrative goods traffic, and until an Act of 1844 enforced its provision, 3rd Class travel was not usually guaranteed.

Where accommodation was provided for 3rd class it was often in open trucks similar to that shown opposite and in fact, at one time the SER removed the seats from 3rd Class trucks to encourage use of 2nd Class! Uncomfortable and draughty, they were sarcastically known as the "Stanhopes", a corruption of "Stand-ups".

They could be perilous to travel in, some of the examples built at Bricklayers Arms in 1847 having sides of only 4 feet in height; a convenient perch, this encouraged the foolhardy to sit there. An unwise practice, this sometimes led to fatal results when passengers collided with line side infrastructure.

However, they were an improvement on walking or riding on a horse-drawn carrier's wagon, the normal method of travel for the less well-off, the only drawback being enduring the locomotives exhaust.

Typical Open 3rd Class carriage of the 1850's

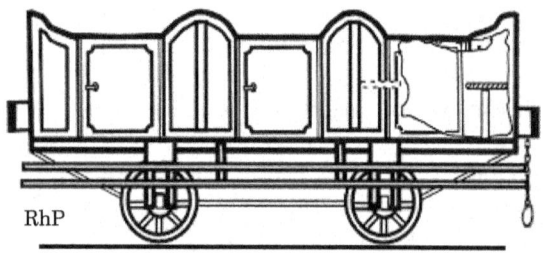

Lewis Gilbert, the local man we met earlier, experienced 3rd class travel from Gravesend in January 1850 and left us this description ¶.

"But the Company (The SER) were then strongly impressed that fresh air was most necessary for common people, so the 3rd Class had no covering at all. The partitions, according to my memory came up to the shoulder. When speed was obtained, it was necessary to put your head to one side to escape the winds, and when it rained to put up an umbrella !"

¶ *Gravesend Reporter 1911.*

A determination to regulate the nation's railways and reduce accidents was behind the 1844 Railway Act. Giving government the power to take over the railway companies, should they not heed its provisions. this legislation, amongst its other requirements, also proscribed for: *"the provision of at least one train a day each way at a speed of not less than 12 miles an hour including stops, which are to be made at all stations, and of carriages protected from the weather and provided with seats; for all which luxuries not more than a penny a mile might be charged"*.

Illustrated above is the SER's answer to this legislation, the "Parliamentary" 3rd. Usually run at inconvenient times, a same day 3rd Class return journey could not always be guaranteed. Without artificial light or heat and with only louvre's to provide light, travelling conditions were grim for the fifty-six persons seated on 12 inch wide wooden benches that were squeezed in around the sides and across the middle of these carriages.

Things did improve however, when the SER, bowing to public pressure, replaced the louvre's

SER closed 3rd carriage of the 1850's

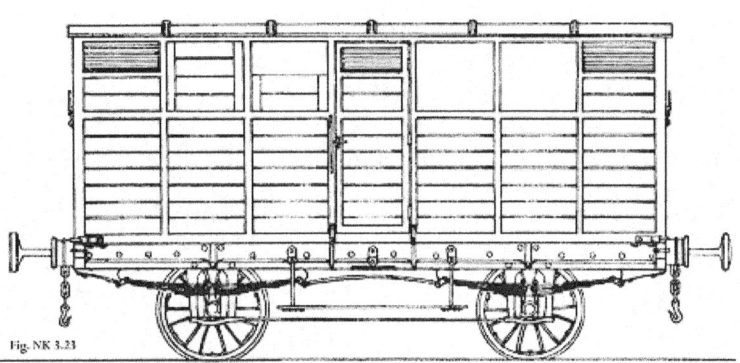

Drawing by J. Greaves South Eastern & Chatham Railway Society

with glazed windows. Various other carriage designs existing, another type used on the NKR was the eight wheeled articulated carriages responsible for the demolition of Gravesend's carriage shed in 1849.

Built by Adams, composed of two 4 wheeled carriages connected by a rubber sealed gangway, they were very intimate when fully loaded, some 120 passengers sitting arranged around the saloon's sides. These vehicles had long lives, with modified examples continuing to run on the NKR until the 1890's.

By way of a contrast to the 3rd class carriage depicted above, shown opposite is a contemporary 1st class carriage. Once again following the style of contemporary road coaches, these were exceptionally comfortable by the standards of the time.

1st Class carriages having separate compartments, each was provided with curtains, carpets, a sheepskin rug and six luxuriously upholstered seats. Illumination provided by day from drop-light glazed windows and an oil lamp by night, an advantage of 1st class travel from Gravesend was the warmth delivered by a personal foot warmer. Honouring the Duke of Wellington, Lord Warden of the Cinque Ports, these carriages were painted in "Wellington Brown".

Travelling conditions for 2nd class passengers were, however, decidedly more basic. Although having the luxury of glazed windows and spring suspension, seating was more basic. The wooden backs only coming up to shoulder height, just the

SER 1st class carriage of 1849

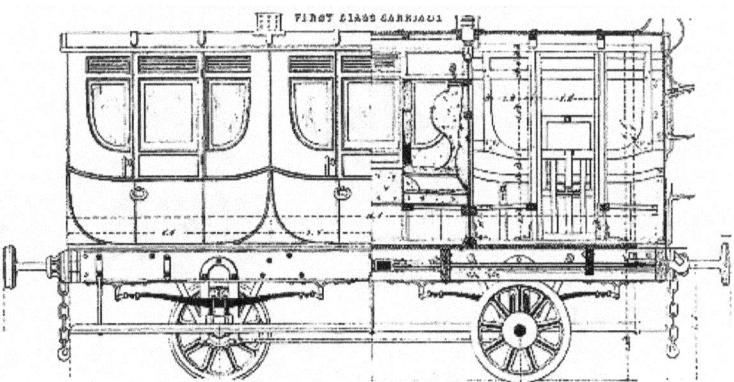

Drawing by J. Greaves South Eastern & Chatham Railway Society

seats themselves were upholstered and their fabric covering looking suspiciously like that of porter's trousers, it was described as "pantaloon". For lighting, open saloon carriages had but a single oil lamp, while those in compartment stock shared a lamp between two compartments.

Derisory, heating was supplied by the ubiquitous foot warmer at the rate of one per compartment for journeys of over 15 miles.

As witnessed by the picture of carriage No. 90 shown to the right, 3rd class travellers on the infant LC&DR had the benefit of both a roof and glazed windows. Not always as comfortable as they may have been, A. E. Ahrons, that noted commentator on railway affairs, said of LC&DR carriages: *"From what nether depths the 'Chatham' excavated most of its carriages, goodness only knows!"*

Obviously unimpressed, he then went on to describe the LC&DR's unheated carriages as *"dog-boxes"*. However, their carriages were soundly built, some specimens remaining in traffic for over 50 years.

Perpetually impoverished, the LC&DR provided illumination by feeble oil lamps, these were to remain a universal feature of LC&DR carriages until a few were experimentally fitted with the novelty of electric lighting in the 1890's.

Nevertheless, the LC&DR had a good safety record, a bonus that was partly due to the use of Westinghouse automatic air brakes on most passenger rolling stock. Some carriages, however,

LC&DR 3rd Class carriage of 1862 *SE&CR Society*

retained hand brakes well into the 20th Century.

Mindful of accidents, in 1871, two emergency rail ambulance vehicles were constructed. Each provided with beds, surgical instruments and an operating table, these could be summoned to give medical aid at serious railway incidents.

The family carriage was another interesting vehicle. Akin to a mobile Victorian parlour, these could be hired by the wealthy for their exclusive use. Also possessing the luxury of a lavatory, its use was denied to the servants who travelled in a separate compartment with the luggage and pets.

Built by Cravens of Sheffield, these carriages sat forty passengers in five compartments. Originally lit by oil lamps, they were later retro-fitted with gas lamps, the gas stored in cylinders beneath the carriage, this was railway manufactured from coal.

Once again possessing neither heating nor toilets, the latter did not appear until 1889 when James Stirling remodelled a few main line carriages to incorporate them.

Construction of SER carriages of this period was insubstantial and largely built of timber, flimsy *papier-mache* panelling was used on some carriages. Their braking systems originally non-automatic, by 1891 automatic vacuum brakes had started to be installed on some stock.

An unusual feature of these carriages was their composite teak and iron wheels. Introduced by Richard Mansell in 1861, they comprised teak segments set between rim and axle where they improved the ride and reduced the ringing sounds made by railway wheels of the period.

SER 2nd Class carriage of 1881 *SE&CR Society*

A. E. Ahrons, describing the motley processions of SER trains with their differing carriages heights and liveries as: *"a moving cavalcade of castellated walls"*, local and suburban trains of the SER made an entertaining sight. Liveries varying considerably the cream and salmon of the 1860's gave way in the late 1880's to a gold lined, purple lake.

Upholstery delineated by class, in 1902, Blue Tashmere was provided for 1st Class, Velvet for 2nd and Tapestry for 3rd.

Life expired carriage bodies often sold off for non-railway uses such as bungalows, cricket pavilions or hop pickers accommodation, some remain in use as homes today.

No. 91, illustrated here, a former four wheeled LC&DR coach of 1862 was a close contemporary of No. 90 seen on page 212. Once resplendent in the teak livery of the LC&DR, when discovered, it was painted a dull green. It's seating now long gone, 1st Class upholstery would have been blue with 2nd Class enjoying a dark red. De-mounted in the 1920's, this carriage body had been used as a chicken run at Cooling Castle, Kent and after removal from Cooling in the early 1980's, it was taken initially to the North Downs Steam Railway (NDSR) at Stone. After a period of storage there, with the amalgamation of the NDSR and TWERPS in 1996, No. 91 was moved to the Spa Valley Railway at Tunbridge Wells.

Moving once again since, it now resides on the Kent & East Sussex Railway, awaiting restoration.

LC&DR coach body at Cooling Castle June 1981 *Dave Fisher*

An unusual feature of some LC&DR carriages was the guards "ducket". A small glazed observation panel protruding from either side of the guard's accommodation, these gave a view along both sides of the train while in motion. Damaged when used on the narrower loading gauge of the SER, many duckets were removed at formation of the SE&CR.

Today, restored LC&DR carriages can be seen at the Bluebell Railway, the Kent & East Sussex Railway and the Isle of Wight Steam Railway.

Harmonisation and updating of the passenger rolling stock of the two companies forming the SE&CR was one of Harry Wainwright's priorities when coming to office and a distinctive style of carriage he introduced was the "birdcage" stock, a nickname it acquired from the glazed look-out superimposed above the guard's brake compartment.

Permanently coupled as three car sets, each set was composed of a brake, lavatory and composite brake lavatory coach. For the uninitiated, a composite coach is best described as a carriage having more than one class of compartment. A universal SE&CR type, examples of "birdcage" stock were occasionally to be found on the "Continental" boat trains to West Street and often on services to Gravesend Central.

An important introduction in these and contemporary carriages was steam heating. Operated by the fireman by a valve from the locomotive's boiler, this important, if soporific, comfort was not to become common until the 1920's when whispers of escaping steam from connecting pipes would indicate its presence.

SE&CR "Birdcage" carriage of 1909.

Lingering on into the BR era, it was finally phased out in the 1980's. Another innovation was carriage name boards, these giving hurrying passengers vital information on a train's route and destination.

The type broken up from the late 1930's onward, by the early 1950's those that had not been withdrawn had been converted for push-pull use. Long-lived vehicles, after passenger service, some were used in engineer's trains into the 1970's. Several escaping scrapping, preserved examples can be seen on both the Bluebell and Kent & East Sussex Railways.

Hundred of Hoo branch push-pull sets.

Usually made up of ex-3rd class vehicles that had been reallocated to 2nd class by the Southern, the Hundred of Hoo branch push-pull sets of the 1950's were mixtures of three types of carriage: compartment stock of either LS&WR or SE&CR origin, or the open saloon carriage portion of the SE&CR's former steam rail-cars.

Converted for push-pull working in 1927, the steam rail-car carriages were briefly allocated to the Isle of Wight. After returning to the mainland, some examples worked for a time on the West Street branch.

When being propelled, i.e. pushed, trains were controlled by the driver from a cab in the front of the leading coach, this cab showing in the photograph of set No. 716 opposite. Here, the driver remotely operated the locomotives regulator, brakes and whistle, while the fireman, remaining on the locomotives foot plate, followed instructions from the driver by bell codes and indicators.

Two systems of push-pull control existing, either pulleys, wires and rods, or compressed air, the auto fitted H Class tank locomotives on the

Laying over on the centre roads at Gravesend Central in the 1950's, set No. 716 of 1937 is coupled to an ex SE&CR steam railcar set. Set No. 716 was withdrawn in September 1960. Photo Society

Hoo branch services used the latter. Still in the red livery of the SE&CR, the photograph of set No. 716 dates from 1955 or earlier as the set had moved away from the Hundred of Hoo branch services in that year.

The SE&CR ex-rail motor carriages withdrawn in 1959 after transfer to the Hundred of Hoo from the Westerham branch, from memory, these sets were not kept particularly clean, a cloud of soot appearing when sitting down!

SE&CR 1921 "matchboard" boat train stock.

Acquiring the name of "matchboard" from the vertical panelling below their waist rail, they were also known as "Continental" stock. One of Maunsell's noteworthy contributions to SE&CR carriage stock, both luxurious and spacious, they featured corridors and gangways that gave access to the full length of the train and importantly for safety, they were fitted with override inhibiting knuckle couplers.

Built by the Metropolitan Carriage, Wagon & Finance Company, only 1st and 2nd Class accommodation initially provided, this was the norm for boat trains of the period. Well appointed, they featured lavatories, comfortable seats, ample luggage racks, coat hooks, tri-lingual notices and a bell to summon attendants.

Running locally on boat train services to Dover Marine from Victoria with two Pullman carriages and a restaurant car attached, they also made appearances at Gravesend West on the "Continental" boat trains. Following nationalisation, a few were repainted into BR carmine and cream livery as

is the carriage No. S1005 shown above. An example from 1924, this carriage is possibly running on a Newhaven boat train service. Remaining in main line service until 1961, electrification relegated them to secondary duties. After conversion for departmental use, the last example remained in service until as late as 1975.

Two carriages survive, one is at the Museum of Rail Travel, Ingrow while the other resides on the Kent & East Sussex Railway.

In contrast to his suburban electric coaching stock, Bulleid's locomotive hauled carriage designs were popular with the public, being appreciated for their comfort and spaciousness.

With deeply sprung and heavily padded seats, they were probably at the time the most comfortable coaches provided in the UK for the ordinary passenger. The soundness of the design recognised by British Railways, they used the layout as the basis for their Mark I passenger coaches.

Although still partially of timber construction, Bulleid's carriages were a step change in design concepts, the use of steel framing and sheeting enhancing the stock's strength. Traditional drop-light windows replaced with wide picture windows that gave passengers clear, unobstructed views of the passing scenery, accessibility to the entire train was provided by corridors and gangways.

With open saloons predominating and the use of compartments reduced, screw couplings were banished to be replaced with the superior and safer knuckle type, examples continued to be built until

SR steam coaching stock of 1946

Bulleid open 2nd carriage, Bluebell railway 30th May 2015. Author.

the early 1950's when the BR Mk I stock came into service. Running on the Chatham main line as four coach sets on semi-fast services from 1949 onwards, sometimes coupled with a collection of BR, pre and post-grouping carriage stock, these trains made an interesting spectacle.

On the Southern Region's eastern division, none received the BR corporate livery of carmine and cream, the stock remaining in the green livery of the Southern Region. Now withdrawn, examples are preserved on the Bluebell Railway.

British Railways locomotive hauled Mark I carriages of 1951

The nationalised railway of 1948 inherited an eclectic collection of coaching stock from its constituent companies and to replace some of this life expired stock, a universal carriage design, able to run throughout the national network was needed, it was the Mark I that fulfilled this.

Incorporating the best features of the former "Big Four" carriage designs, elements of Bulleid's 1946 carriage stock featured strongly in their build. Their steel construction giving better protection to passengers in accidents, as did the override inhibiting, semi-automatic knuckle couplers, the safety advances of the Mk I were praised by the Chief Inspecting Officer of Railways for improving accident survival rates.

Wide picture windows thoughtfully placed to give passengers unobstructed views from their seats, the first production vehicles had veneer panel finishes with labels identifying the type of wood and its origin. A successful design, the only significant modification during their BR service days was the introduction in 1961 of an improved

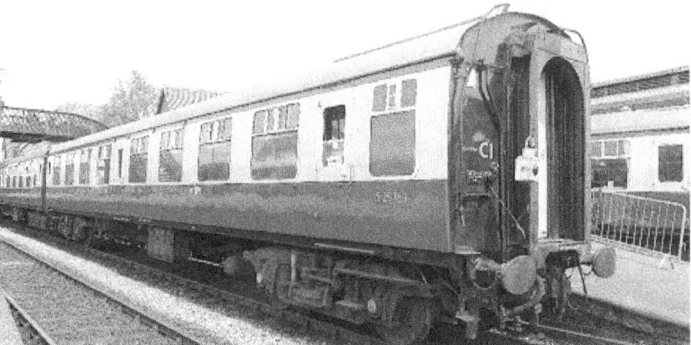

Mk I corridor 2nd, Bluebell Railway 30th May 2015. Author.

bogie, the Commonwealth type. Loco hauled Mark I carriages production ending in 1963, modified examples were built as late as 1974 for Southern Region electric multiple units. Locally used on both the Chatham main line semi-fasts and North Kent line excursions, they were phased out of main line service in the 1990's. Modified to allow running in the modern railway environment, some remain in use today on rail tours. Many having been preserved, the MK I forms the backbone of many preserved railways carriage fleets.

The Southern was nothing if not frugal and rather than purchase all new stock for the electrification of the inter-war period, modified ex-steam carriage stock was reused. Much of it elderly and dating back to the 1890's, these carriage conversions became a part of the 3SUB (SUBurban) electrical multiple units.

SR 3SUB conversion of SE&CR steam stock 1925

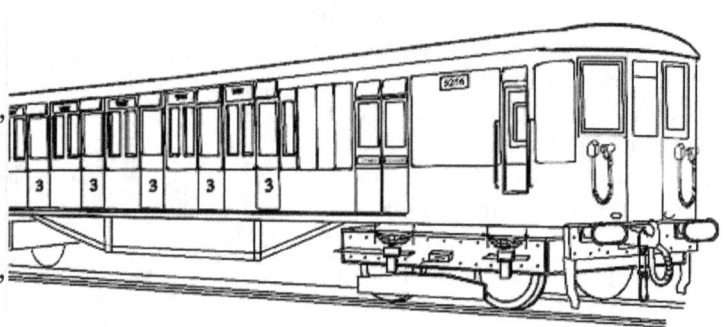

With only the driving cabs, guards and luggage compartments new built, three steam stock wooden carriage bodies were spliced together and mounted onto to new steel under-frames to produce one multiple unit bogie carriage. However, not all were second-hand, new construction of complete train sets was undertaken by private contractors.

Accommodation was as usual in compartments and those conversions produced in 1925 at Ashford works from ex-SE&CR steam stock could seat 56 1st and 180 3rd class passengers in each three car set. Traction motors supplied by Dick, Kerr & Co. Ltd, each motor was rated at 275 HP.

Messages describing the various types stock being sent by telegraph in code, electric stock was referred to by acronyms and by 1932 codes such as 3SUB and 2NOL were in use. With 3SUB identifying a 3 coach suburban set, 2NOL described a 2 coach set with no lavatory's, these codes remained in unofficial use into the 21st century.

By the 1940's, suburban passenger loads were rapidly increasing and to provide more seating, an additional "augmentation" trailer coach was added to the 3SUB's. These becoming known as the 4SUB's, these conversions should not be confused with the 1941 Bulleid 4SUB design.

All 3 car sets having been so converted by 1949, some of these remained in service into the early 1950's as part of five car multiple unit sets. None have been preserved.

Coming into service in 1939, the 2HAL (2HALf Lavatories), the first class of new electric multiple units introduced on the local passenger services, they were set to work on the recently electrified North Kent, Chatham main and Medway Valley lines.

SR 2HAL later Class 402 units of 1939

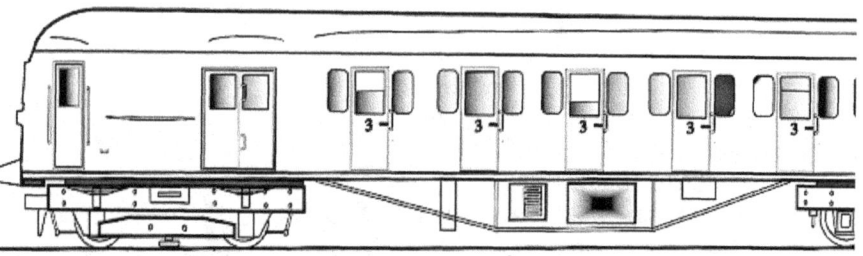

A longer distance, semi fast design by Bulleid, this stock was his first attempt at a maximum capacity design. Noted for their very cramped layout and uncomfortable seating, the 2HAL's were counted by many as amongst the Southern's more unpopular electric passenger stock. However, on the plus side, they did bring the convenience of toilets to the SR's outer suburban rolling stock.

Built by the SR at Lancing and Eastleigh works, they represented a small step forward in safety by being constructed from steel panels on wooden frames. However, screw couplings being retained, they exposed workers to one of the main causes of injuries to railway staff, coupling-up by going between carriages.

Surviving in British Rail ownership just long enough to be assigned to TOPS Class 402, their braking systems incompatible with the new electric multiple stock then coming into service, all had gone from the Gravesham area by 1959,

After providing services on the Central and Western divisions of BR's Southern Region, including a period of duty on the Gatwick services, they finished their days as departmental vehicles in 1972. None have survived into preservation.

Southern Railway 4SUB later Class 405 of 1941

Not to be confused with the earlier strengthened 3SUB units, this was another design from the fertile mind of O.V.S. Bulleid. Wooden roofed, 4-car suburban units built with curved, welded steel body sides, this arrangement enabled cramped six aside seating layout in 3rd Class rather than the five aside norm.

1st class passengers luxuriating with just ten passengers per compartment, this indulgence was to be short-lived; an economy measure introduced in October 1941 unifying all SR suburban services to 3rd Class.

4SUB No. 4731 at Sutton in 1975. RailPicsGB

The early 4SUB units had the highest seating capacity of any of the SR suburban multiple units. Seating 468 passengers at full load, this earned the early sets the nickname of the "Shebas", it was a title taken from the Biblical verse: *"And when the Queen of Sheba heard of the fame of Solomon she came to Jerusalem with a very great train"*.

Achieved by the removal of one compartment per carriage, the later versions had slightly more spacious accommodation. Electrically heated and with toilets once again omitted, their traditional screw couplings and Westinghouse air brake systems precluded their working in multiple with the later EPB and Modernisation era electric stock.

Built in batches up until 1951, they continued to provide stock for the local and suburban services until their withdrawal in 1983. Four examples survive.; unit No. 4732 preserved at the Electric Railway Museum, two others reside at the National Railway Museum with another in private ownership.

British Railways EPB, later Classes 415 & 416 of 1951

Familiar to local veteran commuters, this SR inspired design of electric stock featured all-steel construction, the safer Buckeye couplings and a faster-acting electro-pneumatic brake. Sharing many components with their 4SUB predecessors, BR continued the frugal habits of the Southern by re-using 4SUB under frames in some of the EPB builds.

The first examples built to an SR pattern designed based primarily on seating in compartments, the earliest examples retaining leather strap drop light windows these were replaced in later builds by a friction type window catch.

BR design 2EPB at Shepherdswell on 17th April 2010. Author

Constructed from 1960 onward to a BR design based on the BR Mark I carriage, saloons predominated. Refurbishment of the SR twelve-seat compartment stock starting in early 1980's, they were face-lifted to create open vestibules by removing compartment partitions including new seat trim, fluorescent lighting and public address.

When a young woman was found murdered in a compartment in 1988, the remaining compartment stock was identified with a red stripe above the doors, after 8:00 pm they came out of service. Following withdrawal of the earlier 4SUB units, the EPB then became the mainstay of the area's suburban and local passenger services. Withdrawals starting in 1991, the last examples going by April 1995, two units remained in departmental service until 2005.

A number surviving withdrawal, examples are preserved at the East Kent Light Railway, the Coventry Railway Centre and the Northamptonshire Ironstone Railway Trust.

Post-war, the Southern's passenger loadings, particularly on commuter services had increased significantly, and by the 1948 nationalisation, a solution for increasing seating capacity on suburban trains having become urgent, a potential answer to this issue came in the guise of an experimental double deck train, the unique Class 4DD (Double Deck).

Appearing in 1949, in reality these unusual units were a split level, rather than a true double deck design. Although common in North America and Europe, the UK's C1 loading gauge inhibits carriage designs with two discrete decks.

British Railways 4DD double deck units of 1949

4DD No. 4902 at Hoo Junction after withdrawal in 1971. Authors collection

Unveiled as a plywood mock up at Marylebone station in May 1949, this revealed that each four car unit could seat 508 passengers, some 25% more than a four-car 4SUB unit. The first design to incorporate an version of the Electro-Pneumatic (EP) brake, an "energise to apply" version, this meant that any loss of voltage to the EP brake made it inoperative, recourse then having to be made to a slower acting air brake. Couplings were the screw type, although mountings were provided for the future fitting of Buckeye types.

Formally launched into public service from Charing Cross on the 1st of November 1949 by the Deputy Prime Minister, Herbert Morrison, their designer, Oliver Bulleid, was also in attendance.

The publicity pictures of the event show smiling passengers boarding these unusual new trains. However, the units were not popular with the travelling public, their seating cramped and uncomfortable, the badly ventilated upper deck was also a serious issue in the days of universal cigarette smoking.

Ingress was also restricted, the ratio of doors to passengers being only half that of conventional carriages, access to the upper deck was also very limited with just one short staircase being provided per compartment. Being 4½ inches taller than a 4SUB, their route availability was very restricted and gauging issues prevented their working past Gravesend Central.

All these drawbacks were to be very significant hindrances, with long delays and extended dwell times being experienced while the throngs of passengers struggled to entrain without the benefit of a running board, so tight were the class's loading gauge constraints. While the 4DD units offered the novelty of observing the railway world from a high vantage point, they were unpopular with lady travellers, assaults on young women occurring when trapped on the upper deck.

When these drawbacks became apparent, it was decided to build no more of the type this left the two prototypes, Nos 4001 & 4002 as the sole examples and with this decision made, the alternative, the provision of ten car conventional electric sets was put in hand.

In service the units gave little trouble, requiring little more than routine maintenance. Not acquiring TOPS numbers, near the end of their operational lives the sets were renumbered 4901 and 4902, their numbers re-assigned to the 4PEP (Prototype Electro Pneumatic) multiple units.

The class remained quietly and unobtrusively in service until withdrawal on the 1st of October 1971 after which two driving cars and a trailer car were purchased privately. Unfortunately, only the driving cars now exist, the trailer car wrecked at the Ashford Steam centre. Of the survivors, driving car No. 13003 is at Sellinge with No. 13004 at the Northamptonshire Ironstone Railway. Once slowly deteriorating, No. 13003 is now being restored by the Kent Bulleid 4DD Emu Group.

BR planning to section No. 13004 for display at the National Railway Museum before its private purchase, this may have been a better fate for an important part of railway history. No double deck trains now running in the the UK, they may appear on HS2 should it be built.

Between Downs and Thames - Railways of Gravesend, the Hoo Peninsular and Isle of Grain

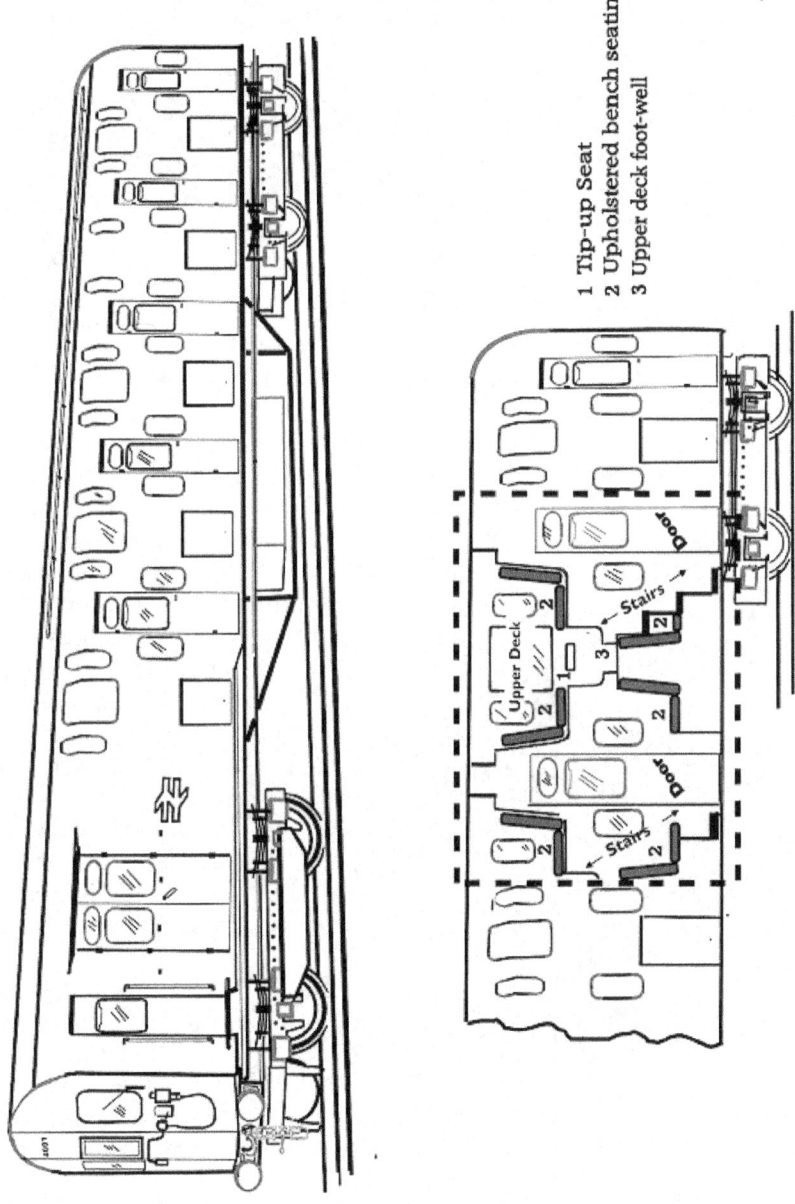

4DD double deck train including a cutaway view of the internal layout

1 Tip-up Seat
2 Upholstered bench seating
3 Upper deck foot-well

In the mid 1950's, with the electrification of the Kent Coast route impending, a family of 90 mph express electrical multiple units was needed to replace the steam trains then running the Kent boat train services.

The inspiration for these new units, the Class 4CEP (Corridor Electro-Pneumatic brake), came from an SR design of 1937, the 4COR (Corridor) units then being used on the London Waterloo to Portsmouth Harbour services. While the 4CEP's body shell was based upon the BR Standard Mark I carriage of 1951, the internal layout was styled as the 4COR units. With 1st Class compartments accessed from a side corridor, 2nd Class, now Standard Class passengers, travelled in open saloons.

With no dining cars provided, only buffet facilities were available from the matching class 4BEP, later the Class 412. Designed to provide operational flexibility, the 4CEP's were capable of running in multiple with the EPB units. By the 1970's the units in need of refurbishment, this work was carried out at the BR Swindon workshops. With withdrawals beginning in 1999 following the introduction of Electrostar units,

British Railways 4CEP later Class 411 of 1955

4CEP No. 1699 stands at Ashford with a special service for BR staff on 29th December 2004. Author

An unidentified MLV unit passes Gravesend on its way to Slade Green Depot 23rd March 1984. Dave Fisher

by 2004 all apart from a handful had gone and making its final run in September 2005, the last example to leave public service was unit No.1698. With a working life of 49 years, the 4CEP's were the longest serving of the former Southern Region's electrical multiple units.

Before their final withdrawal from what was previously the Southern Region's eastern division, a special farewell train for BR staff was run on the 29th of December 2004 from London Victoria to Dover Priory. Fortunate enough to be invited on the trip, this time I wasn't left behind as with the "Farewell to the EPB" rail tour of 1995.

The unofficial intention of the trip being to set a new time record for the class on their former boat train route between Victoria and Dover Priory, travelling on unit No. 1699 during the Down trip, I experienced descending Tonbridge bank at over 100 mph. Unfortunately we were unable to beat the record, a signal check at Brixton on the return journey ending the endeavour, the veteran drivers onboard the train putting the failure down to the lack of the extra power of an MLV in the consist.

Known as the Class 419 or MLV (Motor Luggage Van), these ran as a conventional electrically powered van as part of a boat train's consist and on reaching the dockside they would uncouple and powered from internal batteries, move with the passengers luggage aboard to waiting ships.

Withdrawn at the end of boat train services in 1991, they were used as both departmental tractor units and on postal duties. A regular sight on the North Kent line in the 1980's and 1990's, one was to be seen on regular workings between Gillingham and Slade Green Depots.

Eight MLV units surviving, examples exist on the Chinnor & Princes Risborough Railway, the Eden Valley Railway and the Dartmoor Railway, the MLV unit at the East Kent Railway is occasionally run on batteries at special events.

Perhaps as a legacy from the days of the LC&DR and SER, the Southern Region was seen as the Cinderella of BR, and long after other regions had moved onto more modern carriage concepts with power operated-doors and other refinements, the Southern Region was ordering slam door multiple units based on the venerable Mark I body shell of 1951 into the 1970's.

Examples being built as late as 1974, the 4VEP (Vestibule Electro-Pneumatic brake) units were the last examples of the type. With 'G' representing Gatwick, a variant, the quaintly named 4VEG featured extra passenger luggage racks for use on the Victoria to Gatwick services, .

Intended for working on stopping outer suburban services and rural services in Kent and Sussex, the 4VEP's featured high density seating in Standard Class, with a door to each seating bay allowing rapid entry and egress for passengers. Given a mid-life enhancement between 1988 and 1990, all units were internally modernised when fitted out with fluorescent lighting, public address and other systems.

Withdrawals of the class commencing following

British Rail 4VEP later Class 423 of 1967

4VEP No. 7882 enters Gravesend on a Gillingham to Charing Cross service on 13th April 1985. Dave Fisher

the introduction of the Electrostar units after privatisation, the last of the Southeastern units departed service on the 7th of October 2005.

At the time of writing three are in preservation. One unit having been purchased by the Bluebell Railway, another is at the National Railway Museum at York, while the third is at the Mizens Railway where it is open to the public.

Coincidental with the 1986 birth of Network South East, there was an employment boom in the capital. Leading to even more overcrowding than usual on the venerable slam door commuter trains, consequently the decision was taken to mitigate this by introducing completely new 12-car trains on the Kent commuter routes.

The Networkers, as they were later to be called, were at the time of their introduction a revolutionary design. Featuring automatic sliding doors, sealed toilets, disc brakes, the TightLock automatic coupler and electronically controlled AC drive motors, they were a huge leap forward from their predecessors, the EPB's.

The Networker's body shell being intended to form the basis of the sector's future passenger rolling stock needs, the 1996 privatisation ended the concept, some of the Networkers features have been retained in their Electrostar successors.

Built by both British Railways Engineering Ltd and Metro Cammel, the 750 volt DC Networker derivative comes in two variants: the Class 465 four-car and Class 466 two-car sets. With the first units allocated to Slade Green Depot in 1992, it

British Rail Networker Class 465 & 466 of 1992

No. 466036 at Dartford on 4th March 2010. Author

was intended to use them on 12 car trains. However, it was to be 2014 before 12 car trains appeared locally, the privatisations and the financial strictures of the 1990's having disrupted plans. Dogged by reliability issues, the original Brush drive controllers have been replaced by Hitachi units. With the Class 376 units they now form the majority of Southeastern's Metro, local and outer suburban services.

During the reign of BR, an express version of the Networker, the Class 365 Networker Express, was designed to replace the then almost life expired Modernisation era express electrical multiple units, but when the Class 365 had to be withdrawn from express duties due to serious technical problems, an alternative was sought.

With the first examples ordered in 1998 from Adtranz by Connex, the Class 375 Electrostar was the type they selected to replace their ageing slam-door stock. A family of related designs, the Class 375 is based on Adtranz's *Clubman* design.

Rated for a maximum speed of 110 mph, the air conditioned Class 375 units now provide the majority of the longer distance services on the former Chatham route. Occasionally appearing on the North Kent line, they feature automatic sliding doors, disabled access toilets, space for wheelchair users and CCTV system for the driver. Providing both 1st and Standard Class accommodation, legroom is not as generous as on the former slam-door stock.

As with most modern designs, significant losses are the guard's compartment and catering

Adtranz Class 375 Electrostar of 1999

Class 375 No. 375617 at Paddock Wood. Author

facilities, the recent withdrawal of trolley services exacerbating matters. Updated and refreshed with an interior makeover and livery change, the updated units can be recognised by their overall dark blue livery and light blue doors.

The class making a high demand on traction power supplies, meters have recently been fitted to monitor energy consumption.

A major success, the Electrostar family is also operated in the UK by London Overground, C2C, Thameslink and Abellio Greater Anglia.

From the viewpoint of passengers the Class 376 Electrostar design is a retrograde step. Introduced by Connex South Eastern for suburban routes, they are configured to pack in the maximum number of passengers. The majority of these being standees, they are more akin to a London Overground train than a main line multiple unit.

Harking back to the spartan designs of Bulleid, their passenger spaces have been maximised by dispensing with toilets. An omission apparently agreed to by local travellers in a survey, I personally have no recollection of being consulted in my commuting days.

To compensate for the lack of toilet facilities, Southeastern promised to increase toilet provision at stations and further ease the plight of the incontinent by limiting journey times and with the maximum set at 57 minutes, this brings them to Gravesham.

The design offers better access than the Networkers, their wider doors and dedicated wheelchair spaces improving conditions for the

Bombardier Class 376 Electrostar of 2004

Electrostar No. 376031 at Erith 6th August 2009. Author

disabled. With traction power delivered by 3 phase AC induction motors, they are operated as ten car trains made up of two 5 car sets. Based at Slade Green depot, they occasionally visit Ramsgate maintenance depot. A five car arrangement now a disadvantage on a line dedicated to 12 car trains, it remains to be seen what their future is on Gravesham's rail network.

The design for the Class 373 was produced as a collaborative effort between the British, French and Belgian railways. Constructed by GEC-Alsthom at sites in the UK and on the continent, they are essentially a lengthened version of a French *Train à Grande Vitesse* (TGV) designed for the smaller UK loading gauge.

An eighteen carriage, 1,270 foot long articulated design, with each car sharing a common bogie with it's neighbour and traction power derived from power cars at either end of the train, these develop a combined power output of 12,200 KW.

With accommodation provided for up to 750 passengers with 206 seated in 1st and Business Class and 544 in Standard Class. While 1st and Business Class can have meals served at their seats, a buffet is provided for Standard Class.

International services commencing from Waterloo International station on the 14th of November 1994 using the existing ex-SER "classic" main line to Cheriton, from 2003 services were re-routed to use Phase 1 of HS1 via a link at Fawkham from the "classic" Chatham main line.

Originally a dual voltage design, operating from either the UK 750 volt DC 3rd rail or the 25KV AC supply of HS1, since the opening of HS1 throughout, they now operate exclusively from 25KV AC overhead supplies. An onboard signalling system used to prevent the need to sight conventional signals, they are capable of 186 mph on surface lines and 106 mph in the Channel Tunnel. Holding the UK rail speed record of 208 mph, this was achieved on the Medway Viaduct on 30th July 2003. Refurbished with new interiors and décor in 2004/05, the Class 373 are expected to stay in service until 2020.

British Rail Class 373 Eurostar high-speed multiple units of 1992

Class 373 Eurostar power car, Ebbsfleet 16th November 2015. Author

Siemens Class 374 Velaro e320 high-speed units of 2014

When Eurostar awarded Siemens of Germany a contract for the supply of ten Velaro Class 374 e320 trains in October 2010, the design they chose was based on the ICE 3 (Inter City Express) high-speed trains in use on the Deutsche Bahn.

These 199 mph, sixteen-car, 1,312 ft long train sets have a greater seating capacity than the Class 373. Carrying up to 900 passengers, the Velaro design achieves this by having its 16,000 kW rated traction power equipment distributed along the length of the set below floor level. Featuring state of the art on board entertainment, this includes wi-fi, real-time travel information, videos, music and news-feeds.

Recently placing an order for a further seven e320's due for delivery in late 2016, their higher operating speeds will be used to reduce Paris and Brussels journey times by 15 minutes. Able to operate on the rail systems of Holland and Germany, this is achieved by using one of the train's eight power take-off panto-graphs to collect power from either 25 kV AC, 1.5 or 3.0 KV DC.

A Class 374 Velaro e320 passes the Singlewell cross-over with a Brussels service on 2nd December 2015. J. Townsend

Since late 2015, the class has been running on the St Pancras to Brussels services and by using *Velaro* train sets, additional services to Amsterdam are due to start in December 2017, with services to Cologne, Frankfurt and further French destinations planned to follow.

Hitachi Class 395 Javelin High-Speed electric multiple units of 2009

The 140 mph air-conditioned Hitachi Class 395 trains offer passenger comfort levels usually only to be found on main line UK services. Debuting in the June of 2009, the Class 395 represents the state of the art for multiple units on the medium and short distance electrified rail routes.

Mostly built in Japan, 40% of their components are of a European origin. A multiple unit design, they are based upon Hitachi's "A-Train" concept, the "Super Express", not the "Shinkansen" trains as is widely believed.

Constructed from extruded aluminium body panels for strength and lightness, access is via GPS controlled, automatically aligned sliding doors, GPS is also used to identify the trains locations en route. Normally run as six-car multiple units, an extension to 12-car formations is easily made by use of the automatic couplings located beneath their sleek, bright yellow nose cones.

Only the middle four cars of the six-car units have powered axles, the two end cars being trailers only. Fully accessible to the disabled and wheel chair users, accommodation is exclusively Standard Class. Each six car unit providing seats for up to 340 passengers, on board catering is unfortunately not provided.

A Class 395 departs Ebbsfleet bound for Springhead Junction on the North Kent line on 26th August 2011. Author.

The 29 strong train set fleet maintained by Hitachi at Ashford, Kent in a purpose built depot situated on the site of the former Ashford Down Yard carriage sidings, As a dual voltage design, these units are able to operate from either a 25 KV AC or 750 Volt DC supply.

Starting from St. Pancras, the high-speed services now runs on two main routes using both the "classic" routes and HS1 routes, When disturbing lurching occurred in tunnel, the class was retro-fitted with modified suspension in 2010.

During the July 2012 London Olympic Games, the class was used in its intended role on the "Javelin" high-speed shuttle services to Stratford and to mark this event, twenty-four of the class now carry the names of prominent British athletes, these include *Jamie Staff* and *Sir Steve Redgrave*.

A success since their inception, the journey time from Gravesend to London has now been reduced to just 22 minutes.

A derivative, the Hitachi Class 800, is due to start running services on the GWR, and an electro-diesel type, the Class 801, a replacement for the Class 43, are to enter UK main line service in 2017.

Hitachi's maintenance depot at Ashford. Author.

Gravesend to Tilbury Railway Ferries and Piers

The Paddle Steamer "Earl of Essex" was one the first steam vessels used on the railway owned crossing. A former Thames pleasure steamer, she was In service from 1855 until 1880. Having no bridge to engine room communication, making berthing difficult, a small boy was employed to run between the bridge and engine room to shout orders. Gordon Hales collection.

An oddity of the ferry is how the rights for its use are conferred. Held differently for each direction of travel, this goes back to a time when the ferry rights were held by separate Manors in Kent and Essex.

The northbound ferry rights held by Kent County Council, apart from a period between the 17th and the 19th Centuries, the Crown has owned the southbound ferry rights since the 15th century.

Before the opening of the SER to Gravesend, the London and Blackwall Railway (LBR) had a profitable river passenger trade to the town, their river steamers plying between Blackwall and Gravesend. Resolving to restore this traffic by other means, in a partnership with the Eastern Counties Railway Company (ECR) the two agreed to build a railway to connect London with Tilbury and to then cross the Thames using pleasure steamers to Rosherville and by steam ferry to Gravesend.

The two companies then sought, and in 1852, successfully obtained, a Parliamentary Act ¶ for the formation of a new railway company. To be known as the London, Tilbury & Southend Railway (LT&SR), it was to begin at Forest Gate on the ECR. Opening to the public at Easter 1854, the line ran via Barking, Purfleet and Grays Thurrock to a terminus station at Tilbury. Their Act also giving the LT&SR the desired authority for a new railway steam ferry, it used the wording *"To provide a steam communication to Gravesend"* and by 1855 the LT&SR had opened a pontoon at Tilbury for use by the cross-river ferry to Gravesend's Town Pier and the pleasure steamers to Rosherville.

The ships used on the LT&SR's early ferry service being ex-pleasure steamers, these were the *Earl of Essex*, *Earl of Leicester* and the *Tilbury*.

Provided for the exclusive use of LT&SR passengers only, other travellers continued to use the existing public cross-ferry service. A service going back into antiquity, it used ancient causeways as landing places.

Run by lessees on behalf of Gravesend Corporation, a steam tug was used as the passenger ferry, a towed "float" or lighter transporting cargo and livestock.

The Board of Ordnance also had its own private ferry, and this was used by soldiers based at Gravesend and Tilbury forts. Leased to Gravesend Corporation later in the nineteenth Century, lessees then provided both the public and military ferries.

Purchasing Gravesend Town Pier in 1885 from the then bankrupt Gravesend Corporation, the LT&SR acquired complete control of all the Gravesend to Tilbury ferries. Including the military ferry, they and their successors were to maintain these rights until the privatisation of the service in the 20th century.

Purchasing the LT&SR in 1912 primarily to access Southend and Tilbury Docks, the Midland Railway took over control of the ferry after paying £240 for a £100 LT&SR ordinary share. With the grouping of the railways in 1923, the ferry changed hands once again to become a part of the London, Midland & Scottish Railway (LMSR) and in 1924, a purpose built car ferry, the 371 grt *Tessa* becoming part of the fleet, in 1927 she was joined by a sister ship, the 463 grt *Mimie*.

During the General Strike of 1926 the ferry was operated by the Royal Navy, and unfamiliar with the fast river currents, they damaged both

¶ *Victoria Regina Cap lxxxiv*

the ferries and their berths. Nationalisation in 1948 seeing the ferry come under control of British Railway's London Midland Region, this passed to the Eastern Region in 1949. From February 1961, three smaller, faster and more manoeuvrable diesel ferries took over the passenger services, but with the 1963 opening of the Dartford Tunnel causing revenues to decline rapidly, the car ferry service ending in December 1964, the passenger ferry was privatised in 1984. Subsidised by Kent and Thurrock Councils, lessees now once again run the service and today, the Thames and Medway Passenger Boat Co. currently use the *Duchess M* to provide this vital link.

The screw steamer "Rose" of 1901 seen making the crossing in 1937. Together with her sisters "Catherine" and "Edith," and the car ferries, she helped run the foot passenger service until February 1961. *Tony Riley collection.*

The 1927-built steam car ferry "Mimie". With her sister, the "Tessa", she provided the car ferry service until December 1964. Foot passengers also being able to use the car ferry, "Mimie" was able to carry 36 cars and 300 passengers plus cargo. *Gordon Hales collection.*

One of the three diesel ferries introduced to the crossing in 1961. Known as "Rose", "Catharine" and "Edith" they had ludicrously short working lives, as after the opening of the Dartford Crossing in 1963 they were sold out of service between 1967 and 1992. All have survived; the "Rose" is currently a Malta tourist pleasure vessel, "Catherine" is on the Tyne, and "Edith" is a houseboat in Essex. *Gordon Hales collection.*

Gravesend Town Pier

Gravesend Town Pier, now the worlds oldest cast-iron pier still in daily use is built on the site of the Town Quay. Mentioned in the Domesday Book, this makes this a landing place with a long history. The pier's designer and engineer the same William Tierney Clark we met earlier as engineer for the Higham to Strood canal tunnel, the piers builder was a local man, William Wood. Construction costing £8,700, it opened on the 29th of July 1834 with the usual celebrations.

Originally open to the elements with only small pavilions at the river end for shelter, canvas canopies were used until a covered way was built later in the 19th century. Often used for local entertainments, brass and silver band concerts were a frequent occurrence.

Originally built so that only one vessel could berth at a time, a floating pontoon was added later to allow more vessels to moor alongside.

In the mid-nineteenth century such was the popularity of Gravesend that on the Good Friday of 1854, the public opening day of the LT&SR railway to Tilbury, huge numbers of people crossed to Gravesend. So many were there that the ferry could not cope with the returning multitudes and many were unable to return to Tilbury. Doubtless, the SER profited from this!

The pier once of sufficient importance to have its own stationmaster, Kelly's directory for 1912 lists him as a Robert Cross, "Midland Railway, London Tilbury & Southend section". Holding the status of a railway station, the pier featured in railway timetables.

Apart from a short break during the 1880's, the Town Pier was for 111 years the Gravesend berth for the railway's passenger ferries. The car ferry service finishing in December 1964, the passenger ferry transferred to the West Street landing stage and still lit by gas lamps, the Town Pier closed in July 1965. With the opening of the new Town Pontoon in 2012, after an interval of nearly fifty years, the ferry has returned once more to it former Town Pier home.

The Town Pier in the 1920's with "Rose" alongside. Gordon Hales collection.

The original Town Pier clock. Now at the NRM, York, the original navigation beacon is still in situ. Author.

With the Terrace Pier as a backdrop, a Diamond Company steamer is seen at the Gravesend Town Pier pontoon in the 1840's. Providing a link to the London & Blackwall Railway at Brunswick Wharf, in 1846 there were ten weekday sailings with a rival service also running from the Terrace Pier. The Gravesend magazine.

The now demolished 19th century Gravesend Town Pier pontoon, with the ferries "Carlotta" and "Tilbury" alongside. Although undated, it would appear to be in the Edwardian period. Gordon Hales Collection.

A view taken on the 4th of November 2015 of Gravesend Town Pier, showing in the foreground is the present ferry landing place, the new pontoon of 2012 . Author

Tilbury Landing Stage

The 1855 Tilbury Landing Stage seen circa 1910 with the 1906 Tilbury station in the background. This station was greatly enlarged and modified in 1930. Gordon Hales collection

Tilbury Landing Stage, opening in 1855, it was a modest affair. Only able to accommodate the ferry and one or two small river pleasure steamers, vessels of a deeper draft, such as the Peninsular & Orient (P&O) ocean liners having to moor in the river's mid-stream deep water channel, they used smaller vessels, normally the ferry boats to act as their tenders.

Following the growth of both maritime and railway passenger traffic, in 1906 the LT&SR opened an enlarged new station at Tilbury. Replacing the timber built station of 1854, it's improvements included new platforms, concourse and a covered way to the landing stage.

In the years after the Great War, the Thames ocean steamer traffic greatly increased, and ever more liners lay in the river's midstream. With the Thames becoming unacceptably congested as a consequence, the government of the day decided to resolve matters by making Tilbury London's ocean passenger terminal and passing an Act of Parliament in 1922, this gave sanction for a replacement 1,142 foot landing stage and various other improvements.

This was not the first proposal to increase the capacity of Tilbury's ocean shipping and rail facilities, an earlier unrealised LT&SR plan of 1905 having proposed building a new railway pier to allow boat train passengers to alight directly onto a quay side platform.

Construction starting in 1924 to the design of Sir Edwin Cooper, when complete the complex provided both an ocean terminal, an updated station and new boarding arrangements.

Officially opened in May 1930, the first large ship to use the new landing stage was a P&O liner, the SS *Mongolia,* and from then on, the landing stage became a port of call for many of the leading personalities of the day. An unusual visitor was the ill-fated *SS Wilhelm Gustloff,* Calling in 1939, she took German nationals outside the three mile limit to vote in their national elections.

Ferries and shipping off Tilbury Landing Stage in the 1940's. Gordon Hales collection.

Tilbury was later to became an important emigration centre and until the late 1960's, Australian emigrants, the so-called "£10 POMS", left Tilbury for new lives in the Antipodes.

Immigrants also used Tilbury, the *Empire Windrush* bringing Jamaicans here in 1948. When the last of the scheduled deep-sea services, the Swedish-Lloyd sailings to Gothenburg ceased in 1965, the liner traffic and its associated boat trains came to an end.

Renewal having come to the Tilbury landing stage; now known as the London International Cruise Terminal, it hosts cruise liners such as *Marco Polo* and *Black Prince*.

Closing in 1992, the station is now home to the Tilbury Arts Activity Centre (TRACS).

Circa 1900, the Royal Mail Steamer "India" is seen with the ferry "Sir Walter Raleigh'"acting as tender. "India", while serving as an Armed Merchant Cruiser in WWI, she was torpedoed and sunk off Norway in 1915. Gordon Hales collection.

Gravesend West Street Landing Stage

Gravesend West Street landing stage in 1953, it was then in use for the car ferry. Tony Larkin.

Opened by the LT&SR in 1857 as a goods and livestock station, it was built on the site of the former Three Crowns Jetty, and by 1860 it had acquired both a pontoon and a linking bridge.

The nearby Town Pier was at the time the ferry's passenger terminal. Owned by the Gravesend Corporation, they levied a 1d toll on the LT&SR for every passenger landed there.

To avoid this toll, and possibly in an attempt to ruin Gravesend Corporation, between 1880 and 1885, with the fare reduced to 3d, West Street was used as the passenger terminal for the LT&SR ferries. The ruse working, by 1885 the LT&SR having purchased the Town Pier and the rights to the crossing from a financially ruined Corporation, passengers once again landed at the Town Pier. Before the advent of the car ferry in 1924, the railway passenger ferry continued with the former public ferry's practice of towing a "float" for cargo and livestock. Doubtless some of this livestock was destined for the slaughterhouses and livestock pens once situated to the rear of Queen Street, the name Horn Yard serves as a reminder of the trade.

My mother, who lived in Queen Street, Gravesend in the 1920's, could recall animals attempting to escape, the local children herding them back into the slaughterhouse.

By 1906 a car ferry service had started and post-WWI, traffic had developed sufficiently to warrant providing a dedicated vehicle ferry, the 1924 built beam loading ferry *Tessa*. An early form of roll-on, roll-off ship, she was joined by her larger sister *Mimie* in 1927. Manned by a crew of seven, and carrying both general cargo and vehicles at a maximum speed of nine knots, the car ferry's were by 1928 providing a twice hourly crossing.

Road traffic having grown greatly by the 1950's, during holiday periods the roads leading to the landing stages on both sides of the river witnessed long queues of vehicles waiting to cross.

By the year following the opening of the Dartford Tunnel, with the fare for a car and four passengers on the ferry priced at 10/-6d against a tunnel toll of 2/-6d, the inevitable closure of the car ferry service came on the 31st of December 1964. West Street landing stage, used from 1965 onward, as the passenger ferry's boarding point, in 2013 the ferry transferred to the new Town Pontoon.

The ferries overnight berth, West Street is still used by the first and last ferries of the day.

West Street LC&DR Railway Pier

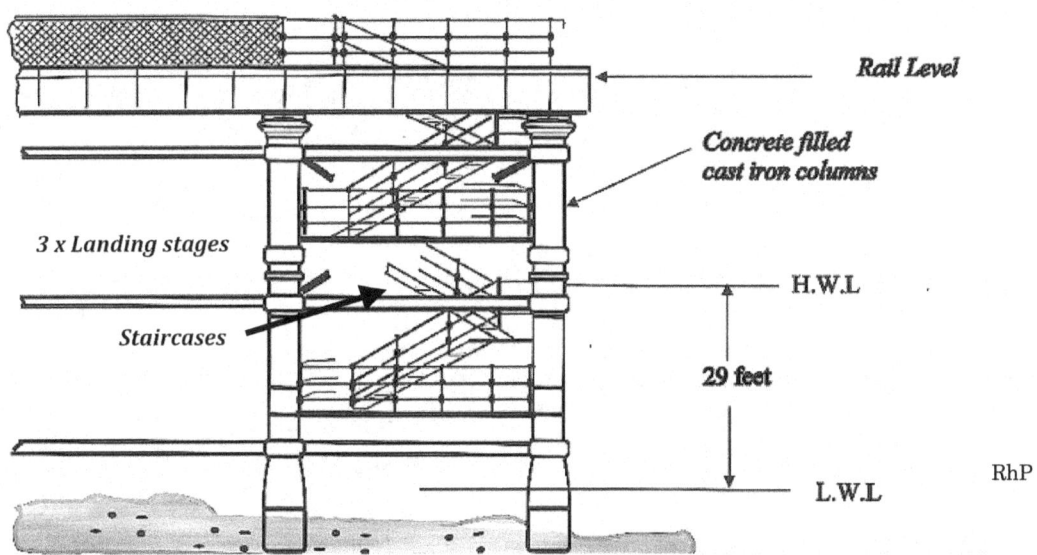

At the river end of Stuart Road, Gravesend, projecting forlornly into the Thames is the remains of West Street Pier. In its early days, known as the "London, Chatham & Dover Pier" after its first owner, together with the Rosherville Gardens, this now rusting structure was one of the main reasons for the 1886 building of the Gravesend Railway.

Plans held in Gravesend library show a short, but sturdy cast iron structure with landing stages at three levels to allow passengers to board ships at any state of tide. Provided with a five track railway layout laid onto steel and timber decking, it was supported by concrete filled cast iron columns sitting on piled timber foundations.

It's construction wasn't without incident. In March 1885 one of its builders, the labourer John Madoe, had a narrow escape when the plank he was walking on moved, pitching him off into a drop of over 30 feet. By sheer good fortune John's fall was checked by a rope sling which prevented him from falling into the river.

The LC&DR had intended to extend the pier further into the river, but the Thames Conservancy fearing this would prove a hazard to shipping in the crowded River Thames of the day, forbade its extension.

The result of this decision was a pier with insufficient depth of water at low tide for the deep sea and ocean trading vessels that the railway had originally hoped to attract here and for a time the pier became something of a white elephant. It had not been cheap to build, the LC&DR having paid a large sum to acquire the river frontage from an existing coal wharfage business. However, local water-men and lighter-men were to benefit from the railway's misfortune by using their smaller vessels as tenders to the large steamers that were unable to moor off the pier at low water.

Nevertheless, for a brief time the LC&DR was successful in attracting shipping to the pier. A short-lived venture being the use of the pier by a steamer service to Norway, the Harwich to Denmark ferry was also tempted to West Street for a brief period before returning to the River Orwell. Another short term user being the Zeeland Company, they used the pier for their Flushing service in WWI.

Becoming a popular place to watch sailing yachts racing on the Thames, the LC&DR encouraged the public to promenade on the pier for a penny a head.

More important visitors, later to become the pier's main source of revenue were pleasure steamers. Calling here on the day excursion trade except during wartime, this was a tradition that was to carry on throughout the pier's working history.

Fishing vessels also using the pier to land their catches for onward travel to Billingsgate fish market by rail, a notable traffic was consignments of local basket-caught sprats.

With only one crane, on the pier, the travelling steam crane mentioned in the 1904 Railway Clearing House handbook proving insufficient for cargo handling, this was a cause of complaint from the local fishermen. Destined for use as railway ballast, another cargo landed here for onward rail shipment was stone from the Channel Islands.

West Street Pier came into its own during WWI when some North Sea and Channel ports were either commandeered by the authorities or had their access severely restricted to merchant shipping due to the proximity of the enemy on the Belgian coast. Alternative ports then sought for both new and existing seaborne trade, West Street Pier became a beneficiary of this.

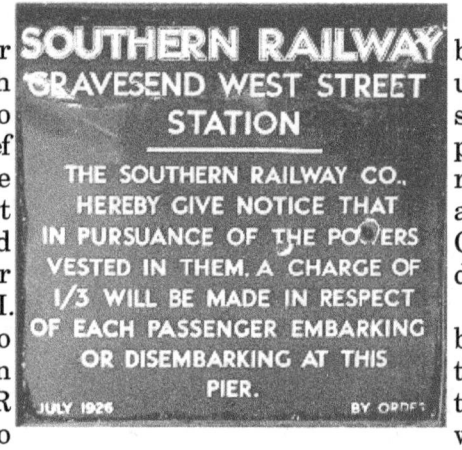

Notice from 1926 once seen on West Street Pier. R.C Riley

The Harwich ferries being once again re-directed here under a Dutch neutral flag, the service was used amongst other purposes, for the transport of repatriated prisoners of war, who after landing, were sent to Gravesend's New Tavern Fort depot for processing.

The possibility of infiltration by enemy spies was not lost on the authorities and the pier then taking on a martial aspect, wooden watch offices were installed together with an armed military presence.

Post-war, in June 1922, the Dutch Batavier Line steamers started to call here. Providing a regular steamer service to Rotterdam, a dedicated connecting boat train service was provided once the steamer service had become established and signs in Dutch appeared on the pier, at Gravesend West station and at some intermediate stations to Victoria.

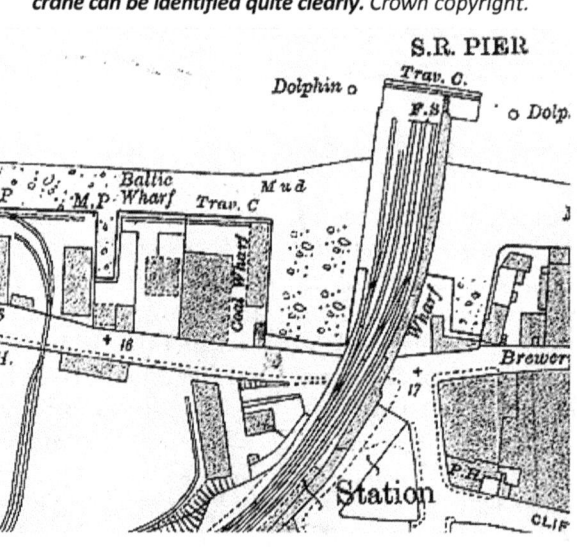

West Street LC&DR Pier's track layout in 1930. The travelling crane can be identified quite clearly. Crown copyright.

In the interval of peace between the two world wars, pleasure steamers continued to visit the pier. Chiefly being vessels of both the New Medway Steam Packet and the General Steam Navigation companies, these ships included *The Queen of Southend* and the *Golden Eagle,* the latter having relocated from Tilbury. Very popular, these excursions induced the SR to offer through ticketing on those trains connecting with the pleasure steamers.

West Street Pier was upgraded in 1930 when a covered way was built to provide shelter for passengers transferring between the boat trains and the Rotterdam steamers. Misfortune visiting the pier in the September of 1932; a steamship colliding with it's cast iron supports, the pier then required heavy repairs.

WWII brought an end to the Batavier services to Holland, but not before some of those fleeing the conflict in Europe had landed here.

On the 2nd of September 1939, a poignant event took place, the evacuation of local children via the pier. Taken off by the MV *Royal Daffodil*, they were taken to the east coast ports of Lowestoft and Great Yarmouth.

Two years after the return of peace, pleasure steamers started to call once again and on the 19th of July 1947, the *Royal Daffodil's* 8:50 am Margate sailing, calling at Southend en-route, was priced at 6/-0d. For the adventurous, an all-day cruise along the Channel coast of France was also on offer for £1. The French coast trips were popular with the imbibers of alcoholic beverages as once safely outside of territorial waters, the licensing laws did not apply.

West Street pier's long association with the pleasure steamers came to an end in the September of 1966 when that veteran of the Dunkirk evacuation, the General Steam Navigation motor vessel *Royal Daffodil*, cast off from the pier for the last time. The fleet then sold off, in February 1967 the *Royal Daffodil* sailed to Belgium for breaking.

In the early 1950's C Class No. 31280 waits on the pier road at Gravesend West having arrived with a local goods. Barry Diplock.

West Street LC&DR Pier seen on 2nd February 1952. By this time the trackwork had been rationalised. In the background can be seen the travelling steam crane, and beyond that, at Tilbury is one of the P&O liners on the Australian service, this is probably the "Himalaya". Lens of Sutton.

With the ending of the pleasure steamer services, the pier went into decline. 1967 bringing a proposal to sell off the pier to a company who intended operating the pier for cargo handling, this came to nought.

The 1968 closure of the West Street branch also closing the pier, its rails later removed, it was to languish out of use.

A visit to the pier in 1990 revealing the covered way to be still largely intact and faded posters advertising the long departed glories of pleasure trips from the pier still in situ, a photo of an example is shown opposite.

Later used for the storage of two small catamarans, *Uriah Heap* and *Philip Pirrip*, these small boats were a forlorn reminder of White Horse Ferries, plan to operate high-speed commuter ferries.

A failed venture, both have now moved away, *Uriah Heap,* briefly worked the Southampton to Hythe ferry in 2016 before heavily damaged in a collision.

By 2006 with the pier's decking removed, and the later removal of the rail viaduct leading to the pier, its demolition seemed inevitable.

However, the pier may yet find a new life, plans announced in 2015 propose developing the area and refurbishing the pier for community use.

Between Downs and Thames - Railways of Gravesend, the Hoo Peninsular and Isle of Grain

1947 poster advertising excursions from West Street LC&DR Pier. Authors collection.

West Street Pier seen on 15th September 2006 just before its landward connection was severed. Author.

Batavier Line steamer service to Rotterdam

WINTER SERVICE BATAVIER LINE
LONDON — ROTTERDAM VIA GRAVESEND
IN CONNECTION WITH THE SOUTHERN RAILWAY
3 SAILINGS WEEKLY

✱

TIME-TABLE

FROM LONDON: TUESDAY — THURSDAY — SATURDAY

London (Victoria Station)	dep. 18.30
Gravesend Pier	arr. 19.23
Gravesend Pier	dep. 19.30
Rotterdam (Jobskade)	arr. abt. 8.— (a)

(a) Motorbus Service for passengers and hand-baggage from Jobskade after arrival of Steamer via Schiedamschesingel (Passenger Office) to D.P. (Central) Station (no charge).

FROM ROTTERDAM: TUESDAY — THURSDAY — SATURDAY

Rotterdam (Jobskade)	dep. 19.— (b)
Gravesend Pier	arr. abt. 8.—
Gravesend Pier (West Street Station)	dep. 9.07 (c)
Victoria Station	arr. 9.54 (c)

(b) Motorbus Service for passengers and hand-baggage at 18.10 from D.P. (Central) Station via Schiedamschesingel (Passenger Office) to Jobskade (no charge).
(c) On Sundays dep. Gravesend 8.50, arrive Victoria 9.35; on week-days when weather conditions enable the steamer to reach Gravesend before the advertised time, passengers are conveyed up to London by an earlier train, reaching Victoria at 9.25.

TRAIN SERVICE — GRAVESEND TO LONDON

Fast electric trains run at frequent intervals from Gravesend Central Station (a few minutes walk from Gravesend Pier) and will be found very convenient for those passengers wishing to get to the City.
Frequent trains also run from that station to Charing Cross (for the Strand and West End).

The times etc. shown above are liable to alteration.

IMPORTANT! In April 1938 the daily service will be resumed.

FARES:

	TO ROTTERDAM From London £ s. d.	TO ROTTERDAM From Gravesend £ s. d.	FROM ROTTERDAM To London fl.	FROM ROTTERDAM To Gravesend fl.
1st class single	2.17.6	2.12. 9	26.60	24.40
2nd " "	2. 5.—	2. 1. 3	20.90	19.10
1st " return	5.14.6	5. 5. —	53.—	48.60
2nd " "	4. 9.6	4. 2. —	41.40	38.—

Return-tickets are available for 60 days.

17-DAY RETURNTICKET:

	From London £ s. d.	From Gravesend £ s. d.	To London fl.	To Gravesend fl.
1st class	4.15.—	4. 5. 6	44.—	39.60
2nd "	3.10.—	3. 2. 6	32.40	29.—

The validity can be extended to 60 days on payment of £ —.18.6 resp. f 9.—.

WEEK-END (NO PASSPORT) TICKETS:

	From London £ s. d.	From Gravesend £ s. d.	To London fl.	To Gravesend fl.
1st class	3.17.6	3.11. 4	35.90	33.—
2nd "	3.—.8	2.15.10	28.10	25.90

These tickets are available for the outward journey on Saturday, for the returnjourney on the following Tuesday.
The tickets may be used without Passports only by persons of "British nationality".

PARTIES 10—14 PASSENGERS:

	From London to Rotterdam £ s. d.	From Rotterdam to London fl.
1st class single	2. 3. 9	20.30
2nd " "	1.14. 3	15.90
1st " return	4. 6. 9	40.20
2nd " "	3. 7.11	31.50

PARTIES 15 AND OVER:

	From London to Rotterdam £ s. d.	From Rotterdam to London fl.
1st class single	2.—.11	19.—
2nd " "	1.12. 1	14.90
1st " return	4. 1. 3	37.60
2nd " "	3. 3. 8	29.50

EXCESS FARE (SINGLE)

	From Gravesend £ s. d.	To Gravesend fl.
for 1st class steamer	—.12. 6	5.80
on Week-End tickets	—. 8. 6	3.90

Cost of food is not included in the above fares. For prices of meals, etc., passengers should refer to the printed tariffs on board.

PARTY TICKETS
are issued on the following conditions:
1. The party must travel out in one group, but individual return is allowed.

Batavier Line timetable from 1937. Simplon postcards.

It was to be thirty-six years after it's opening that the West Street branch finally achieved one of the ambitions of the LC&DR directors of 1886, the attracting of a regular short sea service to West Street pier.

Adding West Street Pier as another port of call to their existing London to Rotterdam service, this was the Dutch shipping firm, William Müller & Co. A service with a long history, sailings had started in 1839 from Wool Quays near Tower Bridge.

Having intermittently used the pier during WWI, in 1916 their steamer *Batavier II* was captured by the Germans and while flying an enemy flag, was sunk by a British submarine.

Müller having kept the Batavier name after buying out the line in 1895, the service was known locally as the Batavier Line. No great thought appearing to have gone into naming the ships used on the service, they were called the uninspiring *Batavier III, IV & VI*.

Batavier III built in 1897 by Gourley Brothers of Dundee, carried 44 First and Second Class passengers plus up to 250 in steerage class. After being sold off in 1939, once again King Neptune failed to smile on the Batavier line and she too became another loss to a submarine when sunk by the German U61 east of the Shetland Isles in 1940.

Batavier IV, also built by Gourley Brothers in 1902, was to have a more fortunate life. A larger vessel, she could carry 75 First and 28 Second Class passengers with accommodation for a further 325 in steerage. In 1939, after being taken off the Rotterdam service, the Royal Navy requisitioned her for use as the training ship, *HMS Eastern Isles.* Re-naming her as *HMS Western Isles* in the following year, she survived until 1970. Lastly came *Batavier VI.* Launched in 1903, she was used as relief ship for the service.

A connecting rail service starting in 1922, the SE&CR Continental Handbook for the year shows a five-day a week service starting from the 15th of June. Departing from Victoria at 5:45 pm and arriving at Gravesend West pier for 6:40 pm, this working was provided by a through carriage detached at Swanley from a main line service.

The carriage was later superseded by a dedicated boat train and services then running directly to West Street pier, it was unofficially known as "The Continental". Normally such a service having its motive power provided by an SE&CR 4-4-0 express locomotive, a humble C Class 0-6-0 locomotive, presumably a member of the class fitted for steam heating, was often rostered for the duty and occasionally, a modest H Class tank locomotive could also deputise.

A service favoured by those wishing to travel discretely, this included the British diplomatic service and members of the Dutch royal family, the Prince Consort of Holland is known to have used the service.

While cabins on the ships could be reserved in advance, those hardier or more frugal souls could spend the journey in the ship's saloons. Passport control was lax in that more leisurely era, they were checked when the passengers disembarked.

The voyage including a meal, a post-prandial activity suggested for passengers by a publicity brochure was:

"spend a few hours on the promenade deck, taking in the wonderful sights of the Thames Estuary and the exhilaration of the bracing air of the North Sea"

By the winter of 1937, with steamer services operating thrice weekly, its returning travellers had a direct connecting train to Victoria at 9:07 am, and should bad weather delay berthing, a substitute train could be provided for 9:25 am.

Departing Victoria at 6.30 pm, the boat trains arriving at West Street pier for 7:23 pm, this allowed just seven minutes to board the 7:30 pm sailing. Depending on the weather and sea state, arrival at Rotterdam was scheduled for around 8:00 am the following day.

Following the invasion of Holland, the service ceased. Never to return to West Street Pier, post war sailings were transferred to Tilbury.

Batavier II of 1897 as rebuilt in 1910, she was sunk by a submarine in 1916. Simplon postcards

Batavier III, also a victim of a submarine in 1940. Simplon postcards

Accidents and Incidents

So far, the area has been fortunate to avoid any major rail accidents, the most severe being the Milton Range Halt collision of August 1922. With all the safeguards of the modern railway, the likelihood of being involved in a major rail incident today is very low.

As this is a theme common to all the local railways, events are set out in a chronological sequence merely for convenience. Most incidents occurring on the SER or LC&DR, the Hundred of Hoo Railway appears to have been remarkably accident free.

Among the most endangered persons on the early railways was its employees and in 1841, on a rail network of 1,775 miles, 28 railway employees were killed and 32 badly injured. Fortunately, the accident rate of more recent times is much reduced and excluding the 207 suicides, in 2007 on a network of 10,072 miles, there were 32 ¶ fatalities, two of whom were railway staff.

¶*Office of the Rail Regulator*
http:/www.orr.gov.uk/statistics

Gravesend G&RR station incident of 1845

Gravesham came close to having its worst railway disaster on the opening day of its first public railway, the Gravesend & Rochester Railway. An incident occurring on the 10th of February 1845, a train derailed and burst through a partition at Gravesend G&RR station.

A large number of spectators were standing behind the partition, and for a moment it looked as if the whole train and its onlookers would be deposited into the murky waters of the nearby canal. Luckily this was avoided. The cause of the mishap later being traced to a late brake application by the guard, *Lloyds Weekly Newspaper* of the 16th of February 1845 reported the event thus:

"Between the terminus and the canal basin (which is from it about 30 yards) is a high wooden partition, with a compartment in the centre, to be used upon occasion as a gateway. Outside of this a great number of people had collected when the train arrived and all at once a crash, and then the protrusion of a carriage through the partition, threw them into the utmost consternation, as they at the instant concluded that the whole train was darting through the aperture, and they would be immersed in the basin which fronted it. Happily, their alarm was but momentary, as the carriage which burst through the partition suddenly stopped, and relieved them from all apprehension of danger to the train of carriages and its occupants in the rear".

Such an event, were it to happen today, would be treated as a serious incident, but in those far-off days it was not even considered worthy of an a investigation. Amazingly, a further derailment occurred at Gravesend station on the following Saturday. Although the local "horse locomotive" proprietor's tried to use these incidents for scare mongering by placing blame upon the train's conductor, this was obviously to no avail, G&RR passenger numbers continuing to increase.

Denton collision and runaway train 1849

An area once notorious for fog, it was during such a weather event in the December of 1849, that a collision occurred at the junction of the former Gravesend & Rochester Railway with the SER at Denton.

Happening when a special train formed of a locomotive and a carriage was struck by a train coming from the ballast pit at Higham, the carriage of the special train smashed, the driver of the ballast train, fearing for his life, jumped clear of his engine. Leaving the engine with it's regulator open, it careered towards Gravesend out of control. A sensational event. the *Kentish Independent* of the 5th of January 1850 gave the following description of the events of the minutes following the accident:

"The train set off at full speed in the direction of Gravesend Station, where the Up train to London, just about to start stood in the platform siding. The switchman, unable to account for an engine turned the points, to send it forward onto the main line, and it proceeded at a rapid pace through the station"

The newspaper's description of events at Gravesend station is probably dramatised, as at the time, the station's centre roads were only sidings.

News of the incident sent by telegraph to London Bridge, the superintendent of the line then rushing to the platforms, commandeered the locomotive from a Gravesend bound express and set off in pursuit. Meanwhile, at London Bridge a locomotive was placed on the station's approach road and sleepers were formed into a barricade. The intermediate stations then sent the details by telegraph, the line was cleared. The superintendent, by now meeting with the runaway at Bricklayers Arms junction, quickly reversed the pursuing locomotive and set off in pursuit of the runaway.

The two eventually colliding, the driver of the pursuing engine bravely leapt into the cab of the runaway to bring it under control. Perhaps not the first use of an electric telegraph for such purpose, it is certainly an early example.

Derailment at Milton Range 1862

Occurring near to the present day Milton Firing Range and uncannily close to the scene of the later 1922 fatal collisions, on the 20th of March 1862 a passenger train, the 3:10 pm departure from Strood to London Bridge left the rails at speed. The unfortunate guard, a George Waller, travelling in the first brake carriage being killed, the locomotive crew were reported as being seriously injured with some unlucky passengers also suffering minor injuries.

The original track laid by the SER in 1847 then still in use, the Railways Accident Inspector, a Captain Tyler of the Corps of Royal Engineers, found the permanent way was in a bad condition. Rail chairs having detached themselves from the sleepers, the wooden tree-nails used as fixings in 1847 having rotted away, improper ballasting, rotting sleepers and loose rail joints were also apparent.

Captain Tyler's report ¶ for the Board of Trade concluded that the oscillating motion of the 2-4-0 locomotive, having finally sheared off the rotten tree-nails, this had caused the rail chairs to come away from the sleepers, the tracks then spreading, the train had derailed.

¶ *Board of trade report August 1862.*

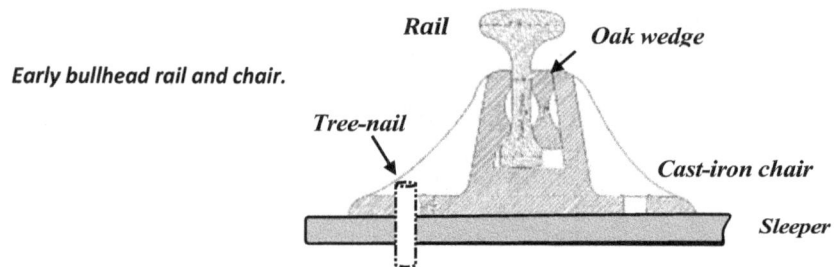

Early bullhead rail and chair.

The Sole Street Bank derailment 1897

On the 23rd of August 1897, the 5:39 am express parcels and goods train bound for Margate and Ramsgate, carrying meat, parcels, newspapers and railway staff, derailed while descending Sole Street bank ¶ at Lower Bush.

The cause of the accident was the derailment of a goods van "jumping" the track. Causing it to slew and disintegrate, it then spewed its load of newspapers and goods over the tracks. Although the driver made an emergency brake application, the train was travelling at speed and could not be brought to a halt before the guards van and five passenger coaches had derailed and torn up nearly a quarter mile of track in the process. Fortunately, no one was seriously hurt.

The breakdown gang, although arriving quickly, took nearly five hours to clear the Up line and the first train to go over the repaired line at 10:50 am was the Up Flushing boat train express from Queenborough. Cleared the same day, both lines were open by early evening.

¶ *The London Standard 24 August 1897.*

The breakdown train is seen arriving at Lower Bush shortly after the 6:25 am accident. Both Up and Down lines were completely cleared for normal running by 6:35 pm. Tony Riley collection

Gomshall incident February 1904

Not a local accident, its story is worth the telling, involving as it did the Northumberland Fusiliers, a regiment that had a long association with Gravesend.

Occurring on Saturday 20th of February 1904 ¶ when the regiment was travelling by troop train from Gravesend to Southampton for embarkation to Mauritius, the train's locomotive, an 0-6-0 tender engine, derailed at some 30-40 miles per hour near to Gomshall, Surrey. The locomotive, slewing around and causing both the driver and fireman to sustain serious injuries, it crushed the trains first vehicle. A brake van, both it and the men's kit it was carrying were destroyed.

¶ *The Times 22nd February 1904.*

Milton Range Halt Collision 1922

The aftermath of the accident, parts of the wrecked train are seen in the Thames & Medway Canal. Jim Greaves collection

Occurring on the morning of the 21st of August 1922, this was the areas worst railway accident and like the incident of 1849, fog was a contributory factor. A major multiple collision, it took the lives of five men and injured many more who were passengers on the 5:45 am workmen's train from Charing Cross to Strood. Upon arrival at Milton Range Halt, the train overran the platform and not content to wait for the train to set back, its impatient passengers, labourers working on the Rochester relief road, now the A226, foolishly jumped directly onto the Up line. Disastrously, just as they started to cross, at 6:25 am, a light engine appeared out of the gloom and ploughed into them.

One man killed outright in the carnage, another was to die of his injuries shortly after. Then remaining at the halt, incredibly, the Charing Cross train was then struck in the rear at 6:35 am by another workmen's train, the 5:55 am departure from New Cross.

The impact of this collision ending the life of yet another workman, in total, five men lost their lives on that disastrous day. Two men dying at the scene, a further three were later to die from their injuries. Another 17 men being injured, some of them were seriously hurt.

At the subsequent investigation by the Ministry of Transport ¶ it was concluded that the driver of the New Cross train having started away from Gravesend Central against a stop signal was at fault. The government's inspector, a Major Hall,

¶ *Report on the accident at Milton Range Halt on 21st August 1922 by the Ministry of Transport, dated 12th September 1922.*

when summing up, recommended the fitting of "whistle" boards either side of the halt to warn anyone crossing of an approaching train.

The fireman and guard of the 5:45 am ex-Charing Cross train should bear some responsibility for the collision with the 6:35 am working as they appear to have failed to protect the train with detonators as proscribed in the company Rule book. Another contributory cause was the absence of a signalman at Denton signal box. Unmanned at the time of the accident, it was not due to open until 7:30 am.

In 1922, Gravesend had no motor ambulance and the towns emergency casualty transport relied upon a handcart operated by the police. The nearest motor ambulance, a naval vehicle brought up from Chatham, had difficulty in reaching the site, finding suitable vans to convey the injured to Gravesend hospital was a significant problem.

In 1922 Gravesend Hospital was little more than a cottage hospital. Run by local doctors, it was inadequate for an accident of this scale and to ensure an emergency vehicle was available in the future, a motor ambulance was donated to the town's St. Johns Ambulance division.

The Runaway Train June 1961

Bemused railwaymen examine the aftermath of the collision at Gravesend West. Gravesend Library

On Wednesday the 21st of June 1961 a nearly new diesel locomotive, ¶ No. D6530, later Class 33 No. 33018, departed from Farningham Road station without its crew after they had failed to secure its brakes. Probably after intervention from a signalman, it was diverted from the main line onto the Gravesend West branch, where

¶ *Now awaiting restoration at the Midland Railway Centre.*

due to the continuously falling gradient, the loco ran the five miles from Fawkham Junction to Gravesend West station. Travelling at speed, upon arrival it smashed into a line of 20 wagons, derailing two, destroying a third and damaging three others. The runaway then obligingly derailing, it crashed down an embankment. Mr. Sharkey, a goods porter the only casualty, he was taken to Gravesend Hospital with an injured knee.

Dreams and Schemes

In the early days of capitalism the finance for most new railway projects was raised from private investors. As yet there were no limited companies in the UK, and an investor buying shares in a company that later declared its costs had risen, had to pay the extra monies or forfeit their shares. A particular form of sharp practice was to float a railway company, watch its profits rise and then sell out before producing anything.

Nevertheless, in the 1840's a speculative craze, "Railway Mania" developed. In some ways comparable to the South Sea Bubble scandal of the 18th Century, its effects were similar, and eager to purchase shares in the technological wonder that were the railways, many investors were either ruined or enriched. Development of the rail network in Kent later in the 19th Century saw two major companies become dominant, the LC&DR and SER. Locked in fierce competition, they constantly attempted to wrest business from each other and a tactic used was to build, or threaten to build, a so called "spoiling" line.

The Gravesend Railway of 1886 being considered to be such a "spoiling" line, an Act of Parliament being obtained to construct a line into a competitor's territory, it was then used to "spoil" the income of the incumbent railway. However, usually dividing revenues, this tactic was usually detrimental to both companies.

Encouraged by advances in building methods in the early 20th century, this period saw the last flowering of proposed grandiose railway schemes before road transport became dominant.

The Northfleet & Farningham Railway 1865

Following the opening of both the SER and the LC&DR, it wasn't long before another local railway proposal appeared. To be known as the Northfleet to Farningham Railway Company, the preliminary step being the obtaining of a certificate for construction under the Railway Companies Powers Act 1864, its rather hopeful intent, to quote the *Kentish Gazette* of November 1865 was:

"To enable the intended Company and the London, Chatham and Dover Railway Company and the South Eastern Railway Company to enter into and to carry into effect contracts to enable the joint working of the said two railway companies"

Commencing from a new station adjacent to the present 1849 SER Gravesend station in the vicinity of Somerset Street, (now Darnley Road) it was then to make its way to Sutton-at-Hone. Planned to connect with the North Kent Railway near Perry Street, an intermediate branch line was to be included to effect this.

Then passing through Northfleet, Swanscombe, Greenhithe and South Darenth, the railway was to form a junction with the LC&DR in the vicinity of Rabbits Road at Sutton-at-Hone. Needless to say the line was not built, but the Gravesend Railway of 1886 in part followed some of the route proposed for the long forgotten Northfleet & Farningham Railway.

Planned SER Rosherville Station 1871

In addition to the construction of the Blackfriars spur and other works, the SER Act of 1872 included authority to build a station for the Rosherville Gardens. To be built on land the SER had purchased in the vicinity of Dover Road, Northfleet, the station was to be sited near to where this road crosses the North Kent line via a skew bridge.

Passing through open countryside, a winding road leading to the gardens part of the plan, its course would have taken it past a smock windmill that once stood here.

Situated just a mile from Gravesend Central station, Rosherville's SER station would have been ½ mile from another potential source of revenue for the railway, the holiday resort of Perry Street village. However, like so many other schemes, it was never to come to fruition, and remains a source of speculation.

Had it been built, perhaps it would have closed after the demise of the Rosherville Gardens, as did the 1886 LC&DR station.

Location map of the proposed SER Rosherville Station.

The Tilbury and Gravesend Tunnel Junction Railway 1882

Sir Edward Watkin, the Victorian railway entrepreneur whom we met earlier, proposed a grand scheme to build a high speed railway to a Channel Tunnel in 1879. Starting to sink shafts in 1877, the construction of Tunnel itself being initially undertaken by a separate company, by 1880 Watkin had extended his control over that project also when buying out the tunnelling company.

Watkin, then the Chairman of the South Eastern and three other railways, could no doubt see that a connection with the Continent would increase the revenues of all these railways.

Starting from the north of England, his high-speed line was to be routed through the Midlands to Dover, where en-route it was to have passed over the metals of those other parts of Watkin's railway empire, namely the Metropolitan Railway and the Manchester, Sheffield & Lincolnshire Railway. Using the SER as its final leg, trains would have arrived at a terminal station by the Channel Tunnel's portal. Although not completed as envisaged, a variation of this high speed connecting line was eventually opened in 1899 as the Great Central Railway. Terminating at Marylebone, it was never extended to the Channel coast.

Travel through the Channel Tunnel was to be achieved by using compressed air powered locomotives, these novel engines being able to draw a train of 250 tons gross weight a distance of twenty-two miles.

Watkin's brainchild was taken more seriously when he set up what to modern ears would have been a venture with a completely different meaning, the Submarine Continental Railway Company of 1882. With work starting at both Folkestone and Dover, boring of the tunnel itself then commenced.

Born into an age when rivalries among railway companies were particularly fierce, these activities caught the attention of other railway entrepreneurs. Seeing that a new rail link connecting the Channel Tunnel to the LT&SR via the SER would be advantageous for both the railways and business's of the east of England, these businessmen proposed a new connecting line, the Tilbury & Gravesend Tunnel and Junction Railway (T&GJR). It's main feature to be a Thames railway tunnel, as it's name suggests, it was to be built between Gravesend and Tilbury. A single track tunnel, in addition to allowing the passage of trains, it was to have had provision for pedestrians.

Accordingly, in 1882 a prospectus was issued for the T&GJR, and an Act sanctioning the scheme was passed into law in the same year. Under the terms of this Act, the LT&SR were

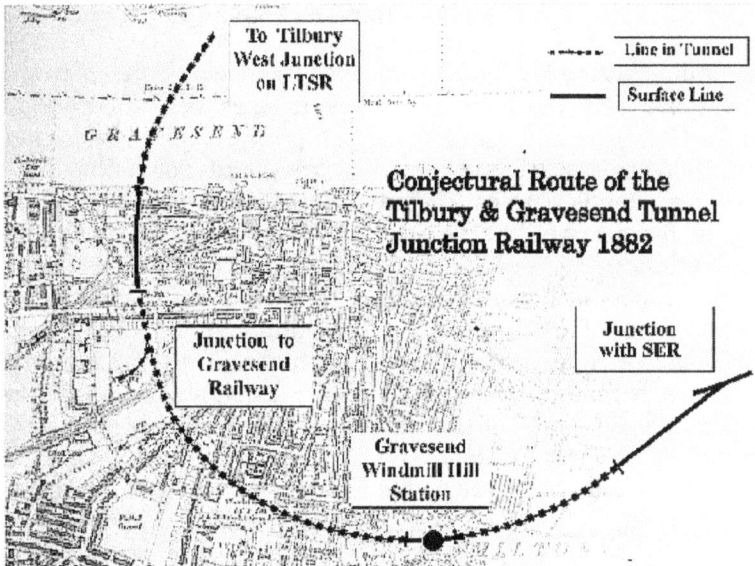
Conjectural Route of the Tilbury & Gravesend Tunnel Junction Railway 1882

to be compensated for the loss of their profits from the Gravesend-Tilbury ferry and their trains given running powers on the T&GJR.

Describing the line as a 3¾ mile long single track railway, the Act of 1882 authorised the line to start from a junction with the LT&SR at Little Thurrock, at a distance of 1,180 yards to the north west of West Tilbury signal box.

A consortium of financiers being the projects main backers, they appointed Messrs Nimmo and Minns as the engineers for the project. Then well known for building the Mersey Tunnel, a John Waddel was selected as the works main contractor. Looking at the route of the line, a drawing ¶ submitted to Gravesend Corporation and Parliament shows the line as entering and exiting a 2,695 yards long tunnel at a gradient of 1:41. Descending to a maximum depth of 40 yards below ground level, the distance between the riverbed and the tunnel roof was to be 40 feet.

Breaking surface in Kent at the site of the present day West Mill Industrial Estate, Gravesend, the line was then to have continued via a curve to pass underneath London Road. From here, by using a spur to Perry Street, an open-air junction was to be made with the yet unbuilt Gravesend Railway. Passing then under Lennox Road and the SER's North Kent Railway, it's route then continuing in tunnel under both Pelham Road and the Bat and Ball cricket ground, it was then to have emerged into the open once more at a new station near to Windmill Hill. Departing from this new station, the line was then to have continued in tunnel underneath Peppercroft Street, Clarence Road, Peacock Street, The Grove and Love Lane. It's final leg taking the line on to Milton Barracks, after emerging at ground level, it would have headed north to a junction with the SER's North Kent Railway.

Although no capital was ever raised, the line's route was, however, surveyed, trial borings undertaken and negotiations started with the landowners on its route. However, the LT&SR, very short of money at the time, showed little enthusiasm for the venture, their main concern competing with the Great Eastern Railway for the lucrative Southend holiday traffic.

With doubts over its viability, given the failure of the Ralph Dodd 1799 road tunnel § and following concerns by the Government and the Board of Trade over the potential use of the Channel Tunnel by an invading enemy, the project was abandoned as was the T&GJR. An Abandonment Bill enacted by Parliament in 1884, it was then wound up. Had the T&GJR been built, the ferries would probably have ceased running by the 1890's and Gravesend and Tilbury become important rail hubs.

¶ Held at Kent History and Library Centre, Maidstone.

§ Reports, with Plans, Sections, &c. of the Proposed Dry Tunnel, Or Passage, from Gravesend, in Kent, to Tilbury, in Essex; Demonstrating Its Practicability, By R. Dodd

Thames Barrage 1905

Building a barrage or dam across the Thames in Gravesend Reach was one of the more grandiose schemes proposed for Gravesham. First mooted in the 1870's, it was 1905 before a scheme finally appeared ¶. It's cost enormous, the estimated construction cost in 2016 values would have been in the region of £500 million.

The barrage's main purpose was twofold, firstly to retain a reservoir of fresh water for domestic consumption and secondly to hold back the waters of the Thames to maintain a constant level of water upstream at all states of the tide. This allowing ships to berth at quay sides, the need for expensive docks and their lock gates could be dispensed with.

¶ *The Great Thames Barrier T.W Barber M.Inst.CE*

To be constructed from mass concrete with four large locks incorporated for the passage of shipping, it was to be located just downstream of Gravesend Town Pier between the Clarendon Royal Hotel and Tilbury Fort. Incorporating land transport links between Kent and Essex, these included a rail tunnel linking the SE&CR to the LT&SR and a road atop the structure. Another benefit claimed for it was as a defence by acting as a barrier to an invading fleet in time of war. Ironically, should a fleet have got that far, the war was probably already lost.

Strong opposition exhibited by both shipping interests and local authorities, its construction was blocked. Proposed In an age when raw sewerage was pumped into the Thames, the consequences of removing the tides scouring effect on the downstream movement of effluent and silt is best imagined rather than experienced!

An artists impression of the abandoned 1905 Thames barrier project

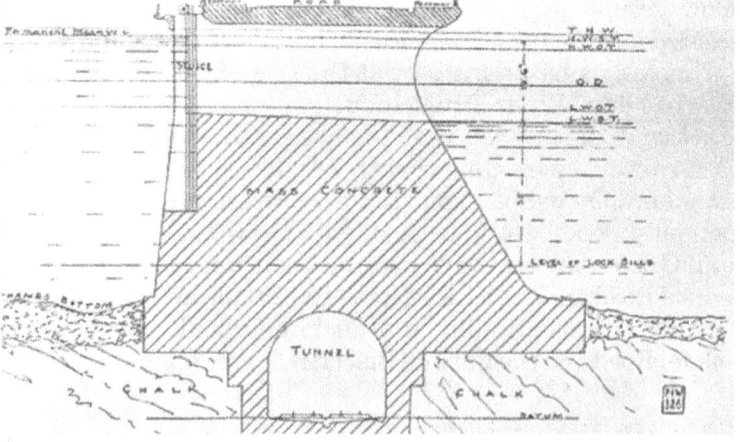

Section through the proposed 1905 barrier showing the railway and road.

The Lower Thames Tunnel and New Connecting Railway of 1921

In the early twentieth Century, before the 1963 opening of the Dartford tunnel, the east London Rotherhithe tunnel was the lowest downstream fixed road crossing point on the Thames. With the coming of war in 1914, also came the threat of invasion and with it, the imperative to have a means of rapidly moving large bodies of troops between East Anglia and the South East without passing through the constricted city.

mile long electrified railway from Gravesend to Luton, this was to pass through the counties of Kent, Essex, Hertfordshire and Bedfordshire. Had it been built, this railway would in part have followed the route of the northern quarter of the present M25 orbital motorway.

Commercially, it was promoted as a means of bypassing the crowded London rail termini and connecting the SE&CR with the Midland,

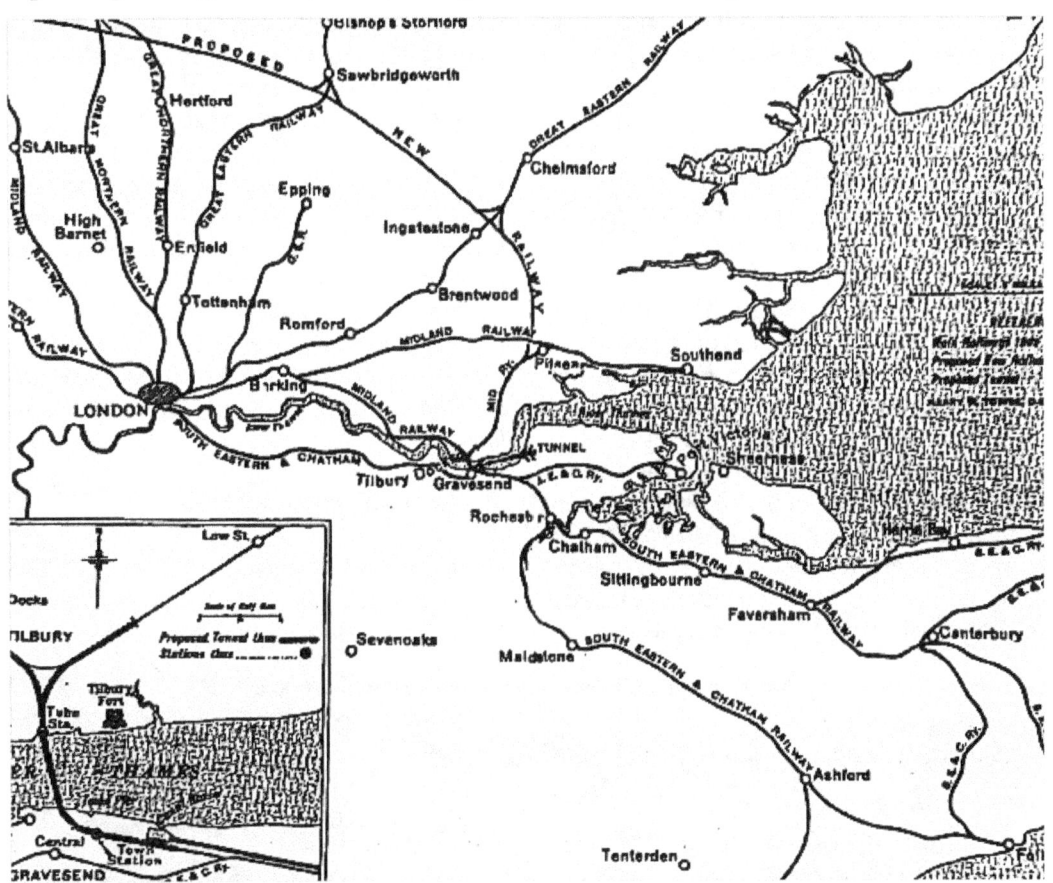

To achieve this, a hastily constructed and temporary wooden pontoon bridge was built by Army engineers between Gravesend and Tilbury. Something of a barrier to the movement of shipping, this 850 yard long floating bridge had been removed by 1920.

After their experiences in the Great War, the War Office, military fore runner of the Ministry of Defence, was mindful of the need for a permanent lower Thames crossing and when a 1921 scheme for a lower Thames rail tunnel was promoted, it received their full backing. The scheme also proposing the building of a new 50

Great Eastern, Great Northern and the London & North Western Railways.

The projects major work being a single track railway tunnel stretching between Gravesend and Tilbury, the tunnel, at its lowest point would have been located at 30 yards below riverbed level. On the Kentish side of the Thames, a tunnel connecting the SE&CR to the Midland Railway starting from a new Gravesend Town station, it was to have had underground stations at Queen Street, Gravesend and Tilbury Riverside station.

Quite popular, the scheme enjoyed the

support of local authorities, manufacturers and those entrepreneurs who could see the opportunity to develop the hinterlands of both Essex and Hertfordshire, interest was also expressed by the coal mining and shipping industries in Kent.

The London Underground railways being then approached for both tunnel building information and support for the project, backing was also sought from the major railway companies.

Expected to be mainly a freight line, some local passenger services also envisaged, these would have included an electrified shuttle service between Gravesend and Tilbury. Longer distance passenger services also being envisaged, Chatham to Barking workings were mooted.

The intended electrification method would presumably have been the 4 rail DC system, then preferred by both the Midland and the SE&CR, this possibility leading to the intriguing likelihood of 3,000 volt, 4 rail electrification becoming the norm on the SE&CR lines rather than the LS&WR 3 rail 660 volt system installed by the Southern in the 1920's and 30's.

At 1921 prices the cost of building the tunnel alone was estimated at £2,600,000, with the new line adding a further £1,000,000. Offices for the project were taken up at 45 Queen Street, Gravesend, where regular committee meetings were held and initiatives were started to seek both local support and inform traders and residents on the schemes advantages.

Gravesend Corporation gave the project their backing, as did Gravesend's MP, Sir Alexander Richardson. To seek government support for the project, a deputation led by Sir Alexander went to see the Transport Minister.

The incumbent at the time being Sir Eric Geddes, a former member of the wartime Railway Executive Committee, he is probably better known as the wielder of "Geddes Axe", a range of austerity measures he introduced to save government spending after the Great War.

The minister being unable to meet them, this policy made his reply by letter ¶ predictable:

"He was gratified to learn that so great an interest was taken locally in transport questions, and that the districts concerned realised to what extent the prosperity of the inhabitants rests upon adequate facilities for the handling of traffic. Unfortunately the times are unpropitious for the undertaking of large works of construction, which under more favourable conditions, would be abundantly justified in the public interest".

And there died the scheme.

¶ *The Times August 12th 1921.*

Model of the 1914 Gravesend to Tilbury pontoon bridge.

Notes on Nationalisation

At the ending of hostilities in 1945, the political climate was one of determination that the fruits of victory should not be lost as they had been after WWI, the Labour government elected in that year believed that the nationalisation of Britain's utilities and major industries was the best way to deliver this bounty.

War weary and run-down, the railways, as the major provider of longer distance public transport were seen as a prime candidate for assimilating into public ownership. Starved of both maintenance and investment during the six long years of war, their fares and freight charges frozen, the railway companies were believed to be in no position to raise the money required for their renewal. This was not actually the case; a fund having been built up by the Treasury for this purpose during wartime, it was treated as excess profits and mostly taken by the post-war government as taxation.

On the railways themselves the track was in a parlous state and the poor condition of the permanent way, rolling stock and infrastructure leading to a series of fatal accidents, line speeds were reduced in consequence. The bad winter of 1947 only adding to the railways' woes, with the passing of the Transport Act in 1947, the legislation was in place for nationalising most of the nation's transport systems, and with the railways as the primary target, government started planning to purchase the £1.7 billion of railway assets.

Acquisition of the railways did not actually cost the government of the day a penny. Achieved by issuing IOU's in the form of British Transport Stock that was not redeemable until 1988, the government defended this by claiming that it would stop a surge in railway share prices. Unsurprisingly, the railway companies protested at their unfair treatment. Demanding a public enquiry, the demand was rejected and on the 1st of January 1948 the nation's railways were vested into the nationalised British Railways.

Obliged to do so by the 1947 Transport Act, one early move of the new organisation was the wholesale replacement of the motley collection of small capacity, privately owned wagons. The mainstay of goods workings, they were also a major cause of operating inefficiency and within a year, 55,000 of these had been scrapped and replaced with modern, BR owned, steel bodied 16 ton wagons. One of the few major investments in railways by the government of the time, in the first seven years of BR's existence, the funds forthcoming from the public purse were of such a sum that they little more than sufficient to maintain the system.

The nation's railways being unable to generate profits from 1952 onwards and serious competition from road and air transport making a return to surplus extremely unlikely, it was acknowledged that change and modernisation was needed on the railways.

To give guidance to the process, the British Transport Commission then published "The Modernisation and Re-equipment of British Railways" in 1955. Better known as the 1955 Modernisation Plan, this envisaged massive investment to eliminate steam traction, extend electrification, modernise the signalling and introduce diesel and electric locomotives to improve the nation's train services.

However, despite the £1.2 billion expenditure of public finance on the 1955 Modernisation Plan, a return to profitably failing to materialise, this was largely due to the Plans failure to change pre-war working practices and banish the obligation to act as a common carrier.

Next to come was the 1962 Transport Act. Dissolving the British Transport Commission, it was replaced by the British Railways board whose chairman was none other than a Dr Richard Beeching. An executive from Imperial Chemical Industries, he was brought in on secondment to provide a fresh view on the railways problems.

Simplifying the process for railway closures, the Act also paved the way for the controversial 1963 report, "The Reshaping of British Railway", the infamous Beeching Plan. Followed in 1965 by its younger companion, "The Development of the Major Railway Trunk Routes", between them these two documents consigned to history 6,000 miles of the railway network and 2,363 stations. Fortunately, the local railways escaped the worst of Beeching's depredations.

In 1965 the British Railways Board changed its name once again to British Rail and the organisation was given a new logo; the familiar double arrow, it is still in use today. Further fracturing of the railways coming with the British Railways Act of 1967, this passed BR's shipping interests to a subsidiary. Known as Sealink, it also absorbed the Tilbury ferry.

1982 bringing the sectorisation of BR, the local passenger railways become a part of the London and South Eastern sector and in the continuing quest for profitability, in 1986 BR's passenger services were again redefined into three core sectors, Inter-City, Regional Railways and Network South East. Gravesham's passenger services allocated to the latter, they then came under the control of its energetic Director, Chris Green.

The railways, however, continued to be loss making and require a public subsidy. To partly alleviate this, BR's subsidiaries were sold off; the hotels going in 1982, they were followed in 1984 by Sealink and by 1989 most subsidiaries had gone, including Travellers Fare, Golden Rail and British Rail Engineering.

In 1991, when the EU issued Directive 91/440, requiring its member states to allow private companies to run services on their nationalised networks, this was to be the catalyst for UK rail privatisation.

Notes on Privatisation

In 1988, the Swedish State Railways were split into two parts. Separating the operation of the train services from the management of the railways' infrastructure, it was on this model that the UK privatisation process was in some part based, although the model for the UK has led to greater fragmentation.

With the political decision to privatise assured by the passing of both the British Coal & British Rail (Transfer Proposals) Act 1993, and the later Railways Act 1993, the fate of the nationally owned British Rail was finally sealed.

The means chosen by government to divest itself of the railways was a new and complex approach. To oversee this process, the separate offices of the Rail Regulator¶ and the Director of Passenger Rail Franchising were created to set about making BR attractive to potential purchasers and lessees.

Splitting up these services, they were turned into pseudo businesses. Becoming Train Operating Units (TOU's) for passenger services, the freight services were divided up into Freight Operating Companies (FOC's), and subsequently, on the 1st of April 1994, Gravesham's passenger services became a part of the Kent Coast and Kent Link TOU's.

Train operations then being separated from infrastructure maintenance with the setting up of Railtrack in the same month, the framework for privatisation was then in being.

¶ *The Office of Rail Regulation is a statutory board which is the economic and safety regulatory authority for Britain's railway network.*

With the ownership of the railways largely remaining with government, the running of the nation's railways was either to be leased or sold off to private companies. Briefly, the structuring of this was as follows:

- Rolling Stock Owning Companies (ROSCO's). [1] After buying most BR's rolling stock, these companies obligation was to lease these to the train operating companies and when required, also purchase new vehicles from train manufacturers.
- Railtrack [2] : As controller and maintainer of stations, signalling, infrastructure and the permanent way, they were also made responsible for providing the pathing and time-tabling of trains.
- Train Operating Companies [4] (TOC's) The holders of the Passenger Train franchises. During their franchise period, they were to manage train services, maintain trains and lease stations from Railtrack.
- Freight Operating Companies. [5] (FOC) Companies who had purchased BR's freight operations including their rolling stock.

[1] Rolling Stock Operating Companies (ROSCO's)

Three companies were set up in 1994; Angel Trains Limited, Eversholt Rail (formerly HSBC Rail) and Porterbrook Rail. Each company being initially sold one third of the former British Rail's passenger locomotive and rolling stock fleet, this sale netted over a billion pounds for the exchequers coffers.

Southeastern using both Angel Trains and Eversholt Rail to provide their rolling stock requirements, Angel Trains is currently the largest ROSCO, owning over 4,600 vehicles.

Some of the original holding companies have since sold out their interests and netting large profits in the process, this has led to claims that the original rolling stock sale price was too low.

2 Railtrack

Railtrack was a grouping of small companies that took control of railway infrastructure on the 1st of April 1994. Following the fatal rail accident at Hatfield in October 2000, its competency put in doubt, it was to be taken over in 2002 by Network Rail, the current infrastructure company.

3 Network Rail

The successor to Railtrack, it is totally owned by Network Rail Ltd; a business limited by guarantee, it is a "not for dividend" company. Using its income for its own operations, it's primary role is to supply services to the TOC's and FOC's.

4 Train Operating Companies (TOC's)

Set up to run passenger services, as the part of the privatised railway most likely to be encountered by the public, an expanded description of their operation may be useful.

As set up in 1994 this was as follows: bidders would prepare an offer for a franchise, then presenting this to the Office of Passenger Rail Franchising (OPRAF), the successful bidder, the new TOC, would then be awarded the franchise for a set period of years with government then paying a previously agreed subsidy until the franchise ended or became either self-financing or profitable. The first round of franchising based solely on awarding franchises to the lowest bidder, in my own experience, this is not always the best method.

Two types of TOC exist. The first type holding franchises for a period of years, the second type are the "open-access" operators who are licensed to provide supplementary services on chosen routes. Both types operate in Gravesham; Southeastern who has a franchise and Eurostar who hold an open access licence as do some FOC's. Operating passenger trains as part of the National Rail brand, these businesses shelter under the umbrella of the Association of Train Operating Companies (ATOC). With some modification this is the model still used today except that franchises are now let by the Secretary of State for Transport.

5 Freight Operating Companies (FOC's)

In 1996 at the dawn of privatisation, three of the six freight operating companies purchased by a subsidiary of the Wisconsin Central Railroad, this was known as North & South Railways. Later renaming the new company as the English, Welsh and Scottish Railway (EWS), by 1997 they had also acquired both Railfreight Distribution and Rail Express Systems.

Deutsche Bahn, the German state railways buying out EWS in 2007, Deutsche Bahn now operate in the UK as DB Cargo (UK) Ltd. In addition to DB, other FOC's include Freightliner (UK) and the two open access freight operators, Direct Rail Services and First GBRf and with other smaller operators, these companies run local freight services.

Summary

Rail privatisation, meant to open up the national railways to competition and reduce the need for public subsidy, this has not quite been the outcome. Having their origins in the deregulation of bus services, some franchises are now in the hands of a few dominant transport groups and in some localities there is a common operator of both bus and train services. Recognised by government, proposals are being considered to increase competition by multiple franchising and open access licensing.

Passenger ridership increasing by 60%, rail freight by a more modest figure, since privatisation, the nations railways have continued to require public support, fares and freight receipts only covering around 50% of running costs.

The hopes for a self financing rail system have yet to be realised, as for the year ending 2005, subsidies for the privatised railway had risen to £5.4bn from BR's £2.1bn grant of 1991.

Bibliography

The Hundred of Hoo Railway – Brian Hart
The South Eastern & Chatham Railway – Adrian Gray
The London, Chatham & Dover Railway – Adrian Gray
The Gravesend West Branch – N. Pallant
The Locomotive History of the South Eastern & Chatham Railway – D. L. Bradley
War on the Line – Bernard Darwin
Southern Railway Halts – R.W. Kidner
The Cement Railways of Kent – B.D Stowel & R.W Kidner
Branch Line to Allhallows – Vic Mitchell & Keith Smith
Southern Electrics, A view from the Past – Graham Waterer
Military Railways in Kent – R.M Lyne
The North Kent Line – R.W.Kidner
Tilbury Riverside Railway Station & Ferry Story in Pictures - Gordon Hales
Hospital Ships and Ambulance Trains -John H Plumridge.
A History of Higham – Andrew Rootes.
The South Eastern & Chatham Railway in the 1914 – 18 War – David Gould.
The Gravesend Branch Railway – R.M Lyme.
The History of Milton Barracks Gravesend and its occupants 1860 -1970 – J Millbank Jones
Gravesend Bomb Damage during WWII - Frank R Turner
The locomotive history of the London, Chatham and Dover Railway - D Bradley.
Carriage Stock of the SE&CR – David Gould.
The South Eastern & Chatham Railway – R..W. Kidner.
Bradshaw's Guides 1863 & 1864.
Working Wagons - David Larkin.
The Hundred of Hoo - Ralph Arnold.
The Canals of South and South East England - Charles Hadfield
Railway life at Ashford - Gordon Turner

Information on The Lower Thames Tunnel and New Connecting Railway of 1921 is sourced from articles in the Times newspaper, an article in the January 2008 *London Railway Record* by Tony Beard, plus articles and news reports by C.Bowen in the Gravesend & Dartford Reporter newspaper archives.

Details of the Southfleet coal handling plant have been obtained from an article in the March 1981 issue of *Model Trains* magazine.

For information on the 2011 spoil line into Lafarge sidings, Northfleet, I am indebted to the publication *Commemorating Northfleet Rail Freight Revival* presented to me by Lafarge.

Information has been taken from archived publications, documents, maps and photos held by the following:

Medway City Ark Kent History & Library Centre
Gravesend Historical Society
Northfleet Historical Society
Dartford library
Gravesend Railway Enthusiasts Society
South Eastern & Chatham Railway Society

Gravesend public library, information sources include:

The Kent Messenger and the Gravesend & Dartford Reporter newspapers archive
The Gravesend Magazine 1911 to 1916
Kelly's Directory
Railway folders.
Gravesend to Tilbury ferry collection
Thames collection

Electronic Sources include:

The Gale News Vault www.gale.cengage.com
Hartley- Kent website www.hartley-kent.org.uk/history
Kent Rail website www.kentrail.org.uk
Cliffe-at-Hoo Historical Society www.cliffehistory.co.uk
Southern Electric Group www.southernelectric.org.uk
Simplon- The passenger ship website www.simplonpc.co.uk
Graces guide www.gracesguide.co.uk
Wikipedia en.wikipedia.org
Industrial Railway Record Society

My thanks also to DB Cargo (UK) Ltd Rail UK for information on their services and Hoo Junction marshalling yard.

Between Downs and Thames - Railways of Gravesend, the Hoo Peninsular and Isle of Grain

Appendices

Site	OS Map ref	Elevation ABSL (Feet)	Next site Up direction	Distance (Miles)	Distance (Miles)	Next site Down direction
Allhallows	TQ844782	20.9	Stoke Junction Halt	1.90	N/A	....
Beluncle Halt	TQ803737	34.3	Sharnal Street	1.11	2.10	Middle Stoke Halt
Cliffe	TQ736747	43	Uralite Halt	2.28	2.40	High Halstow Halt
Denton Halt	TQ664740	10.75	Milton Road Halt	0.54	1.14	Milton Range Halt
Ebbsfleet	TQ614740	16.3	Stratford International	16.80	31.80	Ashford International
Grain	TQ866750	8.5	Grain Crossing Halt	0.25	2.27	Port Victoria
Grain Crossing Halt	TQ863752	3.3	Middle Stoke Halt	1.40	0.25	Grain
Gravesend Central	TQ645740	60	Ebbsfleet	2.22	4.60	Higham
Gravesend Central	TQ645740	60	Northfleet	2.13	0.60	Milton Road Halt
Gravesend G&RR	TQ658742	17.25	....	N/A	3.75	Higham
Gravesend West Street	TQ643743	51	Rosherville	0.71	0.13	West Street LC&DR pier
High Halstow Halt	TQ773751	103	Cliffe	2.40	1.02	Sharnal Street
Higham	TQ715726	41.3	Hoo Junction Staff Halt	1.22	2.63	Strood
Hoo Junction Staff Halt	TQ699735	15.3	Milton Range Halt	2.30	1.22	Higham
Longfield Dust Sidings	TQ620680	273	Longfield	1.33	1.26	Meopham
Longfield Halt	TQ599698	160	Farningham Road	2.95	1.57	Southfleet
Meopham	TQ640678	292	Longfield	2.59	0.93	Sole Street
Middle Stoke Halt	TQ833752	6.5	Beluncle Halt	2.80	1.08	Stoke Junction Halt
Milton Range Halt	TQ682738	4.4	Denton Halt	1.14	1.17	Uralite Halt
Milton Road Halt	TQ656738	42	Gravesend	0.60	1.44	Denton Halt
Northfleet	TQ616744	46	Swanscombe	1.00	2.13	Gravesend
Perry Street Loco Shed	TQ634737	62	Southfleet	1.60	0.39	Rosherville
Port Victoria	TQ876739	13.6	Grain Crossing Halt	2.27	131.00	Flushing
Rochester G&RR	TQ741693	14.5	Higham	2.60	N/A	....
Rosherville	TQ638740	72	Southfleet	1.84	0.71	Gravesend West Street
Sharnal Street	TQ788742	68	High Halstow Halt	1.02	1.11	Beluncle Halt
Sole Street	TQ655675	305	Meopham	0.93	6.86	Rochester
Southfleet	TQ614700	90	Longfield Halt	1.57	1.84	Rosherville
Stoke Junction Halt	TQ842756	0	Middle Stoke Halt	1.08	1.64	Grain
Uralite Halt	TQ701736	20	Milton Range Halt	1.17	2.28	Cliffe
West Street LC&DR pier	TQ644745	11	Gravesend West Street	0.13	191.00	Rotterdam

Appendices

Conversion Chart			
	Qty	Imperial Unit	Metric Unit
Distance	1	Mile	1.61 Kilometres
	1	Chain	20.02 Metres
	1	Yard	0.91 Metres
	1	Foot	0.30 Metres
	1	Inch	2.54 Centimetres
Area	1	Square Mile	2.59 Square Kilometres
	1	Acre	0.41 Hectares
	1	Perch	25.29 Square Metres
Weight	1	Ton	1.016 metric Tonnes
	1	Hundredweight	50.80 Kilograms
	1	Pound	0.454 Kilograms
	1	Ounce	28.35 Grams
Volume	1	Gallon	4.55 Litres
	1	Pint	0.47 Litres
Force	1	lbf	4.448 Newtons
Currency	1	Shilling (-/)	5 Pence
	1	Penny (d)	0.42 Pence

Other early railway proposals

Deptford to Gravesend Railway 1838
Gravesend & East Coast Railway 1840
Gravesend, Rochester & Chatham Railway 1843
North Gravesend Railway 1844
Direct London & Gravesend Railway 1844
North Kent County Railway 1856
North and South Gravesend Tunnel Railway 1876

Gradient profile LC&DR Main line in Gravesham

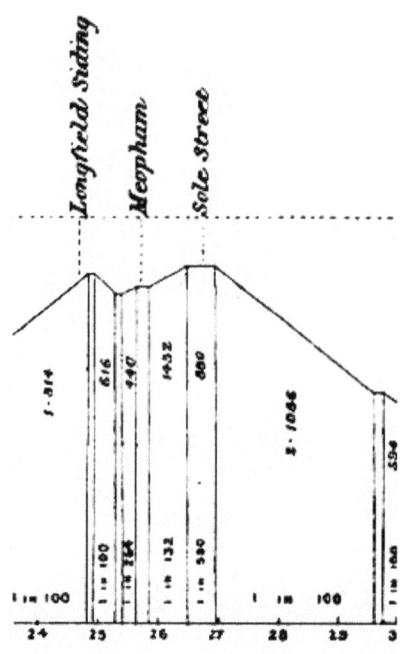

Gradient profile West Street Branch

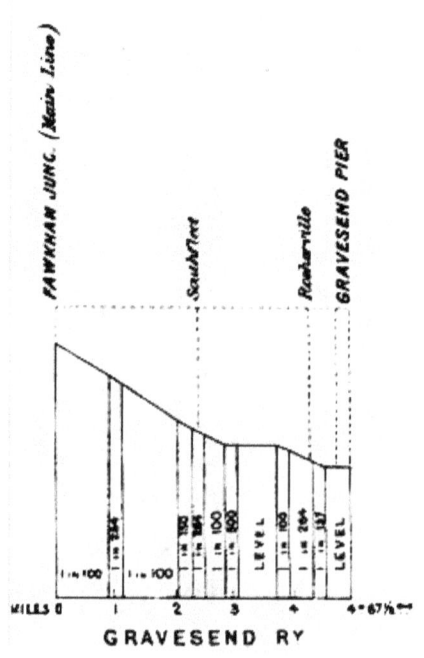

Glossary

2-6-0 Known as the Whyte notation, these numbers classify steam locomotives by their wheel arrangement. The numeric shown identifies a locomotive having two guiding wheels, six driving wheels and no trailing wheels.

AC Alternating current.

APCM Associated Portland Cement Manufacturers, now CRH, a global building materials group, successor to Lafarge.

ATOC Association of Train Operating Companies.

Banking assistance Nothing to do with cash. To provide locomotives sufficiently powerful to climb the steepest gradients (banks) encountered on their journey, would be wasteful. The extra power required to climb a steep gradient was supplied by an additional locomotive, a "banker" pushing at the rear of the train

Bogie An independently swivelling truck supporting the wheels that carry the body of a carriage, wagon or locomotive.

Bothy A term used by railways to describe basic line side storage or accommodation.

BR British Railways, British Rail from 1965.

Chord In geometry a line segment joining two points on a curve. In railway terms this has come to mean a curved section of track joining two railway lines.

C&U Chattenden & Upnor Railway.

CME Chief Mechanical Engineer

CNT Chattenden Naval Tramway.

DC Direct current.

Diesel-Electric The most common type of main line diesel locomotive. A diesel engine within the locomotive drives an alternator, powering the wheels via speed controlled traction motors.

Double heading Describes the practice of having two locomotives at the front of a train to provide extra power. Usually resorted to for hauling particularly heavy trains.

Duplex Lamp Type of oil lamp that uses two parallel wicks.

Edmundson ticket A cardboard ticket stamped with a serial number and originating and destination stations. These were once used as part of an accounting and revenue collecting system and was the standard ticket used by nearly all UK railways from the 1840's until the 1990's. Edward Thompson, a stationmaster on the Manchester and Leeds Railway is credited with their introduction.

EWS English, Welsh and Scottish Railways. A consortium that was headed by Wisconsin Central, a US railroad business.

FOC Freight Operating Company.

G&RR Gravesend & Rochester Railway.

GPS Global Positioning System. Satellite based position locator.

GWR Great Western Railway.

Herepath's Journal A 19th century periodical edited by John Herepath, it is now known as the *Railway Gazette*.

Inter modal The use of more than one mode of transport for a journey that uses a common container for freight.

KLR Kingsnorth Light Railway.

LB&SCR London Brighton & South Coast Railway.

LC&DR London, Chatham & Dover Railway.

LC&NKR London, Chatham and North Kent Railway.

LT&SR London, Tilbury & Southend Railway.

Lock and Block A signalling safety system introduced to railways from the 1870's. "Lock" refers to a scheme of mechanical and electrical connections between railway signals and points that prevents dangerous routes being set-up. The "Block" is a length of railway line, usually between two stop signals, that is required to be clear before a train can enter. The LC&DR was a pioneer in this system.

MPV vehicle Multiple-purpose Vehicle. Usually a diesel powered maintenance vehicle, it is able to carry combinations of modules based on ISO standard containers, these modules can be changed as required to suit particular maintenance needs.

NKR North Kent Railway.

NRM National Railway Museum.

OS - Ordnance Survey.

Railway Clearing House An organisation set up in the 1840's to manage the allocation of revenues between private railway companies for services travelling over the lines of other companies. Disbanded at Nationalisation in 1948.

ROSCO Rolling Stock Owning Company.

SER South Eastern Railway.

SE&CR South Eastern & Chatham Railway.

Special Notice A supplement to the working timetable advising of extra railway related activities.

SR The Southern Railway 1923-1948.

Standard Gauge Refers to track with the horizontal dimension of 4'-8½" (1,435 mm) between rail centres. The most common gauge used on today's public railways including those in Gravesham and the Hoo peninsular, this may derive from the 5 feet (1,500 mm) width needed to fit a carthorse between wagon shafts.

T&GJR Tilbury & Gravesend Tunnel Junction Railway.

TOC Train Operating Company. A company who operates passenger train services, this is most likely part of the railway to be encountered by the public.

TOPS Total Operations Processing System. A computer system used for managing the locomotives and rolling stock on the UK rail system.

TOU Train Operating Unit, pre privatisation BR business unit, fore runner of the Train Operating Company.

Tractive Effort - The force exerted by a locomotive or powered rail vehicle by its driving wheels to produce motion once rolling resistance has been factored in.

U&LR Upnor & Lodge Hill Railway, formerly the C&U.

UIC International Union of Railways. An international organisation that promotes interoperability between rail ways and creates their world standards.

Working Timetable Timetable for internal use by a railway's operating staff which shows all planned train movements.

WWI World War One.

WWII World War Two.

Index

25 KV AC, 147, 224
ACV 125 HP diesel railcar, 78
Aerial attack, 37
Allhallows attractions, 169
Ambulance Trains, 37, 42, 250
An infuriated bull, 118
Angel Trains, 54, 248, 249
Bank Charter Act, 12
Batavier Line, 203, 232
Beluncle, 72, 80, 162-164
Belle steamers, 23
Berry Wiggins, 162, 164
Bomb damage, 109, 250
Bombardier Class 375 Electrostar electric multiple units, 222
Bombardier Class 376 Electrostar electric multiple units, 221, 222
Bradshaw's, 14, 115
Brett Aggregates, 76
British Coal and British Rail (Transfer Proposals) Act 1993, 4, 248
British Petroleum, 77, 174
British Rail, 48, 49, 53, 78, 81, 110, 138, 144, 206-208, 215-218, 220, 223, 248
British Rail 4VEP electric multiple units, 221
British Rail Class 373 Eurostar high speed electric multiple units, 32
British Rail Networker electric multiple units, 57, 126, 221, 222
British Railway Mark I coaching stock, 215
British Railways 2EPB & EPB electric multiple units, 110-112, 200, 220
British Railways Class 33 diesel-electric locomotive, 196, 207, 240
British Railways Class 419 dual powered motor luggage van, 220
British Railways Class 47 diesel-electric locomotive, 120, 209
British Railways Class 4DD double deck electric-multiple units, 218, 219
British Railways Class 71 Electric locomotive, 131, 207
British Railways Class 73 electro-diesel locomotive, 63, 193, 195, 207, 208
Buckeye coupling, 217
Bulleid, 192, 206, 215-218, 222
Car ferry,, 109, 225
Cement wagons, 79
Cement works, 78, 146, 207, 208
Channel Tunnel Rail Link, 58, 60
Chatham Loop Railway, 122
Chattenden & Upnor Railway, ii, 84, 86
Chattenden Naval Tramway, iv, 82
City Express, 128
Class 33, 51, 146, 193, 196, 207, 240
Cliffe Station, 156
Cliffe to Glasgow cement trains, 193
Cliftonville Express, 128
Colas Rail, 56, 193, 208, 209
Connex South Eastern, 111
Continental Agreement of 1863, 22
Continental', boat train service, 203
Crossrail, 4, 55, 118, 121
DB Schenker, 56
Denton Crossing, 151
Denton Halt, 150
East Kent Railway, 18, 220
Ebbsfleet Station, 62, 182

Emergency Powers (Defence) Act 1939., 42
English Welsh and Scottish Railways, 55
Eversholt Rail, 54, 248, 249
Explosion of HMS Bulwark, 180
Explosion of the minelayer HMS Princess Irene, 180
Family coach, 212
Fire Queen, 187
Fireless locomotives 31, 32
Flushing Night Mail, 179
Flying Watkin, 227
Foot warmers, 132
G&RR Long boilered Stephenson 'patentee' locomotive of 1844, 201
GB Railfreight, 55, 208
General Electric Class 70 heavy haul diesel-electric locomotive, 56, 193, 209
General Motors Class 66 diesel-electric locomotive, 56, 63, 121, 176, 207, 209
General Strike of 1926, 225
German Kaiser, 178
Golden Rail, 248
Govia, 54
Grain, 70, 80, 150, 156, 158, 175, 206
Grain Crossing Halt, 172, 173, 180
Grain Station, 173, 174, 180
Granville Express, 99, 161, 204
Gravesend & Rochester Railway, 7
Gravesend and Rochester Canal and Railway Company, 8
Gravesend G&RR Station, 94
Gravesend Railway, ii, iii, 4, 5, 9, 14, 21, 23, 29, 91, 241
Gravesend Station, 1, 13, 100, 101, 111, 113, 114, 116, 218, 237
Gravesend Town Pier, 35, 49, 137, 225, 227
Gravesend West Street, 35, 44, 49, 52, 106, 110, 133, 139, 230, 240
Gravesend West Street Landing Stage, 230
Gravesend, Strood, Rochester & Chatham Railway, 6
Harry Wainwright, 34, 203
High Halstow Halt, 158
High Speed Suburban Service 2009, 64
Higham Station, 97
Higham to Strood tunnel, 11
Hitachi Class 395 Javelin high speed domestic electric multiple units, 64, 65, 111, 113, 224
Hoo Junction, 37, 69, 153, 154, 157, 170, 186, 192, 195-197, 204, 208, 209
Hoo Junction Staff Halt, iv, 49, 153, 154
Hoo Ness Railway, 87, 89
Horlocks Fire Queen locomotive, 187
Hundred of Hoo Electrification Proposal, 79
Hundred of Hoo railway, 199
Hundred of Hoo Railway, v, 66, 69, 178, 192, 237, 247, 250
Hundred of Railway Electrification Proposal 1980, 79
Hutton Vignoles, 13
Imperial Paper Mills, 31, 137
John Rastrick, 8
Kaiser Wilhelm II, 104
Kent Coast Electrification, 124, 171, 204, 206
Kingsnorth Light Railway, 83
Land Clauses Consolidation Act, 14
LC&DR 'R' Class 0-4-4 tank engine, 202
LC&DR 'Enigma' Class, 201
LC&DR 3rd Class carriage, 212
LC&DR 'Adrian' Class 0-6-0, 187
LC&DR Æolus locomotive, 199

Index

LC&DR's bank, collapse, 20
Locopulsor unit, 154
London & Gravesend Railway, 6
London and Blackwall Railway, 225
London Chatham & Dover Railway, iii, 18
London, Tilbury & Southend Railway, 18, 225
Longfield Dust Sidings, 128, 189, 191
Longfield Halt, 30, 144, 146, 147
Market train, 158
Meopham refuse, 128
Meopham Station, 91, 128, 130
Merry-Go-Round, 118
Middle Stoke Halt, 164-166
military trains, 37, 152
Milton Range Halt, iv, 91, 152, 237, 239, 240
Milton Road Halt, iv, 148, 149
Miskins sidings, 163
Motor Luggage Van, 220
Network Rail, 153, 197, 208
Network South East, 221, 248
Night Ferry, 132
North and South Railways, 55
North Downs Steam Railway Society, 4, 26, 98
North Kent Extension Railway, 66
North Kent Railway, 14
Northfleet Station, 14, 50, 115, 117, 119
Omnibus, 92
Omnibuses, 92
Open 3rd Class carriage, 210
Perry Street Locomotive Shed, 187
Port Victoria Hotel, 181
Port Victoria Station, 178, 181
Princes Street station, 21
proposed new station near Windmill Hill, 243
Queen Victoria, 104, 105, 178, 179
Railtrack, 57, 153, 197
Railway Executive Committee, 36
Railway Regulation Act, 36
Richard Maunsell, 200, 214
Robert Stephenson, 11
Rosherville Station, iv, 24, 35, 44, 49, 91, 139, 241, 242
Rosherville to Chatham Railway, 6
Royal Trains, 105
SE&CR 'C' Class, 51, 136, 233, 236
SE&CR E1 Class express passenger locomotive, 204
SE&CR 'H' Class, 110, 160, 171, 202-203
SE&CR N Class locomotive, 50, 204
SE&CR Q1 Class locomotive, 202, 203
SE&CR Rail Motor, 90, 165
SER 1st Class carriage, 211
SER 2nd Class carriage, 212
SER Class 118 locomotive, 16
SER closed 3rd carriage, 211
SER Q Class locomotive, 103, 202, 206
Sharnal Street Station, 80, 160
Singlewell Infrastructure Maintenance Depot, 197
Sir Edward Watkin, 242
Slade Green Depot, 220, 221
Sole Street, 19, 42, 57, 122, 124, 126-127, 204, 207, 238
Sole Street bank, 20, 122, 238
South Eastern & Chatham Railway, 40, 211, 250
South Eastern and Dover Railway, 12
South Eastern Railway, iii, 3, 12, 54, 69, 101, 241

Southern Railway, iii, 39-44, 46, 98, 144, 169, 192, 200, 206, 217, 250
Southfleet Station, 25, 29, 143-144
Springhead Junction, 64, 224
SR Class 12 diesel shunter, 192
SR conversion of ex SE&CR steam carriages to electric stock, 216
SR Light Pacific locomotive, 206
SR Q1 locomotive, 46, 206
SR steam coaching stock, 215
St Vincent locomotive, 201
Staff and ticket, 69
Stoke Junction Halt, 167, 168
Strategic Rail Authority, 53
Thames & Medway Canal, 7, 239
Thamesport, 76, 77, 174, 176
Thanet Belle, 132
Thanet Express, 128
The Lower Thames Tunnel and New Connecting Railway of 1921, 245, 250
Tilbury & Gravesend Tunnel Junction Railway, 242
Tilbury Landing Stage, iv, 229
Trafalgar locomotive, 9, 201
Transport Act 1962, 41
Travellers Fare, 48, 248
U class, 205
Union Rail, 58
Van Tromp locomotive, 201
Vandalism, 10
Veolia, 53
West Street Pier, iv, 23, 231, 232, 234, 236
William Martley, 199
WWI, 38, 134, 148, 172, 178, 179, 204, 229
WWII, 137, 152, 203, 205, 250
Yantlet range, 74
Zeeland Shipping Company, 66

About the author

Rob. as he admits himself is a lifelong railway enthusiast. Recollecting his earliest memories of this passion, these he acknowledges go back to the age of two when he refused to pass Gravesend Central station until being allowed five minutes to watch the passing trains. With school holidays spent wherever a railway presented itself, his particular favourite was code 33B, Tilbury loco. Here, Rob was fortunate to witness steams last hurrah on British Railways LT&SR section. The Hundred of Hoo branch was another favourite, its varied traffic before the withdrawal of passenger services being another fascination.

Since those early days, he has pursued a career as an electrical draughtsman and engineer. Spending nearly twenty years on London Underground, he was involved in major projects, these including his *magnus opus,* the Piccadilly line extension to Heathrow Terminal 5. Still managing to indulge his hobby by volunteering on preserved railways and membership of the Gravesend Railway Enthusiasts Society (GRES), since retiring as engineering design manager, he continues to indulge his passion as the Chairman of GRES and as an established speaker on railway subjects.

His first foray into publishing, this book represents a distillation of his accumulated knowledge of his home areas railways.

www.ingramcontent.com/pod-product-compliance
Lightning Source LLC
Chambersburg PA
CBHW081106080526
44587CB00021B/3465